ASIAN VOYAGES

ASIAN VOYAGES

TWO THOUSAND YEARS OF CONSTRUCTING THE OTHER

O. R. DATHORNE

BERGIN & GARVEY
WESTPORT, CONNECTICUT • LONDON

Library of Congress Cataloging-in-Publication Data

Dathorne, O. R.
   Asian voyages : two thousand years of constructing the other /
O. R. Dathorne.
      p. cm.
   Includes bibliographical references and index.
   ISBN 0–89789–469–3 (alk. paper)
    1. Discoveries in geography.   2. China—Civilization—Occidental
influences.   3. Africa—History—to 1498.   4. America—Discovery and
exploration—African. I. Title.
   G80.D338   1996
   910—dc20   95–39749

British Library Cataloguing in Publication Data is available.

Library of Congress Catalog Card Number: 95–39749
ISBN: 0–89789–469–3

First published in 1996

Bergin & Garvey, 88 Post Road West, Westport, CT 06881
An imprint of Greenwood Publishing Group Inc.

Printed in the United States of America

The paper used in this book complies with the
Permanent Paper Standard issued by the National
Information Standards Organization (Z39.48–1984).

10 9 8 7 6 5 4 3 2 1

Copyright Acknowledgments

The author and publisher gratefully acknowledge permission to reprint the following:

Selections from Ssu-ma Chien, *Records of the Grand Historian of China*, translated by Burton Watson.
Copyright © 1961 by Columbia University Press. Reprinted with permission of the publisher.

Selections from J.J.L. Duyvendak, *China's Discovery of Africa*. Permission granted courtesy of
Probsthain Publishers.

Selections from Chau ju-kua, *Chu-fan-chi,* translated by Frederick Hirth and W. W. Rockhill. Permission granted courtesy of Paragon Book Reprint Corporation.

For Hilde Ostermaier Dathorne
with my usual thanks
for her kindness, help, and constant patience

CONTENTS

PREFACE

Part of the problem for the nonspecialist's study of China exists in the romanization systems for the Chinese language. One, Wade-Giles, put together by two Western Sinologists (Sir Thomas Wade and Herbert A. Giles), is still utilized in printed books, especially in the United States. The other, pinyin, is China's official attempt to help us more closely approximate to Chinese pronunciation. The rivalry between the two has even assumed a degree of "political correctness." I did not want to confuse readers with this, and so I used both, except for retaining the obvious Latinizations of names like Confucius and Mencius, which might have seemed a little strange to Western eyes if presented in any other form. In general, I used the spellings, Wade-Giles or pinyin, of the available printed texts, so that interested people might be able to locate the works with greater ease, and when I include both I have placed the Wade-Giles in parentheses after the pinyin.

In a way, this is a book I had wanted to write since I was a schoolboy. I was very fortunate in that I grew up in Guyana, in what would now be termed a multicultural society. I went to school with Chinese and Indians, as well as Native Americans. My teachers were English, African, Indian, and Chinese. When I reflect on this, I realize with a twinge of nostalgia that this was not part of some master plan on the part of the British in Guyana; it was actually their own recalcitrance, what they came to term afterward "indirect rule." But I never suspected that my Indian friends and classmates like Ali, Banarsee, Dindial, and Persaud, or my Chinese schoolmates like Chan, Chung, Eyre, Fong, Lee, and Yhap were either "exotic" or "oriental." They all seemed to be in the same uncomfortable position that I was—not quite English, despite our English first names, but hoping to make it one day! Alas, of all of us writers in a similar predicament—Jan Carew, Wilson Harris, Andrew Salkey, and Sam Selvon, to name a few—only V. S. Naipaul seems to have "succeeded." He has even been knighted!

My next introduction to the "East," the "Orient," occurred in a less mundane manner. Years later, in England as a student, I was introduced to the European version of the orient by the Theosophical Society, by the occasional lecture at the University of London, and above all, by William Empson. He had suffered the folly of my adolescence gladly, and once, I recall, even as I busily pursued T. S. Eliot's Sanskrit references for my honors thesis, Empson told me about his own very real experiences in China and Japan, particularly as they had affected his personal life. I must say that my own Western acceptance of the intellectualization of the East seemed to bear little resemblance to my former schoolboy personal friendships and experiences. Yes, Shaw was right—youth can be wasted on the young. Only now can I reconcile my own childhood, through which I experienced what today we would call the Eastern diaspora, with the reconstructions of Eliot and Pound that so influenced my generation.

In Europe, despite the reality that Empson's world provided for me, I was caught up in the make-believe monolithization that in some easily comprehensible way readily and conveniently yoked the works of Omar Khayyám and Rabindranath Tagore, Edwin Arnold's *The Light of Asia* and T. E. Lawrence's *Seven Pillars of Wisdom* into one delightful mishmash. It was an easy pill to swallow from the comfort of our London bedsitters but I do reflect that I ought to have known better. After all, I embraced, even endorsed, this Western version of unreality without any reference to the very real "Asians" I had known at home— Chinese men, who at that time still spoke Cantonese, and Chinese women, who dressed in traditional wear. Or Indians, whose weddings we regularly attended because as young men we were always hungry, and Hindus and Muslims had the very appetizing habit of "feeding the poor." Much to out parents' consternation, we endured this brief humility even as we were welcomed into a world of curries and *roti* eaten off a large palm leaf in lieu of a plate.

This world of the Chinese and Indian diaspora seemed to have little or nothing to do with the unpeopled reconstructions of England. I say "unpeopled" because until relatively late in the fifties, only a few indigenous spokespersons existed. And these few, like Jiddu Krishnamurti (declared to be the incarnation of Buddha by an enthusiastic theosophist leader), seemed to help contribute to the make-believe of Western invention. Thus Shelley's "Ozymandias" and Coleridge's "Kubla Khan" seemed to be, in this context, the right and relevant response.

Later, in America still another version of the East would be revealed, one that became monolithic in the nineties, when the assumption became that all

"Asians" are computer literate and attend Berkeley. Our short memory has helped us forget the time, just a few decades ago, when Chinese and Japanese were virtually locked out of the United States and those who did get in were forced into tasks such as building the railroads, or running laundries. By the nineties there was another version of India in Britain too—Indians and Pakistanis were "coloured" or even "Black," ran restaurants, drove buses, and were either liked or disliked by the populace at large, but never, thankfully, romanticized.

When I did finally visit China, I observed something completely different. This was Home, the Center, and from here there seemed to exist a confidence about a people's role and their place in the world, which diasporan experiences could never replicate. I had the feeling of being totally alone, lost in a sea of faces going about their business in Hong Kong, Taiwan, and on the mainland, with little or no concern for those like myself on the periphery. That is when the point became so clear and valid that it is not enough to dub the non-Westerner as "Other" and to assume that he somehow acquiesces to this distorted imaging of him. Within the framework of a Chinese conceptualization (something the West has never been able to alter) was the firm assurance, realization, and knowledge that China, Malaysia, Indonesia, Japan, Korea, and Vietnam were not "East," but lay at the very center of the world. Whatever Western incursions have done, this one perception they have never been able to alter there. On the other hand, I think that Western conceptualizations have altered indigenous perceptions in Africa; certainly they have in the Americas and the Caribbean, but not in China.

Today, many of us feel that we know China and the South Pacific, India and even the so-called "Middle East," because we associate place with anecdote and easy mnemonics. And these anecdotes (oftentimes taking their origin from a single fact) are expected to tell the whole story of place: Tianamen Square is supposed to do just that for China; and Don Ho and Pearl Harbor to do as much for Hawaii. If this book has a major thrust, perhaps it is my attempt to rediscover, to renew the whole, to establish that there exists no important link between our misconceptions and their realities, and to demonstrate that very often we are wrong and they are right.

Particularly, in the case of China, I have attempted to show that a certain model works whereby the Chinese seem not conscious of their supposed "Otherness," but instead implant their own ordering of Otherness on the world as they encountered it. I have argued about what I have termed degrees of this otherness, whereby at one extreme exists the "odder" and the "oddest" and, at another point, the "uttermost." The varying extent of some types of ultimate otherness, I contend, has been sanctioned from ancient times. Therefore, both

Europeans and Africans can be fit into just such a pattern.

I try to argue that Europeans, recognizing a degree of similarity between their own and Chinese institutions, never claimed to either "explore" China, as they had in the case of Africa, or "discover" it, as they had in the instance of the New World. As "travelers" they approached the land and its people with a greater humility than they had shown with regard to other continents. And this does not even alter in the nineteenth century with the advent of the Jesuits, who never really achieved wholesale conversion, or with the rise of nineteenth century European imperialism, when it could be contended that the Chinese still maintained a psychological distance from the "barbarian" Westerners, keeping them virtually on the coast.

In the instance of the Pacific Islands, the European influence is entirely different, but one with which I am more familiar. There, place is invented even before it is encountered, as an eighteenth-century response to what had not yet been found in the New World. So, although we are discussing the relatively sophisticated people of the Enligtenment, we must keep in mind that they were still very self-conscious, seeing themselves as playing the roles of founder, discoverer, and civilizer. In the process, not only were the islands occupied and owned, but additionally, what limited barriers had existed were quickly surrendered, sometimes even voluntarily. Once the area was "discovered" and named, it quickly became Western—British, French, or American—something that to this day has never happened in China.

Therefore, even as I attempted this book, I became very aware that my mind, like any Western mind, was entrapped within the multiple associations of what constitutes "Asia." Perhaps, unlike most, I carried additional baggage. After all, "race" in Guyana is not Black/White but Black/Indian, Black/Chinese, all considerably exacerbated by the actions of a postindependence government that stressed this, leading to violent confrontations and years of unrest. So that today, the ease with which I recall Ali, Banarsee, Dindial, and Persaud, or Chan, Chung, Eyre, Fong, Lee, and Yhap is itself a fictionalization, for they have mostly left, not for some distant "homeland," but for further extensions of the diaspora, particularly Canada and America. Here we meet as still newer and different constructions, so-called "ethnics."

As I attempted this study, I became more and more conscious that there are three or four Asias in my head; one is the quiet one of my homeland, unrecognized as different or apart. Yet, to be truthful, there was something a little tenuous about the way in which the so-called Asians seemed to exist, as if they were always on the verge of extinction, going about very quiet lives, in a very noisy country, living in homes where there seemed to be never a sound above a whisper. This is the first Asia of my mind, people existing in a small corner of the world, all of us strangers and scavengers, but some seemingly more at home than others. The second Asia is the reconstruction from Europe, which I had to be taught about—it was almost de rigeur, one which I failed to connect (unknowingly, but very wisely) with the people I had known at home. My third Asia is one of aloof and distant people; in America, I had inherited the label and attributes of being Black in a hostile world, and the Chinese and Indians I met, casually but carefully gazed at me, and I at them, from across a wide gulf.

My fourth Asia arose from the direct experience of going there, and of being totally lost. There was not even a street sign you could recognize, a symbol you could scrawl that would aid in mutual intelligibility. I recall that even to get back to the hotel from some mad adventurous dash by cab, my wife and I often took the name and address card of the hotel manager. We would point (and hope we had not encountered an illiterate taxi driver!) and thus secure our way back. These four concepts of the the Asian world are the ways I must unapologetically assert that I have continued to see the area of this study. I can only hope that this does not detract too much from what I have tried to say.

There are a relatively small number of scholars working with Chinese materials, and I must acknowledge my deep gratitude to them, since I depended on their translations (and often their eyes and ears) to do my own interpretations. In particular, I will remain in the debt of the late Arthur Waley for the constant interest he displayed in Chinese letters and for his serious commitment. At a more contemporary level, Burton Watson and William de Bary have been indefatigable in producing source material for a large number of works. Vikram Seth, the Indian novelist, has returned to the older poets Li Bai (Li Po) and Du Fu (Tu Fu) for a second look. More recently, Patricia Buckley Ebrey has revised an earlier book for student use, and many of her selections help provide a living reality to China and its people.

Of course, I have been familiar with the translations of Ezra Pound since my undergraduate days—however, the problem remains that he is more a "poet" than a translator, so one has to be cautious. Equally, but for different reasons, James Legge is another translator who has done an enormous amount of work, yet Sinologists tend to be wary of him—I think partly because of his unusual orthography and his Christian bias. I must add that Edward Said has been most instrumental, from the date of our first meeting a decade and a half ago, in helping me to see, through his spoken and printed words, how the West, where both he and I have spent our adult years, has formulated not only its perceptions of the East, but conditioned our responses as well.

As usual, I wish to thank Dr. Lynn Flint who helped make me feel that some of this mattered, and who was always willing to offer practical advice. I also owe much to everyone who helped during the two-year stint of researching and writing this book—Emily Carpenter, who assisted with the research and with organizing the manuscript; Columbia University Press and SUNY Press, which assisted with books; the *Journal of Asian Studies* and the Association of Asian Studies; The School of Oriental and African Studies, University of London, which fired my imagination some forty years ago and proved a useful repository at the present time; the libraries at Harvard, Berkeley, and my own home University of Kentucky, whose librarians remained always helpful, eager to answer questions from a curious researcher. Finally, as always, my special gratitude to my wife, Hilde Ostermaier Dathorne, whose unstinting assistance has made my continued work possible. I will be forever in her gratitude, for none of this would have been possible had she not contributed so generously and freely of her time and committed herself so fully to my small aims. I assume full responsibility for whatever shortcomings exist in this text.

1

THE WEST AND THE REST

At first sight, Chinese, Africans, and Native Americans seemingly possess few commonalities. One could reasonably argue that they are all literally continents apart and, as such, from prehistorical times have undergone a variety of experiences that have shaped each into distinct kinds of identities. Furthermore, they are geographically removed, even inhabiting ecologically dissimilar areas, and, as such, would have required different and varied types of stimuli to help them adjust to the process of human adaptation.

Yet they all may be considered within a specific context. It would be too easy to categorize them within a kind of generalized nomenclature as "victims" or "colonized" or even as denizens of the "Third World" (if one can still make such a distinction). Of course, it is demonstrably quite true that in each instance we are describing areas that have suffered degrees of "colonization," varying from total imperialism on Africans to economic suzerainty on Chinese to the relentless ghettoization of Native Americans. But this is not going to be a major concern here; instead, I wish to examine ways in which these three areas of the world intersected not so much with Europe but with their own "West"—what was outside, external, even alien, and certainly beyond them—and how they, to some extent even unwittingly, altered their own indigenous world view and passively had it changed in the process.

There is a specific historical moment we can easily identify when we note the manner in which this alteration dramatically takes place, a change from a kind of relaxed monoculturalism to a newer, radical consciousness of global multiculturalism. This could ordinarily be regarded as part of the process through which peoples and nations "grow," evolving beyond themselves into a grander and larger comprehension of the scheme of human reality. Chinese, African, and Native American societies can all identify specific time and place, occasion and reason, when this cultural collision has taken place. In fact, it is not just a "moment," for it may be protracted into centuries, nor is it objective "history," for it may be told differently by the various players. But since the occurrence is very much *in time*, and *in place*, we may safely regard it as an event that seems to have taken place with a kind of rash, sudden and explosive force.

Before this "meeting," there is no larger identity that will be later defined by the West. At the earliest point of precontact, the societies exist within borderless areas, circumscribed merely by the limitations of language groupings or the physical constraints of landscape. Therefore, when European scholars contend that the very names (China, Africa, Native America) are Western concoctions, they are right, but not for the jingoistic reasons frequently asserted. What names we find tend to devolve around ethnic groupings that share specific commonalities, such as the Qin (Ch'in), the Afer, or the Ameriques, and these terms may well have supplied names and identity to China, Africa and America. But it is precisely at this point that the first contention begins, since some researchers assert that Qin is but an early "Chinese" name for China, "Afer" an old name for Africa, and "Ameriques" an indigenous Nicaraguan term for America. Thus, we have it on no less an authority than the *Encyclopaedia Britannica* that "the Ch'in from which the name China is derived, established the approximate boundaries and basic administrative system that all subsequent Chinese dynasties were to follow for the next 2000 years."[1] As we shall see, this is only partly true.

For Africa, the UNESCO-authorized African history series suggests the plausibility of various versions:

The word 'Africa' is thought to come from the name of a Berber people who lived to the south of Carthage, the Afarik or Aourigha, whence Africa or Africa to denote the land of the Afarik.

Another derivation of the word Africa is that it comes from two Phoenician terms, one of which means an ear of corn, a fertility symbol in that region, and the other, Pharikia, means the land of fruit.

It is further suggested that the word comes from the Latin adjective *aprica* (sunny) or the Greek *aprike* (free from cold).

Another origin might be the Phoenician root *faraqa*, which suggests the idea of separation or in other words diaspora. It may be pointed out that the same root is to be found in some African languages, for instance Bambara.

In Sanskrit and Hindi the root *Apara* or *Africa* denotes that which, in geographical terms, comes 'after', in other words the West. Africa is the western continent.

An historical tradition subscribed to by Leo Africanus has it that a Yemenite chief named Africus invaded North Africa in the second millennium before our era and founded a town called Afrikyah. But it is more likely that the Arabic term *Ifriquiya* is the Arabic transliteration of the word 'Africa'.

One version even suggests that Afer was a grandson of Abraham and a companion of Hercules.[2]

We are left, therefore, with eight possible derivations, but are none the wiser.

Regarding Native Americans, the origin of the word "America" has been seriously disputed from as early as the latter part of the nineteenth century. Jules Marcou, in "L'Origine du Nom d'Amérique," asserted quite definitely "that Amerrique is the Indian name of the mountains between Juigalpa and Libertad in the province of Chontales, in Nicaragua." The word *Amerrique* signifies, in the Maya language, "the country of the wind."[3]

On the one hand, therefore, serious and credible scholars have argued that the names were not invented by Europeans but derived from units within the areas themselves. Therefore, China, Africa, and America acquire an *indigenous* significance when located in these local contexts. However, European scholarship in general has tended to be less concerned with these factors and, in any event, would argue that "naming," even if derived from a local reality was, in effect, a deliberate European act, meant to indicate both ownership and cultural ascendancy.

What else are we to make of J. M. Roberts' *The Triumph of the West*, a title both slanted and certainly ill-chosen? Roberts' book is not only given the official seal of approval by the British Broadcasting Corporation, its publisher, but, in addition, received a wide audience through the television documentary of the same name. At one point, Roberts is quite categorical, albeit here only with reference to Africa, but in other contexts the same argument is advanced for the world. He affirms quite definitely that "until Europeans took the idea [of Africa] to Africa, no African knew that he lived in a continent which could hopefully be thought of as a whole. No African knew he was an African until his European schoolmaster told him so."[4]

One cannot merely dismiss *The Triumph of the West* as a nostalgic clarion call for British imperialism. Certainly it is this, but embedded in the sentiments which Roberts expresses are ideas which go to the very heart of identity, of declaiming who and what Chinese, Africans and Native Americans represent. For if, as Roberts suggests, they are merely images (rather imaginings) of Europe, then from the very beginning of our considerations, we are up against an enormous problem. In a few words, how can we be sure that the non-West exists independent of the West? How can we speak of China, Africa, or America, if, by definition, the West claims a cultural monopoly in not merely influencing events, but inventing these continents? The problem lies at the heart of the entire question of "perception," for it flows over from the "agent" who promulgates the notion, to the "object" who begins to believe in and to accept the mythology. But a major part of our consideration will be to inquire as to who is the "perceived" and who the "perceiver."

"TRAVEL" IN CHINA

A closer look reveals that within the areas of our concern, these are hardly relevant issues for average, everyday people. "China" (like the "Asian flu," "Chinatown," and "Chinese fortune cookies") is very much a western idea. The People's Republic of China knows itself as "Zhonghua Renmin Gonghequo" in the common speech of *putonghua,* which we still insist on refering to as "mandarin."[5] As among Africans and Native Americans, identity occurs at the more basic level associated with group affiliation and language despite the wishes of any nationalist government. "Africans" and "Native Americans," again despite government inclinations, view themselves quite rightly as members of a "tribe" (an unfortunate word when *we* use it to describe *them*). Indeed, for villagers in Africa, organized opposition to European presence, as Michael Crowder argues, was most effective at this local level, indeed providing "some of the stiffest resistance the colonial forces of occupation experienced."[6] Confucius himself never advocated nor indeed could have advocated, nationalism, especially given the fierce internecine disputes of his time. His loyalties were to the state of Lu (modern Shandong) where he was born. As he confided to his disciples, at one stage, "Let us go home. Let us go home"[7]—the youth, he argued, were in need of guidance.

"Home" in the minds of the peoples under consideration has a fixed locus independent of whatever any autonomous national governments might assign in terms of "state" or "country." "Home" also tends to be an identifiable place with a given language, agreed cultural norms, acceptance of specific mores, and a distinct suspicion and caution toward populations beyond its immediate borders. Although the "West" means different things to different areas, what is of demonstrable instance is that all these societies do encounter the West in certain clear specific ways. First, the West (at times a synonym for the outside world) comes on the routes of trade—on the Silk Road to China, on the Sahara routes and Atlantic Ocean to Africa, and on earlier Columbus/conquistador transatlantic ocean voyages and, later, the Lewis and Clark land incursions toward Native

Americans. Different names identify different types of perceptions as the West moves closer, as Europe saw its relationship with these areas.

For Europeans, China has its "travelers," Africa its "explorers," the New World its "discoverers." The "traveler" assumes that there exists a substantive and concrete manifestation at the end of the journey. Marco Polo never claimed to be a "discoverer." In 1271, when seeking out Khubilai (Kublai) Khan, he and his party were reduced to the position of subordinates, hoping that the Great Khan would see them, speak with them, accept the pope's greetings, which a less agreeable khan had rudely refused but a few years earlier when John of Plano Carpini was sent by Pope Innocent IV.[8] Travelers to the East may have exaggerated what they saw, their statements fueled by overripe imaginings sanctioned by church and popular belief, but they never claimed to "found" or create the East. In a way, this had less to do with the unarguable antiquity of what they encountered than with the complete alienation and amazement of the visitors. One major plus was the existence of a written language (not an issue in the New World or Africa, as we shall presently see), in a form that was recognizably different and unintelligible to the visitors.

"Explorers" and "discoverers" of the New World thought of the people they encountered in a totally different way, as *not* even possessing language. In this way, what Stephen Greenblatt calls "misnaming" takes place, from which "the linguistic appropriation of the land" is the next logical step. Explorers, he adds, "had little practical interest in immersing themselves in native culture and no desire to do so. To learn a language may be a step towards mastery, but to *study* a language is to place oneself in a position of dependency, to submit." When the Maya, for instance, respond to the query regarding the name of their land by saying *"uic athan* (we do not understand you)" their "expression of incomprehension becomes the colonial name of the land that is wrested from them."[9] Similarly, Aztec and Inca are named in quite arbitrary fashion.

There is no similar opportunity to "rename" or "misname" China. Medieval European travelers encountered lands where they truly witnessed civilizations possessing all the cultural accoutrements with which they were themselves familiar, or indeed, elements that clearly surpassed what they had left behind. For instance, the Franciscan friar, John of Plano Carpini, journeying east between 1245 and 1247, was very conscious of the need to observe custom and ceremony, recognizing the absolute requirement to be humble. He and his party were brought "into the tabernacle of the prince," and after bowing and taking care not to walk on the threshold, they spoke "kneeling upon [their] knees,"[10] as they would before an altar.

William of Rubruck, who traveled to Asia between 1253 and 1255, attempted some dubious philology, but did conclude regarding Cathay that "the people have received their name from one of their cities."[11] This almost reverent attitude prepares the way for Marco Polo, who, in addition to the circumstances of his travel as a kind of papal petitioner seeking Mongolian help, must have been aware (as his audience certainly was) that much of the cultural territory had already been charted. Marco Polo related his account (true it possessed some of the tall stories of his time) always with a desire to situate Mongolian royalty within a cultural European context. We learn of Chingiz (Genghis) Khan, of the sumptuous lifestyle of the Mongols, of their physical prowess in battle, and of Chingiz Khan's superiority even in battle with the legendary Prester John.[12] From the very beginning of the West's encounter with China, there seems to have been a fairly healthy respect.

I do not want to suggest that degrees of demonization were absent in the West's encounter with China, for travel accounts are replete with the fantasies of Plinian and Alexandrian lore. What I do wish to emphasize is that for Europeans, China presented three problems not shared by Africa or America. First, its very size and grandeur, historical scope, art, literature, and language completely overwhelmed the travelers.

Next, China made few accommodations. Much, much later, in the nineteenth century, Europeans would be restricted to a few external ports such as Shanghai, Hong Kong, and Macao, and today their presence is still evident to the most casual visitor. Europeans, even at the height of colonizing fever (incidents such as the Opium Wars, the Taiping Rebellion, and the Boxer Rebellion notwithstanding)[13] never effectively penetrated into the heart of China, as the Japanese later did. Somehow, unlike Africans and Native Americans, Chinese kept Europeans at arm's length, thereby securing a degree of autonomy and cultural longevity for themselves. Even today, visitors to China feel *their* own alienation, not the other way around. None of the recognizable "signs" work, not even "Arabic" numerals so useful in bypassing the language barrier in Europe.

Finally, a major Western acceptance of China's "remoteness" probably lies in the history of Western conquest. When Alexander the Great conquered, as we are so often told, the "then-known world," China was clearly excluded from the "known." And I suspect that an important reason why China, at least until the Japanese invasion, remained virtually beyond European imperial hegemony must be found in its early successful attempts to come to terms with molding a nation free from the splintering effects of ethnicity that have so wracked the last few years of the twentieth century.

Peter Worsley sees this as the logical development of ethnic group and state:

Historically, there have been three main ways in which the relationship between the State and its constituent ethnic groups has been resolved. They emerged in different epochs, and therefore embody different conceptions both of society and of the State. The older ones, however, did not simply disappear, but lived on, now overlaid and synchronic with the newer ones.[14]

Worsley identifies these as three types: one, "hegemonic," with one dominant culture; a second, "based on uniformity" with a nation-state; and a third, "pluralist," made up of various cultural identities. For China (Tibet is an obvious exception), Worsley's first model, reinforced by the ties of a modern socialist state, has obviously served as a way of maintaining its oneness, apartness, and uniqueness as a culture, thereby preserving aspects of the hegemonic. But not all China is Chinese, and China as geographical space and political concept may often run counter to ethnic determinants.

In addition to having the concept of "Otherness" inflicted on them by the West, the Han Chinese applied this concept to the inhabitants to their north and west. The Great Wall, is physically very real but symbolically represents attempts on the part of occupants within its orbit to *restrict* the alien and the hostile and to *inhibit* the familiar and the well-disposed. Whenever tribesmen from the north breached the wall, the Chinese solution was simple; over a period of time they sinicized them, even their Mongol rulers.

In the New World, the case was radically different. Hernán Cortés's appearance was disturbing and frightening, even if we discount later accretive inventions of him as a returning god. Those who first witnessed his presence note in a frightened cryptic manner, "We must tell him [Motecuhzoma II or Montezuma II] what we have seen, and this is a terrifying thing: nothing of the kind has ever been seen."[15] We do not know how the Chinese reacted to Marco Polo, but we do know that Chinese records do not even mention his presence, despite his statements regarding his closeness with the khan and his being sent back to Europe as a special envoy.

On the other hand, Cortés had come to a world which was still locally "hegemonic" (to use Worsley's concept). As a result, each splintered group identified an "Otherness" in their neighbors, as Tzvetan Todorov rightly observes:

The first, spontaneous reaction with regard to the stranger is to imagine him as inferior, since he is different from us: this is not even a man, or if he is one, an inferior barbarian; if he does not speak our language, it is because he speaks none at all, cannot speak, as Columbus still believed. It is in this fashion that . . . the Mayas of Yucatán call the Toltec invaders *nunob*, "mutes"; and the Cakchiquel Mayas refer to the Mam Mayas as "stammerers" or "mutes." The Aztec themselves call the people south of Vera Cruz *nonoualca*, "mutes," and those who do not speak Nahuatl they call *tenime*, "barbarians," or *popoloca*, "savages"; they share the scorn of all peoples for their neighbors, judging that the remotest ones, culturally or geographically, are not even suitable to be sacrificed and eaten .[16]

As our investigation will show, perceiving and recognizing "Otherness" is not directed solely from the Western "One" to an alien non-Western "Other," nor is it the sole purview of any single participant. Rather we note that "Otherness" may be particularly observed as the non-West describes its own differences, not from the West, but from other elements that the West also categorizes as non-Western and, therefore, similar in their degree of difference. In other words, more differences and greater degrees of Otherness seem to exist between groups which the West would normally lump together, in a hasty attempt at distinguishing them from what the West would consider as its own intrinsic values. These first "distinctions," the earliest evidences of Otherness, are not only directed from Western "victor" to non-Western "victim," but seem to be identified among the so-called victims themselves.

Such delineations of apartness, difference, "Otherness" are mutually observed and identified, for instance, between the inhabitants of Sung China and the earliest Mongol invaders, between Yoruba and non-Yoruba (Igbo, Hausa, Tiv, and so on), and between Inca and non-Inca. Quite naturally, these real and imagined distinctions make the role of the imperialists a much easier one, for they can and did exploit the differences, promoting at will those who seemed to adhere more closely to their own style of governance and order and their agreed and accepted view of the world.

If the terms *évolué* and *assimilado* have anything in common, it is surely an agreement on the part of French and Portuguese colonizers that progress lay in evolving into and/or assimilating the Weltanschauung of the West, thereby in this process establishing an even greater degree of distinctiveness from other groups. In general, though, the mass of people are anonymous, of no account, or, as George Orwell put it, "when you see how the people live, and still more, how easily they die, it is always difficult to believe that you are walking among human beings. All colonial empires are in reality founded upon that fact."[17] One should add at this point the reminder that Chinese, Africans, and Native Americans all practised forms of enslavement and even "colonization."

The point with which most sensitive and progressive modern scholars would concur is that the perception is usually from colonizer to colonized, from European to Chinese, African, Native American. While admitting that our culture accounts for a great deal of the misconceptions that arise out of such a distorted image, I must still insist that equally detrimental have been the Chinese, African and Native American views, first within the orbit of the larger configuration of colonizer/colonized and, second, as directed between their own indigenous major formations. So, even when there is an attempt at muting differences within the larger concept of "nation," degrees of hostility still continue to be directed among elements of these inner groups (the "tribes") themselves, which feel a greater affinity one with one not the Other.

One seeks in vain to identify special sympathetic concerns that would supposedly exist during Zheng He's (Cheng Ho) fourth expedition, in 1413, to Africa[18] or the Afro-Spaniard Estabanico's incursions among Native Americans from 1528 to 1536.[19] In other words, when we look at the Chinese encounter with Africa, or the African encounter with America, we do *not* find moral lessons that help guide us along some exemplary path. I can therefore unequivocally proclaim a degree of remission from the life sentence of guilt imposed on the unfortunate White male, since he is by no means the sole offender.

Interestingly, therefore, the very ways in which the West seeks to define its approaches to China, Africa, and the New World mark out not only the manner in which the West itself perceives itself and these places, but also ways in which the areas may come to view themselves. This has been due not so much to colonialism, but to the effects of acculturation, particularly in Africa and the New World. To a large extent, its own firm belief in the sanctity of its indigenity saved the East, for there was always a *written record* that could be set against anything that the West could devise. This is not to say that there were not Western incursions; the history even of revolt against the West in China is replete with the utilization of the Western text as symbol for the attack against the West itself. For example, the nineteenth-century so-called Taiping Rebellion, in which the leader proclaimed himself to be the younger brother of Jesus Christ, is but one example.[20] And despite any arguments that might be made to show that Marxism is a logical extension of indigenous Chinese belief, the truth still remains that Marxism is a Western import.

"EXPLORATION" IN AFRICA

The case of the African continent is a little different. First, there is the pride and proclamation of varied ethnicity. Despite this, the colonial powers drew boundaries at will, borders that often ignored the validity of language and custom. If there had occurred a point at which, say with the advent of independence, some rectification had taken place, one could readily have asserted that the colonial boundaries were merely artificial. But considering the reality of the permanence of the national borders (largely unrecognized by poachers and refugees), and the manner in which they are fiercely defended by newly independent African nation-states, we see how the western presence has left a permanent imprint.[21]

Second, another type of "border," more important for our concerns, is the artificiality of the language boundaries. Not only have the colonial languages, English, French, Portuguese, and even Spanish, been zealously maintained, but also very often these languages have served as ways of dividing the new nation-states from one another. Thus, the respective countries are closely linked in postindependence unions with the former metropolitan centers of their colonizers.[22] As a result of these national and linguistic boundaries in Africa, what has emerged are nations without a center, nationalities without a base, places where "home" is somewhere else, London, Paris or Lisbon, where important decisions are made and taken, and where any actions there have seen and felt ramifications back in the African homeland.

This then brings us to the enormity of a problem, which Kwame Appiah has dealt with in his 1992 study, *In My Father's House.*[23] There he posits the intriguing conclusion that Africa might well be a fiction of the "Negro" mind, a point anticipated by Taban lo Liyong in his provocative 1969 essay "Negroes are Not Africans."[24] In other words, in Africa itself, there is little empathy for the concept of a continental diaspora, especially a nationalistic one, since both are conceptualized from the West, albeit for different reasons. Therefore, the Western European colonizing process that established language and nationhood is merely akin to Black diasporan yearnings for Africa, seeking to justify an artificial unity based on the concept of a nation with which Blacks of the New World diaspora can associate, thus providing a ready-made panacea Somewhere in the middle of the two extremes—the Eurocentric imposition of a distorted reality and the Afrocentric cravings for a romantic belief in a holistic past—lies the "truth" of a village, a people, a continent.

When the German Duke Anton Ulrich von Braunschweig-Wolfenbüttel and the British Duke of Montagu decided that they would take part in an enterprise to guage African humanity, they did not act from the viewpoint of good and benign benefactors. Wilhelm Amo (c. 1703–1755), Eliza Johannes Capitein (c. 1717–1747), and Francis Williams (1700–1770), were subjected to their rather misguided attempts at re-forming the Noble Savage. They were sent to the best schools in Germany, Holland, and Britain, respectively, and I suppose they must have accomplished what their benefactors had hoped for. Amo became a professor of philosophy, Capitein went back for a brief spell to Ghana as a missionary among his own Fanti people, and Francis Williams, after pursuing a degree at Oxford, returned to Jamaica as a teacher.[25]

However, their accomplishments speak volumes when we try to concern ourselves with cultural impact. Amo distinguished himself by ably proving in his dissertation that slavery was not contrary to the laws of God and could therefore be justified. Capitein, as Janheinz Jahn commented in *Muntu,* sought fit to translate the Ten Commandments of the Bible with an introduction that proved to be too much even for his sponsors—"I am Jan Company that brought thee out of the land of Egypt."[26] And, according to the 1774 *History of Jamaica* by Edward Long (himself grantedly a racist), Francis Williams often described himself as a "white man acting under a black skin," copiously executing Latin panegyrics to successive British governors of Jamaica.[27]

Davison Nichol, a poet from Sierra Leone, has suggested in "The Meaning of Africa" that from the vantage point of Hyde Park oratory on a given Sunday in London, Africa was a "concept," in which, he said, Blacks could "hide our separate fears" and "dream our separate dreams."[28] But it should be noted that he spoke as a special kind of African person, a Creole from Sierra Leone, much like Americanized Liberians, both of whose ancestors had shared the historical experience of having lived in the New World. For surely if being an Africa "Creole" means anything it is this: during the nineteenth century, persons of color had returned from the United States, the United Kingdom, Nova Scotia and Jamaica to take part in the practical invention of a "dream." I say this because even the place names are an indicator of utopian fantasies: Liberia and Freetown would represent the liberty and freedom not necessarily found there, but which hopefully would be created by New World returnees.[29] Indeed, as late as May 1951, President William Tubman of Liberia would stress that it was Black repatriates who brought "civilization, education and religion that were to be imparted to the natives . . . [From this] everything that is here has sprang forth and grown ."[30] Perhaps this helped hasten his downfall.

Of course, there was instant disillusionment. The new "tribe" in general despised the old indigenous ones. For instance, the early Black pioneers often persisted in seeing Africa as a place that had to be reformed. They were themselves Christians, and for them one of the most important tasks was evangelism, since through this the continent could be redeemed and, incidentally, they themselves could be made to look much better in the eyes of their Western sponsors. Of course, I am not suggesting that they were motivated solely by reasons of cultural placation, pleasing the White managers of the American Colonization Society. But I am arguing that the contrast helped to make them look better mand also indicated that the possibility of cultural upliftment for Blacks was not a mere theory but a definite option.

This was part of a larger debate that had gone on since the eighteenth century. Would it be possible for an African to be "civilized," schooled like a European and exposed to a European environment? The question may strike us today as being merely rhetorical, but it remained a burning issue and we see elements varying from outright rebuttal to the theory of the eternal savage, as in Countee Cullen's rather strange proclamation, "They [Africans] and I are civilized." This was written at the height of the Harlem Renaissance in the 1920s.[31]

Therefore, the exposure to Africa merely seemed to confirm an abiding superiority in Blacks who had been part of the Western educational system. How else are we to understand the much touted adage of W.E.B. DuBois that White America should help train and recognize a "talented tenth"? These would obviously be the elite who would serve as intermediaries between the White superstructure and the unwashed Black masses.

White "explorers" like David Livingston and Henry Morton Stanley had confirmed also that there was only tribulation and the hope of redemption (perhaps he meant self-redemption) out there in Africa. The continent became a spiritual challenge, part "discovery" undertaken by them and later by John Henning Speke and Richard Burton. Also, apart from the consolation of exploration and soul saving, there was the backdrop of an enormous continent that presented still another great challenge—hunting—through which White males sought mastery over landscape and life. Despoliation of the environment continued well into the twentieth century, as witness the adventures of Winston Churchill in 1907[32] and Theodore Roosevelt in 1909.[33] Both of them, like earlier explorers, move across a cultureless void, where the only human perception is the ever-faithful "boy" (they quickly acquire the terminology), the passive landscape, and the toll of carcasses.

One can obviously see the "explorer" and "hunter" as two sides of the same adventure. They both fail to recognize the intimacy of human encounter, being content merely to visualize people and land as one large enormous trope. What is more is that both explorer and hunter come, albeit unknowingly, seeking some type of replenishment, although they would be the last to admit it. And in the course of their own search, they iron out all differences, smooth over all specificities that would challenge the idea of a single Otherness, much as the diasporan Blacks do. The entire continent is backdrop: "The best sky was in Italy and Spain and Northern Michigan in the fall and in the fall [sic] in the Gulf of Cuba . . . . All I wanted to do now was get back to Africa," Ernest Hemingway, a latter-day hunter, muses in *The Green Hills of Africa* (1935).[34] Even for Hemingway, who was relatively sophisticated, Africa was one place, a pretty picture, and, of course, an endless hunting ground, a *country* which he says "was always better than the people."[35]

This idea of Africa as monolith trickles through in modern European and American texts like Joseph Conrad's *Heart of Darkness* (1902), Saul Bellow's *Henderson the Rain King* (1959), and Graham Greene's *A Burnt Out Case* (1961). In all of these, the prevailing myth is that Africa as "place" exists solely for the fortification of souls in distress. All the protagonists become "heroes" in the process of traveling to Africa. In *Heart of Darkness,* Marlow is able to rescue not only the dying Kurtz, but also to save Kurtz's name from oblivion, and bring back to the Intended his own fabrication of Kurtz's failed life. In *A Burnt Out Case,* Query seeks and finds his own redemption at a leprosarium. And in *Henderson the Rain King,* Henderson grows to heroic stature as, he, too welds together all the unstated differences of language and nation, rising, much like Robinson Crusoe, to a new status in the indigenous society itself. Surely the significance of Kurtz, Marlow, Query, and Henderson must be that failure in the West is the chief prerequisite for leadership and success in the non-Western, African world.

In encountering the Other in Africa, New World Blacks and Whites both become explorers as they shrink the continent to manageable terms and then seek to find ways in which this very minimization becomes the manner through which they achieve saving grace. Both are employing a creative mythology, in that they seek to construct an imaginary edifice for themselves, one that they can briefly inhabit and reject or embrace as they see fit.

In *Homecoming* (1972), Ngugi wa Thiong'o says as much when he asserts that for many Black writers Africa is merely the backdrop against which an inner drama may be played out. For instance, Ngugi faults Afro Caribbean writers who "use physical Africa as a symbolic backcloth."[36] And in *Hopes and Impediments* (1989), Chinua Achebe attacks Conrad, as he might have done to any number of other writers, for failing to understand that the landscape he described was peopled and that, for instance, the sight of a French gunship apparently pointlessly firing into the jungle was clearly absurd, since Conrad failed to understand that living African human beings were very much part of the environment. Conrad's work, Achebe says, celebrates the dehumanization of the human race.[37]

In the instance of the African encounter with the West, the situation is much more complex than, say, with China or Native America. One major difference is that there were Black spokespersons in the diaspora who had neither understood nor experienced Africa, and who very often adopted causes with little understanding of their consequences. One issue that has become tremendously sensationalized is the latter day debate over female circumcision. For instance, Alice Walker, in *Possessing the Secret of Joy* (1992), relates the issue in terms of the West, with the chief character harboring lifelong ill feelings against "genital mutilation." The narrative is replete with the fantasy of an African woman who now lives in North America, and filled with references to a "witchdoctor," a mother who prays to a "little idol," "Hottentot" women who love their genitalia, and "clay figures of African gods and goddesses from Ancient Egypt"[38] Clearly Alice Walker is taking the issue out of its cultural context, and once again, Africa is reduced to a single place, a point of view, a debate. Again, those who speak mythologize the Other, and, in the process, the Other becomes distant, inhuman, "odder," even as they seek to identify.

"DISCOVERY" IN THE NEW WORLD

At this stage, it would be useful to visualize, from the point of view of the Native American, what precisely occurred when the "New World" was "discovered." Such an attempt is fraught with enormous problems, for one is centuries removed from the events, and more importantly, there is a relative lack of indigenous "evidence," especially "Western"-type written records. Also, in attempting to reconstruct this past from a Native American perspective, any investigator runs into the immediate problem of language bias in surviving texts.

From the incept, "language" presents itself as a major issue, since all languages, including English, have obviously built-in prejudices of ancient misconceptions. There is this very basic issue: For instance, even when referring to the land which indigenous peoples inabit, how can one claim neutrality? The very terms like the *otro mundo* of Columbus or the *nuevo mundo* of Amerigo Vespucci are fraught with unfortunate nuances. Other worldliness suggested the name "Antilles" as a concept, not only of an anti-island or a non-Europe, but of a Europe turned on its head, where European norms are capsized. We have already noted that European newcomers to the continent assumed that such a condition existed.

Using Vespucci's terminology, New World, even though it has received acceptance, causes a larger problem.[39] The continent is only "new" with reference to a "norm" that is supposedly traditional, stable, and ancient. Newness also carries with it certain kinds of expectations, embedded very often in what the seekers saw: either a world of pristine beauty and abundance, or else a place that was rife with the possibility of restarting human development.

Terminology therefore plagues us, and, in this context, the names we use for native inhabitants unwittingly force us to arrive at conclusions before we even venture on a discussion. Nomenclatures like "Indian" rehash the old European mythologies of the "Indies," confounded by the emergence in later fiction of the "Noble Savage."[40] On the other hand, use of a term such as "Native American" provides us with two unfortunate problems: First, the term "native" has been much maligned in our language, and it suggests much more than "natus." Second, beyond its literal meaning, there are associative correlations of "native" with being backward, incapable of art or industry (except, perhaps, in a very basic form), and, above all, "uncivilized."

Martin Waldsemüller's unfortunate naming of the southern part of the continent as "America" in 1507 also carries unfortunate ramifications. For it is associated with "discovery" and "ownership."[41] Any such nomenclature divests indigenous people of their individual group names and, for simplicity's sake, renders them, with one sweeping motion, into a kind of monolithic identity that is purely fictional.

Furthermore, to use fashionable terms such as "victor" and "victim" or similar synonyms assumes a view of the world that we force on the indigenous inhabitants. Thus, in a much larger context, beyond the merely superficial aspects of Western culture, we have the right to enquire as to who is the "perceiver" and who the "perceived," who is the "colonizer" and who the "colonized." For we do not know that either definition, or the status itself, has ever been accepted by indigenous people as a way of self-definition.

However, since we "gotta use words," and since both "verbal" and "visual" territory have been mapped out by European texts we must acknowledge the problem we face, the manner in which the language itself stereotypes, and yet pursue as diligently as is humanly possible an attempt to recall the nature of the times of the young world we seek to explore. We have to fall back on old clichés as we endeavor to make sense out of the meaning of "Encounter," and if we are to come to terms with its psychological ramifications.

At least, from one viewpoint, we can historically catalogue a series of initial encounters which began with Columbus in 1492[42] and lasted until Samuel de Champlain "discovered" the Great Lakes in 1615.[43] Having done this, we will then, hopefully, be in a position to consider at least one "case study," the "encounter" between Emperor Xocoyotzin, Motecuhzoma II, and Hernán Cortés in an attempt to understand the nature of the meeting from both viewpoints.

Before doing this, I should like to itemize the significant European encounters in the New World that come after Columbus's. I have largely excluded Portuguese travel since, by agreement, with the exception of Brazil, it tended to be concerned with the East. In any case, just five years after Columbus, John Cabot, an Italian sailing for the British and seeking a northwest route to Asia, landed in "Kanada," and staked a British claim, which was eventually resolved by war with the French. By 1513, Vasco Núñez de Balboa was exploring Panama, Juan Ponce de León was traveling through Florida, and Francisco Pizarro (with Balboa) had crossed the continent to the Pacific, and would soon begin his domination of the Inca.

Following Ferdinand Magellan's circumnavigation of the globe between 1519 and 1521, Hernán Cortés (whom we shall discuss later), conquered the Aztec town of Tenochtitlán (present day Mexico City) in 1521 and later explored southeast to Honduras. In 1524, Giovanni da Verrazano, an Italian, explored the Atlantic coast from "Cape Fear," "discovering" New York Bay in 1524. Between 1528 and 1536, Alvar Núñez Cabeza de Vaca wandered the southwest of North America, in what was a type of non-Conquistador exploration, reversing tropes of mastery.

Jacques Cartier, a Frenchman, penetrated the Gulf of St. Lawrence between 1534 and 1535 in search of the elusive Northwest Passage. Diego de Almagro, who had himself earlier, in 1532, joined Pizarro, explored the Andes Mountains in northern Chile between 1535 and 1537. Between 1539 and 15[44], Hernando de Soto, another Spaniard, explored the American Southeast, "discovering" the Mississippi River. Francisco Vásquez de Coronado also explored the present day United States, "discovering" the Grand Canyon. Francisco de Orellana, noted by then for his famous contest with Amazon she-warriors, gave their name to the South American river and region in his own explorations between 1541 and 1542.[44] Germans also attempted to stake their own claims, particularly in Venezuela and Colombia.[45]

Despite later claims to empire, the British do not actively enter the picture until 1576, when Martin Frobisher again sought a Northwest Passage and "discovered" a bay he prudently named after himself. Another Englishman, John Davis, between 1585 and 1587 made three voyages seeking the Northwest Passage and sailed into Baffin Bay, departing from a bay to which he also gave his name. Sir Walter Raleigh traveled south to the Orinoco River, where he located El Dorado in 1595, but on failing to find it again in 1616, was executed. Early in the seventeenth century, French exploration of Canada continued with Samuel de Champlain's "founding" of Quebec Colony in 1608 and his "discovery" of "Lake Champlain" in 1609, as well as the Ottowa River and the Great Lakes.[46]

After this, Europeans would devote their travels during the eighteenth and nineteenth centuries to "discoveries" in Asia, the Pacific Islands, and Australia. The same derring-do is apparent; "discovery" is followed by naming, ownership, and settlement. By the nineteenth century, Americans join Europeans: between 1804 and 1806, Meriwether Lewis and William Clark also embarked on an "epic" journey, as their biographers remark.[47] Indeed, their exploration across the fledgling United States, which was initiated by President Thomas Jefferson, was officially termed the "Corps of Discovery."

In general, we can assert that all the "encounters" related above follow guidelines identical to those of the Motecuhzoma/Cortés meeting. This arose not out of some attempt at identical patterning, but from the very important fact that the worlds of both the Europeans and indigenous ethnic groups had not been historically prepared for this enormous discourse. As such, the encounters moved through a series of clearly definable stages. These stages, even in the more sophisticated Lewis/Clark era, made assumptions that often bring about an irreversible and mutual "mimetic blockage," as Stephen Greenblatt terms it, which remains with us today.[48]

In order to arrive at what we might perceive as an objective truth, we should seek differing versions of the events. On the one hand, Cortés's *Five Letters* to Emperor Charles V gave his version.[49] But therein lies a problem, for Cortés was attempting to ingratiate himself with his sovereign, who already had an "Indian" affixed to his royal emblem as the "Wild Man."[50] Furthermore, Cortés had to give the type of account that, for reasons that go even beyond his own mutiny, must at all times present the appearance of a "civilized" European dealing in a firm but sensitive way with "wild" Indians. He must also always remember that Motecuhzoma was not a commoner, but one of royal blood, with which Charles could relate—an incident that Cortés's friend and companion, Francisco Pizarro would unfortunately fail to remember in his own later dealings with the Aztec emperor in Peru.

We are fortunate in that we do not have to rely solely on Cortés for the "conqueror's" view. Bernal del Castillo Díaz was a soldier in Cortés's army, and he compiled his own version of events, *The True History of the Conquest of New Spain,* in five volumes.[51] But Díaz did not, at least so far as we know, keep a diary; these events were recalled from memory several years after the event. In addition, both Cortés and Díaz, whether implicitly or explicitly, were writing for the greater glory of Spain, to exalt themselves and their nation. Their material was published in Spain, to be read by the nobility and the learned, and both writers must have had this sobering reality of a specific and special audience in mind.

On the other hand, we would like to think that we have, at least to some extent, a degree of minority discourse in the various Aztec codices—both pre- and post-Cortésian.[52] Among the earlier ones are included the *Codex Bologna, Codex Borbonicus, Codex Borgia, Codex Columbino, Codex Cospiano, Codex Fejérváry-Mayer, Codex Laud, Codex Nuttall, Codex Vaticanus A and B, Codex Vienna,* and *Codex Vindobonensis.* Of these, the *Codex Nuttall* seems to be the most typical. It once belonged to Lord Zoncke of Hakynworth and is available in an edition with 88 color plates, edited by Zelia Nuttall,[53] after whom it was named. Generally speaking, it concerns itself with Aztec religion and rituals and includes information on sacrifice, temples, and kings.

Of the post-Cortésian codices, the following list includes most of those known: *Codex Azcatitlán, Codex Bodley, Codex Boturini, Codex Chimpalpopoca, Codex Dehasa, Codex Dresblen, Codex of 1576, Codex Florentino, Codex Ixtilxochitl, Codex Magliabecchiano, Codex Mendoza, Codex Mexicanus* (also known as *Historía de los Mexicanos por sus Pinturas*—strictly speaking a book by an anonymous Aztec chronicler), *Codex Mixter, Codex Paris, Codex Ramirez, Codex Rios, Codex Telleriano-Ramensis, Codex Tudela, Codex Xólotl,* and *Codex Zouche.* The editors of the *Codex Mendoza* have described it in language that is applicable to most others, and representing it as; "a pictographic writing system that comes down to us in a few remaining books made of fig-bark paper or deer skin. The manuscripts were used to record genealogies, histories and tribute tallies and to serve as ritual, divinatory and calendrial manuals."[54] In addition, there are indigenous written versions of the events, composed under Spanish supervision. The most famous is the *Codex Florentino* or *Florentine Codex.* What is noteworthy in both pre- and post-Cortésian accounts is the relatively limited space accorded to the encounter that is the hallmark of Spanish and European history; instead, the chroniclers relate

the historical events of their own battles, martyrs, victors, and tribute. By
omission, the codices suggest that the constantly-related meeting between Cortés
and Motecuhzoma was a very infinitesimal part in the long tradition of Aztec
historical existence.

While we are relieved that we possess versions of the discourse from the
Aztec side, we soon discover that after zealous Spanish priests had destroyed
most of the older books, they rigorously set about preparing new ones. So many
that survive are in no way "authentic"—they are only re-creations of a seemingly
agreed upon event. Some of these were composed a generation or so after the
actual event and are tainted by the Spanish version of history. Therefore, even
such a noble undertaking as Fray Bernardino de Sahagún's *Florentine Codex*
must be treated with special care, since its own supposedly indigenous version of
events tallies too closely with the European view.

Codices do have an extra dimension, for, much like European maps, they
have a "visual" aspect. Particularly because we are faced with the European
accounting of themselves as incoming gods, it becomes all the more important
to see the Aztec books as a "final authority,"[55] within the limitations I have tried
to outline. José Rabasa adds in a very perceptive essay that the visual version is
not "an illustration of the text, but a mode of writing the event."[56] Certainly,
when the Aztec account is combined with subsequent anthropological work, we
may attempt to seek some kind of reconstruction.

Could we relive history, it would be possible to assert that Encounter
involves two clearly defined stages. At each separate end, one could claim that a
state of pre- and post-encounter exists. In the former instance, most typical in
the Motecuhzoma/Cortés meeting, the drama was present as a mental picture in
the minds of both players. In Motecuhzoma's case, November 8, 1519 had
already been assigned as a fateful day according to the Spanish version of the
Aztec calendar. In Cortés's case, he had been dispatched by Diego de Velázquez de
Cuéllar, governor of Cuba, with specific orders to "conquer" the Yucatán
peninsula. Before the drama unfolds, we therefore observe that the two parties
were predisposed to its final execution;[57] they are almost playing from a written
script

Even before their meeting, Cortés was not unknown to Motecuhzoma, for he
was expected. One has to be a little suspicious regarding the profuseness of
legends in the New World that associate the coming of Europeans with the
arrival of gods—later to be fictionalized, as part of the same thematic concerns of
Caliban toward Prospero and Friday toward Crusoe. In any event, Cortés is
expected, and somewhere at the back of the European's mind, we are told, he is

about to assume the destined role of god-conqueror that history had worked out for him.

Cortés himself knew of Motecuhzoma. His expedition had been the third one dispatched by Governor Velázquez from Cuba, the first having been an exploratory slave-hunting expedition in 1517, and the second having been led by Juan de Grijalba, who reached the northern outskirts of the Aztec empire, and brought back the gold he sought. John Greenway notes how the Grijalba expedition learned of Motecuhzoma:

Grijalba visited several points along the coast, giving Spanish names to various bays, islands, rivers, and towns. On arriving at the river which they named Banderas, because of the numerous Indians carrying white flags, whom they saw along the coast, they first heard of the existence of Montezuma, of whom these people were vassals, and by whom they had been ordered to keep a look out for the possible return of the whitemen, whose former visit to Cozumel had been reported to the emperor.[58]

So even before any personal physical contact, Cortés and Motecuhzoma knew of each other's existence and were conscious of the fact that they would physically meet. In many ways, this foreknowledge of the Other, admitted by both sides, deprives the actual occurrence of their meeting of any later imposed mystique.

This mutual preknowledge of Encounter is not very evident in the reported Motecuhzoma/Cortés meeting, but is nonetheless manifest. Perhaps only in this way can we explain the much debated "light" Columbus allegedly saw, in his 1493 encounter with the Taínos people, long before the sailor's cry of "Tierra! Tierra!" In any event, the Taínos would have been warned of Columbus's coming when the Europeans fired a cannon and hoisted a flag.[59] Even before this initial encounter, the distant light and cannon fire assume almost the force of some large primordial impact. At Guanhani—present-day Watling Island in the Bahamas—Europe and the New World were both ready for Stage 1 of the drama of Encounter.

Some of what takes place in Stage 1 of the Cortés/Motecuhzoma Encounter is also part of what occurs to Taíno, Maya, Inca as well as Aztec. At this stage, in order to be completely neutral, we see not a "Conqueror" and a "conquered," for this would be to anticipate later historical judgment; instead, we witness the "Great Silence" as an initial part of the coming together. The two "sides" do not have even the basic currency of "language" and, indeed, their very "humanity" is in doubt. Europeans, to some extent, carry in their heads notions regarding the monstrous races. Indigenous peoples, specifically here the Aztec, perceive the possibility of a return of Quetzalcoatl, or perhaps this is only what the Europeans think that the indigenous people think.

In any case, there is an enormous silence, since "spoken" sounds are useless, and "written" words as yet have no place. Here only the physical movement of body, the exaggeration of gestures and facial expressions, can have any meaning. Stephen Greenblatt adds that even "gesturing" can have no universal meaning within the context of what I have termed the Great Silence. Therefore, much will be misunderstood: "The paradox of the meaningful—or perhaps the full—sign is that it is empty in the sense of hollow or transparent; a glass through which Columbus looks to find what he expects to find," Greenblatt comments.[60]

In truth, no communication has taken place. Here, as Greenblatt recognizes, there is an attempt at the interpretation of signs, hence the unfortunate tendency to misinterpret. This leads to "appropriate nemesis, imitation in the interest of acquisition," on both parts, which need not have entailed "any grasp of the cultural reality of the other."[61] At Stage 1 of Encounter, there is even a limitation in the employment of the human senses, for all player/participants are restricted to seeing, hearing and smelling, and those only to a small degree, since in all instances, cultural self-containment would prevent the "translation" of sense apprehension into any larger comprehension.

If Stage 1 of Encounter is typified by the Great Silence and modification of the senses, Stage 2 might by categorized as the utterance of the "First Sound." Note that there can, as yet, be no "discourse," no real communication; instead now, although the sense of hearing is predominant, there is a failure on both sides to comprehend. Body language and sign language have given way to movement, the physical lessening of the distance between parties. Because discourse at this stage is unintelligible, it will obviously be misunderstood. But the "we" versus the "them" (and at this point we have to introduce those terms) is what Marianna Torgovnick terms "a shared illusion"[62] that disguises, indeed represses, fragmentations of gender, class, and political affiliation. But this is truly the moment when distinct world views are present, both for Motecuhzoma and Cortés.

At Stage 2, there is no One or Other. Although sound is heard, dialogue is not yet possible. What is stated becomes not merely a "monologue" but a type of soliloquy, spoken to the self alone. In his "Second Letter," Cortés reported very quickly past Stage 1, where "we were received by that lord, Montezuma, with about two hundred chiefs all barefooted, and dressed in a kind of livery, very rich," to Stage 2. Cortés descended from his horse and attempted to embrace Motecuhzoma, but was warned off by Motecuhzoma's retinue. But "they, and he also, made the ceremony of kissing the ground." Here we are in for a disappointment because, despite the presence of Cortés's mistress, Doña Marina, his "ear," Cortés only reports words that apparently derive from signs, actually gestures. Even when Motecuhzoma speaks, Cortés states it as a speech act of the Unreachable Other buried in the past, writing "After he had spoken with me.[63]

When they do speak, it is therefore not a "conversation." Motecuhzoma, according to Cortés, seats himself on a hastily prepared "platform" near Cortés and begins what can only be described as a monologue. This is when Cortés apparently hears the strange legend about the return of Quetzalcoatl which Grijalba had supposedly already taken back to the Spaniards. Yet according to Cortés, Motecuhzoma declared:

we have always held that those who descended from him would come to subjugate this country and us as his vassals; and *according to the direction from which you say you came,* which is where the sun rises, and *from what you tell us* of your great lord or king, who has sent you here, we believe, and hold for certain, that he is our rightful sovereign, especially *as you tell* us that since many days he has had news of us.[64] (Emphasis added)

Independent of any Aztec version of the events, more problems arise. First, according to Cortés himself, he and Motecuhzoma had just met and had not yet spoken. Second, there is no mention of the presence of Doña Marina, when Motecuhzoma is speaking, so how could Cortés possibly have understood such a long narration much less reproduced it verbatim in his letters? In any event, it is not at all certain that Doña Marina could have understood the Aztec language so well, and then translated all its diplomatic niceties into Castillian for Cortés to understand and later report. Third, the story itself is too pat, the account of a god come back home, one that was part of European imaginings and would be played out in fact and fiction throughout the domain of the New World. Fourth, Motecuhzoma's entire speech seems geared toward Cortés's design, namely to flatter Charles V and gain concessions for Cortés himself. Motecuhzoma's instant admission, a few hours after they have met, that Charles is his "rightful sovereign," smacks of downright nonsense. Motecuhzoma would have no way of understanding any links that existed between the bearded stranger standing before him and an emperor in a faraway land, especially if Cortés was a returning Aztec god. Certainly, his subsequent actions against Cortés would dispel any such illusions.

Our tentative conclusion must therefore be that in China, Africa, and Native

America, there were various barriers that prevented any kind of total understanding. We have noted that these issues do not derive so much from ethnic apartness, as from an inability to see through the cultural haze and affirm a common humanity. When in China, the "traveler" encounters the "traveled," in Africa, the "explorer" meets the "explored," and in the New World, the "discoverer" finds the "discovered," it is the very lens of looking out that prevents identification. Therefore, travelers to China sought not what was there but what was in their heads, the legendary leftovers of the European medieval period, its monsters, gold, Prester John, Amazons, the Fountain of Youth, and, indeed, Paradise itself.

Likewise, those who "explored" Africa carried preconceived ideas of the "Dark Continent," and these notions were easily located, identified, and even named. Prester John was thought to be in Ethiopia, the cache of wealth may have been in the "Gold Coast," and Plinian pygmies were found in the Ituri forest of Central Africa. The naming signified both authenticity and location, both the realization of legend and justification for it. The situation was compounded by the slave trade, which, by transporting millions of Africans to the New World, brought them into contact with mythologies that contributed to their despisal of self and their construction of new mythologies, partly in a desperate effort at self-revival.

Among Native Americans, the "discovered," the distortion was just as acute. Since Europeans brought the selfsame medieval beliefs and mythologies to the New World, they again identified and named their own monsters. The Caribs, cannibals, are a case in point; the Amazons, another. As the New World was "discovered," it receded into the background of old misbegotten European notions. To some extent, Native Americans, like Africans, began to believe at first in the more charitable version of the imposed mythology, the Noble Savage, and later in the less flattering interpretation of the "Wild Man." Part and parcel of the way in which the mythology was both justified and normalized lays in the manner by which traveler, explorer, and discoverer conscripted the encountered into this new idea of the world. We shall also see how this occurred with reference to the Pacific islands.

In a way, all European colonizers were "missionaries," expounding faith, fashion and fusion, a spiritual credo and a cultural belief. Christianity became part of the basis through which these worlds—by sign, gesture, and pseudo-language—could be further traveled, explored, mythologized, and "discovered." Although China was less affected by this in the narrower sense, in the broader interpretation of Christianity as Western culture, all of the three areas were tremendously influenced. Christianity gave new names and symbols to indigenous people, and often there arose from this a hierarchy of Western values that had little to do with spiritual welfare, but a great deal to do with material success. This adds a new and important dynamic to the concept of the Other in a world where China, Africa, and Native America never meet except through the intervention of the West. In a curious way, each begins to define its own Otherness in terms of Ultimate Otherness, in a dark and shady bypath of history where their own shadows loom. Each victim is conscious of one thing only—this is not what I want to be. For in the the ultimateness of the Unreachable Other he recognizes himself and grows afraid.

This study will focus on China and the Pacific Islands as quite arbitrary examples of a process whereby the Other established his own degrees of Otherness. I have termed these imposed differences—Odder, Outer, and Utter—in an attempt at showing not only the establishment of latitudes of separation, but also in demarcating how Western-conferred Otherness was partly accepted, then partly passed on to neighboring or distant peoples, so that the very terminology often indicated the plight and wretchedness of both the Namer/Other and the named/other.

2

LEGENDS OF EARLY CONQUEST

China's contact with and incorporation of its West may be seen in a number of distinct, yet overlapping, ways. First, there was a period, quite early in China's history, when this West was perceived as odd, macabre, and mysterious. Second, there was a period of deliberate expansion from the area that was originally China westward, in which some of the old notions were challenged but nonetheless survived in mythology, especially in Daoist belief. Third, there occurred a period, as in the time of Confucius and Mencius, when this area which we shall call China underwent unrest and civil strife; Buddhism then became the spiritual route through which China's West was let in. Fourth, through middlemen (mainly Parthians), China and Rome met each other. At this point, commerce was the major activity that introduced the West, and, of course, this continues until the present. Fifth, China embarked on its own overseas exploration, through which it came into contact with India, the Persian Gulf, and the east of Africa as far south as Zanzibar. Sixth, Mongol conquest of the various states which constituted China expanded the area's cultural horizons and brought peoples of various languages and backgrounds within the province of China. Finally, following the admission of Jesuits beginning in the sixteenth century, and with the advent of Western military might, China was free to open its doors to Western powers.

All of these will be considered in some detail, particularly to demonstrate how China changed from being "perceiver" to becoming "perceived," and how in the course of time the Chinese "Other" perceived the non-Chinese "Other," until all of this new territory, now termed China, was itself constructed as a monolith and acquired an Otherness imposed on it by the West.

QUEEN MOTHER OF THE WEST AND THE EMPEROR MU

In the distant parts, China's "West" was an amorphous undefined area, the abode of Xi Wangmu (Hsi Wang Mu), Queen Mother of the West. Formerly, she had been a semihuman, with the teeth of a tiger and the tail of a leopard. She possessed a beautiful garden filled with exotic birds and flowers, and a fruit, the *pan tao* or peach of immortality.[1]

C. P. Fitzgerald has pointed out in his *China: A Short Cultural History* that among the motifs on base reliefs have been found on Han tombs in Shandong province "are hunting scenes, battle places, notable historical happenings such as the attempt to assassinate First Emperor, Qin Shi Huan Di (Ch'in Shih Huan Ti) (259–210 B.C.), when he was still only King of Ch'in, and legends such as the visit of King Mu of the Chou dynasty to the divine ruler of the far west, Hsi Wang Mu, 'Royal Mother of the West.' Fitzgerald adds that the legend has intrigued western scholars, who wrongly attributed a western origin to China. He rightly suggests that Xi Wangmu most likely belongs to the stuff of legend.[2]

Emperor Mu (1961 B.C.) is mentioned in *The Annals of the Bamboo Books* (c. 200 B.C.), which was written on bamboos slips.[3] It may, in fact, have been a method of preserving in legendary memory the actual journeys of earlier Chinese voyagers by crediting them to Emperor Mu. There we read that Emperor Mu "went on a punitive expedition of mount [Kunlun]; and saw the western Wang-moo [Wang mu]."[4] The suggestion made in this translation by James Legge, and subsequently taken up by other sinologists, is that the Wang-mu may well have been a people.

The Annals of the Bamboo Books further tells us that "the chief of Wang-moo [Wang mu] came to court, and was lodged in the palace of Chon." Apparently Emperor Mu's journey must have been extensive: he "travelled over the country of the Moving Sands . . . and that of 'Heaps of Feathers.' "[5] In all, his journeys had been 100,000 *li*—one *li* is about one-third of a mile. This route sounds very much like a path between the Kunlun Range and the "Moving Sands" of the Taklamakan Desert. Indeed, this is the very direction that later Han travelers would take in search of the unknown West. Interestingly, "Kunlun" was a name for the exotic that would later be applied to regions in Tibet, India, Malay, and finally Africa.

Emperor Mu's journeyings are a mixture of fantasy and fact. For instance, when he ascended the Kunlun Range he visited the palace of Huang Di (Huang Ti), the Yellow Emperor (supposedly fl. 2697–2597 B.C.),the legendary founder of China. There he paid appropriate traditional respects to Huang Di's grave by heaping piles of earth on it. But as he went toward the Chun Mountains, from which he could survey the wild and desolate scenery to the West, he noted (at least the compiler of the *Annals* did) that here was a place of near perfection where existed "a store of precious stones and valuable jade" and "where the most flourishing crops grew and the trees were tall and the bushes beautiful."[6] At the foot of the mountain he spent five days listening to wonderful music and being entertained by beautiful women.

As Emperor Mu traveled on, he finally came to the domain of the Queen Mother of the West. The account speaks of a marvelous courtship, as he offered her silk and other fabric. At a banquet on Emerald Pond, she toasted Emperor Mu begging him to return. He gallantly replied in song that he would indeed be back in three years. The chronicler added that Emperor Mu rode on to a mountain, upon which he planted a tree, naming the place in her honor, "Mountain of the Royal Mother of the West" or "Hsi-Wang-Mu-Shan."[7]

Although this delightful legend is not verifiable history, it does indicate the possibility of a very early contact with China's West, long before religions could synthesize the legends or history might render them dubious. But as late as the time of the composition of *The Tso Chuan* (or the commentary of Tso), we still find an independent reference[8] to Emperor Mu and the Queen Mother of the West. *The Tso Chuan,* written in the third century B.C., mentions a lost ode to Emperor Mu and adds, "They say that long ago, King Mu wished to give free rein to his heart by traveling all over the world, leaving his carriage tracks and horses' hoofprints in every region."[9] Obviously the ancient people of China thought that Emperor Mu at least symbolized an early attempt at world exploration.

What is fascinating about the Queen Mother of the West is that she progressed from folk belief to become also a representational figure, first in Daoist belief and later in Buddhist religion. Since Chinese alchemy was forever engaged in the search for immortality, it was not unnatural that she would become on par with the Daoist Eight Immortals who are usually identified with positive human attributes, and very often associated as the patrons of guilds. Emperor Han Wu Di (Han Wu Ti) (156 B.C.–87 B.C.) was granted the famous peach of immortality by her, as was the founder of the Ming dynasty in the fourteenth century. This was precisely because both Daoism and Buddhism maintained her mysticism and magic. J. C. Cooper adds in *Chinese Alchemy* that, "In Daoism the Western Paradise was presided over by Hsi Wang Mu, Queen of Heaven; in Buddhism, the Amida Buddha resided in the Pure Land."[10]

Regarding Daoism, the Queen Mother of the West, along with the Spirit of the Northern Region, the second Sage King (Shun), and other great and auspicious figures, became one of the mutual recipients of the "word."[11] We read in the second important Daoist work (after Lao Tzu's *Dao de Ching (Tao-te*

Ching), the *Chuang Tzu,* attributed to the author of the same name, that "The Queen Mother of the West attained it [The Way] and took her seat on Shao Kwan Mountain. No one knows her beginning and no one knows her end."[12]

Daoism, which dates from the sixth century B.C., quite early therefore reinforced the older mythological association with the West, lending it religious support. However, the Queen Mother of the West did not exist in folk belief and Daoist philosophy and religion merely because of her link with the West, but specifically because she became associated with the peach of immortality. A Qing (Ch'ing, 1644–1911) account is given in Yan Lan's *Record of the True Lord Wu*. There we read how Wu Dao, the Divine Doctor, goes through the second of seven stages before achieving immortality. Yan Lan's undated stele inscription reads, "Hitching up his robes, Wu Dao climbed to the highest peak, where he saw the Queen mother of the West. He stayed for seven days. [She] transmitted to him divine methods of saving the world, and the arts of exorcising demons and driving away evil influences. Upon setting out to return he suddenly found himself back home and thus attained enlightenment."[13]

The major point about Lord Wu's achievement of divine status was that he was able to accomplish it through his meeting with this mysterious female in the furthermost Kunlun Mountains. Through her, he gained the tremendous ability to save the world and banish evil. As a result of being with her, he was able to achieve enlightenment.

Interestingly, an account was also given of the historically real Emperor Han Wu Di. The description of Han Wu Di's meeting with the Queen Mother of the West became of additional significance since, historically, he was the real motivator for travel and expansion westward. The narrative is related of how Emperor Han Wu Di was given the famous peach, but warned by the Queen Mother of the West not to bury it in Chinese soil. Not only was Chinese soil not suitable, but the peach tree of immortality only blossomed every 3,000 years.[14]

Emperor Hong-Wu (Hung-wu) (1328–1398), founder of the Ming Dynasty (1368–1644), had provided a period of indigenous rule between the Mongols or Yuan (1206–1368) and the Qing (Ch'ing) or Manchu dynasties (1644–1911). Despite his undoubted skills as a military leader and his ability to organize a new bureaucracy, and despite his concerns about undue Confucian influence, Emperor Hong-Wu still sought some legitimacy for his own continuity in the legend of the Queen Mother of the West.[15]

Her favor, again in the form of a flat peach stone, was presented to Hong-Wu. The stone was supposedly the original given to Han Wu Di and passed on through the Yuan dynasty which Emperor Hong-Wu had overthrown. Thus the Queen Mother of the West came to stand for a new legitimacy, one which supposedly established the new peasant-emperor as a direct descendant of the ancient Han dynasty.

In addition to being associated with Daoism as philosophy and religion, alchemy and the quest for immortality, the Queen Mother of the West was listed in one account as the one who "transmitted the scriptures."[16] In a way, she thus became almost an archetypal originator of the Buddhist bodhisattva, a person who postpones Buddhahood to help others. It is no accident that this sacred person was *feminized* in China.

THE XIONGNU AS ULTIMATE OTHER/UTTER

Westward expansion from Han times onward did not therefore end the unfamiliarity of the mysterious West. As a case in point, we should note that the Xiongnu, ancestors to the Huns, seemed to represent an almost metaphorical fear of the unknown. China's preeminent historian, Sima Qian (Ssu-ma Ch'ien) (c. 145 B.C.–c. 85 B.C.) devoted considerable space in his *Shi chi* (*Historical Records)* [17] to this fascinating mirror image of the Han Chinese "Other's" perception of the "Other."

Sima Qian asserts quite categorically that "the Hsung-nu [Xiongnu] have been a source of constant worry and harm to China."[18] Although he readily admitted that since he was a court appointed historian (and, indeed, had been castrated for what was thought to be a lack of empathy), like Confucius he had to use "subtle and guarded language" when "writing about his own times."[19] Nevertheless, Sima Qian sees the Han "Other" as crude and nomadic and without fixed dwellings or cities. Unable to acquire even permanent leaders, they had neither writing nor contracts, nor they did even obey the basic caveats of military warfare: "If the battle is going well for them they will advance, but if not, they will retreat."[20]

This denunciation of the implied cowardice of Han Otherness is particularly intriguing, if only because we know that as early as the fourth century B.C., Sun Tzu advocated this very type of warfare. Sun Tzu's *Art of War* states quite categorically, "If weaker numerically, be capable of withdrawing," but "If equally matched you may engage him [the foe]."[21] Mao Zedong made this a cornerstone of his own guerilla tactics.

Sima Qian's remarks two and a half centuries later than Sun Tzu cannot therefore place the Xiongnu in a bad light, particularly since they obviously provided the Han with constant harassment. According to Sima Qian himself, they had done this for a considerable period of time. Yet the Han did not hesitate to demonize them; Sima Qian cited the *Shih jing* (*Shih Ching*) or *Book of Odes*, one of the "Five Confucian Classics," in which it was stated that "We smote the barbarians of the north"[22] as ancient proof of Chinese might and power.

Part of the problem with the attempt to dismiss the Xiongnu as "barbarians" is that the submission of the barbarians was only possible with the help of one Yu Yü, himself a barbarian, who spoke the language of the early Qin (Ch'in) (221–206 B.C.). To a great extent, therefore, the glorious account which Sima Qian gives of gradual Qin encroachment into these areas is somewhat lessened by the manner in which the distant Other actively cooperated with the Qin.

Another way in which one may quite clearly observe early attempts at keeping the "barbarians" without is the construction of the Great Wall, which predates the advent of the so-called First Emperor, Qin Shi Huang Di (Ch'in Shih Huang Ti).[23] Sima Qian described the beginning of the Great Wall's construction as guarding against the attacks of the barbarians. Clearly, the Great Wall became an attempt to lock out the Otherness so dreaded by the Chinese.

What is particularly ironical and worthy of note at this point is that the Great Wall may have served more to restrict China's inhabitants than to prevent encroachments. For it certainly did not deter either the Mongols in the thirteenth century, or the Manchus in the seventeenth from becoming part of the fertilizing seed of contemporary China. Additionally, those very invaders served to extend and define China as the area we would recognize today. The "China" of Qin Shi Huan Di was confined to a fairly narrow strip bordering the Yellow River on the north and the Yangtze to the south.[24]

The Xiongnu and the Great Wall became physical manifestations of Chinese fear of Ultimate Otherness. But the fortifications could not totally withstand the encroachments of the world outside. So although Sima Qian was at great pains to describe the total alienation of the Xiongnu barbarians, time and time again during the Han Dynasty, the Xiongnu triumphed. Even as Han generals deserted, the Han were forced to make concessions to begin to recognize the Xiongnu not just as "barbarians" but as a viable presence with which they had to coexist.

One important fact, historical and yet very symbolic, is the gift exchange and the presentation of a Han princess to the Xiongnu imperial family, as the Han paid subsidy to their despised Other. As Sima Qian expressed it, "The Han agreed to send a gift of specified quantities of silk floss and cloth, grain and other food stuffs each year, and the two nations were to live in peace and brotherhood."[25]

The frequency with which women found themselves part of the pawns of peace has become a staple in much Chinese poetry. If, as Arthur Waley states, Chinese poets tended to disregard male/female relationships as trite and overdone,[26] then perhaps the plight of the Han princess living abroad became an acceptable avenue to express love, yearning, nostalgia and *Heimweh*. The "Lament of Hsi-Chün" is typical of this genre of poetry. Finding herself with a decrepit and aging Central Asian nomad, K'un Mo, Princess Hsi-Chün looks with some scorn around her habitat. As she muses on the dire predicament of a princess forced to live in a felt tent and consume uncooked food, she yearns for her home, the heartland, wishing she could fly back away from this "far corner of Earth."[27]

Because the account is Han-centered, the norm remains, through the eyes of the poet or historian, that of what ultimately became the basis of China. Therefore, despite apparent concessions to the alien outsiders, the Han emperor in 174 B.C. is portrayed by Sima Qian as a kind of arbitrator. Indeed, the emperor even tells the *Shan-yü* or leader of the Xiongnu, how he ought to conduct his own civil strife with an errant king. Sima Qian showed the Han emperor as generous, citing a letter in which the emperor sympathetically wrote, "Your envoy tells us that you have led your troops in person to attack the other barbarian nations. . ." and that the Xiongnu leader had even sent various items the enemy "from our own wardrobe"[28]—presumably gifts given to the *Shan-yü* by the emperor himself.

What is most peculiar about this letter is that there is blatant assumption of Qin superiority. The problem is that surely the Xiongnu could never so readily admit to their own barbarism, even had it actually existed. And bearing in mind a Confucian adage that "Barbarian states with their rulers are inferior to Chinese states without them,"[29] it would seem fair to conclude that Sima Qian's account of this early contact between Han Chinese and their own Other reveals an early documented attempt at marginalizing what was different, odd, strange, and, in the final analysis, completely outside the province of Confucian reason and norms.

ZHANG QIAN AS DISCOVERER OF THE WEST

Not unnaturally, when Zhang Qian (Chang Ch'ien) (d. 114 B.C.) ventured west in 138 B.C. under direct orders from Han Wu Di, he took with him the legends of his Han center. Han Wu Di's reasons were most pragmatic; he had heard of the Yuezhi (Yüeh-chih or Rouzhi) people of the Gansu corridor who had been driven west by the Xiongnu. They had settled in Bactria, in contemporary northern Afghanistan. Han Wu Di wished to ally himself with the Yuezhi so that he might be able to have additional help in battling the feared Xiongnu.[30]

Zhang's exploration is in itself a fascinating narrative. He was captured by the Xiongnu and imprisoned for ten years. When finally released, he still undertook the continuation of his mission, only to find the Han emperor's requests for alliance roundly rejected by the Yuezhi. On his way back, he was again captured and held for a year. Only after thirteen years did he make his way back to his emperor. His report, as related by Sima Qian, was the first factual account that the Han had of "Western lands."

Since Zhang was a creature at the center, as he reached out to Ferghana (now Xinjiang Province), Bactria, and Sogdiana (now in western Turkistan), he combined facts with mythology and exoticism as he categorized what he encountered. Thus, he became the prototype of all "discoverers" in that he assumed a degree of proprietorship (of course in the name of the emperor).

His informers had told him that "T'iao-chih" (Mesopotamia) "is situated several thousand *li* west of An-hsi (Parthia) and borders the Western Sea [possibly the Persian Gulf]." Even though our latter-day translations are attempts at approximation, clearly this is, on the face of it, an attempt at objective reckoning. As is the further description of Mesopotamia being "hot and damp," a place where "the people live by cultivating the fields and planting rice."[31]

Accompanying apparent fact is the mythologizing process. In encountering the An-hsi, Zhang even harked back to a time that anticipated his own real presence and which, nevertheless, he still ignored. Zhang felt that he was so far away from the Han norm that he had to depict the unusual and the absurd. So, he wrote that in this country "live great birds which lay eggs as large as pots."[32] The haphazard manner in which this is thrown into the "objective" rendering of T'iao-chih Otherness, confirmed the reader's suspicion that it all constituted part of a larger "fact," different to be sure from any that could be experienced at home.

What, however, clinches the total Otherness/Outerness of the T'iao-chih is reference to ancient Han belief, which we have discussed before. According to the "old men of An-hsi," along with the marvel of the River of Weak Water, on which even a goose feather could not float, was to be found "the Queen Mother of the West, though they admit that have never seen either of them."[33] Since, as we noted, Xi Wangmu had been grounded in folk belief and authenticated by Daoism and even later by Buddhism, few would have difficulty in understanding the total alienation of such un-Han abnormality.

Zhang's report added two other noteworthy points concerning this area on the periphery. First, its inhabitants did not have a knowledge of governance: "The people are very numerous and are ruled by many petty chiefs."[34] The order which Confucius preached, attainable by adherence to rites and proper conduct, had contributed to the idyllic nature of the era of the Sage Kings, Yao, Shun and Yü. Clearly, the legendary natural perfection that existed in Yao's (supposedly reigned c. 2357–2256 B.C.) abdication in favor of Shun (supposedly reigned c. 2255–2206 B.C.) and Shun's succession by Yü (supposedly reigned c. 2205–1766 B.C.), tamer of the Great Flood, was lacking.[35] Early Han Chinese would have recognized an absence of a sense of order in the conduct of these Western people beyond the Han periphery.

Second, the inhabitants have been given an inversion of Han norms. The ruler of An-hsi, Zhang reported to his emperor, regarded his chiefs as his servants. In a Han universe in which there was a definite delineation of hierarchy, members of the nobility could never revert to the status of peasants. As Mencius (371–289 B.C.), expanding on Confucius, would state: "When the world declined and the Way fell into obscurity, heresies and violence again arose." With the departure of the legendary Sage Kings, "feudal lords do as they please," "the way of Confucius is not proclaimed," and "sooner or later it will come to men devouring men."[36]

Zhang accorded to the Western peoples a degree of nimble animal dexterity. Saying that they were "very skillful at performing tricks that amaze the eye," he was almost certainly referring to his party's encounter with acrobats and jugglers.[37] They are amusing, odd, and even macabre and, as Irene Franck and David Brownstone add in *The Silk Road*, "would prove most attractive to the Chinese and would later be specially imported—giving rise to the acrobatics tradition that is still so popular in modern China."[38] Especially, I would suggest, a major staple of Beijing opera, alas now slowly falling on tough times.

Above all, Zhang's expedition was actually one of surveillance, even espionage, that would later help Han expansion and, through carefully controlled population transfer, begin to define the China we recognize today. Sima Qian introduced Zhang's report by stating that, "in person [he] visited the lands of Ta-yuan [Ferghana], the Great Yüeh-chih [Indo-Scythia region], Ta-hsia [Bactria], and K'ang-chü [Trans-Oxiana region], and in addition he gathered reports on five or six other large states in the neighborhood. All of this information he related to the emperor on his return."[39] Therefore, Sima Qian intends us to see this not merely as a fact-gathering mission, but as a prelude to conquest.

In the report, Zhang listed the position of different places, their proximity to other countries and to Han China, the fortification of the cities, the wealth of the inhabitants, and what obstacles lay between the Han capital and the various areas he described. He narrated the relationship between the neighboring countries and their attitude toward the Xiongnu, the state of their army, and the geography of the area. Zhang was able to provide a verbal map for his emperor so that, at a later stage, those who followed in his footsteps in future encounters with the West were able to rely on the insight and information this early "discoverer" provided.

Quite in keeping with the traditions of imperial hegemony, the "discovered" were also conscripted into service. On his first expedition, Zhang took Kan-fu who, Sima Qian reliably informs us, was a Xiongnu "barbarian. " Obviously, Kan-fu must have acted as both cultural liasion and interpreter for Zhang, yet he is never commended for this either in Zhang's report or Sima Qian's commentary. Instead, his Otherness is stressed, as we read of his natural ability to live off the game of the forests and to feed Zhang and himself. This failure to recognize Kan-fu for his accomplishments is even more appalling since Zhang had himself married a Xiongnu "barbarian" woman and started a family during his period of captivity. Even Kan-fu's return to Han China with Zhang is meant to sound odd, for we learn that he is the sole surviving member of Zhang's original expedition. Seemingly, Zhang's contacts with the Xiongnu, his marriage, and his relationship with Kan-fu are merely intended to portray Zhang as the Han expert on the Other—the "discoverer" and his "discovered."

Eleven years after his first expedition, Zhang Qian, despite a temporary period of imperial displeasure, was again dispatched to the West. Sima Qian wrote that those who followed him "in later times relied upon his reputation to gain them a hearing." For Zhang's success as diplomat and envoy, he would be given the position of "grand messenger," ranking him "among the nine highest ministers in the land."[40] We read no more of Kan-fu.

Although he did not seem to have heard of the Roman Empire as later Han travelers would, Zhang's lasting contribution was to have brought back news of India, which the Han called "Shen-tu." In Ta-hsia, he observed that there were "bamboo canes from Ch'ung and cloth made in the province of Chu [present-day Sichuan]." When he inquired as to how these articles had been obtained, he was told, "Our merchants go to buy them in the markets of Shen-tu." He was able to add that India was "said to be hot and damp," that "the inhabitants ride elephants when they go into battle," and that "the kingdom is situated on a great river,"[41] no doubt a reference to the Ganges.

Sima Qian added two important points. First, it was because of Zhang that the emperor knew of these countries "rich in unusual products" but "militarily weak" and prizing Han "goods and wealth." Second, after his defeat of the Xiongnu with General Li Guangli (Li Kuang-li), and other expeditions to the West, Zhang was able to return, like any conqueror: he brought back specimens of his conquest, "accompanied by twenty or thirty envoys" and "a similar number of horses,"[42] from still another defeated people, the Wo-sun.

A present day Chinese historian concludes, again in the spirit of Conquest, that the "Western Barbarians" were thus able to learn of Chinese technology such as "know-how about making iron and drilling deep wells,"[43] and that by 60 B.C. the areas were brought under Han control. A governor was appointed "in charge of military and political affairs [thus] protecting traders and travelers."[44] Han Wu Di had earlier even "encouraged settlers to move to the edge of the desert," where "they converted large tracts of wilderness into farmland."[45]

If Zhang's "discovery" and "conquest" seem familiar, it is because the pattern is the same. Much like Africans and Native Americans, the Xiongnu left no written record of Han activity and conquest. So we must depend on the narration that Sima Qian constructs to make any sense of "history." However, it is very obvious that Han "expansion" obviously meant Xiongnu "contraction," and Han "victory" meant Xiongnu "defeat."

Indeed, Sima Qian focused on his and his emperor's own ethnocentric realities to describe the inevitability of Wo-sun defeat. After all, the *I Ching* (which is also called *Y jing* or *Book of Changes*), the earliest of the "Confucian Classics," had predicted as much.[46] The emperor had consulted the ancient system through which eight trigrams in pairs formed 64 hexagrams, each with a name, a root meaning, and a symbolic equivalent. The emperor had been told that "divine horses are due to appear from the north-west," so that when Zhang brought the horses from the Wo-sun, he saw this as the logical fulfillment of Han destiny. Indeed, the emperor even called them "heavenly horses." Later on, when other horses arrived from Ferghana, "blood-sweating horses" which "were even hardier," the emperor simply changed names. The horses from the Wo-sun he now called "horses from the western extremity," and for those from Ferghana, he reserved the name "heavenly horses."[47]

Obsession with the "heavenly horses" was not a mere aesthetic delight on the part of the emperor, nor even some religious exultation at seeing the fulfillment of the prophecy of the *I Ching*. The tough horses were needed for further conquest, for traveling the length of the empire, and above all, for battle. If the Western Territories were to be maintained, the Han had to have a superior fighting force there. So, wisely, they beguiled the Wo-sun with the promise of still another princess and offered them silk. Long after Zhang's death, the leaders of Ferghana willingly handed over "their finest horses and allowed the Han officers to choose the ones they wanted."[48] This was to prevent General Li Guangli from attacking them.

General Li Guangli discovered something important during his siege of Ferghana: not only did the area have contact with Trans-Oxiana, but also the Han were not united in their efforts at demonizing the Other. One reason why Li Guangli did not readily attack was that, as he told his aide, "I have received word . . . that the people within the city have just obtained the services of a Chinese who knows how to dig wells."[49] This meant that the siege could be endlessly protracted, but even more that not all Han Chinese were of the same disposition toward the alien West.

Additionally, on grounds of sheer pragmatism, one unnamed high court official was totally against the expansion and occupation. Relying on the commonly accepted wisdom of the Sage Kings, he argued that the legendary ancients "devoted themselves to the nine provinces and the five concentric zones, caring nothing about what was outside."[50]

Indeed the *Shu jing (Shu Ching)*, or *Book of History*, had laid out a plan that would supposedly last for all time.[51] This was one in which Yü, the third Sage King, had assigned a specific order to the universe. Yü had stemmed disorder as he had held back the Great Flood. Now he created "the imperial domain" at the very heart of his ideal world. This was surrounded by "the domain of the nobles," "the peace securing domain," and "the domain of restraint." At the next edge, far beyond the innermost area where the emperor dwelt, existed the "wild domain" with "wild tribes which had not yet been merged in the conquering race, nor driven by it from their original seats,"[52] as James Legge explains. Finally, the *Shu jing* relates Yü's renown: "On the east reaching to the sea; on the west extending to the moving sands; to the utmost limits of the north and south: his fame and influence filled up all within the four seas."[53] Somewhere, beyond the specificity of boundary, outside the perimeter, Yü's work had ended, as he too recognized and banished the non-Chinese alien to these outer wastelands.

However, even though the argument was made that the wise ancients were content to rule within the boundaries nearer the core, Sima Qian noted with approval that what the ancient text "states about the mountains and rivers of the nine ancient provinces of China seems to be nearer the truth."[54] Consequently, one should note how the ancient texts were used both to justify and to oppose imperial expansion. We can be certain, however, that since Sima Qian is writing an official history, his view of conquest and the civilizing nature of Han culture is very much in keeping with imperial wish.

Expansion meant that there were two other related themes that become basic to Chinese poetry. Like the story of the sad princess, forced to live with barbarians far away from her land, the Emperor Han Wu Di's infatuation with the "heavenly horses" became the subject of a Chinese hymn as early as 101 B.C. In a version translated by Arthur Waley, their arrival, repeated choruslike five times times in the short text, confirms their importance for Han Chinese strategy. But as the hymn progresses, not only do the horses stress that "the barbarians are conquered," but they provide the means through which Emperor Han Wu Di himself would be able to achieve perfection by passing through,what Waley translated as, "the Gates of Heaven" and "the Palace of God."[55] Thus does the expanding empire fulfill the prophecies of ancient texts and, in addition, point the way forward to spiritual tranquility, ultimately fulfilled by its contact with Buddhism.

However, just as the Han were engaging, almost textbook style, in the usual imperial distortion of both demonizing and romanticizing their conquered, internal and external factors brought a temporary end to the Former (or Western) Han dynasty in 9 A.D. Not until the defeat of the "usurper" Wang Mang by the "Red Eyebrows" (which is how the peasants painted themselves), did the Later (or Eastern) Han dynasty establish itself in 25 A.D. When, in 70 A.D., the Later Han were able to attempt some new control of the West, the period belonged to a new general and new historian. We shall next look at their view of China's Other world.

3

CONQUERORS AND PILGRIMS

Only when the Han Chinese were able to restore some order to their own domestic situation did they reembark on their Western adventure. When they did, the players were new and even a trifle more sophisticated.[1] One family is identified most notably with this period of renewed expansionism. Ban Chao (Pan Ch'ao) (32–101 A.D.) was a scholar and writer who traded in his robes for a general's uniform. He was the son of historian Ban Biao (Pan Piao) (3–54 A.D.) and twin brother of Ban Gu (Pan Ku) (32–92 A.D.). Ban Gu completed, with his equally famous sister, Ban Zhao (Pan Chao), the *Hou Han Shu* or *The History of the Former Han Dynasty,* around 82 A.D. This dealt with the period 206 B.C. to 25 A.D.[2] When, between 73–76 A.D. and 91–101 A.D., General Ban Chao journeyed west, it should also be remembered that the Han, in a way, were retracing a familiar path, so his task was much easier than that of the earlier "discoverers" and "conquerors," such as Zhang Qian and General Li Guangli. But although, at this stage, we find few references to the Queen Mother of the West, we nevertheless note the continuing demonization of the Xiongnu and other area peoples, and the unabated Han feud with them.

Although Ban Gu and Ban Zhao's history does not deal with their brother's life, we should not even expect the superficial objectivity that Sima Qian sought to render, for now the ties of Han kinship are reinforced by the bonds of true Confucian sibling love. As General Ban Chao embarked on his exploration and reconquest of western lands, bringing them under the suzerainty of a dominant Han empire, the persons who unofficially noted his success and kept score were none other than his historian brother and sister. They were bound to view the explorations of the Former Han in the light of their brother's conquests. A contemporary account states that at one stage the emperor was so piqued that he had the historian Ban Gu imprisoned, and only the intercession of the general himself could restore Ban Gu into the emperor's good graces.[3]

Thus, because they wrote the history of a former era, Ban Gu and Ban Zhao were therefore very conscious of their brother's achievements. Very much like other educated Han Chinese, they saw the Xiongnu barbarians as completely removed from Han norms and realities. After all, the historians would have been familiar with much of the learning Confucius had helped assemble concerning the sanctions against the barbarians, traditionally banished, as previously noted, to the outer edge, far from the center where the emperor dwelt.[4]

Also, since Ban Gu and Ban Zhao reproduced much of Sima Qian's *Shi chi* and many of the official travel documents of the Former Han were clearly at their disposal, they would not have wished to have departed too radically from Sima Qian's sentiments.[5] Although, as I have already suggested, they were obviously too sophisticated to repeat some of Zhang's absurdities, they were nevertheless inheritors of his world. Particularly after the fiasco of the Wang Mang interregnum from 9 A.D.–23 A.D., when civil strife had brought about the temporary cessation of the Han, they would have yearned for a return to the old stability.

The Xiongnu, as well as other peoples west of the Pamirs, continued to represent the opposite of what was most desirable in Han Chinese society. The historians would already have read in Zhang's report that the Xiongnu apparently abjured order and good government, preferring instead to exist in a topsy-turvy world, with no adherence to Confucian rites, little regard for social order, and no concern for their diet.[6] Therefore, both the chroniclers of Ban Chao's reconquest and the new conqueror himself would have been predisposed for the further discovery of a sub-Han species of people whose only hope for welfare and good governance would have been their ultimate acceptance of Han subjugation. And the point is worth repeating that, as with the earlier conquests and descriptions, we have no written sources from the Xiongnu or other groups on which we can draw. Therefore, they remained as "barbarians" providing the continuity of the narrative thread of official historical marginalization from Sima Qian's time.

Ban Chao and his family obviously saw the advantages of trade, even with barbarians, and a letter exists from his historian brother asking him to purchase certain items in Central Asia.[7] At the same time, the Xiongnu remained the enemy, and neither Ban Chao nor the generals who came after him would permit themselves the slightest display of sympathy or generosity. Although they did not formulate a concept of "empire," they certainly exercised all aspects of it as they sought to crush people after people in the relentless Han expansion westward.

At the center, the family's norms could always be identified as Han, as part of a belief system which the emperor himself represented by virtue of *tian ming*

(T'ien Ming) or "The Mandate of Heaven"[8] True, Confucianists had attempted to explain imperial loss of power as a moral flaw, but not until the seventeenth century would there be any serious challenge to the authority of the emperor, particularly in the work of Huang Tsung-hsi whose *Waiting for the Dawn: A Plan for the Prince* (1662) spelled out what was required of each sector of government, including royalty.[9] In a way, the reasoning of Confucius and Mencius was circular: if the emperor held on to power, this was proof that Heaven had smiled beneficently on him; but once he had lost authority, this was evidence enough that he deserved his fate.

Although neither Ban Gu nor Ban Zhao explained their world in this critical light, as relative sophisticates they must have been aware of some of its shortcomings. Above all, they knew firsthand that there were other worlds, not necessarily better ones, beyond the Kunlun Mountains and the Taklimakan. Indeed, we recognize in General Ban Chao not merely the avid greed of the conqueror, but the curiosity of the traveler.

GAN YING GOES WEST

One of the most significant acts on General Ban Chao's part was the dispatch of Gan Ying in 97 A.D. to what was probably the Persian Gulf.[10] Gan Ying, one of Ban Chao's trusted officers, was able to learn not only about areas further west, but in addition he got to know about the "Western Sea," and to learn about the eastern reaches of the Roman empire. Although Gan Ying did not complete the journey, he nevertheless opened up the possibility of other kingdoms beyond the smaller ones that the Han Chinese had encountered.

The area of the eastern Roman empire, about which Gan Ying learned, was called "Ta Ch'in" by the Han. In a way, the name, which apparently means "Greater China," says much about the manner in which the Middle Kingdom continued to perceive itself in relationship to the rest of the world. But the irony of Gan Ying's journey is that he was forced to substitute the potential of real knowledge about Rome for a myth—seemingly one that could explain away his failure and his fears. Historian Jacques Gernet says bluntly that Gan Ying had been "discouraged by the Parthians from continuing his journey."[11] But Gan Ying's own version of events is a little different.

When he arrived at the Persian Sea (or perhaps the Black Sea, as some writers contend), Gan Ying wrote as follows, in what was probably a later report delivered to the emperor, much as Zhang's had been. This is what he claimed he had been told by the seamen at a major port:

This sea is very wide. With a favorable wind one may cross it in three months, but if the winds are adverse the voyage may take two years. Moreover, there is about this sea something which gives people such a longing for their own country that many die of it. For these reasons those who embark take at least three years' provisions. If the Han ambassador is willing to forget his family and his home, he can embark.[12]

Gan Ying was obviously expressing his own fears about the West. It seemed very far away, and the possibility of the loss of home, departure from the center, could well result in death. The last part of his statement appealed to the norms of Han sensibility, "family" and "home." At the very center of Confucian belief, indeed inscribed within the Five Confucian Classics themselves, side by side with the heroic deeds of kings, proper rituals for propitiation, and appropriate rites for ancestors, lay the duty of filial piety.[13] This would be meaningless away from the center where the emperor dwelt.

An enormous problem is that had this been a reconnaissance mission like Zhang's, it would have failed miserably for one major reason: the Parthians were loath to cut themselves off as intermediaries in the profitable trade between east and west. By scaring off Gan Ying, they managed to maintain their own position, at least for a brief period, thereby severing the possibility of Han contact with Rome until the Romans came by sea. Yet because of middlemen, from Han times on, the Chinese even knew of the existence of Byzantium, which they called "An Tu" after its official name, Augusta Antonia.[14]

In the *Hou Han Shu* or *History of the Later Han Dynasty,* this "Land West of the Sea" is described in splendid terms, as "discoverers" are wont to do. The area is extensive, possessing four hundred cities with walls constructed of stone. The land is abundant, and the people enjoy a comfortable life. Over all, a wise and honest king presides who metes out justice fairly. Kings deemed unworthy through the manifestation of signs and portents are deposed. This is an idealized version of Han society.[15]

The Han account also describes these people of the West as tall, with "an air comparable to those of China, and for this reason they are called Big Ts'in or Big Chinese." This is a land of gold and rare gems, and "every foreign thing, precious or strange, is produced here." Yet the people are honest. From this place, a traveler may go on to the north via a high bridge. Again, note how the area is a model for China, possessing gold that would aid in the alchemists' search for immortality.[16]

What is of particular interest, reinforcing the perception of the alien as strange, exotic, unreachable, is that this account is directed from Han Chinese to an Other—in the West—that is so removed, so fanciful, that the West has to be rendered in these most fantastic terms.The *Hou Han Shu* even falls back on the legends of a bygone era—the resuscitation of the ever elusive Xi Wangmu, Queen Mother of the West: "Some say that to the west of this country there are vaporous flowing sands near to the dwelling place of Hsi Wang Mu . . . nearly at the place where the sun sets."[17] Thus the West is fictionalized beyond any mundane reality.

In fact, it may be argued that this early Han document "orientalizes" the West, looks at the West as distant, apart, inscrutable, and strange, much as Westerners, also in pursuit of the macabre, would later envision China. Intriguingly, at the historical moment when this meeting of East and West takes place, neither recognizes the One or the Other, instead perceiving in each other the extremities of their own worlds. This situation was compounded by the fact that, for a long time, the West mistook entrepreneurial middlemen traders for the Chinese.

For instance, although Pliny is himself often personally guilty of making great exaggerations, especially in his treatment of non-Europeans, much of what he writes about in his *Natural History* of 77 A.D. is at least based on current beliefs of the time.[18] Some of the information was gleaned from older records, parts of them now lost, but there are also accounts from supposed travelers of the period. Pliny called the Chinese the "Seres," after the silk they supposedly manufactured from a tree that was specially cultivated there.[19]

With respect to the "silent" barter, Pliny recounts that the Chinese and middlemen often shared a mutual suspicion of one another and the Chinese "wait for the trade to come to them."[20] Goods would be placed on one side while the Chinese withdrew; the middlemen would inspect them and then leave their goods in exchange before they also withdrew. In this way, they avoided contact with one another. A Chinese account in the historical annal by Zhao Rugua (Chau Ju-Kwa) concurs, adding that:

In the Western Sea there is a market where a [silent] agreement exists between buyer and seller that if one comes the other goes. The seller first spreads out his goods; afterwards the [would-be] purchaser spreads out the equivalent, which must lie by the side of the articles for sale till taken by the seller, when the objects purchased may be carried off. This is called the "Devil or Spirit Market."[21]

Pliny adds a curious note, in which his description of the Seres clearly does not match the faintest description of what Chinese may have Looked like then or

now. They "resemble wild animals,"[22] Pliny states, "surpassing the ordinary
stature of mankind, [and] having red hair, blue eyes, hoarse voices, and no
common language to communicate by."[23]In addition, Pliny is quite unhappy
about the excesses that the barter system in silk caused among Roman women.
Their finery and silk embroidery was much too costly, Pliny complained, and
not worth the expense, merely for them to deck themselves out in gaudy
apparel.[24]

Obviously, what his statement does show is that a few years after the
beginning of the Christian era, Chinese goods were finding their way into
Europe. One may argue that this demonstrated a second stage of cultural contact
between West and East, namely one in which, even in areas where neither
Roman nor Chinese armies had marched, there was a thriving contact through
trade. This, along the so-called "Silk Road," would result in enormous benefits,
not the least of which was the wholesale importation of an Indian religion into
China

By 102 A.D., after thirty years' service in Central Asia, Ban Chao had
returned to Luoyang, the capital of the Later Han, where he died. Not until the
period of the Tang (618–907 A.D.) do we see any more attempts at contact
between East and West. By 643 A.D.,Tang Tai Zong (T'ang T'ai Tsung), who
was the second emperor and considered the real founder of the Tang dynasty,
supposedly received envoys from the "King of Rome"; they allegedly told of
Arab incursions into their territories. Indeed, in the early decades of the eighth
century, Muslim armies had begun to push west.[25] But before that time, the
West itself had come to China in the form of Buddhist holy books or sutras and
holy relics, borne on the backs of pack animals. India had begun to export
Buddhism to China, and the Chinese themselves had become eager pilgrims
seeking after Nirvana. Physical conquest had given way to religious surrender as
China once more met its West.

QUEST FOR NIRVANA

When Zhang Qian had was sent west in 138 B.C, and Ban Chao in 76 A.D.,
after the Han restoration, they embarked on military expeditions of which the
purpose was to seek alliances with and ultimate control over the non-Han Other.
But by the time of the great Buddhist pilgrimages to India, the motivating
factors for travel had moved beyond military conquest or trade alliances. Instead,
with the advent of continued civil unrest in China, the Chinese began to seek
more than the Confucian requirements of good order and appropriate ritual. They
wanted more internalized forms of spiritual satisfaction, associated with the type

of spiritual nonmateriality that would satisfy the Chinese, and yet required a ritual that reflected more than good governance. In this quest for spiritual order, the Chinese were seeking pragmatic answers to their own problems, so that not unnnaturally, over a period of time, the Buddhist religion in China would be Sinicized, in addition to bearing traces of influences from along the routes that brought Buddhism from India through Central Asia to China.[26]

For instance, one example of Western influences along the trade routes was uncovered by the archeologist and inveterate traveler, Aurel Stein. He demonstrated the manner in which the image of the Buddha himself bore traces of Greek Alexandrian contact before the time Buddhism had even arrived in China. Stein also noted that some of the coloration of Buddhist figure representation, particularly the use of blue, was a consequence of the intersection of Alexander's world of the West and the Indian world of the East, directly resulting from the manner in which these two cultures met following the Alexandrian period.[27] By his defeat of Darius and conquest of Persia, Alexander had extended his empire between 334 to 323 B.C. from the shores of the Aegean to the Indus River. We read that, at a certain point, those whom Alexander could not conquer, he locked away from the known world:

Some of the enemy Alexander's men killed, others they pursued northwards for fifty days, until they came to two mountains in the unseen world, which they called the Breasts of the North. . . .He saw that the two mountains would be suitable for closing up their exit, so he stayed there and prayed to God to help him close up the mountains to keep them out. . . .Immediately the mountains came together. . . .When Alexander saw what had happened, he praised God. Then he built bronze gates, fixed them in the narrows between the mountains and oiled them. . . .So Alexander shut in twenty-two kings with their subject nations behind the northern boundaries—behind the gates that he called the Caspian and the mountains known as the Breasts.[28]

This was the symbolical locking off of the Ultimate Other, lest its very presence should disrupt. Later, in the thirteenth century, during the time of the Mongol invasions of Europe, it was very much feared that the tribes beyond the Caspian had broken out of hell.[29] This area of the world, unknown to Europeans, was securely detached from the rest of the world by Alexander's actions. Therefore, even as the Chinese were quite active at creating their own marginalized humans, the West had already secreted the East in an area beyond human habitation.

Alexander's empire was not of course merely the cycle of legends that so fired the Greek imagination. Indeed, it was more a union of ideas rather than a political reality, since long after his death and well into the Roman period, it continued to extend the Hellenistic worldview into India and areas west of China. In the process, since many of Alexander's soldiers had married local women, Hellenistic concepts both altered and were altered by the people and cultures with which they came into contact.[30]

Aurel Stein was mainly concerned with Greek influence on Buddhist art. But the Buddha representation was traditionally iconic, making use of his footprint, throne, or the Bo tree under which he had obtained enlightenment. There were two independent artistic efforts to humanize the Buddha; one movement dating from perhaps as early as 1 A.D. or as late as the second or third centuries, was centered in the region round Gandhara, now in Pakistan and Afghanistan, and the other from around Mathura in present day India. The Gandhara sculptors were influenced by Hellenistic models, as Stein rightly asserted, and so Buddha was shown often resembling Apollo, dressed in a Roman toga.

The Mathura depictions followed traditional Indian designs,[31] depicting the Buddha as a type of ancient nature deity, whether as a huge standing figure or enormous seated one displaying a broad chest and shoulders and firm legs planted wide apart. Mathura images quarried from red sandstone also employed the same style for representation of kings and gods of the Hindus, as well as the saints of Jainism.[32] Most likely the two schools influenced each other, and by importing Buddhism, Chinese culture came into contact with two aspects of its West—the eastern outskirts of Greek and Roman culture, as well as the civilization of India.

Therefore, in China, in traditional representations the Buddha would now be depicted as a full-bodied human being.[33] The figure of the affable "Smiling Buddha," for instance, is peculiar to China; it is not a product of North India where the Buddha was born a Hindu prince, turning away from the old religion of his ancestors to found a new faith.[34] China then inherited, in part, a synthesis that history had already worked out, but China also developed that synthesis into its own image in art and in religion.

There is a Chinese legend about how how Buddhism arrived in China. It concerns Emperor Han Ming Ti (29 A.D.–76 A.D.). It was during his reign that General Ban Chao had succeeded in restoring Han control to the western lands. Emperor Han Ming Ti had a dream of a flying golden god, which was identified with the Buddha, and as a result, he dispatched envoys to India to enquire into the Buddhist religion and to bring back books.[35] It is claimed that this is how the *Sutra in Forty Two Sections* found its way to a temple just outside Luoyang.[36]

Historically speaking, the points of cultural contact may be traced more directly to some of the early purveyors who arrived from Kushan and India proper, along the trade routes, and who, having noted the Chinese interest in the Buddhist religion, began the serious task of translation of texts and conversion. Particularly influential at this stage was King Kanishka (c.78 A.D.–103 A.D.?), whose subjects, the Kushans, were mentioned in detail by Zhang Qian. Since it is believed that Kanishka's kingdom stretched from the Pamirs to central India, he may well have brought parts of the western area (for a time under Han control) into his own domain.[37] As a result, Buddhist beliefs may well have penetrated into China directly from there.

Early travelers to China from its West[38] included Kumarajiva (344–413 A.D.). Kumarajiva was brought from Tibet to China by the Qin emperor Fu Chien in 383.[39] He embarked, at this early stage, on the task of rendering Buddhist scriptures from Sanskrit into Chinese and also introduced the important branch of Mahayana (or the Greater Vehicle) Buddhism, which the Chinese would later follow in preference to what is derisively called Theravada (or the Lesser Vehicle).[40]

Among the early Indian missionaries to China was the semilegendary Bodhidharma (c. 6th century A.D.), who traveled from near Madras to Canton around 520 and became the founder of what the West knows as the Zen (in Chinese, Ch'an) school of Buddhism.[41] Bodhidharma is credited with such profound and prolonged meditation that on one occasion he spent nine years looking at a wall; so intense was his concentration that his legs fell off. On another occasion, when he grew angry with himself for falling asleep during meditation, he cut off his eyelids, and from them grew the first tea plant.[42] Zen monks justify this as an important basis for their tea ceremony. Another well-known Indian missionary and translator was Paramartha (c. 6th century A.D.), who expounded on the Ideation school, according to which all apparent reality was seen as illusional. His views were later taken up and expounded by one of China's most important Buddhist pilgrims, whom we shall next consider.[43]

Among the famous names of those from China who ventured out to north India to visit the holy places and collect relics and holy books, the best-known is Xuanzang (Hsüan-tsang) (602–664 A.D.), whose journey abroad was partly motivated by the internecine strife that marked the transition between the Sui (581–618) and the Tang (618–907) dynasties. But long before his time earlier disciples had visited India, in particular Faxian (Fa-hsien) from 399 to 412, Sung Yun and Hui-sheng between 518 and 522. And after Xuanzang, still others followed, in particular, between 671 and 695, I-Ching, who also left a record of the travels of fifty-six monks to India. What they all were attempting to do was to situate Buddhism, not as legend, not as an aspect of Confucianism or Daoism, but as a religion with its own original strength and flavor.[44]

When we examine their accounts dating from 399 to 695 A.D., we find that one fact is most pertinent: They are all embarking into the unknown and fearful West. They go willingly, but their main purpose is not to give accounts of their contact with India from the beginning of the present era but to record what had become of holy Buddhist places, to relate the present state of Buddhism in India, and, above all, to bring back with them specific relics of the Buddha (his tooth, washbowl, and sweepingbrush, for instance), as well as ancient sutras, which they later proceeded to translate into Chinese. Indeed, some of the Sanskrit originals have still not been found; so, in many ways, modern researchers remain grateful to Xuanzang and others for the journeys they undertook under what must have been the most arduous of circumstances.

Our major interest in these travelers, moreover, is to examine their mindset, the psychological framework of their minds, and the way in which they too carried with them various beliefs, legends, and myths concerning the world beyond the center. Although, for obvious religious reasons, they did not view Buddhists in India as monstrous outsiders, their journeys were still fraught with the intervention of monsters and ogres, as well as the presence of an Other that was often strange, unsettling, and full of foreboding. As Xuanzang put it, when describing a group of people living near the Hindu Kush: "The people are cruel and fierce. Their language is coarse and crude. Their marriage rites a mere intermingling of the sexes. . . . For clothing they use hair garments."[45] At a later stage, Xuanzang described how he had suffered at the hands of Hindu pirates who wished to sacrifice him to "a ferocious goddess"[46] who annually required a victim. Only his goodness saved him, on account of which a storm arose thus causing the pirates to realize the error of their ways.

Faxian traveled between 399 and 414 A.D. His *Fo Kuo Chi* or *A Record of Buddhistic Kingdoms* is an early example of Chinese venturing out not as conquerors, but as seekers, not as the sole possessors of civilization, but as converts to another. As such, his attitude is different from that of Zhang and Ban Chao. Fear of the unknown still remains and is seen in Faxian's journey across the Gobi Desert. There Faxian noticed the dried bones of the dead in a trackless wasteland. The picture he painted was one in which there remained the omnipresence of death and the possibility of the traveler's own imminent mortality. Surrounding it all, Faxian noted the absence of birds and animals and the pervading presence of evil spirits.[47]

Xuanzang made his own pilgrimage between 629 and 645 A.D. He also pointed to his own experiences in the Gobi desert, which is described as "endless," and as "a murderer of whole herds and caravans," in which he, like Faxian, had also noted the omnipresence of death.[48] In the desert, Xuanzang had experienced a mirage of "barbarian" hordes riding toward him, only to disappear as he drew nearer. He was equally afraid of the landscape and the portentous indicators of death. Also, much like Faxian, he was both impressed and totally terrified by the snowcapped mountain tops to the north of India.

The record of Xuanzang's journey was compiled by two of his disciples as *Ta-T'ang Hsi-yü-chi* or *Records of the Western Regions of the Great T'ang Dynasty*.[49] Further details exist in a biography published after his death. According to an account of Xuanzang's life translated by René Grousett, Xuanzang is described as a figure of striking nobility. His elegance and grace are compounded of "his intimate partnership of the ancient wisdom of Confucianism with the tenderness of Buddhism."[50] Xuanzang also had a dream, in the manner of Emperor Han Ming Ti, in which the saw the holy Mount Sumeru rising from the sea and

desiring to reach the holy summit, he had no hesitation in throwing himself upon the bosom of the waves. At that moment a mystic lotus appeared beneath him and transported him effortlessly to the foot of the mountains. . .a mysterious whirlwind lifted him up and he found himself at the top. There he discovered a vast horizon clearly visible in every part, a symbol of the countless countries which his faith was to conquer. He was filled with a joyful ecstasy and woke up. A few days later he left for the great West.[51]

The point of the dream is to authenticate Xuanzang as a divinely chosen pilgrim, suggesting that his journey was inspired by conditions beyond human control.

In his account, Xuanzang is passionate in describing the decline of Buddhism in India, but he was also an eager participant in Indian culture in general. He was called upon to dispute with local scholars and traveled the length and breadth of India before returning home. He observed in detail Indian names, climate, astronomy, dress, habits, written languages, and hygiene. Little escaped him, and he even considered the methods for enforcing laws, burial rites from place to place, and forms of greeting. Like other pilgrims, he was very critical of the Brahmins, although he was most definitely repelled by the Jains, whose "skin is a livid white," whose "bodies are unclothed," and whose "feet are chapped and calloused."[52]

Xuanzang was most empathetic when describing the India of the "historical" Buddha. His prose is very reverential, as he observes the ancient holy sites of the

Buddha's life or notes the presence of former Buddhas who had preceded the historical Buddha. Xuanzang captures in these references not mere piety but a severing of the boundaries of time, going back and forth and yet remaining part of his own present.

For instance, when at a holy site where he identified "secret spiritual influences,"[53] as he terms them, Xuanzang was able to show their meaningfulness for Buddhists who believed in the continuity of Buddhas into the far future. Thus Xuanzang's account may be that of a seeker's, but he was no mere novice. His text shows his familiarity and expertise with Buddhist theology and the beliefs of the various schools. Since he could converse in various Indian languages and was obviously well read, Xuanzang also exhibited an understanding of the more immediate history of Buddhism in India, especially the enormous debt owed to Emperor Asoka (d. 238 B.C.) of India for his personal faith in, and dedication to, the growth and extension of Buddhism.

In 645, Emperor Tang Tai Zong welcomed Xuanzang back to China, even though he had left without official permission. The emperor provided him with the means and personal assistants he needed to study and translate the six hundred sutras he had brought back with him, as well as to write and expound his own views of Buddhism. Because of pilgrims like him, China would become the mainstay of Buddhism following its decline in India and would export the religion to other lands, particularly Japan.[54] But the Buddhism that survived and survives even in the China of today continued to demonstrate the influence of Confucianism, Daoism and Western beliefs.

Over the years, the Chinese have retained a fascination with Xuanzang both as historical figure and legend. His adventures became the stuff of folklore, opera, and even a television series. His journey was fictionalized in the monumental Chinese novel *Journey to the West* (1592) by Wu Ch'eng-en.[55] In an early preface to Xuanzang's work, he is even likened to the "discoverer," Zhang Qian, and to the earlier pilgrim, Faxian. "Compared to him," we are told, "Po-wang [the title under which Zhang Qian was enfeoffed] went but a little way, and the journey of Faxian was short indeed."[56]

Time and time again, what emerges from these texts is an unwavering love for, and loyalty toward, China. As the pilgrims traveled, they made constant comparisons with their homeland, reminding us that they were never spiritually removed from the norm, even though they might have been physically distant. In a description of their own voyages between 511 and 523, Sung-yun and Hui-sheng compared a country they had visited with China. It is a place with "no walled towns," where its inhabitants "use felt garments." They described with some trepidation the lives of nomads, who were unskilled in the art of writing, had no knowledge of astrology, and, worst of all, lacked in courtesy.[57] Xuanzang put it this way, in an aside probably added later to flatter Emperor Tang Tai Zong, his major sponsor once Xuanzang returned: "With regard to the rules of politeness observed between the prince and his subjects, between superiors and inferiors, the Land of the Lord of Men [China] is generally considered in advance."[58]

In one instance, Faxian saw what seemed like a vision of home in an image of a Chinese roadside merchant:

Seven years had now elapsed since Fâ-hien [Faxian] left the land of Han; the men with whom he had been in intercourse had all been of regions strange to him; his eyes had not rested on an old and familiar hill or river, plant or tree: his fellow-travellers, moreover, had been separated from him, some by death, and others flowing off in different directions; no face or shadow was now with him but his own, and a constant sadness was in his heart. Suddenly (one day), when by the side of this image of jade, he saw a merchant presenting as his offering a fan of white silk; and the tears of sorrow involuntarily filled his eyes and fell down.[59]

These are words of understandable human longing, full of pathos and sorrow. They reveal that Faxian was certainly a Chinese nostalgically recalling the land of his ancestors.

In another instance that displays the patriotic sentiments of the missionaries, Xuanzang delivered an impassioned address to his fellow Indian monks. They had wanted him to stay, arguing that China was a "barbarian" land since it had not produced the Buddha. But Xuanzang would have none of it, pointing out the goodness of the emperor, his fairness to his subjects, and the achievements of the Chinese in science.[60] Not unnaturally, one suspects that this is of later addition, particularly after Xuanzang was welcomed back triumphantly. But its sentiments are in keeping with much of the literature, which may send seekers to a spiritual abroad but which still celebrates a very physical home.

Nearly always, the pilgrims were all too eager to identify the Other as "barbarians" once they did not practice Buddhism. When Xuanzang was entertained by a Turkish ruler, he noted how the numerous attendants and the profusion of gold all contributed to a dazzling spectacle of barbarian splendor and wealth.[61] Later, in 518, Sun-Yung was equally fascinated by the Huns. He tells us that they too possessed no walled cities, use garments of felt, "kill living creatures and eat their flesh," but "possess gems in great abundance."[62]

The Chinese pilgrims constantly displayed this fascination with the horrible as they observed humans at the periphery. One supreme irony about their descriptions is that they fit almost verbatim those of later European missionaries who attempted to make contact with the Mongols, who were rulers of the Chinese in the thirteenth and fourteenth centuries.[63] Thus, the European method of demonizing the Mongols is anticipated centuries earlier in the accounts of some of these Buddhist missionaries venturing westward. Perhaps the Chinese Buddhist pilgrims had forgotten one of the most important injunctions of King Asoka, inscribed on his Rock Edicts and Pillar Edicts, "All men are my children."[64]

If Zhang had furthered the mythologizing process whereby Han prejudice was transfered to the new lands, what occurred with Buddhist travelers was only a little different. Additionally, they were all too ready to accept the local accounts they heard of magical occurrences, provided of course that these bore some relationship to the Buddha's life. This does not make these travelers simplistic, but demonstrates their unwavering faith in trying to come to terms with the alien and the abnormal, with a foreign religion that in the course of time would even be banned in China, when it seemed to be seriously threatening indigenous Confucian and Daoist beliefs. Even the more recent Communist ban has only been partly lifted, and if Tibet is an example of how far the Maoist state is prepared to go in order to accommodate Buddhism, then we know that Buddhism will remain only a touristy showpiece on the mainland of China.

These were certainly not the surveillance expeditions of earlier Han times but forays of faith that ran counter to the prevailing mythology of Han cultural mastery.Their goals were more wide- ranging than those of European adventurers in that they did not merely suspect the approximation of Paradise on earth, but often traveled with a very clear concept of what it was. Indeed, the very concept of the "Pure Land of the Western Paradise" was born from the journey Buddhism made over the Pamirs and the Taklamakan once it had left the Hindu Kush.[65]

Painters and sculptors were enthusiastic in their depictions of this idyllic place, which they constructed in all its elaborate detail on the ceilings of the Caves of a Thousand Buddhas, as well as in Buddhist *stupas* or holy places found in the westward area. For the "Pure Land" was certainly, even at its most prosaic a utopian ideal, and at its most spiritual, Shangri-la, the literal representation of permanent existence in an eternal Nirvana.

Once the Pure Land of the Western Paradise had traveled to China along the so-called Silk Road, it introduced the concept of the Blessed who would be able to exist forever in an eternal place of happiness. The two relevant Mahayana texts, translated into Chinese in 252 A.D., offer the promise of the Western Paradise even to "those beings who are in the ten quarters," outside the Buddhist norm. Hence the promise of this ideal place "in the Western part, a Buddha country, a world called Sukhâvati (the happy)" represents a haven where there is "neither bodily nor mental pain."[66] It is adorned with palm trees, precious gems, and lotus lakes, surrounded by the wonderful harmony of continuous music.[67]

Pure Land Buddhism, which was merely a branch of Buddhism in India, made rapid progress in China. It stressed the worship of Amitabha, who the Chinese called O-mi-t'o. Through hearing the name, meditating, and showing a desire for spiritual rebirth, the believer could be reborn in the Western Paradise or *Sukhavati*. The feminized bodhisattva known in China as Guanyin (Kuan-yin) constituted an aid toward achieving this end.[68]

In some ways, Buddhism freed the Chinese from too rigid an adherence to the Five Confucian Classsics and too close a concern with their legendary Sage Kings, Yao, Shun and Yü. Buddhism also provided an inner spiritual satisfaction that both Confucianism and Daoism lacked, and it thus appealed to large numbers of people beyond the privileged. Most importantly, Buddhism let in the outside world, since throughout the first few thousand years of Chinese history, until the period of the Han, the Chinese had seemed to need little outside interaction. The Middle Kingdom represented the place of perfect balance, harmony, and security, the super norm that outdid all Others. Buddhism would, for a time at least, seriously challenge China's belief in itself. Yet when all was said and done, Lord Buddha was Indian, distinct from the Chinese and traditionally dwelling on their periphery.

Perhaps this is why it became necessary to Sinicize Buddhism. We should again stress that there were interpretations of Mahayana Buddhism in China that developed there; in particular, the development of the acceptance of the Western Paradise, and the feminization of the Indian Buddhist Avalokitesvara as the Chinese Guanyin. Guanyin was the willing bodhisattva who postponed her own Nirvana in order to help others. In China, she was no mere copy of an Indian original, but instead a Buddhist godhead, in a religion without a god, who had her own rites and rituals.

The point at which Buddhism truly came into its own in China was with the publication of Buddhist texts. First, China was unique in that it had produced *The Diamond Sutra,* the first printed book in the world and a Buddhist classic as well.[69] Printed in 868 by Wang Ch'ieh, *The Diamond Sutra* became essential to the understanding of Zen, but remained a typical sutra. Lord Buddha preached to the converted, in India, within an Indian setting. The place was Shravasti in north India, and many allusions were made to the sands of the Ganges, as well as to Hindu personal names and astrological concepts of space and time.

Of course, the faithful could easily comprehend what the Buddha so eloquently summed up in chapter 5 of *The Diamond Sutra* that "wheresoever are material characteristics there is delusion; but whoso perceives that all characteristics are in fact no characteristics, perceives the Tathagata [another name for the Buddha]."[70] He was speaking about the extent to which thought may be freed from form, image, and dualism—hence the name of the sutra, since it supposedly cuts away all dualistic thought like a diamond. Chinese converts were told to memorize the text (and they did), but the Chinese could still only envision the Buddha as a foreign proponent of the Eightfold Path to Righteousness.[71]

Second is the more pertinent point relating to the Sinicization of Buddhism in China. *The Sutra of Hui-Neng* or *The Platform Sutra* is the only Buddhist sutra that is concerned with someone other than the Buddha, and it remains the only sutra in which a Chinese holds center stage. Basically, this sutra is supposedly the biography of the Sixth Patriarch, Hui-neng (638–713), himself a man of very humble origin, who was able to embark on the typical Buddhist archetypal journey toward wisdom, all within China. Having made preparations for the care of his mother, in the fulfilment of the filial obligations that Confucius would have recognized, Hui-Neng went to visit the Fifth Patriarch. He had previously listened to a recital of *The Diamond Sutra* and, feeling instant enlightenment, sought to work more closely at the source of spiritual power. When he arrived there, he was conscious that he was still very much in the world and was reduced to the lowliest level possible by being constantly dubbed a "barbarian." The Fifth Patriarch, although recognizing Hui-neng's promise, in order to protect him from jealous rivals, set him the task of pounding rice.[72]

Slowly Hui-neng managed to make himself worthy of the mantle of Sixth Patriarch. Only Hui-neng was able to understand the Fifth Patriarch's teaching, as the close disciples tried in vain to respond to the request to compose an appropriate poem. Hui-neng instinctively realized that illusion was the very basis of the human condition. But he could not write, so he had to tell his thoughts to another who penned them for him. His success was very Chinese for, as his mentor the Fifth Patriarch expressed it, "When the patriarch Bodhidharma first came to China, most Chinese had no confidence in him.[73] And as the Chinese inherited the patriarchy, they passed on the word and the faith within a Chinese context. Hui-neng adds that he was the thirty-third patriarch in the world, and the sixth patriarch in China. Thus his ascent showed continuity with the past and a desire to authenticate a true and lasting Buddhism for China.

When Faxian was in India, he heard a story in which, after many thousands of years, the supreme relic, Buddha's begging bowl, would go to China and return to India before rejoining the Buddha and the Blessed.[74] This account was personalized in Hui-Neng, the illiterate, fatherless, outsider, who, however, was unmistakably very Chinese, and who became the supreme symbol through which Chinese were assured that an outsider's promise of Nirvana and the Pure Land of the Western Paradise could be realized by them.

4

THE MONGOLS AS OTHERS SAW THEM

Interestingly enough, the next important culture contact between China and the West was brought about by the conquest of the much feared "barbarians" to the North. The invasion of a divided China that began under Chingiz (Genghis) Khan (1167–1227) would have two important effects that bear on this study. First, it would introduce a major foreign element into Chinese society, which would continue the process of cultural cross-fertilization initiated by the Han. Second, the Mongols would move Chinese armies and manpower much further west than they had ever been, to the gates of Russia, Hungary, and Poland. In this process, China once more would open itself to the world, becoming an international global center for trade and commerce, as well as a very receptive area for the importation and development of cultural ideas.[1]

In considering the advent of the Mongol invasion, we shall attempt to see how Mongols viewed themselves and how others viewed them. Although, in the earliest account of their origins, they used the Chinese script, they did construct an elaborate mythology about themselves that is very often at variance with both how the West and how the Chinese perceived them. In addition, more often than not, they saw themselves as justifiers of the wrath of God, claiming that the proof of their military success identified them as executors of a divine punishment against both Muslims and Christians.

Their arrival in the three states that could then be considered as constituting China—Xi Xia (Hsi Hsia), Jin (Chin) and Song (Southern Sung)—had the effect of altering an almost endemic disorder. Additionally, they were able to achieve many accomplishments for which they are not often accorded any credit. Often we view them from a strict European framework, as Alexander's tribes lately let out from their imprisonment. After all, both the Bible and the Koran refered to the tribes of Gog and Magog, and early European visitors, dispatched as papal or imperial emissaries, often reacted with fear that they were, indeed, monsters. European travelers bore with them certain myths about the Mongols—whom

Europeans dubbed Tartars or Tatars—which helped even more in the process of Mongol demonization.

At the onset, it should be stated that the Mongols, beginning with Chingiz Khan and extending through the establishment of khanates that would rule the Golden Horde of Russia, vast areas of the Muslim world and, indeed, China itself, had to have achieved a degree of administrative sophistication. For they were able, in an age in which communication skills had to be invented, to maintain an administrative center at all times. It required no small amount of planning to execute some of the battle strategies for which they were best known.

Furthermore, they were able to conscript the conquered into their own frame of reference. Not only did they recognize and utilize the talents of their Chinese subjects in siege warfare, but additionally, they oftentimes used Chinese bureaucrats as intermediaries to help them control their vast empire. One such individual was Yelü Chucai (Yeh-lü Ch'u-ts'ai) (1189–1243), whom Chinese history credits with convincing the Mongols to spare the Chinese and not simply reduce their vast land mass to fodder.[2] Obviously, Yelü would have had to have been more than a mere spokesperson for the rights of Chinese pastoral farmers against their nomadic conquerors. He must have had to demonstrate that the use of the land for cultivation of crops rather than for grazing would be beneficial to the Mongols.

Mongols conducted diplomacy at the highest level. They did not seek out the current rulers of Europe, but were avidly sought out by them. They were also people who were quick, in the space of a few generations, to realize the advantages of a settled life. They must be credited, at least in China, with extending the canals,[3] so that produce could be brought inland, and also with architectural achievements. At first, they built Karakorum, which represented, by its very situation on the Mongolian steppe, their attempt at isolating themselves from the Chinese. In the course of time, they became more and more integrated, but never totally Sinicized. By the time of Khubilai Khan (1214–1294), not only did the Mongols erect a summer retreat at Shentu (the "Xanadu" of Coleridge's poem,"Kubla Khan"), but also they constructed China's first national capital. The city of Khanbalik, called Dadu (Tatu) by the Chinese, was a contemporary marvel. It was built in 1267 on the site of present-day Beijing by a Muslim architect under the administrative charge of an ex-Buddhist priest. It reflected both the grandeur and sumptuousness of the Mongol overlords, as well as their wish to preserve their own homesteads in felt tents. Additionally, they adopted the name "Yuan" ("Yüan") meaning "origin of the universe," from the

Confucian divination classic *I Ching.*[4]

Furthermore, as patrons of the arts in China, they encouraged the development and flourishing of Chinese theater. Under the Yuan dynasty, established by Khubilai Khan, theater became a popular form of activity. The songs, acrobatics, and acting perfected during this period are still very much a staple of Chinese theater.

Additionally, the Mongols were responsible for the introduction of a currency that had validity throughout much of the world conquered by them. This aided in the transfer of goods, services, and people, helping to establish Yuan China as a truly international venue, or as Jacques Gernet put it:

The Mongol domain was traversed by men of every nation—Moslems of central Asia and the Middle East, Russian Orthodox subjects of the Chagatai, Il-Khan and Golden Horde empires, subjects of the former Liao and Chin empires of North China, and Genoese and Venetian merchants whose commercial relations with Russia and the Near East involved journeys to Mongolia and even Peking.[5]

In Mongol cities, for the first time China was truly cosmopolitan with the presence of Arabs and Russians intermingling with the Chinese. With the newcomers came their own cultures and religions, food and dress, thus helping to contribute something of a multicultural flavor to Yuan China.

Because they were interested in trade, the Mongols were quick to seize opportunities for utilizing skills and commodities across the broad frontiers they had established. Chinese pottery was now glazed with materials imported from the El-Khanate, and silk had worldwide distribution.[6] Indeed, the Ming would continue the traditions after the demise of the Mongols in China.

If, in this study, we are seeking to explore ways in which cultures come into contact with each other and redefine themselves, then the Mongol model is perhaps the most outstanding that we have. The Chinese were abruptly moved out of their purely parochial considerations; indeed, it might be argued that the China of the Yuan was more recognizably like modern China than was the China that had resulted from any of the previous attempts at unification, including that of First Emperor Qin Shi Huang Di. But as a result of their own reaction against the "barbarians" from across the Wall, from the much feared North, the Chinese vowed that they would never again be conquered in this way. Although this did not come true, Mongol presence did serve to unify the Chinese, especially when they realized that, despite the presence of Chinese intermediaries, Yuan laws more often than not reduced them to second class status.

AS SEEN IN EUROPEAN CHRONICLES

Whatever the rest of the world may have thought, the Mongols saw them-selves in a heroic and advantageous light. In *The Secret History of the Mongols,* in which Chinese written characters and the Mongolian language are used, they describe their own origins.[7] Those beginnings are, quite appropriately, shrouded in legend and mystery, going back to the animal world with which the Mongols were so familiar. Tracing the ancestry of Chingiz Khan therefore quite naturally begins with the world of the steppe: "There was a bluish wolf which was born having [his] destiny from Heaven above. His spouse was a fallow doe. They came, passing over the Tenggis [the Sea]."[8] Whatever others may have thought of them, the Mongols at least had a self image of a people whose ancestry, deriv-ing from the animal world, was positively linked to sky and ocean.

Europeans viewed the Mongols in terms of the destruction inflicted by them. We should recall that, for Europe at least, the Mongols became the first indication of an eastern presence, after Europeans had been assured for centuries that there was no one living in that direction. In the surviving fragment of a thirteenth century Russian epic, "Orison on the Downfall of Russia," the Mongols are represented as "a great misfortune."[9] In another Russian epic which related Batu Khan's invasion of Russia, the Mongols are described as "godless, false, merciless."[10] In this fictitious account, Batu Khan is most impressed when he learns that Prince Fedor's wife comes from the Byzantine imperial family. But Batu is roundly upbraided by the Russian prince who points out to him, just before losing his own life, that their wives were not at the disposal of savages.

In the Russian chronicles, Batu is called "accursed" and "godless," and his victories are described as the "terrible letting of Christian blood."[11] Therefore, the degree of Batu's success, indeed Mongol achievement itself, varies in direct proportion to the Mongol's state of savagery. Indeed, a favorite Russian theme was to pit a pious Russian knight against the godless invaders. When, in 1237, Batu was unable to subdue Smolensk, a legend emanated that Batu's inability was due to the direct intervention of St. Mercurius of Smolensk.

St. Mercurius is relayed in terms that leave no doubt about his Christian faith and goodness:

There used to live in the city of Smolensk a young man called Mercurius who was very pious, who studied God's commandments both day and night, who distinguished himself by his holy life, and who, because of his fasting and prayers, shone like the star which announced the birth of Christ to the entire world.

Batu and the Mongols are, of course, in diametrical opposition. The text is very carefully worded, clearly stating that St. Mercurius was one who would often "pray before the cross of Our Lord for the whole world."[12] The suggestion is that the Mongols are outside this frame of relevance, reverence, and reference, thae is they are not even part of the world. As such, many of the medieval writings, even independently of Pliny or Alexander, depict the Mongols as diabolical incarnations.

In 1241, after devastating southern Russia, over which the Mongols would rule, Batu turned his attention to Hungary. The epics pay little attention to truth, and in one instance kill off Batu before he can even leave Russia. Actually, the chroniclers are recording the absolute alarm of the period, and even though some accounts were written several years after the events, they reflect mirror images of hostile feelings toward these rank outsiders. This is why the marshalling cry, indeed the most evident European unifier, is Christian solidarity against pagans.

Even the most casual chronological reference may have a pointed slant. This occurs in the *Chronica de Gestis Hungarorum,* which was published around 1358, but refers to events almost a century before:

In the reign of Bela, in the year of our Lord 1241, the Mongols or the Tartars invaded the kingdom of Hungary with five hundred thousand armed men. King Bela gave battle against them on the river Seo, but he was defeated, and the military might of the kingdom of Hungary was there almost wholly destroyed. Bela himself, with the Tartars in cruel pursuit, fled towards the sea. The Tartars remained in Hungary for three years. And because during that time they could not sow their fields, the number of the Hungarians who perished of hunger after the departure of the Tartars was greater than the number of those who were carried away into captivity or fell beneath the sword.[13]

King Bela is the Hungarian equivalent of St. Mercurius. God is on his side, and he is a brave and hardy warrior who manages to fight, even despite the large numbers of invading Mongols. Furthermore, it is the Mongols who are in "cruel pursuit," and their very presence has blighted the land and stunted its growth.

The *Chronica* records that later on, in 1285, the Mongols again invaded "and spread a terrible devastation of fire throughout the whole country."[14] Once more the language suggests an otherworldliness; this is not a battle of equals, but a random series of cruel and vindictive acts. Again the language of the plague occurs in the "terrible devastation of fire." Also, there is something here that hints at pentecostal destruction, suggesting that the mere appearance of these "tribes," securely locked away by Alexander for so long, was signalling the end of the world.

The view of Mongols as monsters and devils spread far beyond areas where they had any actual contact. For instance, the English Benedictine monk Matthew Paris (d. 1259), used his official contact with Henry III to relate something of the fear and trepidation the Mongols had caused. Punning on the Latin word, "Tartarus" meaning Hades, Paris contended that the Mongols had indeed come from hell; his historical publication *Chronica Major,* available in English as *The Illustrated Chronicles of Matthew Paris,* utilized visual representations to show the extent to which the Mongols were clearly outside the pale of civilization.

In one illustration, "Tartars Eating Human Flesh," the familiar portrayal of Plinian Anthropophagi is shown. There, much as Native Americans would be depicted two and a half centuries later on, the Mongols are shown hacking at humans and roasting them over an open spit. On the right side of the illustration a shocking picture of perversity is shown. An enormous Mongolian horse, as tall as the tree near which it stands, nibbles away at the tree's branches; below the horse lies a naked woman, legs open, hands tied behind a tree, awaiting the inevitable act of bestiality.[15]

Another illustration shows the Mongols on the warpath. In this depiction, an enormous horse and rider crush two hapless victims. The face of the Mongol is cruel and distorted, even as he jabs at the prostrate creatures with an enormous spear. They lie prone and helpless, whereas the Mongol horseman is very much in a kind of wild and savage control, oblivious to the poor creatures being trampled beneath the hooves of his horse.[16]

Matthew Paris neatly summed up the Western view in a 1238 entry by describing the Mongols as

a monstrous and inhuman race of men [who] had burst forth from the northern mountains, and had taken possession of the extensive, rich lands of the East; then they had depopulated Hungary Major, and had sent threatening letters, with dreadful embassies, the chief of whom declared, that he was a messenger of God on high, sent to subdue the nations who rebelled against him.[17]

What is of particular interest is that Matthew Paris knew none of this firsthand, for even his official sources could merely have provided him with hearsay. Why his accounts are of interest is that we may note in them a European view of the Mongols, as the ungodly, the cruel, the barbaric, which far outstripped anything that was stated about the usual European enemies of the time. The Mongol presence brought together all the fears and phantoms that were part of the entire mythologizing process. It is almost as if the legends existed merely awaiting an object for their actual realization.

Lacking this kind of mythological baggage, the Chinese tended to have a different, not necessarily better, view of the Mongols. Chang Chun (Ch'ang Ch'un) (1148–1227), a leading Chinese Daoist master and alchemist, was summoned to the court of Chingiz Khan. Between 1219, when he set out from Beijing, and 1224, when he returned, he had traveled across the whole of Central Asia. First, he crossed the much feared Gobi Desert on an initial visit to Chingiz's younger brother in Mongolia. Then he set out to meet with the khan, finally arriving in Samarkand in the winter of 1221. But Chingiz Khan was encamped for the spring in the Hindu Kush mountains, and so Chang who was seventy-three years old at the time, was forced to push on. He died three years after he returned to Beijing, but a disciple left a record of his sojourn, the *Hsi Yu Chi*, (literally "Journey to the West"), translated by Arthur Waley as *Travels of an Alchemist.*[18]

Through the eyes of Chang, we see a different, but not necessarily more favorable interpretation of the Mongols. Of course, the writer had to be cautiousl, since he was composing a contemporary account of his Mongol overlord. Moreover, although Chang's version is more sophisticated than that of Zhang Qian or Gan Ying, it nevertheless still examines the Mongols from the viewpoint of a center, which here had more to do with Daoism than with China itself. This is not the journey of a discoverer or conqueror, such as the early Chinese explorers undertook, not the holy pilgrimages of Faxian nor Xuanzang; instead a rather unwilling Daoist master is summoned by a new conqueror. This definitely marks a role reversal for the Chinese.

In Chang's account, his journey is the familiar one undertaken by earlier Buddhist monks, across desert and mountain. Since Chang is composing contemporary history, he is very careful not to paint the Mongols in a negative light. He does, however, come over as a rather crotchety individual, constantly complaining of the difficulties of the journey, the food the Mongols attempted to give him,[19] and their harsh way of life. All of this is said in the context of his own religion, implying thereby that he was merely following the wishes of the Dao, the Way of Daoism, which the Mongols, since they were so eclectic, were supposed to understand. We shall look at some further ramifications concerning this at a later stage. What is of some concern to us is the manner in which the Mongols tried to seek, through their many multinational conquests, linkages with a variety of spiritual forces. True, they dismissed and eventually outlawed

Daoism, burning many Daoist books, merely because Daoists did not seem to deliver on the much sought after alchemic cure for mortality. Yet what the Mongol quest shows is that, despite their zeal for battle and conquest, they still found the time to satisfy intellectual and spiritual curiosity. Indeed, Khubilai Khan had requested Chang's presence in order to hear him discourse on the very important questions of life and longevity.

On November 19, 1222, Chang spoke as follows to Chingiz, "Tao is the producer of Heaven and the nurturer of Earth. The sun and moon, the stars and planets, demons and spirits, men and things all grow out of Tao. Most men only know the greatness of Tao. My sole object in living all my life separated from my family and in the monastic state has been to study this question."[20] He went on to discuss how the world originated, in a kind of rural environment that Chingiz himself would have known from *The Secret History of the Mongols,* then still unwritten and at an oral stage. But in more than one way, the remarks were intended to rebuke the warrior's way of life and to affirm monastic devotion.

Man lost the light, his radiance, Chang continues, because he failed to understand the Dao. As he warms to his subject, we note a direct repudiation of what Chingiz stands for: "Those who study Tao must learn not to desire the things that other men desire, not to live in the places where other men live, " Chang exhorts Chingiz.[21] Here he is, of course, delivering standard Daoist sentiments, but in addition, he is stressing the need to avoid what he later condemns as "lust." There are obvious parallels between an intense desire for the worldly, which is to be avoided at all cost, and Chingiz' embarkation on semi-world domination. The picture of the aging seer addressing the almighty conqueror reinforces the contrast between powerlessness and power, victim and victimizer. The intriguing question remains this—at the moment when Chang is speaking, who is the powerful and who the powerless?

Chang is a skilled diplomat. While making a reference to the *Dao de ching* (I shall refer to it as the *Tao te ching*) one of the few Daoist books that escaped Mongol burning, he adds a very pointed remark, "If common people, who possess only one wife can ruin themselves by excessive indulgence, what must happen to monarchs, whose palaces are filled with concubines?. . .It is hard indeed to exercise self-restraint. I would have you bear this in mind."[22] Here Chang is preparing his audience of one for his final, and very pragmatic, remarks. A suitable official should be appointed by the Mongol khan, he tells Chingiz, to oversee a plan to help relieve the Chinese from too heavy a burden of taxation. But, as already noted, Daoists were to fall into disfavor, particularly after their feuding with Buddhists increased.

The same kind of spiritual curiosity that had made Chingiz summon Chang is evident in the Mongol interest in Buddhism. An account is given of a young Zen priest, named Haiyun (Hai-yün), who had so impressed the Mongol conquerors in 1219 that a report of his fearlessness in the face of danger was sent to Chingiz. In turn, Chingiz dispatched a response in which he ordered that the monk and his companion were to be well treated and should be ranked as Mongol freemen. He added, "Feed and clothe them well, and if you find any others of the same sort gather them all in and let them 'speak to Heaven' as much as they will."[23]

Of course, much of the attitude on the part of the Mongols may have arisen purely from fear of the unknown rather than any kind of respect for other cultures and religions. But I suspect that their very healthy attitude toward things spiritual was due to both their own doubts regarding their ancestral religion and a concern that they could well profit from learning about others.William of Rubruck related a great disputation, in 1254, among Christians, Buddhists, and Muslims,[24] and in 1258, Confucianists, Buddhists, and Daoists debated at Kubla Khan's summer residence in Shentu.[25]

This type of interest will hopefully show that the Mongols were helping to extend the cultural borders of China in more ways than one. They were not merely the ruthless conquerors, as relayed in the European chronicles, but in addition, seemed to have been—for reasons that may well have had to do more with fear than faith— interested seekers in a search for the spiritual.

AS VIEWED BY CHRISTIAN TRAVELERS

Perhaps, because they ever sought the spiritual, Mongol leaders had no hesitation in declaring themselves as spokespersons for God and Allah. Here again we note the manner by which they made use of a type of activist assimilation to suit their own purposes. In 1245, fearing the worst after the capitulation of Russia, and especially in the face of a divided Europe, Pope Innocent IV dispatched two Franciscan friars to visit the Mongols. These were Lawrence of Portugal and the better known John of Plano Carpini, who actually compiled the report. These were the first Europeans to journey East; indeed, they became the primary European witnesses of the Mongol Other at this time.

The further east they journeyed, the more they became aware of the strength and power of the Mongols. They observed the pomp and ceremony of the installation of Guyuk as Great Khan, an occasion at which they witnessed at first hand the coming together of peoples as far afield as the Golden Horde of Russia and the incipient khanate of China. The European travelers were curious, but, as they traveled, the notes they kept regarding the Mongols were affected in no small measure by the mythologies that traveled with them.

Quite early in Carpini's account the norm was established. The Tartars, as he terms the Mongols, are "quite different from all other men, for they are broader than other people between the eyes and across the cheek-bones."[26] The ethnocentrism witnessed here and in their other initial observations would have been understandable, even pardonable, did we not realize that this was still another way of imposing the traditional Western view of the Mongol. Carpini is not about to describe the Mongols in terms far different from those of the Medieval chroniclers, although unlike Matthew Paris's and the Hungarian and Russian descriptions, this is not a "public" document, with an inevitable layer of propaganda; rather, it was intended for Innocent IV.

When Carpini comes to issues regarding morality, he is at his preachiest and his most distorted, reminding us again of the images of fear that defined the Mongol presence in Europe. He paints with a broad brush, asserting that:

to kill men, to invade the countries of other people, to take the property of others in any unlawful way, to commit fornication, to revile other men, to act contrary to the prohibitions and commandments of God, is considered no sin by them.

They know nothing of everlasting life and eternal damnation, but they believe that after death they will live in another world and increase their flocks, and eat and drink and do the other things which are done by men living in this world.[27]

Carpini states that the Mongols were obviously unworthy of any claims to real human nature since they neither knew nor acknowledged the Ten Commandments, nor had any concept of Christian belief in an afterlife. To return for just a brief moment to the Mongols' own sacred text, *The Secret History of the Mongols,* recall that Chingiz himself was descended from a wolf with a destiny in "Heaven." Indeed, when Chingiz first wielded the warring bands of steppe nomads into a nation, the history states that he recognized, "the might of Everlasting Heaven, [my] might and power being increased by Heaven and Earth."[28]

I suppose that this is what gave the Mongol khans their supreme faith in themselves, so that they were able to accommodate others and conscript the large diversities of their cultural conquests into a unified whole. As such, Guyuk Khan had little trouble in dismissing the pope's two Bulls of March 1245, written just eight days apart.[29] In the first, he merely urges the khan to receive Carpini and his companion. But in the second, he climbs off the pulpit to point the bitter finger of accusation at the khan, in language made familiar to us by the chronicles, arguing thusly:

it is not without cause that we are driven to express in strong terms our amazement that you, as we have heard, have invaded many countries belonging to Christians and to others and are laying them waste in a horrible desolation, and with a fury still unabated you do not cease from stretching out your destroying hand to more distant lands, but, breaking the bond of natural ties, sparing neither sex nor age, you rage against all indiscriminately with the sword of chastisement.[30]

This was written before Carpini could even have brought back his account, and, not unnaturally, Guyuk Khan regarded these as fighting words.

Considering that Guyuk Khan had only just recently been installed as Great Khan, he should be praised for not seizing hold of Carpini and beheading him. In response to the pope's urgent plea that after such "savagery," the Mongols should observe some kind of penance, Guyuk Khan, in a 1246 response, ironically enquired of the pope, "How dost thou know that such words as thou speakest are with God's sanction?" Then he added the punch line, at once a blend of indisputable logic and theological injunction, "From the rising of the sun to its setting, all the lands have been made subject to me. Who could do this contrary to the command of God?"

Guyuk's response closes with an absolute clincher:

Now you should say with a sincere heart: "I will submit and serve you." Thou thyself, at the head of all the Princes, come at once and serve and wait upon us! At that time I shall recognize your submission.

If you do not observe God's command, and if you ignore my command, I shall know you as my enemy. Likewise I shall make you understand. If you do otherwise, God knows what I know.[31]

To this Guyuk Khan affixed his seal, with the added words "by the power of the eternal Tengri [God]."[32]

Other Europeans would travel, in equally futile attempts. In December 1253, William of Rubruck, for instance, was sent as an emissary of Louis X to the original Mongol capital of Karakorum. Among his party was a Muslim, Abdullah, although they refer to him as "Homo Dei." We learn little of what he thinks or sees, since he is dismissed, much as Estabanico "the Negro" would be

in later Spanish incursions into the New World. However, the presence of
Abdullah and Estabanico is living proof that there existed degrees of Otherness;
some were not quite as startlingly alien as others and could be accorded limited
acceptability, even if their capability went unrecognized.

In a way, Abdullah's presence prepares the reader for the transition into the
area beyond the Crimea, which is reached in early June, for he is the constant
reminder of the unfamiliar. As Rubruck stated, "when I came among them [the
Mongols] it seemed indeed to me as if I were stepping into some other world."[33]
Several pages later this is repeated as if for emphasis, "When we arrived among
those barbarians, it seemed to me, as I have already said, as if I were stepping
into another world."[34] It is, rather like Columbus's "otro mundo" or Amerigo
Vespucci's "mundus novus," a place that is startling and indeed unworldly.

Even as Abdullah makes us ready for the encounter with the outermost, he is
a presence, but not a third eye.We never witness events through him or because
of his presence. We never see him act; perhaps, he is evidenced most strongly as
a trope. Never do we glean a small degree of perspicaciousness, even from his
conversation, which is usually reported in the past perfect, third person. But, in
addition to his real presence in the travel narrative, and his symbolical presence
in the text possibly as an indicator of an acceptable cultural alternative, we can
deduce certain specificities from how he is portrayed.[35]

First, he was obviously an accomplished person, in that he had a definite
role in the travel encounter. In addition to his own language, he had learned
French, or he would hardly have been able to understand what the people of his
party were attempting to communicate. Second, the languages into which he was
translating, were not merely "Persian" or Arabic; he played a major role in
interpreting what the Mongols said. In no small measure, therefore, we are
entirely dependent on him for any success or failure at understanding, which
constitutes the raison d'être for the journey. Any conclusions arrived at by
William of Rubruck and his party depended solely on the accuracy or inaccuracy
of his interpretations. And, since Rubruck does not state anywhere, as Carpini
had, that he had observed any failure in the communication process, we can be
reasonably certain that Abdullah was able to comprehend both Mongol signs and
utterance and to make them understandable to his party.

Third, Abdullah must himself have been a fascinating representative of
cultural marginality. He must have been a convert from Islam to Christianity,
from Muslim mores to European norms. Or if not a complete convert, at least
on the surface someone who was able to project European Christian beliefs, so
that he both made the members of his party comfortable with his presence and

convinced the non-Christians whom he addressed that he was in all ways representative of the Europeans.

Fourth, Abdullah was obviously a much traveled person, more familiar with the cultural diversity of the area than anyone else in the party.[36] As such, he was not startled, like William was, by the otherworldliness of what he encountered since this was part of his own cultural provenance. Additionally, because of his background, he could not have been unfamiliar with different diets or clothing, which William and Carpini (at an earlier stage) had taken great pains to point out.

Finally, as someone born outside Europe and not part of the inheritance of Alexander or Pliny, he traveled without the prejudices and mistaken beliefs that were part and parcel of the cultural baggage of his party. True, part of the *leitmotiv* of Arab narrative texts does assume that beyond a certain point the earth became uninhabitable, and earlier references, in keeping with Ptolemy (2nd century A.D.), assumed a degree of disparity between areas of the world.[37] Recall that Ptolemy was an astronomer and geographer from Alexandria, but since his time, especially following the death of Mohammed, Arabs had become familiar with the East, particularly through trading ventures.

Yet all of the above only constitute a projected view from Abdullah's standpoint. In the text, over which he had no control, he is rendered at times as irresponsible and on other occasions as possessing a degree of infantalism that European readers would have expected. For instance, on one occasion, fearing that he would be separated from the party, he breaks down into uncontrollable weeping.[38] Only William's intervention, explaining that he was required as a faithful servant, convinces the khan to let Abdullah accompany them. Ironically, all of this is done through Abdullah himself; in other words, he seemingly faithfully translates both the khan's command for his own unhappiness and William's solution for its surcease. In a way, this more than any other incident demonstrates how, beneath the superficial texture of the text, Abdullah acts as the agent for his own welfare.

After Carpini and William of Rubruck, others would follow who would leave accounts of the Mongols and their way of life. These would include Jewish, Arab, and African travelers,[39] who seem to a large extent free from the effort at marginalizing the Mongols and Chinese. This should not imply that there were no distortions, only that the center had shifted from Europe to Jerusalem and Mecca. However, one must not generalize too much, since many of these medieval travelers, whatever their faith or ethnicity, often drew from a well of fairly standard and accepted beliefs, as I have shown elsewhere.

This is why common motifs that occur in Carpini, Rubruck, and even Marco Polo, and that doyen of plagiarists, John Mandeville, tend to be similar. In most instances, we read of an East that has an agreed mythological specificity. It is a land of abundance, with gold digging ants, spices, and pearls. Often the legendary figure of Prester John personalizes the wealth and power found there. Later this symbol would be transferred to the New World, in the search for gold and the Fountain of Youth. At the center of the utopian mix of abundance and wealth would be the resuscitated figure of Prester John, now dubbed Manoa d'El Dorado, or just simply El Dorado, in the New World.[40]

The travel narratives of the period also contain references to Amazon women, pygmies, giants, Anthropophagi, Wife Givers, monstrous creatures, and so on. Although, as John Bloch Friedmann has shown,[41] these can be traced back to Alexandrian and Plinian accounts, what is of greater interest is that by the time of travel to the East, they had become stock representations fixed in the popular mind. As such, more often than not these figures of popular imaginings are encountered and described, and later on, when new travels—now "discoveries"— begin in the New World, they are often sited, situated, and named. Hence, we are left with the province of Amazonia in Brazil, where Spaniards first saw and battled a band of female warriors, as well as a host of place names that attempt to concretize legend.

For instance, Plinian Anthropophagi gave way to Columbus's "Canabs" or "Canibs," fierce maneaters he is told about on his First Voyage.[42] The account is made all the more interesting since Columbus, perhaps following the likes of William of Rubruck, had embarked on his adventures with an Arab-speaking interpreter. Again, in the absence of any evidence, apart from the legends Europeans carried in their heads, a whole race was branded "Carib," and an entire region, "Caribbean." We should stress at this point that Columbus's "interpreter" would obviously not have had the advantages of Abdullah, for this was territory far way from the familiar. Hence, he would have been forced to invent acceptable interpretations within the parameters of European cultural expectations.

As the travelers moved eastward, they opened up for us not only territory that was to receive its first accounting in European texts, but also the state of mind of contemporary Europeans, who, in the New World, would soon come face to face with West Africans possibly from the ancient kingdom of Mali, and original indigenous inhabitants like the Taínos and Arawak. Thus, as we read their narratives of the East, we have to be ever mindful of an important linkage between China, on the one hand, and Africa and the New World, on the other. Since Abdullah does not speak and we rely on the European narrators to chart our course, we must always recall that what they tell us is what they had been conditioned to expect. In a curious way, the East becomes indirectly responsible for the invention of the New World, through the mindset of its Western "discoverers."

Arab and Chinese contact with the East African coast. is next relevant to our considerations. Some have contended that allusions to "Black Dwarfs" in the Shang period, between the sixteenth and eleventh centuries B.C., indicate an even earlier presence of Africans among the Chinese.[43] However, this will not be of major interest to us, although further archaeological investigations should assist in determining how far back we can go to examine the barbarian Other even in an incipient China.

At another level, we should mention in passing that later European contact also shows varying degrees of symbiosis in Chinese society. First, European missionaries came into contact with China, and particularly of interest here is Matteo Ricci (1552–1610),[44] the first Jesuit priest to visit China. Second, European contact on a larger scale is a matter of the nineteenth century, with European acquisition of so-called "Treaty" ports. At a still later stage, one should add that the triumphant Marxist revolution of Mao Zedong is perhaps the final and most dramatic example of the confluence of cultures—China takes from the West, and in familiar Chinese pattern, models Marxism after its own image. So that up to today still the West persists, particularly in local and foreign demands for market reforms and political change. Yet, despite some change, China still clings to itself, to an image that seeks to assert a China compounded from its own ancient historical role, not to be overtaken by the West, but to find and discover the West for itself.

5

CHINA AND AFRICA: MUTUAL DISCOVERIES

Official Chinese contact with Africa took place around the time of the decline of the Yuan dynasty (1271–1368) and the accession of the Ming (1368–1644). But, although this iwas the period when the famous "Star Raft" expeditions of Zheng He (Cheng Ho) (c. 1371–1433) took place, what became very clear was that Africa was very much known to the Chinese. This is because they were not traveling into unknown territory, as Columbus had done. The two societies had already met through Arab middlemen, and even more face to face, as we shall see. Additionally, Chinese travelers did not need to have too much fear of the unexpected, for they basically knew where they were going, having invented the compass.[1]

One important way in which knowledge is acquired is by hearsay. I shall be looking at Chinese evidence for verification of some of this kind of knowledge, which was part rumor and part actuality. It occurred as a result of Arab middlemen who plied the shores of the South China Sea from very early times and not merely introduced talk about Africans, but physically brought Africans to China itself; and also as result of Africans themselves who came, as the Chinese saw it, to pay "tribute," but in actuality to trade.

As the two cultures met and intersected, whether through middlemen or by direct contact, they began to form certain beliefs and notions about one another. These ideas were based more on speculation and secondhand rumor than on actual knowledge—in other words, once more there were certain notions the Chinese had about the world which they expected to see fulfilled among those with whom they came into contact. As we have noted so far, they also held certain peculiar notions about the Middle Kingdom, and they were often hard-pressed when these beliefs were challenged by an unexpected world. Certainly there was nothing in Confucian or Daoist texts that prepared the Chinese for contact with Africans.

On the other hand, as we have noted the "barbarians" had been expected from the north and the west. Their contact with the Chinese, whether as Xiongnu victims or Mongol conquerors, had been anticipated; the Great Wall was physical testament both to Chinese fear and the impossibility of avoiding the inevitable.

However, the meeting and contact first with the Islamic world,[2] and then with Africa, had not been scripted and was not officially part of Chinese expectations. Islam had entered China hesitantly—not militarily as it had invaded the West—in the form of trade and barter, with early Chinese converts meeting and interacting with peoples from their west, along the same thoroughfare that had brought Buddhism. True, Islam never had as direct a hold on the Chinese as Buddhism. The reasons are not difficult to find: Islam was always foreign, centered on Allah and the Holy Prophet, Mohammed. Buddhism seemed part of the Chinese psyche because it called on neither God nor Allah but depended solely on meditation and instant enlightenment. One could even argue that aspects of Buddhism became incorporated into both Confucism and Daoism.

From Muslims in the south of China, particularly in Canton, China was introduced to another area known by the Arab and Muslim traders. Part of this was the strange and bewildering world of the "K'un-lun-ts'öng-ki"[sic], or the "Zanj (or Blacks) from Kunlun."[3] The term itself is a mixture of wild Chinese speculation, as seen in the word "Kunlun," and accommodation to Arab usage, as seen in "Zanj," the Arab designation for "Blacks," from which Zanzibar derived its own name. In Han times, the word "Kunlun" had been used to describe a faraway and seemingly inaccessible mountain range that was the habitat of barbarians.[4] In later times, before the introduction of "Zanj," the word still signified an Africa that was equally distant and remote.

Part and parcel of Chinese thinking from time immemorial assumed that the Middle Kingdom occupied a place at the very center of the earth. The *Shu Jing,* one of the Five Classics of the Confucian canon, had assumed as much. When China, perhaps the entire earth itself, was first made habitable by Yü the Great, tamer of the Great Flood, he had constructed nine provinces. As noted earlier, the "barbarians" (then, non-Han and other Asians, and later, Westerners, and Africans) had been placed in the outermost of the nine provinces, "the most remote" of the various areas, "THE WILD DOMAIN," as Legge translates it in capital letters.[5] This area was nine times larger than the inner sanctum of the imperial domain and was occupied by barbarian tribes.

Confucius, even while eschewing violence toward those who inhabited the inner sanctum, does not condemn its use outside the core. He even argues for an ethical superiority at the center, stating that, "When distant subjects are unsubmissive one cultivates one's moral quality."[6] Therefore, the norm that prevailed at the center had to be both morally and physically strong—it was assumed that these qualities in themselves would defeat the barbarians.

For Mencius, the further one lived away from the imperial domain, the greater the degree of alienation. He, like Confucius, was primarily concerned with variants within an agreed norm, that is, areas that were immediately contiguous. In the abode of the barbarian outsider, Mencius asserted, dwellers would only be entitled to smaller property sizes, would have no direct access to the emperor, and would have "to affiliate themselves to a feudal lord." In a word, Mencius termed such areas "dependencies."[7]

KUNLUN SAVAGES

One must, of necessity, bear all this in mind (particularly the slanted version of the world) when attempting to visualize the precise way, the fundamental manner, in which the Chinese must have regarded their Ultra-Ultimate Other, the Black Kunlun savages. They lay beyond the Other, were obviously odder, living even apart from the Outer, and inhabiting the extreme fringes of what was truly Uttermost. The term "Kunlun" carried with it none of the mystique of the Mother of the West or the search for the Daoist tree of Immortality somewhere in the West. Indeed, the magic and mystery earlier associated with the term had been dubbed nonsensical by no less a renowned figure than Sima Qian, Grand Historian of China.

In tracing the origin of the word and how it was first given to the range of mountains in Han China's West, Sima Qian wrote,"The emperor also sent envoys to trace the Yellow River to its source. They found that it rises in the land of Yü-t'ien among mountains rich in precious stones, many of which they brought back with them. The emperor studied the old maps and books and decided to name these mountains, where the Yellow River had its source, the K'un-lun Mountains."[8] In his summing up of this portion of his work, the Grand Historian cited two ancient texts which the emperor had consulted: *The Basic Annals of Emperor Yu,* now lost, and a geographical work, the *Classic of Hills and Seas.* These texts assert, Sima Qian tells us, that the source of the Yellow River in the Kunlun Mountains lies in an area "where the sun and moon in turn go to hide when they are not shining. It is said that on these heights are to be found the Fountain of Sweet Water and the Pool of Jade."[9]

This was the very course, Sima Qian adds, that China's first explorer, Zhang Qian, took. But according to Zhang, there were no such wonders, and, therefore, Sima Qian concludes, "I cannot accept them."[10] But he does argue that the order established by Yü was more to his liking and belief. All of this helps us understand how the concept of "Kunlun" lost its magical connotation and became solely associated with the barbarian tribes. Hence the Chinese had mentally prepared themselves for an encounter with demons which they themselves had created.

Chinese may well have been in contact with Africans as early as the Han dynasty (206 B.C–220 A.D.) during the same era that had marked the advent of westward expansionism. It has been contended by Chinese writers that the kingdom of Kush, at Meroë in present-day north Sudan, displayed stylistic influences in its pottery and bronze that may well have resulted from Indian or Arab trade between China and northeastern Africa. Also, in Axum, in present- day Ethiopia, it has been asserted that some of the goods from the port of Adulis may well have found their way to China, possibly through Roman middlemen.[11]

Faxian had mentioned, as early as the fifth century, that there was brisk trading in Sri Lanka, noting that merchants came even when the island was only inhabited by spirits. The place became populated "through the coming and going of the merchants" who spread the word "in various countries" of the land's bounty.[12] Cosmas Indicopleustes (c. sixth century A.D.) would concur in *Topographia Christiana*. Although he was born in Alexandria, his Latinized variant last name tells us that he was familiar with the Indian Ocean, and his account reveals that he took part in some form of trade between Ethiopia and Asia. In one part, even as he waxes eloquent on otherworldly matters, as is his wont, he specifically mentions "some who to procure silk for the miserable gains of commerce, hesitate not to travel to the ends of the earth."[13] Specifically he mentions traders from China and Axum interacting at Sri Lanka, stating:

The island being, as it is, in a central position, is much frequented by ships from all parts of India and from Persia and Ethiopia and it likewise sends out many of its own. And from the remotest countries, I mean Tzinista (China) and other trading places, it receives silk, aloes, cloves, sandalwood and other products, and these again are passed on to marts on this side, such as Malé, where pepper grows, and to Calliana, which exports copper and sesame logs and cloth for making dresses, for it also is a great place for business. And to Sindu (Diul Sindh at the mouth of the Indus) also where musk and castor is procured, and *androstachys* (possibly spikenard), and to Persia and the Homerite country (Yemen) and to Adulé (Zula on the African coast of the Red Sea). And the island receives imports from all these marts which we have mentioned, and passes them on to the remoter ports, while, at the same time, exporting its own produce in both directions.[14]

Up until the time of the Tang (618–907), when renewed Chinese expansion west came into violent and disastrous collision with Islamized Arabs, there was no direct record of Chinese views toward Africans. But when a Chinese traveler named Du Huan was captured by the Arabs, he spent some twelve years abroad. When he did return in 762, his book, *Record of My Travels,* now lost but partly preserved in an encyclopaedia, told of

a country called Molin [Malinde] which he reached after 'crossing the great desert' in a south-westerly direction. . . . Molin was inhabited by black people. It was approached through mountains where a variety of religions were professed, Islam, Christianity and 'the Zemzem teaching'. It seems to have lain not far from the coast. The climate was not appealing. There was little grain and no vegetation, and malaria was endemic.[15]

Philip Snow believes that the area Du described was none other than Axum.

Even at this early stage, before the introduction of Kunlun as a pejorative term, we note the compilation of negatives. The area, much like the West in Han times, was almost inaccessible, over desert and mountain, lying, it would seem, beyond the outer rectangle of Yü's demarcation. Next, it clearly lacked any semblance of order; rival established religions contended with one another, none of which was Chinese or even Buddhist. Additionally, Du shows the beginning of an influence that is going to doubly darken Africans; the early Chinese bought into Arab mythology the cocept of the "Zemzem" (sometimes called "Lamlam") as a term denoting the general worthlessness of African indigenous language andbeliefs. As late as the fourteenth century, Ibn Khaldun (1352–1406), a man born in Moorish Spain and educated in North Africa, would describe a southern Africa of "Lamlam" slaves, "nearer to animals than to reasonable beings."[16]For years he remained an official spokeman on matters pertaining to the African continent.

AFRICA THROUGH AN OTHER'S EYES

The Chinese had only very hazy notions of Africa. As noted before, early Buddhist pilgrimages to India had helped provide some basic ideas of the West and the Southwest. But since the Chinese depended on middlemen for trade, their interpretation of the world tended to be at best sketchy and at worst uninformed. In their introduction to Zhao Rugua's (Chao-Ju-Kua) *Chu-fan-chi* (in pinyin, *Zhufanji)* a work on Chinese twelfth and thirteenth century trade, editors Frederich Hirth and W. W. Rockhill find that from the fourth to the seventh century, "all the products of Indo-China, Ceylon, India, Arabia, and the east coast of Africa [were] classed as products of Persia (Po-ssï), the country of the majority of traders who brought these goods to China."[17]

There was no Chinese authority then in a position to correct Du Huan. By 618, the majority of foreigners living in Canton were Persians and Arabs.[18] Not long afterward, Muslims also established settlements along the islands off the east coast of Africa as far south as today's Tanzania. They had unintentionally created a kind of trade monopoly through which they would be able to secure local representation, in both China and Africa. Hence the *UNESCO General History of Africa,* in dealing with Africa of this period, concludes that given the nature of the fragmentary representation of Africans in Chinese sources, the Chinese even "came to think of the Africans as subjects of Muslim rulers and of their countries as forming part of the Arab empire."[19]

What is particularly intriguing at this point of our discussion is that the Chinese constantly seemed to view their Others through the medium of a Second Other. We have noted that this was certainly the case with the exploration of the West, and so, despite Gan Ying's journey to the Persian Sea, in all probability the Chinese continued to imagine that the Parthians were the Romans. In much the same way, the Chinese saw Africans, who were unknown to them, though Arab and, later, Muslim intermediaries. Why was this situation duplicated?

One can merely hazard the guess that in all probability the very topography of China had enclosed it; and its cultural aloofness, the very concept of the Middle Kingdom, had placed it as thing apart from the rest of the world. The Chinese were not particularly eager, as a result of their cultural containment, to "explore," to "discover," to "convert," or to "conquer." This by no means suggests that they were lacking in the push and aggression that European historians oftentimes claim as a genetic European birthright. Nor does it suggest that the Chinese were peaceloving and less rapacious. All that one may assert, given the evidence, is that Chinese geography, history, language, and culture had placed a stamp of apartness on them. As such, they were not interested in world conquest or domination, but merely in demonstrating the power and might of China. This was the real meaning of the "Star Raft" expeditions of Zhang He in the fifteenth century.

The evidence is clear that China was not self-sufficient, a thing unto itself. Two Arab historical accounts from as early as the ninth century have been collected in the *Salsalat-al-tewarykh.* According to one of these narratives, by a trader named Soleyman, favorite Chinese imports were ivory, frankincense, copper, tortoiseshell, and rhinoceros horns. Chinese chronicles of the time concur: The *Wei-shu*, which deals with history between 385 and 556, and the *Sui-shu*, which is concerned with the period from 581 to 617, mention coral, amber, pearls, glass, diamonds, steel, cinnabar, quicksilver, black pepper, dates, gold, silver, lead, sandalwood, sugar, and indigo, among other items. By the end of the tenth century, the *Sung-shi*, or chronicles of the Song dynasty (960–1270), significantly, had added elephant tusks, ivory and scented woods to the list.[20]

Most likely, therefore, Africa had become a significant partner in the "silent barter" by the time of the Song. Additionally, ivory tusks seemed to be heavily prized. Chu Yu's *P'ing-chóu-k'o-t'an,* a twelfth-century document, shows that imports of ivory over a specific weight "besides paying the 'clearance dues' must be disposed of exclusively at the official market, since they are 'licensed articles.'" Merchants tried to avoid the stiff customs dues by cutting up their ivory. But the entire cargo was considered very valuable, Chu Yu added, obviously from firsthand information: "Should anyone, before the ship has paid its clearance dues, presume to remove from it any part of the cargo, even the smallest bit. . ., all the remainder (of the cargo) is confiscated, and he is in addition punished according to the gravity of the offense. So it is that traders do not dare to violate the regulations." [21]

In "The East African Coast and the Comoro Islands," historians F. T. Masao and H. W. Mutoro have demonstrated that much of these valuable imports came from the coast of East Africa. They argue that:

Although there is no evidence of direct contact, some African products were known and in demand in China during the Tang period. . . .The East African coast was known as a prolific source of ambergris [from whales] which was introduced to China by the end of this dynasty [906]. By the seventh century, sweet oil of storax, tortoiseshell from Bambara, 'dragon's blood' (resins of *Draceaena schizantha*, and *D.cinnabari*) and aloes (plant juice) were among the exports to China. [22]

These writers also mention the exportation to China of ivory, gold, incense, perfumes, and aromatic oils. Marco Polo noted that in Zanzibar, "the staple trade of the island is in in elephant's teeth, which are very abundant; and they have also much ambergris, as whales are plentiful."[23]

The most basic of comparisons between Chinese imports and African exports show that trade could not have been one-sided. What is usually stressed is that the evidence of Chinese porcelain and pottery artifacts show an African importation; but little is ever written about the manner in which, through trade, the two continents, albeit through intermediaries, began to share in the appurtenances of one another's culture. Moreover, often African imports carried prestige; the ivory palanquins and belt buckles of officials were status symbols. Other material from Africa, such as powdered rhinoceros horn, was considered an aphrodisiac. Ambergis and frankincense had medicinal value and were used to improve blood circulation.[24]

Therefore, it is quite reasonable to suppose that African and Chinese entrepreneurs would attempt to bypass the middlemen. Zhao Rugua's entry under "Zanzibar" stated that each year from China "localities along the sea-coast send ships to this country with white cotton cloth, porcelain, copper and red cotton."[25] The *Sung-shi* recorded that in 1071 a visiting delegation, most likely from Africa, visited the Chinese court. The journey and country of the envoy are described as follows:

Traveling by sea, and with a favourable wind (the monsoon), the envoy took a hundred and sixty days. He passed by Wu-sün (presumably some place near Maskat), Ku-lin (Quilon) and San-fo-tsi (Palembang), and came to Kuang-chóu. The ruler of the country was named A-meï-lo A-meï-lan. They (the A-meï-lo) had ruled the country for five hundred years (during which time there had been) ten generations. The language sounds like that of the Arabs (Ta-shï). The climate (of Ts'öng-t'an) is warm all the year. The wealthy people wear turbans of *yüé-(no)* stuff and clothes of flowered brocade, or of *po-tié* cloth. They go forth riding elephants or on horseback. They have official salaries. According to their laws light offenses are punished with the bamboo, serious crimes with death.

Of cereals, they have rice, millet and wheat. For food they eat fish. Of animals they have sheep, goats, buffalo, water-buffalo, camels, horses, rhinoceros and elephants. Of drugs they have putchuck, dragon's-blood, myrrh, borax, asa-foetida, frankincense. Of products, pearls, glass (*p'o-li*), and three kinds of drinks called *mi* (wine) *sha* (sherbet) and *hua* (?). In commercial transactions they use coins made by the government only; three parts are of gold and copper in equal proportion, the fourth of silver. The people are forbidden coining them themselves.

This was not a onetime visit, for twelve years later Zhao tells us that the same party "came again to court." This time the emperor was most impressed and "considering the great distance he [the delegate] had come, besides giving him the same presents which had been formerly bestowed on him, added thereto 2,000 ounces of silver."[26]

From the Chinese side, apparently there was also some unorganized and unfettered trade, not trade disguised as tribute; Philip Snow postulates in *The Star Raft* that Jia Dan, a ninth-century prime minister and geographer, could have known of a route to Africa, possibly from Chinese sailors, possibly from Arab traders.[27] But we can definitely assert that by 1226 Zhao Rugua had gleaned enough from seamen of all nationalities, Chinese included, to be able to put together a two volume work on travel and exploration. This was almost two hundred years before the Ming launched Zheng He on his famous seven voyages, the last three of which included East Africa.

By 1320, a hundred years before Zheng He, Zhu Siben had produced a world map. One of China's officially sponsored histories, *Ancient China's Technology and Science,* describes Zhu as an "avid traveler" and one who made use of his personal findings "to correct previous cartographical errors."[28] As a result, he produced a map of Africa that anticipated European knowledge by almost a century. Zhu Siben's map shows the southern portion of Africa in rounded form, whereas at that time, Europeans believed that the southern tip of Africa extended to Asia through a large land mass.

INFANTILIZATION OF WOMEN AND AFRICANS

Despite these thirteenth-century Chinese representations—one visual, depicting the world on a grid on Zhu Siben's map, the other verbal, in Zhao Rugua's *Chu-fan-chi*—it would be incorrect to assume that the Chinese possessed objective and factual views of non-Chinese society. True, they were luckier than most European countries in that their immediate past history was partly made up of interaction with the much despised "barbarian." Not only had the Mongols ridden off the steppe and ruled them until 1368, but in addition, the presence of foreigners for trade or religious purposes in the capitals and major cities of China harked back at least to the time of the Han emperors. Yet, as we shall see, legends and misrepresentations continued to be actively pursued in the *Chu-fan-chi* .

Women, standard fare for a type of permanently displaced generic/gender Other, fare equally as badly as in European texts. References to a Kingdom of Women abound, representing the same kind of male fears that forced Marco Polo and Sir John Mandeville, among others,[29] to express econstantly their own apprehensions in a similar reference. Here, as with the Kunlun, the area constantly shifts, moving further and further away from the Chinese known. It is a place where norms do not apply, where men may be put to death for adultery and are often subjected to mere sexual exploitation; where, indeed, even the natural way of conception may be ignored: Thus we learn that, "The women of the country conceive by exposing themselves naked to the full force of the south wind, and so give birth to female children."[30]

In such a society, just as the role of nature is usually distorted, so also, not infrequently, are various matters relating to the small number of available women, their governance of males, the hierarchical order, and even matrimony itself. Such women are very threatening, as the following excerpt makes clear:

In the Western Sea there is also a country of women where only three females go to every five males; the country is governed by a queen, and all the civil offices are in the hands of women, whereas the men perform military duties. Noble women have several males to wait upon them but the men may not have female attendants. When a woman gives birth to a child, the latter takes its name from the mother.[31]

All of these must have been doubly shocking to Chinese men (and women), schooled in the etiquette of Confucian "filial piety," with nary a word for the daughters of the household.

One may easily perceive how because of the oddness of the Other world out there, situated beyond any traditional reference point, the invention and embellishment of the Kunlun become de rigeur. On the "good" side, Kunlun people were expert divers, particularly suited for servitude. On the "bad" side, they could be easily caught and lured away, since (the reference is again plainly intended to shock traditional Confucianist views) they had little love for their families. Their appearance was quite odd: "In the West, there is an island in the sea on which there are many savages, with bodies as black as lacquer and with frizzed hair."[32]

The Ta-shi (Arabs), according to an account cited by Zhao Rugua, recognize their simplicity: "They are enticed by offers of food and then caught and carried off for slaves to the [Arab] countries, where they fetch a high price. They are used for gatekeepers. . . . It is said that they do not long for their kinsfolk."[33] From these words, we gather that the Kunlun are a stupid people, not unduly concerned with their own freedom, and indeed prepared to barter it for a snack. They are unskilled and, most condemnatory of all, once away from their families, feel no sense of loss or longing.

People in Africa are prone to perform magical deeds; sorcerers are able to change themselves into animals and use this feat to keep their own people in ignorance. Yet a curious addendum follows this blanket assertion, which is that the sorcerers had the power to hold up foreign ships when disputes arose. The account solemnly concludes that the "government has formally forbidden this practice."[34]

Naturally, the environment of such a strange and unusual people must itself be weird. So in the land of "The Zanj (or Blacks) from Kunlun," the traveler will encounter "great *p'öng* [sic] birds which so mask the sun in their flight that the shade on the sun-dial is shifted."[35] These birds are so large and monstrous that they feed on wild camels. Along the Somali coast, there exist birds so huge that they cannot fly, a strange creature (a giraffe) that is part camel and part ox, and an odd animal (a zebra) described as "a kind of mule with brown, white and black stripes round its body."[36] We shall later note how the gift of a giraffe to the Ming emperor in 1414 resulted in unusual consequences.

Zhao Rugua was not compiling an official history. He wrote down, like Marco Polo and Mandeville, the current beliefs of the day. But we need to stress that as Zhao moved away from the Arab intermediary to observe the Ultra-Ultimate Other through Chinese eyes, he was still utilizing agreed norms of viewing the world. In other words, the Arabs were passing on their notions of the world both to the Europeans and the Chinese, and the Chinese were intermingling this with their own imaginative excesses.

Perhaps the hotchpotch of cultures on the East African coast confused the monocultural Chinese even more. In considering literary work from a much later period, when Swahili was synthesized as a language from African, Arab, and European influences, Jan Knappert described Swahili culture as being this kind of amalgam: "The Persians taught the Swahili the beginnings of political organization; the Arabs brought Islam and with it all the learning they had accumulated; and the Indians brought their finery and artistic products."[37] But quite rightly, Lyndon Harries questions this sweeping generalization, arguing that "without some experience of the African background of Swahili poetry, the Arabist may not appreciate all that the poetry has to offer."[38] Put differently, "all immigrants—never very numerous—underwent a process of Bantuization," in the words of Masao and Mutoro.[39] In looking at the world, first through the Arab/Muslim intermediary, and later still under their influence, the Chinese failed to understand the full complexity of the Africa they visited in the fifteenth century.

In 1413, 1417, and 1421, the Chinese embarked on their grandest effort to interact officially with Africans. In doing this, they were coming face to face with their own fears, as expressed by Zhao, and, at the same time, turning their backs on their own isolation. Although still not approving trade, the third emperor of the Ming who was called the Yung-lo emperor, reigning from 1403 to 1424, tacitly endorsed trade. The Chinese were responding to their own curiosity and, as I have tried to show, attempting to distance themselves from the cultural intermediaries who not only traded for them, but also had begun as well to interpret their world for them. These expeditions were led by an Muslim eunuch under the auspices of an emperor committed partly to Daoism, partly to Confucianism, a warrior prince who had supported the publication of the world's largest encyclopaedia. These expeditions from China to the world outside had all the makings of a kind of cultural diversity that seems more in keeping with the aspirations of our own time.

AFRICANIZATION OF THE KUNLUN SAVAGE

Part of the Chinese interest in travel seems to have been purely domestic. In 1402, after a palace coup that deposed his own nephew, Chu Ti, who afterwards became known as the Yong-lo Emperor (or Ch'eng Tsu (pinyin Cheng Zu) to Chinese historians), began his reign. The former emperor vanished, and one of the ostensible reasons for the expeditions of Zheng He, sometimes called the "Three Jewelled" eunuch, was to find the dethroned emperor and bring him back.[40]

If this were the initial purpose, it soon expanded into something much grander. As *The Cambridge History of China* points out about the expeditions:

They were probably not organized to search for the dethroned, perhaps fugitive Chien-wen emperor, as some have suggested; the [Yong-lo] emperor was more likely looking for allies and perhaps probing new horizons for conquest, although these experiments had no military objectives. He undertook the expeditions for a number of reasons: to search for treasure,. . . to display his power and wealth, to learn about the plans of Timur and other Mongols in western Asia, to extend the tributary system, to satisfy his vanity and his greed for glory, and to make use of his eunuch staff. In any event, these activities reflected this restless emperor's concept of imperial world order and of foreign relations as applied to the South seas. [41]

However, all of this is only partly true. Zhao Rugua's *Zhufanji* itself borrowed about a third of its contents from the *Ling-wai-tai-ta* (pinyin *Lingwaidaida)* which was written by Zhou Qufei (Chou Ch'ü-fei) written in 1178.[42] Zhou had shown quite clearly that the Chinese had already been in contact, both directly and indirectly, with a variety of places, including Africa. We have already noted the manner in which Africa came to be formulated in Chinese thinking; new contacts by Zheng He would not dramatically alter this perception.

In a way, therefore, one may assert that Zheng He knew what he was seeking, or rather that he had already been told what to expect. At this stage, it would be useful to recall some of the images of the "Pi-p'a-lo,"[*sic*] or the Somali coast, as recounted in the *Zhufanji* following the earlier description in the *Lingwaidaida*. There was an area where people fed on dairy food (quite obnoxious to the Chinese of this time), where there existed monstrous animals like the giraffe and the zebra and the gigantic "camel-crane" (the ostrich).[43] In a nearby area called "Chung-li," itself a corruption of the medieval Arabic *Zing, Zang,* or *Zenj*—land of the Blacks—there was a great deal of sorcery, and, again, it was a place where people's eating habits were most unsavory. Often they were simplistic, not even realizing that they could actually eat fish.[44]

Recall also the great *p'öng* birds of Pemba and Madagascar, the place the Chinese called "K'un-lun-ts'öng-k'i." This too was the land of "savages," where people did not value their own freedom and were easily enticed with food. It is almost as if the further south one traveled the more twisted the people, the more distorted their values, and the more inverted the Chinese norm. Indeed, as early as 863 A.D., Duan Chengshi (Tuan Ch'eng-shih) had noted some additional points, not reprinted in later works. In describing Ma-lin (Malinde), Duan observed the following:

after one traverses the desert for two thousand miles is a country called Ma-lin. . . . Its people are black and their nature is fierce. The land is pestilentious and has no herbs, no trees and no cereals. They feed the horses on dried fish. . . . They are not ashamed of debauching the wives of their fathers or chiefs, they are (in this respect) the worst of barbarians.[45]

It would seem then that, to any informed Chinese, the Africans had been marginalized for a long time, as truly savage living in an environment that provided them with little or no sustenance, eking out their existence as brutes in a scenario of unbounded sexual license.

When Zheng He embarked on his voyages to Africa, he would therefore have been familiar with much of all this that he had already heard, read or been told. Because he was a Muslim, whose father had been to Mecca on the *hadj,* he could not have been unfamiliar with Africans. But he would also have inherited much of the lackadaisical Arab attitude toward Africans. For even as Zheng may have had his own beliefs of the Ultimate Other, he himself was being subjected to careful scrutiny by the indigenous Chinese scholar-bureaucrats. For they distrusted the eunuchs in particular, and at the end, they would win out; China would withdraw after Zheng's seventh expedition and leave the sea to the Portuguese.

One consequence of Zheng's voyages was that there could no longer be any doubt regarding where Kunlun lay. As the journeys expanded Chinese global knowledge of geography and peoples, Africans came to represent the nadir of barbarism and savagery. J. J. L. Duyvendak has summed up how the term Kunlun shifted from early Chinese exploration of Asia to be securely repositioned in Africa:

The word *k'unl-un* [*sic*] has an interesting history. Used early on as the name of the fabulous mountains in the West, the home of Hsi-wang-mu, the word originally seems to mean the round vault of the sky, in which as it were, these gigantic Tibetan mountains seem to lose themselves. Etymologically, it is connected with the binom *hun-lun,* "chaos." The K'un-lun mountains are also identified with the Anavatapta mountains and the Sumeru in India, well known in Buddhist literature. Now the Chinese have applied the term *k'un-lun* to the peoples, mostly of the Malay race, whom they found at the ends of the earth. At first chiefly confined to the races of the South-West, later as the geographic knowledge of the Chinese expanded, the same term was applied to the native races of the countries around the Indian Ocean, including the negroes.[46]

The term thus denoted the extent of utmost demonization beyond the outer parameter of the Great Yü's demarcation, as we have seen. It is almost as if the Chinese took with them a brand to show ultrabarbarism and finally decided to mark Africans with it.[47]

In our discussion of the *Bamboo Books,* we noted the Chinese prehistorical fascination with the inaccessible and the distant. Emperor Mu had journeyed over an enormous distance, over the desert and the mountain of Kunlun, to visit the mythical Xi Wangmu, Queen Mother of the West. In the seventeenth year of his reign, the ancient chronicle states that, "the chief of Wang-moo came to court, and was lodged in the palace of Ch'aou."[48] From the beginning of their history, therefore, the Chinese had considered the concept of Kunlun as something distant, unreachable, afar, and, as a an idealistic goal, even unattainable. But by the time that the word came to stand for the land of the Blacks and was linked with Arab and perhaps even European beliefs, it had lost much of its pristine significance and had been reduced to the concept of disorder and darkness, to something menacing and undesirable. We have noted the means through which this became more and more apparent both in the *Zhufanji* and the earlier, *Lingwaidaida.*

In spite of their belief in the utter damnation of those existing at the extremity of the world, the Chinese, as noted, ascribed to the Kunlun magnificent powers, like being able to dive and remain under water for long periods at a time, and also of being unusually strong. But along with this, the eleventh century *P'ing-chóu-k'o-t'an* (pinyin, *Pingchouketan*) has added that:

in Kuang (Canton) rich people keep many devil slaves, who are very strong, being able to carry several hundred catties. In their language and tastes they are strange. Their disposition is gentle, and they do not run away. They are also called "wild people." They are black in colour, as black as ink. Their lips are red, their hair curly and yellow. Both sexes are found among them; they are natives of the islands beyond the sea in China. They live (in their native land) on raw food; when caught and fed on food cooked with fire, it purges them daily and this is called "changing the bowels." Many during this treatment sicken and die, but if they do not they may be reared and become able to understand human speech (i.e., Chinese), though they themselves cannot learn to speak it.[49]

Duyvendak has added that this translation omits the white teeth of the Kunlun and that the terms used to describe gender are nonhuman; as he says, "the term for animals is used." Additionally, Duyvendak also translates the reference to the Chinese tongue as "people's language,"[50] that is *all* human speech.

Zheng He traveled south to this land of semihuman barbarians who had to be caught like animals and were are unable to learn or speak probably any other human tongue. The Ming voyagers sought out a people who ate raw food, who were wild but simple, oddly formed, with a strange coloration of hair, eyes, and skin. These were the people who would be chronicled by the Muslim interpreter Ma Huan, who actually did not reach East Africa, and Fei Xin (Fei Hsin), a scholar who traveled as a petty officer. Their views tell us something of how the Chinese, given the significance of their mythology, reacted to the world they set out to explore—and how even as a European Other they first situated and related their own outermost Other, then "discovered" them.

6

CHINA'S "DISCOVERY" OF AFRICA

Zheng He's made seven expeditions, most for the Yong-lo emperor, who reigned between 1402 and 1424. Having usurped the throne, the new emperor no doubt felt obligated to establishing the Ming as one of China's most illustrious dynasties. In keeping with his lofty aspirations, he had moved the capital from Nanjing to Beijing, expanded territory, and rebuilt the Great Wall. Under him, China attempted to amass what was the greatest collection of literary texts—the *Yongluo Dadian (Yung-lo ta-tien)* or The Great Canon of the Yung-lo era—over 11,000 volumes, some of which might well have been lost, were it not for this praiseworthy attempt at preservation. Although he was the third Ming emperor, his overwhelming deeds have often caused historians to regard him as the true founder of the Ming.[1]

The Yong-lo emperor's missions abroad were undertaken against a partly personal need for self-fulfillment, but in other respects a very national concept of mission. There was need for trade, to bypass the Arabs and to proclaim the power of the emperor. This latter was most important, since the emperor no doubt felt a sense of insecurity, having wrested the throne from his own family. But on a grander scale lay the need to demonstrate that China without the Mongols could still be glorious. Indeed, from the very foundation of the Ming dynasty, it became apparent that both change and continuity were necessary. Yong-lo was a Buddhist yet realized the need to control both Buddhism and Daoism. Although Islam had been given some support by the Mongol Yuan rulers, the Ming founding emperor tended to judge Muslims by their individual loyalty and usefulness, rather than by their religion.[2] No doubt Zheng He fitted into this category.

The African connection was made on Zheng He's fifth (1417–1419), sixth (1421–1424), and seventh (1431–1433) voyages.[3] In addition to Zheng He's main fleet, subsidiary fleets were also used; so, rather than going south down the coast of Africa from Arabia, on at least one occasion a separate fleet cut across west from Sumatra and moved past the south of India to the East African coast. The fleets visited Mogadishu, Brava, and Giumbo and went as far as Malindi. What did they learn or unlearn in the process?

Zheng He's records were destroyed following internal dissension in the Chinese court against the influence of the eunuchs.The attack was chiefly led by scholar-bureaucrats who resented the eunuchs' influence and power, which dated back to Han yimes. Therefore, in reconstructing the voyages, we have to rely on two major sources. The most important of these does not even deal with Africa, and the second is a visual rendition.[4] An examination of tthe work of Ma Huan and Fei Xin (Fei Hsin), as well as the famous map of Mao Kun (Mao K'un), should help tell us more about Chinese attitudes toward Africa and the world.[5]

MA HUAN

Ma Huan's *Ying-yai sheng-lan* (pinyin, *Yingyai shenglan) or Overall Survey of the Ocean's Shores* (c. 1433) assists us, in that it is a description of eyewitness encounter. But, although also a Muslim like Zheng He, Ma was obviously quite indoctrinated into indigenous Chinese culture. He tells us in the 1416 foreword to his book that he had read Chinese travel literature. As a result, he had enquired, "How can there be such dissimilarities in the world?"[6]

He therefore begins with an assumption not so much of diversity, but of deviation from the norm, one that is very Chinese. Born around 1380 of rather humble parents, Ma Huan, in addition to Chinese books, had read Buddhist literature and, later on, adopted the Buddhist faith. He learned Arabic as a second language, then joined Zheng He as an official translator in 1412. He also sailed with Zheng He on the sixth expedition, 1421–22, and again in 1431–33, during the last expedition. He did not go to Africa, quite naturally opting for Mecca instead. But, it is from his account that we know that Zheng He's fleets often split up into subsidiary sailing expeditions, and we obtain an inkling of how Zheng, a fellow Muslim Chinese, may have seen the Islamic world outside China.[7]

Ma Huan's travel account exists in three different manuscripts, the original 1451 edition having been lost.[8] An attempt to reconstruct the actual text of Ma Huan may be found in the J.V.G. Mills translation, which includes a foreword and a poem by Ma Huan, as well as another foreword by Ma Jing (Ma Ching).[9] Critics argue as to whether or not Ma Huan wrote the poem or the foreword, but whatever the final assessment, both show Chinese attitudes (as reflected by a Muslim) toward the unknown.

Ma Jing's foreword, like Ma Huan's poem, is couched in flattering language and is meant to appeal to the emperor. But beyond the excessive praise lies the undertone of foreign barbarism, which is contrasted with the Yong-lo emperor's munificence and power. We read about how barbarians to both the north and south would recognize the emperor's precepts, "causing every person with a soul throughout the world" to be imbued with "virtue and civilizing influence, so that all would know their emperor and respect their parents"[10]—obviously good, safe Confucian wisdom.

In the poem, Ma Huan writes that he is but an envoy of the emperor. The emperor is quoted as having urged Zheng He's fleet to "proclaim abroad the silken sounds"[11] to the barbarians. Present in the poem are many of the adverse Chinese attitudes to foreign people that we have already encountered among a whole plethora of authentic Chinese writers: lands of strange people, with "unkempt heads and naked feet," who speak a barbarian language, lacking in virtue and the ability to understand true ritual—again a reference to Confucius. What surprises us is the zeal with which Ma Huan embraces them.

Since Zheng He left no literature,[12] it is necessary to attempt to view the world through the eyes of his fellow Muslim traveler, Ma Huan. What we note, as we travel with him, is that the fifteenth-century Chinese are very much creatures bound to a specific locality and time. Perhaps the Muslims could have been conscious of Chinese insularity and, especially in this post-Mongol period, attempted to set the natavistic minds of their Chinese audience to rest. In this context, Ma Huan, in his dedicatory poem, mentions the early explorations of Zhang Qian during the Han Dynasty, and he argues that the present sea voyages, being greater, can only serve to increase the reputation and glory of the emperor.

Ma Huan well understood also the fiction of the diplomacy of the time; these were supposedly not trading ventures. They were expeditions to a savage world to make known the good name of the Chinese emperor and to have all people recognize his authority. At the same time, as part of their recognition of Chinese might, they would be expected to pay "tribute"—Ma Huan lists gold and rare gems. From this we may extrapolate the fact that the encounter with Africa was no different than those with Vietnam or other parts of southeast Asia, India, or Arabia, all areas visited by Zheng He's fleets. These were all thinly disguised trading missions.

Among the places Ma Huan visited were Champa (in Central Vietnam), Java, Thailand, Malacca, Sri Lanka, Aden, Bengal, and Mecca. As we examine his attitudes to the non-Chinese, we must constantly remember that his is a view reflected by the Other itself. The further Ma Huan travels away from the Chinese locus, the greater the discrepancy. Constantly one gets the opinion that

Ma Huan was attempting to flatter the Chinese, particularly with his references to the negative. In Champa, we are told, "they have no paper or pen" and "no intercalcary moon."[13] How seriously could the Chinese take a people who were illiterate and unable to calculate time itself? There also, the locals are compared with older Chinese immigrants who emigrated during the Tang period (618–907) and about whom Ma Huan comments, "the food of these people, too, is choice and clean; many of them follow the Muslim religion, doing penance and fasting." Interestingly enough, when the mirror image reflects back the Muslim Self, Ma Huan can be quite complimentary. But, in the same place, beyond China proper, marginalized people must be found. Hence, the indigenous people "have very ugly and strange faces, tousled heads, and bare feet; they are devoted to devil worship."[14]

Thailand is full of loose women who control their husbands. Here again, the Chinese are painted in a good light, as desirable suitors: "If a married woman is very intimate with one of our men from the Central Country, wine and food are provided, and they drink and sit and sleep together. The husband is quite calm and takes no exception to it; indeed he says 'My wife is beautiful and the man from the Central Country is delighted with her.' "[15]We seem to be almost back in the European travelers' fantasy world, spawned from the Plinian Wife Givers.[16]

What is most evident is that Ma Huan's account, if not totally propagandistic, is at least slanted in a very Chinese direction. It takes in the Chinese world view and values, and constantly contrasts them with the habits and customs of other people. In the attempt, non-Chinese fare very badly, unless they are of immediate Chinese descent, or at least Muslims. Why this seems so unusual is that when European travelers of the same period are faulted, arguments may be made that they were never exposed to anything outside monocultural norms. But Ma Huan, like Zheng He, as we noted, existed in an Arab-centered world, had learned Arabic and possibly Persian, and had become a Muslim as an adult. In other words, he had been exposed to a degree of Otherness that ought to have made him more accepting and less denunciatory of the world outside China.

Often Ma Huan's attitude can be downright dangerous if we depend on what he sees and interprets in order to make sense of the non-European world of the period. A particularly good example of his attitude exists in his rather clumsy accounting of the religion he finds in Sri Lanka. There he describes how

both the great personages and the common folk each morning take cow-dung, mix it thin with water, and smear it all over the surface of the ground underneath the house;

after that they worship Buddha. Both hands are stretched out straight in front of them, both legs are extended straight behind them, and both breast and stomach are glued to the ground—and [so] they perform their worship.[17]

Obviously, what is occurring is that Ma Huan is confusing the simple task of cleaning house with Buddhist and Hindu ritual.[18] Additionally, he seems to be throwing in his knowledge of Muslim prayer in order to make these people seem even more absurd, for no Buddhist can be said to worship Buddha.

THE AFRICAN GIRAFFE

No wonder after the Chinese emperors learned of these strange customs among the barbarians, they seemed more than ever confirmed about their own omnipotence. Indeed, one "tribute" from Africa even assured them of the truth of their wildest expectations. The account is given of the arrival of a giraffe from Malinde in 1414. A first giraffe had been brought back to China on one of Zheng's excursions through Bengal, where it had apparently been sent as a gift from Africa. In 1415, a delegation arrived directly from Africa to present another giraffe. Duyvendak argues, not totally convincingly, that Zheng He's fifth trip to Africa was intended to return the visiting delegates, although I am not certain why, if they had made it to China, they could not have returned to Africa on their own.[19]

Why the fuss about a giraffe? It seems that the giraffe was not just a giraffe; the Board of Rites and no less an august body than the Imperial Academy had asserted as much. It was a *gilin (k'i-lin)*—a mythical animal with a dragon's head, two prominent horns, a scaly body, cloven hooves, and a bushy tail. Shen Du (Shên Tu), a prominent member of the academy, was moved to pen some lofty lines to the Yong-lo emperor:

I, Your servant have heard that when a sage possesses the virtue of the uttermost benevolence so that he illuminates the darkest places, then a K'i-lin appears. This shows Your majesty's virtue equals that of Heaven; its merciful blessings have spread far and wide so that its harmonious vapours have emanated a K'i-lin, as an endless bliss to the state for a myriad myriad years.[20]

Then followed a long, laudatory poem that related, in no uncertain terms, the solemnity of the occasion of the giraffe's presence and its portent for a wonderful future.

At first the Yong-lo emperor seemed a bit reluctant about accepting all this praise, but he was soon able to cast reservations to the wind, and placing all this in the most ethnocentric context, he soon saw the giraffe as relevant to his recognition as world sovereign. As he put it, "This event is due to the abundant virtue of the late Emperor, my father, and also to the assistance rendered me by Ministers. That is why distant people arrive in uninterrupted succession, From now on it behoves Us even more than in the past to cling to virtue and it behoves you to remonstrate with Us about Our shortcomings."[21] The Yong-lo emperor was not inventing this reasoning. Confucius had said as much: "If the ruler of the state is drawn to benevolence, he will be matchless in the Empire."[22] And Mencius, even more pertinently, had stated that: "Whatever commands the admiration of the noble families will command the admiration of the whole state; whatever commands the admiration of the state will command the admiration of the Empire. Thus moral influence irresistibly fills to overflowing the whole Empire within the Four Seas."[23] Ironically, then, the barbarous Kunlun had provided the means through which the emperor and the aristocracy could best reassure themselves that the Mandate from Heaven had been extended to encompass the entire world.

This is the sharp irony that stands out in Chinese culture regarding their perplexing view of the different, distant, and distinct Africa. For, even as we look at the reasoning here, allowing for differences in time and culture, we still must be acutely aware that the foreign only seemed relevant with reference to China itself. Once the alien confirmed the sanctioned views of emperor and subjects, once the Other could understand and accept his own uttermost alienation, even as he bore the giraffe to the center, then there was no problem of acceptance there. The situation only became tense when non-Chinese refused to see themselves as a subject people paying tribute. On these occasions, Zheng He was moved to fire his weapons, as we shall see.

ZHENG HE AND THE KUNLUN SAVAGES

Everywhere the Chinese fleet sailed, it was supposedly welcomed with much ardor by the local inhabitants. In Aden, "The king of the country was filled with gratitude for the imperial kindness;"[24] In Malacca, the "treasure-ships" were carefully guarded; two stockades were erected and manned.[25] But as Ma Huan's foreword makes abundantly clear, the most important purpose of the various expeditions was to show "how the civilizing influence of the Emperor has spread to an extent which could not be matched during former dynasties."[26] This kind of praise would have fit in perfectly with the designs and pretesnsions of the Yung-lo emperor.

Unfortunately, modern-day scholars are not agreed that there was a uniform degree of euphoria regarding the arrival of these Chinese fleets. Indeed, on the very first trip to Africa in 1417 (although it seems that Zheng He himself did not go, but instead one of the subsidiary expeditions), the Chinese were "compelled to make a display of military force at Mogadishu and at La'sa."[27] This seems very surprising—the lengths to which the Chinese would go simply to display the grandeur and prowess of the Ming emperor.

Citing Chinese sources, Edward Dreyer mentions that even the first expeditions "involved 27,800 men sailing in sixty-two 'treasure ships' of which the largest carried nine masts and were 440 feet in length and 180 feet in the beam."[28] Yap Yong and Arthur Cotterell, in *The Early Civilization of China*, stress that the tonnage of these ships far exceeded that of the Portuguese vessels of Vasco da Gama.[29]

As early as 1178, Zhou Qufei in *Lingwaidaida* had related how the vessels that sailed to Africa were constructed on a very grand scale:"The ships which sail the southern sea and the south of it are like houses. When their sails are spread they are like great clouds in the sky. Their rudders are several tons of feet long. A single ship carried several hundred men, and has in the stores a year's supply of grain. Pigs are fed and wine fermented on board."[30] One possible reason, though, why the first expedition, despite its opulence, may not have been greeted with the dumbstruck awe that the Chinese expected was this: the Chinese had not ventured into a backwater, but into an area that was rife with trade, where already Arabs and Africans had intersected, and where, as already noted, Chinese imports had been known via middlemen for several centuries.

The sight of Zheng He's fleet off Mombasa, demanding tribute and the recognition of the Ming emperor, might well have stirred some laughter, and afterwards a degree of hostility. After all, Africans were familiar with the courts of the Chinese and had visited and, as thirteenth-century Arab documents make clear, frequently plied the waters of the Indian Ocean.[31] The supposedly avid welcome of the Chinese fleet and the continued demonization of Africans were therefore from the Chinese viewpoint. Most likely Africans had little knowledge of their "Kunlun" status and merely viewed the Chinese as traders who had come, much as they themselves had gone to India and China, and much as the Arabs before the Chinese had arrived on the East African coast.

This is why on March 2, 1498, when Vasco da Gama came from a different direction round the Cape of Good Hope, *he* was the surprised person, as he met his first Arab speaking Africans, decked out in fine clothes, who afforded him great hospitality from their leader, the Sultan of Mombasa. Furthermore, Portuguese efforts would have foundered were it not for the helpful technical assistance provided them by the pilot, Ibn Masdjid al-Din Ahmad, who guided them to India.[32] Ibn Masdjid's sea charts have been published.[33] Additionally, historians now contend that a large amount of scientific and technological knowledge had been amassed by the Africans and Arabs. This, they assert, aided the Portuguese in their seafaring conquests.[34]

African and Arab knowledge also aided the Chinese in their own ventures; and it is likely that African seagoing crafts of some magnitude were known to Chinese. Whatever the Ming emperor may have thought, this much is evident: culture (like trade) is not one way but flows in both directions. In the 1340s, both Ibn Battuta and Nicolo de Conti were passengers on board Chinese vessels, and they both remarked on their astonishment; the vessels were "so much larger," Daniel Boorstin adds, "than any they had seen in the west."[35] Obviously, therefore, before Zheng He there must have been major Chinese/African contact. But it remained unofficial since, for the Middle Kingdom, only "tribute" could be understood.

We might therefore argue that both Zheng He and Ma Huan were embarked on a journey, not to meet the Other, but to see the One, namely their own Arab Self. Africanized Arabs and Arabized Africans in East Africa had been part of a process through which Arabism had been synthesized with another culture and, as result, had given birth to different people in the process. Equally, the sinicized Arab or the Arabicied Chinese had undergone a process during which two cultures again blended. A major contrast between, say, Ibn Masjdid and Zheng He was that the former existed in a majority African culture and the latter as a Muslim minority in a majority Chinese culture. Hence, the encounter between Africans and Chinese on the coast of Africa during the early fourteenth century would have been one in which these two countervailing viewpoints would predominate, even given the fact that Africa and China were both "encountering" each other through the dramatis personae of the Arabs.

Perhaps this is why the Chinese never completely understood who the Africans were and continued to believe, even after Zheng He's visit, in the type of mythology that allowed the Chinese to maintain their fantasy about the barbaric Kunlun. For instance, take Fei Xin in *Hsing-ch'a sheng-lan* (pinyin, *Xingcha Shenglan)* or The Overall Survey of the Star Raft (c. 1436).[36] Fei Xin was not unduly burdened with the cultural pluralism of Zheng He or Ma Huan; instead, he was a criminal who was simply trying to expiate his misdemeanors and curry favor to the powers that be. As such, he prepared not only the work by which he is known, but also a book of illustrations for the emperor.[37]

According to Mills, Fei Xin mentions twenty-four more places than Ma Huan, which would suggest that he played a greater role in the expeditions.[38] But although Mills included Giumbo, Mogadishu, and Brava, he seems to feel that these were not areas actually visited, but "places known by hearsay."[39] In any case, Fei Xin returned to the old lore of the Chinese as he attempted to flatter the emperor and to contrast the sad lot of the miserable Africans with the happy life of the fortunate Chinese. In the case of some unknown country called "Djubo," Fei Xin writes that the "people live in solitary and dispersed villages." and "the country is situated in a remote corner of the west."[40] We are back in the familiar territories that the earlier Chinese travel texts had imaginatively explored, faeaway lands where the very environment was hostile to social growth.

The account of Djubo continues, regarding the people: Their "customs are simple"; they grow "neither herbs nor trees," and live in an area "where the mountains are uncultivated.[41] This is confirmation, were any needed, of Kunlun status—here the failure to live a settled life (much like the Mongols) condemns the Kunlun as a nomadic, barbaric people. Duyvendak adds that:

There are similar descriptions of Mogadishu and Brava, all equally cheerless. Of Mogadishu it is specially stated that the houses are four or five stories high. The inhabitants are quarrelsome, and practise archery.Wealthy people engage in navigation and trade with distant countries. Camels, horses, cattle, and sheep all eat dried fish.[42]

We have heard the language before in Zhao Rugua's *Zhufanji* and other similar works. But here it is "confirmed" by a specific traveler, authenticated in a way that continued to establish the Kunlun savage as identical with the African terrain. Indeed, Gong Zhen's (Kung Chen) *Xiyang fanguo zhi (Hsi-yang fan-kuo chih)* or Records of Foreign Countries in the Western Ocean (c.1434) reproduced Ma Huan almost verbatim, thereby further authenticating the oddness of the Chinese Ultimate Other in Africa.

MAO KUN'S MAP

Mao Kun (1511–1601) had worked for the governor of Fujian Province. He found and published maps which are dated around 1422.[43] Duyvendak cites a reference to an introductory note (alluding to Zheng He) that Mao Kun's "maps record carefully and correctly the distances of the roads and the various countries."[44] Therefore, these maps should presumably help us to adduce more clearly the objective nature of the expeditions and the people with whom the

Chinese came into contact.

Yet again, we must note the presence of the Arab influence in the construction of the maps, although Mills asserts that in all probability the maps' mythology, their literal legends, were "an independent invention of the Chinese." [45] Whatever may be the truth of this, a glance at the map reveals the continued presence of inventions, through which visual reproductions sought to authenticate the verbal renditions of travel. For instance, on Folio 19v, the Mao Kun map prints, running from left to right, across the lower end, Chinese approximations for African names: Pu-la-wa and Mu-lu-wang (for Brava), Man-pa-sa (for Mombasa), and to the right hand corner Ma-lin-ti (for Mozambique).

In this context, Ma-lin-ti is especially significant, given the fact that earlier Chinese records had already noted the presence of a country called "Ma-lin." This was one of the places, it will be recalled, which was the repository of savagery. Mao Kun's map is further compounded by the problem of the researcher not being able to authenticate the place names with any definite degree of certainty, since as Mills adds, the accompanying Chinese text was "written by an illiterate person and is corrupt."[46] All identification must therefore be tentative. Add to this the problem of the compression of the chart, especially with regard to the East African coast,[47] and the map becomes even less helpful.

Yet it must be stated that this map remains of great historical interest. As Mills rightly comments: "This is the earliest Chinese map to give an adequate representation of southern Asia, and the representation extends as far as Persia, Arabia, and East Africa." Earlier maps had tended to concentrate on China itself. *Ancient China's Technology and Science,* compiled by the the the Chinese Academy of Sciences in Beijing, makes this very point. In a chapter by Cao Wanru entitled "Maps 2000 Years Ago and Ancient Cartographical Rules," the author shows that from the Qin Dynasty (221–207 B.C.) until the time of cartographer, Jia Dan (730–805), maps tended to emphasize local topography. But Jia produced a map (now lost) that included both China and the known "barbarian" states. Even Luo Hongxian (1504–1564), following Zhu Siben (1273–1333), although making use of a grid scale, concentrated mainly on the "border regions and the river valleys" of China itself, Cao contends.[48]

In comparing the Mao Kun map with European maps, Mills makes a very important point:

The radical difference in substance between Chinese maps and European maps lies in the fact that the former become less complete and exact as they progress westward, and the latter as they progress eastward. We expect each of them to be superior in their own homeland. In respect of the half-way region, that is the coasts of Africa and Arabia, this Chinese map is immeasurably superior; the European mappers knew little specific about this region.[49]

As Mills shows, the Portuguese had only just embarked on their exploration of the West African coast and had no knowledge whatever of areas further south and round the African coast. This would have to await Vasco da Gama and the aid of Ibn Masjdid. But, in the meantime, the Chinese, with some Arab help, had developed a definite idea of the northeastern and southeastern coast of Africa, even if their maps still betrayed aspects of Chinese mythological marginalization of the Kunlun.

In *Star Raft*, Philip Snow attempts a reconstruction of a map such as Chinese might have produced between the twelfth and thirteenth centuries. His illustration includes much of what had already been mentioned in the written texts—some factual, some fictional. Side by side with the real fact of Islamized coastal towns complete with mosques (which Zheng He would most definitely have noticed), Snow also placed the unreal fiction of the incense bearing trees of Somalia, and the enormous bird with a camel in its beak, supposedly native to northern Madagascar. [50]

What, however, is even more significant is Snow's modernization of Zhu Siben's map of Africa.[51] There, we observe the pictorial presence of the Arab legend—the word for "Zang slaves" written in Chinese, some Arab place names, and Arab assertions about the presence of a large lake in the central portion of southern Africa. Of course, Zhu Siben's map predates Mao Kun's, but what remains intriguing is that, despite Zheng He's voyages, the cartographical legend persisted. What seems very certain now is that the Chinese attempted to incorporate their own visualization of the Kunlun barbarian with the Arab view of the Lam-lam slaves. Since Chinese history had prepared them for this very kind of assertive arrogance, they would have no compunctions about imposing their own narrow ethnocentrism on an isolated and distant Other.

It would have been useful to utilize East African sources, were they extant, to relate something of what the Africans saw, how they viewed the Chinese, and what occurred. But, at this stage of our discussion, this must remain a mere theoretical supposition, since East African oral records do not describe this encounter. Perhaps the Chinese were just another one of the many visitors to the coast, or perhaps their visits were not considered significant enough. Apart from the presence of porcelain shards, which many archaeologists have identified on the East African coast, the African record is silent on this matter. And, as already noted, the Chinese goods may have come through middlemen.

China's "discovery" of Africa thus merely confirms its long held assumptions. As a result of Zheng He's expeditions, little reality enters into the Chinese account, although we cannot blame Zheng overmuch since his records were intentionally "lost" following the bureaucratic conflict with the eunuchs. What again we must stress is the manner in which "encounter" is often just another stage of imaginary endeavor through which long-cherished notions about the Other are looked for and identified.

The Chinese were not global adventurers or they might well have done the same. All that they were able to do was to identify the fearful outsider, name and describe him in terms that suited their own ethnocentric history and time. They could not impose this burden on the unknowing Other, as the West could and did. Instead, ironically, this would be done to them by the West, who would see in the "heathen Chinee" and the "Yellow Peril," reasons for demonization and even exclusion. By the mid part of the twentieth century, it mattered little what Zhu Siben had drawn or Ma Huan or Fei Xin had written; instead, the Chinese were attempting to portray themselves as bound together in an historical link with peoples of what used to be called the "Third World." European history had branded them, too, these very inhabitants of the Middle Kingdom, as outsiders. Hence, their only refuge was to accept this status, and try to opt for a common association with those whom Frantz Fanon—in seeking to explain the miserable condition into which the colonized had almost passively fallen—had called the "wretched of the earth."

7

THROUGH ARAB AND MUSLIM EYES

We have observed the extent to which the Chinese were at first only able to visualize and describe Africa and Africans through Muslim eyes. Even when China embarked on its first full-fledged expedition to the East African coast, the fleet was led by a Muslim, and one of the surviving accounts was composed by another Muslim. Additionally, we have seen how Africanized Muslims, as in the case of Ibn Masdjid, were familiar with the realities of African and Asian travel. We have noted that the Chinese attempted to merge their version of Africa with the Arab one and, in so doing, very often came up with a further device which distanced them even more from Africans. The Kunlun concept was moved further and further away from China, until finally this belief in one of complete outsider was positioned in East Africa. Seemingly, real Chinese contact with Africa needed some mythical attempt at justification of reality—hence the persistence of the legendary concoction. The Chinese, it may be said, as late as the fifteenth century, on the eve of the opening up of the New World, had securely locked themselves away from attempts at facing external reality.

FAXIAN AS EARLY VOYAGER

From no less an authority than Faxian, the Buddhist pilgrim who traveled to India between 399 and 414 A.D., we know that a thriving sea route had existed between Sri Lanka and the China coast, for this was how Faxian attempted to return to China in the company of merchants. The disciple who accompanied him wrote: " he took passage in a large merchantman, on board of which there were more than 200 men, and to which was attached by a rope a smaller vessel, as a provision against damage or injury to the large one from the perils of navigation."[1] When they encountered a storm, the merchants "took their bulky goods and threw them into the water."[2] It would be safe to argue from this example alone that the ship was of some considerable size and was equipped with the means to transport a fair amount of cargo.

In the description that follows the abatement of the storm, we learn a little about fourth century navigational styles and techniques:

The great ocean spreads out, a boundless expanse. There is no knowing east or west; only by observing the sun, moon and stars was it possible to go forward. If the weather were dark and rainy, (the ship) went as she was carried by the wind, without any definite course. In the darkness of the night, only the great waves were to be seen, breaking on one another, and emitting a brightness like that of fire, with huge turtles and other monsters of the deep (all about). . . . But when the sky became clear, they could tell east and west, and (the ship) again went forward in the right direction.[3]

Seemingly to the pilgrim, as well as the more seasoned merchants and crew, the ocean was a mysterious presence. They could sail once they could observe the sun, moon, or stars, but in the absence of a compass, they were unable to have any real sense of direction. The ship had a life of its own, and thus it was that Faxian arrived in Java.

He tells us that he remained there for five months, apparently waiting for another vessel. This is also described as "another large merchantman, which also had on board more than 200 men." The itinerary may not have had clockwork regularity, but Faxian relates a series of interconnecting routes that allowed him to eventually get back to China. He gives us some additional information about this vessel, for instance, that it "carried provisions for fifty days."[4] However, again because they encountered another storm, they were sailing for some seventy days, but still had enough water and provisions to allow them, with some rationing, to subsist for an even longer period.Thinking that they were probably on a wrong course, "they directed the ship to the north-west, looking out for land."[5]

With some inspired guessing and a great deal of very basic navigation, Faxian eventually reached a port on the Shandong peninsula, from which he was able to set out by land for the capital, Xian. He concluded that the return journey had lasted some three years. The types of vessel in which Faxian traveled were regularly used to ply the course of the Indian Ocean and the China Sea. Since Faxian returned to China with many Buddhist texts, which he had managed to preserve on both of the two hazardous sea journeys, as well as the overland route, these ships must have had the capability of carrying a fair amount of cargo in relatively safe conditions. Faxian spent the remainder of his life translating these texts.

ARAB/MUSLIM CONTACT

Arabs had made contact with China long before the advent of Islam. According to Marshall Broomhall in *Islam in China*, this contact may well have occurred prior to any actual historical recording. Using the October to April monsoon winds to sail their dhows, the Arabs appeared off the coasts of China in the early part of the first century. But even greater contact with China took place soon after the advent of the Holy Prophet Mohammed (born c. 570 A.D.). After the Hegira, or the Flight of Mohammed from Mecca to Medina, which took place in 622 A.D., early Muslim converts began to make their first appearance in China. Broomhall indicates that the Tang Dynasty (618-907 A.D.) was the earliest period during which there was actual historical verification from a Chinese source, namely the Annals of the Tang Dynasty. [6] He even suggests that Arabs had established a factory in China by 622 A.D.

Under Tang Tai Zong (Tang Tai Tsung), the second emperor of the Tang dynasty, China became a flourishing center of what today we would call a truly multicultural society. And, as the Chinese looked outward at the new arrivals, those new arrivals in turn looked inward at the Chinese, wrote about them, and were very often surprised at the high level of Chinese tolerance. As a result, China became caught up in the growing pains of the expanding Islamic world— indeed even giving at times a curiously odd rendition of the origin of Islam:

At the time of the Sui dynasty, 610 A.D., a man from Persia was feeding his cattle on the western mountains of Medina *(Mo-ti-na)*. A lion said to him, "On the western side of the mountains are many holes. In one of these is a sword, and close to it a black stone with the inscription in white, 'Whoever possesses me becomes ruler.' " The man went and found everything as the lion had said. He proclaimed himself king on the western frontier and overcame all who withstood him.[7]

A devout Muslim would have some difficulty in recognizing that these are references to Mohammed's visions in the cave at Hira, recounted in the Koran, Sura x and liii, where Mohammed received a divine messenger who assured him of his holy mission.

However, by 872, an Arab account does relate (albeit with a degree of surprise) some knowledge of Islam on part of the Chinese Emperor I Tsung. Ibn Wahab of Basra recalled his experiences in China soon after his return to Iraq. When he visited the emperor, he had been asked how he would recognize the Holy prophet. The emperor passed round a series of rolls to him with the words, "Let him see his Master." What is puzzling about the account is that Ibn Wahab allegedly recognized the "portraits of the Prophets," even though he came from a religious background that expressly forbade the depiction of human beings. Furthermore, when he replied to the emperor that he recognized Noah, the surprising reply that I Tsung supposedly gave was that, "As for the Flood, we do not believe it. The Flood did not submerge the whole world. It did not reach China or India."[8] This is surely a distorted image of China as reflected by its Other; the Muslims, now secure in their new belief, were clearly attacking Chinese agnosticism or even their ignorance of the Word. Muslims would not have known of intrinsic Confucian faith in the Great Flood stemmed by Yü.

On the other hand, the emperor seemed to be knowledgeable enough to recognize the force of Islam and its mighty origins. Ibn Wahab has him say about Mohammed: "He and his people founded a glorious empire. He did not see it completed, but his successors have."[9] Ibn Wahab then adds that he also saw other pictures, with inscriptions in Chinese which he presumed gave an account of the pictures, thus stressing the overall sophistication of the emperor, his knowledge of the West, his interest in the various religions of China and India, and yet his confirmed belief as a kind of stubborn pagan.

The trading ventures of Arabs resident in China would remain a virtual monopoly until the arrival of Europeans in the sixteenth century. But, interestingly enough, the advent of Islam, the arrival of first generation Muslim converts, and even the conversion of resident Arabs and Chinese, did little in terms of altering Chinese customs. Certainly Islam never impacted on China in the manner of Buddhism, or even later, Christianity, to a lesser extent. Perhaps this was in part due to the military rivalry that arose between China and incipient Islamic nationalism, especially in China's northwest. As early as 751, at the battle of Talas, Tang troops were routed by Muslims, thereby bringing about the loss of Kashgar.[10]

An indirect result of civil unrest may well have been the 755 rebellion of An Lushan (703–757 A.D.).[11] An Lushan had achieved the position of general by the age of thirty-three. By 744, he held total control over North China, and by 755, he was ready to attack the Tang leadership itself. He was aided in this by natural disasters that had occurred in China, which were seen as clear evidence of the emperor's unsuitability and as portents of the withdrawal of the Mandate of Heaven. In the poetry of Li Bai (Li Po) (701–762) and Du Fu (Tu Fu) (712–770), there are many contemporary references to the suffering of the people in contrast with the excessively luxurious lifestyle of the court.

Following the capture of Luoyang and Xian and the escape of Emperor Tang Huang Ming, An seemed poised for success. But internal strife brought about his own murder, in 757, at the hands of his second son. Although the rebellion began by An was eventually suppressed, the Tang never completely recovered their losses. Indeed, the area to the northeast, originally under An's control, was not really reconquered until the time of the Ming (1368–1643).

Constant Chinese battles with Arabs and Muslims, coupled with internal Muslim uprisings, confirmed Chinese suspicions and meant that although Arabs and, later, Muslims became a visible feature of Chinese life, they were never wholly integrated into Chinese society, nor did they become sinicized. This was due to the prevalence of strict Muslim religious beliefs that offered little compromise. Muslims could trade with the Chinese, but they found Chinese food, for instance, utterly objectionable. And since the Chinese, despite their own philosophical approach to life, could hardly be included as "people of the Book," like Jews and Christians, the rift, even when not openly hostile, remained very pronounced.

In assessing Arab travel between 1000 and 1500, T. W. Arnold has rightly argued that the motivating factors were an interest in geography, a religious urge to perform the *hadj*, and a desire to engage in commerce.[12] Where China was concerned, the need for trade was the most stimulating factor for Arabs, but commerce also introduced concomitant interests such as geographical and religious concerns.

Pre-Muslim geographical knowledge regarding areas bordering China shows that Arabs certainly possessed superior knowledge to Europeans. Nafis Ahmad has cited at least three geographers who "began to play a leading part in the administration, commercial and cultural life of Central Asia"[13] during the ninth century and whose works are fundamental to our understanding of the period. He has even contended that during the time of the Mongols, Muslim geographers had an enormous influence on Chinese geographical knowledge in general. Furthermore, Ahmad Zaki Validi has stated in *Islamic Culture* that the official Chinese map for 1331 was either very dependent on Muslim cartographers or was composed by Muslims.[14]

A tenth-century account by Buzurg ibn Shahriyar, *Kitab 'aja'ib al-Hind,* relates the care and concern with which the pilots took their responsibilities. In speaking to one of his passengers while trying to calm him during a storm, a pilot argued:

"You must know," he said, "that travelers and merchants have to put up with terrible dangers, compared with which these experiences are pleasant and agreeable; but we who are members of the company of pilots are under oath and covenant not to let a vessel perish so long as there is anything left of it and the decree of fate has not fallen upon it. We who belong to the company of ships' pilots never go on board a vessel without linking our own life and fate to it; so long as it is safe, we live; but if it perishes, we die with it. "[15]

In addition, Arnold also mentions al Maqdisi (he refers to him as al-Muquaddasi), who also wrote during the tenth century. Yet although his book *Ahsan al-taqasim* is a spirited revelation of life in Islamic territories during the period, the writer "made no attempt to describe the countries of the unbelievers."[16]

Arab and Muslim writers and travelers therefore suffered from the same kind of misguided bias as their medieval European counterparts. They all imagined the fantastic and often invented or retold outright fabrications about the areas they encountered. Also, Muslims were often prejudiced against non-Muslims, not deeming them worthy of consideration in what they wrote. Not all, thankfully, were like this, or we would have great difficulty in being able to locate and trace the Arab concept of the Chinese.

Among some of the travelers and compilers of accounts, most important is Ahmed Ibn Masdjid al Din's *Nautical Instructions and Arab Routes between the Fifteenth and Sixteenth Centuries.*[17] There Ibn Masdjid (without whom the Portuguese would not have reached India) mentions that he had followed in the footsteps of his grandfather and father. He himself had personal experience navigating the Red Sea area for some forty years. But, in addition to the very real marvels that he and others mentioned, there was the usual degree of inventiveness. Unable to distinguish between the blatantly false and the amazing, they all simply set everything down.

These are the serious limitations that we find in the works of the twelfth-century writer Ibn Jubayr and the better-known fourteenth-century author Ibn Battuta. Ibn Jubayr helps us understand, if only for reasons of comparison with China, the extent to which Islamic beliefs and customs had penetrated Europe. Ibn Battuta was a Spanish-born Muslim who was determined to make the *hadj* to Mecca, after he had been forced to consume wine.[18] He interests us mainly because he provides an insider Islamic view of the Crusades, describing, for instance, the enthusiasm with which the name of Saladin was uttered in Mecca. Ibn Battuta had gone to the East between 1183 and 1185 and once more, after the fall of Jerusalem in 1187, he attempted to travel there. We learn from him about the inroads Islam had made, particularly in Sicily. Even King William II of Sicily (d.1189), one of the first kings to embark on the Third Crusade, could read Arabic. And today, in contemporary Sicily, the presence of the Muslim world is very evident to the most casual of visitors, in language survivals, food, music, and architecture.

As already noted, the Muslim impact on China was far less, but in the work of Ibn Battuta, there is present some of what has already been observed—the view of the Chinese as pagans and a constant looking out for the marvelous. This quest for the wondrous concerns us even more, since Ibn Battuta came to be regarded as *the* alternative voice, *the* accepted viewpoint of the Other. He more often than not tends to be very condemnatory in his view of both Africa and China, whereas he is not nearly as harsh when he writes about other places. I have suggested elsewhere that one reason could well have been that he, like other Arab and Muslim writers of the period, tended to be engaged in two purposes.

First and foremost, they wished to distance themselves from the European concept of the Other, the barbarians and "lam-lam" slaves of Africa, and the descendants of Gog and Magog in China. After all, the Arabs who did write tended to understand quite clearly their role; they were or may have been antagonists with Europeans, but rightly saw themselves as their equals. And those Muslims who lived in Europe would have clearly known that they existed in a life- threatening situation, as their future expulsion from Granada in 1492 would make abundantly clear.

Second, Arab travelers and geographers drew from a common source. Their view of the world had been shaped by the same forces as those they eventually would give back, enriched, to the Europeans. Not only was Ptolemy part of the common heritage of belief, but also, in addition, Ptolemy could truthfully be seen as a pre-Islamic grandsire, much more related to the Arab world than the European. Additionally, Arabs, having freely drawn from European sources in their illustrious libraries in Timbuctoo, Toledo, Alexandria, Bagdad, and Damascus, had not merely performed exercises in the translation of European texts. Indeed, what added to their achievement and their knowledge was a delicate balancing act of synthesis, whereby they drew from both Arab and European traditions and molded them together. It was therefore quite logical for them to envision themselves as the progenitors of medieval culture. This was not a world in which they saw Africans or Chinese as active participants.

IBN BATTUTA GOES TO CHINA

It is against this background that we have to understand Ibn Battuta's opening salvo in his *Travels in Asia and Africa: 1325–54,* where he comments: "The Chinese themselves are infidels who worship idols and burn their dead.[19] Between 1342 and 1354, Ibn Battuta had presumably gone to China after visiting

North Africa, Egypt, the Middle East, and India.But the journey to China was disputed from as early as his own time for a number of reasons. In the first place, it was felt that the accounts he narrated tended to be a little too fantastic and, in some instances (especially in the descriptions of Mecca), too heavily reliant on the work of Ibn Jubayr.[20] Furthermore, the chronology of his itinerary, in addition to his confusion of place names, does not aid in any assurance of authenticity. Yet, according to Ibn Battuta, he had landed at the great Chinese port of "Zaytun", traveling to Beijing and back by using the canals.

The greatest degree of condemnation is derived from the work of his own contemporary Ibn Khaldun, who related that on Ibn Battuta's return to Fez, his account of China was received by the sultan and his court with much disbelief. The issue is further compounded by the fact that the travel narrative was not written by Ibn Battuta himself, but by one of the sultan's secretaries, Muhammad ibn Juzayr, who embellished it and often mistakingly transcribed non-Arabic words and phrases.[21]

We may interpret the work of Ibn Battuta as presenting a commonly accepted and agreed viewpoint, a mirror image, of how Muslims saw the world round them and, for our purpose (whether he actually went to China or not), of what Muslims would have accepted about China during this time as factual, albeit a little titillating. He expressed a very pro-Islamic stance, contending that even the power shift from Arabs to Turks was merely a divine manifestation within a singular Islamic world. Bernard Lewis has pointed out that the Muslims were the first to create an "intermediate civilization" of both space and time, one that spanned the physical continents of Africa and Asia, while straddling the time span between Hellenistic antiquity and modern times. Thus, for Ibn Battuta, the very pro-Islamic foundations of his beliefs saw no contradiction in the cessation of Arab domination and the rise of Turkish power. Ibn Battuta "saw the coming of the Turks as a sign of God's providential concern for the Islamic faith and the Muslim community."[22]

Only in this way can we make sense of what Ibn Battuta supposedly saw and concluded about China. For him, the base of the world was located at an Islamic core, not an Arab center, and when he looked out beyond the confines of this area, renowned world traveler though he might have been, he saw nothing but deviation from the Islamic norm. I suppose we can argue that he was therefore particularly harsh on African "barbarism" and Chinese "paganism," not because he was merely judgmental (although he might have been), but because he saw these peoples as living on the outskirts of European/Arab, Christian/Islamic belief. As such, all he could do was to record what any Muslim of his time might have felt, and if in the process he seemed less charitable toward the Chinese, we should recall that his viewpoint was merely an inversion of what the Chinese themselves had concocted about others. Thus, both Chinese and Arabs visualized each other as *the* Other, even before the harsh gaze of European scrutiny would render their considerations of otherness moot and obsolescent, as Europeans began to apply their own finger pointing, their own concept of marginality, on the entire non-European world.

In the work of Ibn Khaldun, we find what we expect: for instance he acknowledges that in China he is at the very extreme of the world, confessing that "beyond the city of Sín-kalán there is no other city, either infidel or Muslim. It is sixty days' journey, so I was told, from there to the Rampart of Gog and Magog, the intervening territory being occupied by nomadic infidels who eat men when they get hold of them."[23] In fact, the view is not an extreme one; one may even argue that the proviso "so I was told" makes the statement even a little cautionary. The comment is the standard fare of orthodox Islamic belief, for the Koran itself had described how Dhul-Quarnayn, an Islamized Alexander the Great, had heeded the cries of a people who spoke no known tongue and imprisoned behind two enormous hills the frightful monsters Gog and Magog.[24] On this Jews, Christians and Muslims could all agree—that somewhere on the eastern edge of the known world, beyond the purview of civilization, the Ultimate Other had been securely locked away. The Chinese, se-cure at their own center, could not possibly have recognized this as a representa-tion of themselves. Yet, for a people who tended to be always condemnatory of the alien Other, this seemed a just and fitting reprisal.

According to Ibn Khaldun, whose *Muqadimah* constitutes the preface and first book of an examination of universal history, the Chinese were not human outcasts. He divided up the world into seven zones and argued that the major difference was between what he termed "temperate" and "intemperate" societies. To the latter category belonged the Zanj; there is some little hope for them, for when they settle in temperate latitudes, Ibn Khaldun affirms, they "produce descendants who gradually turn white in the course of time." Those who remain in the intemperate latitudes "are in general characterized by levity, excitability and great emotionalism." The Chinese are not part of this extreme; they were even spared the excessive ravages of the fourteenth-century plague because of their "more affluent civilization." Indeed, what distinguishes China is that it may at least be pointed out and identified, unlike the region south of Mogadishu which is inhabited by "other nations beyond which there is nothing but waste and empty areas."[25]

What we witness in Ibn Khaldun and Ibn Battuta is both a synthesis of Arab and Greek thought and a new individual application. For instance, Ibn Khaldun roundly rejects, even condemns, any acceptance of environmental conditions in development, opting instead for genetic factors as the only logical explanation for the excesses he finds. In Ibn Battuta, we do not see closely reasoned arguments, but instead the results of the blending of two traditions. Thus, the "negrolands" of West Africa constitute a brutish place where it is difficult to find an educated slave girl or to discover people who have good manners, or who even know and understand how to prepare palatable food. The women are immoral, giving themselves freely (as in every male European travel fantasy of the period) to all and sundry. It is an area seemingly abandoned by Allah, and Ibn Battuta even writes of the Sahara:

That desert is haunted by demons; if the *takshif* [guide who travels ahead with messages] be alone, they make sport of him and disorder his mind, so that he loses his way and perishes. For there is no visible road or track in these part—nothing but sand blows hither and thither by the wind. You see hills of sand in one place, and afterwards you will see them moved to quite another place. [26]

All that is occurring here represent the usual negative response to the unfamiliar. We have already noted this with reference to the Gobi Desert and early Chinese pilgrims, who also noted monsters and strange sights. But Ibn Battuta's bewilderment in the Sahara seems surprising, given his birth in Spain and the Muslim links with North Africa.

Concerning the Chinese, Ibn Battuta constantly asserts their strangeness, their oddness. Indeed, it very often seems that he is only able to make his foray into China with the generous help of Muslims who live in the various cities he visits. The highlight of his arrival in one city is encountering a Muslim whom he had previously met. For all the beauty of the buildings, and the spaciousness of the avenues, set amidst fruit trees, Ibn Battuta sourly remarks, quite early in his account after visiting only two cities in China: "The land of China, in spite of all that is agreeable in it, did not attract me." We know the major reason why he finds China so repulsive: "I was sorely grieved that heathendom had so strongly a hold over it."[27]

Because of remarks such as these, some scholars have concluded that Ibn Battuta may not have seen China. For, in some respects, the visit to China becomes a celebration of what it means to be Muslim in the fourteenth century. Ibn Battuta confesses without remorse that he was so distressed by what he saw in China that he prefered to stay indoors and, in his words, "go out only in case of necessity."[28] Perhaps precisely because Ibn Battuta seems so averse to China, we are able to learn, if not understand, the extent to which the Muslim world engaged its Chinese Other with a degree of contempt. What seems quite evident as the narrative progresses is that the Muslims who had settled in China were doing quite well—at least those with whom Ibn Battuta associated. Furthermore, they had managed to preserve elements of their culture and religion, although they seemed able to relate very easily to the Chinese, in many cases speaking Chinese and enjoying the entertainment of Chinese jugglers.

When Ibn Battuta comes into the jurisdiction of the Mongols proper, he exhibits much more enthusiasm. This part he calls "Khitá," an Arab version of Cathay, both words being a corruption of "Qitay" or "Qitan" the name of the Altaic Turkic ethnic group that ruled during the Liao Dynasty (907–1101 A.D.). Cathay is poetic territory, where Marco Polo, like Ibn Battuta, looked for and discovered wonder. Indeed, Cathay was passed down into European lore as a place of magic, often having little to do with any eastern or Chinese reality. Much as we observed before the constraints under which both Ibn Battuta and Ibn Khaldun were operating in non-Muslim areas, we should note also the extent to which Ibn Battuta and Marco Polo were considerably freer from the need to demonize the Other, once they entered the magical territory of Cathay.

There are other examples of Cathay as a trope for the beyondness of even the accepted exotica of China. After his journey between 1316 and 1332 had been completed, Odoric of Pordenone would write about the wealth and religious zeal of the "Emperor of Cathay."[29] Later on, Marco Polo would envision Cathay and the court of Khubilai Khan with idyllic fervor; there the emperor was the idealized embodiment of a perfect European king, ruling over a land "more valuable and healthy" than any in Europe, "with no evil deed done in the city."[30] Christopher Columbus would either hear or read about the wonders of Cathay in a famous letter written by Paolo dal Pozzo Toscanelli.[31] Columbus both inherited and passed on Cathay as a figment of European imagination to be felt, and a fact to be sought after. After all, Cathay was the major impetus for his journey. We should therefore note at this point that the term Cathay was taken over by the West and redefined quite independently of China. In a way, this separation and the manner in which "oriental" fantasy was both distinct from, and yet part of, the concept of China in the West may be situated within the general schema of a narratology that constitutes both European and Arabic attempts at constructing China.

Cathay, Ibn Battuta said, was "the best cultivated country in the world." At

Khanbaliq, modern day Beijing, even though "there are no Muslims to be found," there are "villages, and wide spaces, covered with corn, fruit-trees, and sugarcane."[32] The power of the khan, even a dead khan, was absolutely stupendous. The corpse of one was brought to the funeral, as Ibn Battuta relates,

with about a hundred other slain, his cousins, relatives and intimates. A great *ná'ús,* that is, a subterranean chamber, was dug for him and richly furnished. The Qán [Khan] was laid in it with all his weapons, and all the gold and silver plate from his palace was deposited in it with him. With him also were put four slavegirls and six of the principal mamlúks, who carried drinking vessels. Then the door of the chamber was built up and the whole thing covered over with earth until it reached the size of a great mound.[33]

It should come as no surprise that neither descriptions of a still-unbuilt Khanbaliq, nor that of the burial of the Mongol chief lend credibility to the narrative. For, although both instances are historically accurate; the events depicted occur *after* 1356, the date of the earliest extant copy of the manuscript.[34] Nor should we be even mildly disappointed, since either Ibn Battuta or his copyists and transcribers are using the manuscript as a kind of palimpsest. On it are the accretions of Muslim beliefs about the Chinese and the Mongols.

If we are to judge by Ibn Battuta's intoxication over Cathay as imagined China, we may point to this as an early verification at orientalizing of the Orient, to use Edward Said's phrase. After the fourteenth century, after Columbus, indeed after the conquistadors had verified the possibility of an orient, a utopia, in the New World, all these ideas coalesced in the European mind. It was no more possible to distinguish between Cathay and Arabia, say, than between supposed Carib barbarism and African cannibalism. I am suggesting not only that "good" and "bad" came to have clearly definable localities in the European mind, but also that it was downright impossible to distinguish one Other from another other. In time, with European penetration into various areas, it became not just difficult for colonials schooled in European norms to establish or recognize differences among others, but they Asians, Africans, and Native Americans themselves all succumbed to the new and seemingly authoritative mythology. Thus they were forced to see even themselves (not just each other) in this new way.

This was quite a triumphant act of conscription on the part of Europeans, for they had validated the mirror image of themselves and imposed distorting features on the countenance of the Other. Europeans had also reawakened in the Other some nightmarish glimmer of recognition that this might indeed be them, that, in some respects, lowly though they were, they could in time represent the latent apotheosis of Europeanism. Thus, in one fell swoo, incipient colonialism, before it became full blown in the nineteenth century, had already marked out its victims.Those who would subscribe to the dispositioning, the ordering of the Other, could aspire perhaps eventually to becoming part of a new imperial way. Of course, then, no one knew how the history of the twentieth century would alter in very profound ways this crude design of rewarding only those who spoke with their masters' voices.

Today, all of this should be quite evident. What now seems less obvious is that no European or American power (even with superior weaponry) could have colonized Native Americans, enslaved and later ghettoized Blacks, demonized the Chinese and Arabs, and marginalized the Africans, without the assistance, even the active cooperation, of these very "victims." There had to be more than a small degree of complicity, even at times grave doubts about self-worth. Therefore, when in precolonial times, Chinese, Africans and Arabs saw their worlds split up, or they themselves began to separate and divide their own worlds along lines that were purely ethnocentric, bearing no resemblance to any norm outside of self, they were sowing the seeds of their own demolition.

The closer we examine Chinese isolationism before the twentieth century, the more we look at Muslim overconcern with religious apartness, the nearer we come to understanding what ethnocentrism means within these configurations, and the closer we are to realizing how easy it became for Europe to define its Other. Since the Chinese, Africans, and Arabs had already defined each one's Otherness, Europe then merely had to educate each fledgling wannabe into a clear understanding that the Other was located not just there, but here as well, particularly among they themselves. Once this was accepted as fact, it would take centuries to unravel even the most basic kernel of truth and awareness. The process is still ongoing, for it never fully reversed itself. In a way, the concept of Third Worldism is the final irony with which the One brands the Other. At one stage, Mao even declared that China was leader of the Third World. Now that the Third World can no longer logically exist, the question that should be asked is whether the acceptance of victim status is indeed a commonality. Or is it just another hoax perpetrated by the One on the Other, and by the Other on itself?

8

IMAGINING CHINA

In attempting even the most cursory examination of Chinese culture, what becomes most apparent is that the Western classification of Other clearly does not fit. First and foremost, in any encounter, there is a One and an Other, but the One defines itself purely in terms of power with respect to the Other. Second, the One simply applies concepts, usually negative ones pertaining to its own culture, to the Other. This is quite independent of Western concepts and seems to be related merely to the imbalance in any relationship that exists. Finally, as the One encroaches on the Other, what often emerges is that the Other seeks to define itself in terms of the more powerful One, thereby willingly subscribing to any notions of deficiency ascribed to it. The large picture therefore involves the One and the Other not so much in a collision but in a collusion, whereby differences may not be ironed out but become subsumed within the larger format of a new concept, of "tribe," "group" or "nation."

As Benedict Anderson has so ably shown in *Imagined Communities,* nationhood can possess little meaning beyond the artificiality imposed on it by political convenience.[1] Dominance on the part of the One, with its sacrosanct norms and conventions, becomes the prevailing factor. And when the Other simply opts to dress, act, and behave as the One, this is merely a version of the pragmatism of Napoleon's pigs in George Orwell's *Animal Farm* (1945), as they simply grow into the same conventions they affected to despise.

This is why from the beginning of this study, we observed just how the process moved through various degrees of difference. Perhaps China is a particularly striking instance of this, but long before it could even be defined by its present-day boundaries, an inner definition of self-depiction seemed to have been at the core of encounter. Hence even in legendary times, even as Emperor Mu embarked on his fabled visit to the West, Xi Wangmu is depicted both as semihuman and consort. This perception of difference as a type of conjoining of polarities is usual in the early stages of encountering the Other.

DEGREES OF OTHERNESS

Otherness by itself seems more than a little arbitrary, since there are degrees of alienation, as noted, from the normalcy of the One. A way of observing this in the instance of China's encounter with its West is to note degrees by which the Other, having been encountered and defined (perhaps even partly understood), gives way to the Odd, which has to exist because it is positioned outside the norms of representation, comprehension, and incorporation. Beyond this is the Outer, more removed, and far, far beyond the Outer is located the Outermost/ Uttermost—remote, unreachable, never understood, and animal like with no hope of ever being understood even as the Other.

Once Xi Wangmu was incorporated into the Daoist canon,[2] which was partly ferreted out of folk belief, and resuscitated as the Queen Mother of the West, she became a comprehensible Other, mysterious, living apart from the recognizable, but within the belief boundaries of "home." Her association with the peach of immortality assured her role as both necessary to the sustenance of home and essential to the awe derived from distance. To maintain her "mother" status, she had to be maternal but godlike, and to accomplish both characteristics, she had to signal the differences between "us" and "them" and provide the way through which "them" became essential to the preservation of "us." It was, therefore, a mutually interdependent relationship.

Therefore, when *The Bamboo Annals* assert that Xi Wangmu came to court in the seventeenth year of Emperor Mu's reign, it must be noted that this was done after he had "mounted a punitive expedition to Mount Keun-lun [Kun-lun]."[3] She therefore seemingly came to pay homage to her conqueror, or at least sent an emissary to acknowledge Emperor Mu's superiority. She was admitted, at least temporarily, to normalcy.

Otherness, within the confines of the Known, the familiar, "Home," becomes acceptable, even within the realm of the legendary. But the Kunlun concept, as noted, was merely shifted further and further away from the Chinese center until it became implanted in Africa during the Ming voyages. Of course, there is another side to this, a fascinating one, but it is an issue that remains clouded with controversy and needs more solid research. This concerns the contention that some anthropologists make that "an African presence existed in China from a most remote period."[4]

Indeed, this would be a most interesting line of pursuit, if only because the concept of the pre-Shang legendary Other might well have been the One, only once removed.[5] In such an instance, we could well come to an interesting psychological theory not unconnected with political theories regarding colonized peoples who often exhibit a contempt for one another, even as they all copy the colonialist's models of action, thought, and language.

Whether Africans were present or not in ancient China, what is evident from the earliest Chinese sources is that there was a strong distinction between "us" and "them," even though the "us" obviously had to be defined. Yet in their haste to distinguish between a Chinese norm and a non-Chinese reference point, even sympathetic Western critics tend to identify supposed dissimilarities as a lack of sophistication that Chinese would have noticed with reference to, say, African art. Thus, Roger Fry insisted at the turn of the century that: "If we imagined such an apparatus of critical appreciation as the Chinese have possessed from the earliest times applied to this negro art, we should have no difficulty in recognizing its singular beauty." Yet "the negro," Fry adds, "has failed to create one of the great cultures of the world."[6] One of Fry's major faults, as Mariana Torgovnick points out in *Gone Primitive,* is his inability to see in the very works he utilizes "the full display of cultural hegemony established after conquest."[7]

What should be stressed is that there is seemingly little empathy from the Chinese viewpoint as the Chinese encounter their Ultimate Others, the Kunlun. The Chinese speak nowhere of works of art by their Others which seem to possess any inherent beauty, nor do they even grant an iota of normalcy to the people who inhabit the edge of their world. Instead, as we have noted particularly in the *Zhufanji* by Zhao Rugua, since the Africans cannot all be brought "home" to the center, they remain outside, always described in pejorative superlatives. This comes as even more of a surprise since the Chinese had seemingly known of a "real" Africa, partly, it is true, from Arab sources, although Zhu Siben's map of 1320 did not act as a corrective device to the fanciful *Zhufanji.* The Kunlun existed in a land of large and monstrous animals, and as we have noted, had particularly un-Chinese concepts of the world: little personal regard for each other and no family loyalty. It is within this vacillating concept of the grotesque (Xi Wangmu's resemblance to a tiger and leopard and her godlike status) that the difference between the "Outer" and the "Utter" becomes most apparent.

At least in Xi Wangmu's acceptance into the court of the emperor (albeit possibly as a petitioner), there seems to be the probability of redemption to humanhood. No such hope is offered to the Utter, for it exists in a world beyond normal discourse, apprehension, and understanding. There is no way of incorporating such a disparity into one's own cultural belief system. And particularly because Africans were observed through Arab intermediaries, they took on an additional foreboding quality—the Other's Other, so to speak. We noted that the condition of being beyond the Other involved being wild and unkempt, consuming raw food, and not possessing an ability to speak— although we read that the Kunlun could be taught simple words.[8]

Somewhere in between the "Odd" and the "Utter" was located the "Outer." I have argued that this lay within the realm of Chinese conscious conception, but not necessarily acceptance. So if Xi Wangmu could be received within the confines of the norm and the Kunlun existed in eternal banishment without, then the Xiongnu probably could be more closely equated with the "Outer," and the possibility of eventual redemption. The Kunlun concept was a horrendous and horrifying trope for the most remote "Utter," absolutely condemned to eternal difference, and everlastingly polarized against all that the Chinese represented.

Yet despite what China may have seemingly advocated, it was always part of the world. Also, contrary to what is constantly affirmed by the West, the only way in which China could define itself was first by physically becoming part of its western areas and, second, through the spiritual importation of Buddhist scriptures from India. Both foreign lay ideas and religious beliefs underwent a process of Sinicization, but we could argue that even when, as with Islam, the effect was slight, we must nevertheless acknowledge the extent to which China, as a result of these incursions, became part of a larger world. During this process we should note how the advent of the outside world affected Chinese music, dance, opera, and particularly the novel and poetry. It goes without saying that early Confucian literature, despite the inventiveness of later Chinese interpretive criticism, sometimes reads very much like the parochial expressions of quotidian issues, concerned with platitudes about a moral life in an ideal state. With the movement outward, it seems as if Chinese culture also expanded spatially, embracing themes and issues beyond the previously omnipresent ones like the celebration of filial love and nature.

CONFUCIUS AND MENCIUS: THE INWARD LOOK

There is, seemingly, even from these earliest times, when Confucius presumably first put together his anthologies, a backward look. And this tradition of nostalgia for a perfect past continued up to the advent of the Communist Revolution.[9] It seems strange, almost ironical, that Confucius himself, who was the symbolical embodiment of the ideal past, would have constantly looked back, but this he certainly did, to a time remote in mythology when the Three Sage Kings were alive. For Confucius, this had been the era of perfection and ideal government. And for those who followed, Confucius's own time would itself achieve these very idyllic proportions. For instance during the period of the Han Dynasty, the era of the Three Sage Kings and the time of Confucius seemed almost coeval and were certainly romanticized out of all reality. Over and over again, we observe in Chinese culture and thought this hankering back to a past that was never present, but which could presumably be reconstructed and brought to life for the future. It is a curious conundrum, even a quandary, in that the writers and artists never seemed at ease with their own age until the twentieth century when the Chinese Communist Party officially renounced the past, thereby mandating that perfection lay in the present and the utopian possibilities of a perfect future.[10] Of course, today, all this is once more subject to intense debate, of which, thanks to government controls, we hear only a small whisper.

The ancient Confucian Classics seem to have had a number of clearly defined goals in mind. The *Book of History (Shu jing)* was not so much concerned with history per se, as with describing the manner in which the god-kings attempted to maintain order, both in terms of keeping out the ever-encroaching wilderness and imposing a sense of order on the land and its people. This idea of the "norm" has pervaded Chinese society until the present time, and in this respect the Chinese have been both fortunate and unfortunate: fortunate, since the idea of an agreed norm helped establish a buttress that the Chinese could erect against the encroachments not only of the northern barbarians, but also of those barbarians who would invade from the European West; unfortunate, in the manner through which the idea of normalcy constantly tended to erect blockades against the entrance of new ideas, particularly as they came through the religious activities of those who promoted Buddhism, Islam, and Christianity. Ironically, this cultural insularity did not prevent the entrance of one type of Western political thinking, namely Communism, which came to dominate Chinese life in the twentieth century.

The *Book of Odes (Shih jing)* set the tone for poetry, both from the point of view of subject matter and in terms of its heavy reliance on music. Additionally, as in the *Book of History*, there is a tendency toward the glorification of the race. What is of some interest is that both these classics are only "Chinese" with reference to how they were seen at a much later date. When they were composed, even written down, China bore little geographical or cultural resemblance to what it would later become. Therefore, what both these books show is a rather narrow view of a small part of China, yet one that would become the measure for all of China in the years to come.[11]

Another example of the manner in which the local became a representation of the national, of how the locally ethnic was intentionally applied to a multiethnic community, may be noted in the *Spring and Autumn Annals (Ch'un Ch'iu* or pinyin, *Chun qui)*. There is little in the brief entries that seems (at least to the non-Chinese twentieth-century reader) to contribute to the making of a canon, much less one that bears Confucius's name or is at least identified with him.[12] The entries, which are terse, are presumably very relevant for Lu, Confucius's home state, but do not seem to have any import beyond the mere recounting of facts relating to the ascension, deeds, and demise of a multiplicity of dukes who ruled the state.[13]

What is of even greater significance in these volumes is that they confer a sancrosanct authority on the famous Sage Kings of legendary fame. The Sage Kings are important since, unlike the earlier Legendary Emperors, they seem to exhibit attributes that are both human and divine. The Legendary Emperors were the more ancient ancestors of the Sage Kings, and their origin probably belonged to Han-dynasty Daoism. They tended to be deities who performed etiological functions. For instance, Fu Xi, who supposedly reigned around 3000 B.C., was said to have been the inventor of the eight trigrams that constitute the basis of the *I Ching*. But scholars seem to feel that the very concept may have been an invention of the Zhou Dynasty (1122–256 B.C.). The second of the legendary emperors, Shen Nong (Shen Nung), invented agriculture, whereas the third, Huang Di (Huang Ti)—whose name was afterwards appropriated by the Jesuits to mean "God"—was responsible for introducing the sixty-year cycle to the calendar.[14]

By the time we encounter the Three Sage Kings, Yao (who supposedly reigned 2357–2256 B.C.), Shun (who supposedly reigned 2255–2206 B.C.) and Yü (supposedly reigned 2205–1766 B.C.), we are a little closer to human history. But elements of the divine continue to exist in them; for instance Yao, praised by both Confucius and Mencius, passed over his own son in favor of Shun. Shun, enduring the hatred of a wicked stepmother and a foolish father, always exhibited filial piety and was also constantly commended by Confucius and Mencius. There are even allusions in the *Mencius* which often equate Confucius with the Sage Kings.[15] Yü drained the lands after a great flood and set up a system of hierarchical boundaries. The Sage Kings, according to Confucius and Mencius, are anthropomorphic ancestors from whom we should be able to glean something of correct behavior.

Because Yao and Shun are mentioned in the *Book of History* and Yü in the *Book of Odes,* what becomes evident from the earliest commentators is that history is a moral lesson for China. From its examples, humans must seek to extract what is good and bad, pertinent and irrelevant, attempting to live by these moral guides. This is why the rites become doubly important, since as laid out in the *Book of Rites (Li Chi),* and constantly articulated by Confucius, they become the means through which humans could best avoid the pitfalls of repetitive historical error. Confucius edited the *Spring and Autumn Annals,* Mencius tells us, "When the world declined and the way fell into obscurity." History was expected to contribute a moral corrective.[16] Perhaps these were among the aspects of Confucianism that, according to David Bonavia, were seen as "embodying some of the best national characteristics of the Chinese."[17]

The importance of Confucius, therefore, is that he authenticated rites and rights as they would later become accepted as central factors in Chinese identity. Confucius had himself passed on much of their importance through composing or editing the Five Classics that bear his name. His *Analects,* although they do not present a prolonged thesis on the human condition and certainly never ever delve into things of the spirit, show us the life of a wandering teacher/scholar who could provide thoughtful, pithy answers to questions that were asked of him. To the Western reader, he seems inoffensive, apolitical, but a Chinese official history describes him thusly: "Confucius propounded a Confucian ideology with 'ren' (humanity) at its core. Imbued with a conservative and reformist air, it was an ideological transition corresponding to the change from slavery to feudalism in the later Spring and Autumn Period."[18]

Confucius was less interested in matters pertaining to the spirit than he was in the circumspect behavior of humans. He addressed such issues as how sons should relate to their fathers, and thus the manner in which subjects could and should regard the emperor. For Confucius, even at this early stage of Chinese thought, the backward glance provided the best answer. Although he lived from 551 to 479 B.C., for him the golden age lay far back in the past, during the time of the dukes of Zhou in Western Zhou (1122–771 B.C.). To bring back this age of perfection, Confucius stressed the importance of *jen* (benevolence) and *yi* (righteousness) although since "it was conceived of as the totality of moral virtues . . . we can say that *yi* is rooted in *jen.*"[19] And since we have contended that the concept of what today we call China expanded spatially, we could equally argue that for Confucius, the beginnings of expansion were temporal. Perhaps since he stands at both the beginning and midpoint of history, this was a most understandable course to chart.

A well-known legend states that Lao Tzu departed from China through the northwestern gate and was never heard from again. What is interesting for us is a possible interpretation we can give to this. He did not, for instance, compose his alleged work, the *Tao te ching* (pinyin, *Dao de ching),* after he left China, but before.[20] Nor are there any references in his early work, just as with Confucius's, to attempts at exporting the beliefs of China abroad. Lao Tzu simply disappeared, that's all. His work was done, and he was no evangelist.[21]

Nevertheless, there does seem to be one important difference between Confucius and Mencius when compared with Lao Tzu and Chuang Tzu. Not only did Daoism incorporate large elements of folk culture, but also, as noted, it attempted to take in a world outside the narrow borders of the then "China" proscribed by Confucius.[22] By utilizing folk belief and mythology, particularly from the mysterious "West," Daoism borrowed both externally and internally from a region beyond the immediate. In a sense, therefore, Daoism opened up, like Confucianism, in a temporal direction, while also expanding spatially. Thus, much as with later Chinese physical exploration and "discovery," Daoism was able to physically transplant itself outside the borders of the then understood China.

CHANG CHUN AS SYNTHESIZER

In this respect, it was not unnatural that Daoism would become the first important Chinese culturally homegrown idea that traveled west—true, not with its alleged founder, Lao Tzu, but with a figure whom we can clearly demarcate as "historical." This was Chang Chun who, as noted before, visited the court of Chingiz Khan between 1221 and 1222.[23] We shall later look at the content of the message he took with him.

Chang Chun is particularly significant because he traveled as a kind of missionary from 1219, first to Beijing, then northward to the camp of the khan's younger brother in the heart of Mongolia. After visiting and instructing him, Chang turned southwest, across the familiar terrain traversed by Buddhist pilgrims like I-Ching, Faxian and Xuanzang to Tashkent, Samarkand, and, finally, to Chingiz's camp in the Hindu Kush. The account of his journey, the *Hsi Yu Chi* (Journey to the West), translated and referred to here as *The Travels of an Alchemist,* was meticulously kept by one of his disciples.

Everywhere Chang traveled, he spread the Word, but what is of greater significance is that his message was not pure, unadulterated Daoism, but, in fact, a synthesis of Confucianism, Daoism, and Buddhism. This gave it a truly "Chinese" significance, for nowhere else had this fusion occurred. Chang's role was, additionally, truly unique in that he became the spiritual equivalent of Zhang Qian (d. 114 B.C.) who first ventured west under the direct orders of Emperor Han Wu Di.

For Chang the concept of place had obviously widened. Of course, his world view was still centered at a recognizable place. But what place was this? At the time before the Mongol total invasion, any resemblance to a China concept actually constituted three states—Qin, Song, and Xia—all of which, in time, the Mongols would defeat and unite. But the unity was not one that brought about a Chinese "nation," except insofar as there were what could be termed "nationalist" outcries against the Mongol "barbarian." What the Mongols did do, however, was to link an incipient, amorphous, China, its concepts and ideas, into a larger cultural and economic format. At the center, however, was the Yuan Dynasty.

At least Chang Chun's journey meant that China, as a recognizable space, was now actively partaking in world affairs. Not unnaturally, Chang nostalgically recalled "home," much as I-Ching, Faxian, and Xuanzang before him had done. But their absolute center was scarcely China, for they had been motivated by differing religious reasons to identify with areas beyond their base. Also, their own familiar associations with the specific religious sub-base of Buddhism made them obviously regard India, to a very great extent, also as the place they thought about as "home"—a mixture of given geographical place and specific religious and spiritual linkage.

None of the three great Chinese philosophical schools of thought—Confucianism, Daoism, or Legalism—had altered what was basically a local, albeit differing, view of the familiar. This meant that their concerns tended to be with the local state and the family—hardly issues that would lend themselves to foreign adoption.

Confucianism, as already noted, tended to be place-centered in the narrowest of terms. Because Daoism, by Chang Chun's time, had incorporated (at least in his sect) foreign elements, it could offer some iota of appeal to Chingiz, even though he never became a Daoist. Legalism, with its strict conformity to the Chinese state and its insistence on an anti-Confucian stance, said more about the altercation taking place within China at a given time than about Legalism's relevance for elsewhere.

LEGALISM AND THE CENTER

By stressing that human nature was self-centered and even inimical to society, Legalism continued to emphasize a very internalized view of China, since all its examples and prescriptions related to that specific part of the world. Hence, the entire philosophy is ruler centred (not unlike that of Machiavelli at a much later time); the very actions of the prince define what is good, as his aversions indicate what is wrong.

Arthur Waley argues that with Legalism, "law should replace morality." [24]

Waley identified Mozi (Mo Tzu) (c. 479–438 B.C.) as an earlier proponent of this pragmatism. But Mozi, with his view that the ideal state existed among the Xia (Hsia) Dynasty (2183–1752 B.C.?) seems mild by comparison with the later Legalists. Although at odds with Confucius, for whom, Wing-Tsit Chan states, moral life was desirable "for its own sake," Mohists (or followers of Mozi) stressed that moral life was needed "for the benefits it brings." But that which distinguished the Mohists from Confucianists and Legalists was their "doctrine of universal love: other people's parents, families and countries are to be treated like one's own."[25] This is a startlingly radical concept, in view of the extreme ethnocentric narcissism thus far observed.

By abolishing the Confucian emphasis on the "way of the Former Kings" and substituting "the facts of the world as it now exists,"[26] the Legalists even sought a way of omitting the past. Thus, there is little of the temporal growth noted in Confucianism, and none of the spatial growth of Daoism. Because Legalism in its most pragmatic assertion localized all issues, it obviously had little chance of ever being exported or accepted by foreigners. The three major concepts, as Paul Thomas Welty points out in *The Asians,* were *jen* (benevolence), *shih* (power, position, authority), and *shu* (statecraft, or methods of government). These three fundamental factors also point to how a strong, centralized government, supporting agriculture and war, "would simultaneously increase the power of the state in relation to other states and in relation to its own citizens."[27]

Major Legalist scholars [28]included, among others, Guan Zhong (Kuan Chung) (d. 645 B.C.) to whom the *Guan Tzu* is attributed; Lord Shang, reputed author of *Shang Tzu (The Book of Lord Shang);*[29]and Han Fei Zi (Han Fei Tzu) (d. 233 B.C.), a Han prince, whose work is named after him. As with Confucianism (where the ideal state was Lu), and Mohism (where the exemplary kingdom is the Xia), with Lord Shang, the realization of perfection was in a "Chinese" state—here the Qin. Therefore the center is again firmly secured, not in a distant land mass that we could even retroactively call China, but in a specific placethat is localized, defined, and very, very definite.

With Han Fei Zi, there seems to have been every logical reason why a prince should himself advocate the virtues of totalitarianism. But for us, what is of supreme significance is the manner by which Han Fei Zi acknowledges the outer parameters while at the same time assuming Han overlordship. Han Fei Zi warns the emperor:

Do not let your power be seen: be blank and actionless. Government reaches to the four quarters, but its source is at the center. The sage holds to the source and the four quarters come to serve him. In emptiness he awaits them, and they spontaneously do what is needed. When all within the four seas have been put in their proper places, he sits in darkness to observe the light. When those to his left and right have taken their places, he opens the gate to face the world. He changes nothing, alters nothing, but acts with the two hands of reward and punishment, acts and never ceases: this is what is called walking the path of principle.[30]

From the viewpoint of the Han Other, there is obviously a problem here in accepting the Chinese emperor as a godlike figure to whom service is due and whose function (and this Han Fei Zi borrowed from the Daoists) is merely to alter nothing, a little like Jean-Jacques Rousseau's potrayal of Émile's teacher.[31]

Legalism was very pragmatic; according to Han Fei Zi, "as circumstances change the way of dealing with them alter too."[32] Often, therefore, the ways of the past must change and adapt. When Yao ruled the world, he dressed in deerskin and ate coarse millet. When Yü took charge, he worked as hard as any slave. No wonder the ancient kings "thought little," as Han Fei Zi argues, "of handing over the rule of the world to someone else." King Wen, he asserts, could have won over the Western barbarians with "benevolence and righteousness." But alas, "benevolence and righteousness served for ancient times, but no longer serve today."[33]

Han Fei Zi's philosophy obviously appealed to the ruler and was adopted literally by Qin Shi Huang Di as he attempted to wield together an early version of what would later become China. But within the very concepts of Legalism lay its own doom: For, if quite clearly it was anathema to foreigners, could it with its equally stifling approach appeal to home and thus outlive its early founders? By the time of the Han Dynasty (206 B.C.–221 A.D.), Confucianism, despite its home-based appeal and Han foreign adventurism, was back in favor. However, some do contend that, despite its official renunciation, Legalism remained at the base of much of the philosophical and political debate in China until the fall of the imperial family in the twentieth century, and very possibly afterward.[34]

CHANG CHUN AND CHINGIZ

Chang Chun, Arthur Waley writes, "claimed to have broken down the barriers that divided the three religions and shown that Taoism was the original starting point of both Confucianism and Buddhism."[35] Waley adds that Chang Chun was not the originator in this regard, but clearly he moved the ideas out of

China proper, some of them back in the very direction from which they had come. Hence, when we look for a true spatial expansion of Chinese culture, one that by the time of the Mongol ascendancy had assumed, in part at least, a tricultural approach, we may very easily identify Chang as a major symbol. And, of course, Chingiz, ever curious, pragmatic, and not a little fearful about his own afterlife, was the eager recipient of what Chang preached.

On November 19, 1222, when Chang first delivered his sermon to Chingiz, stressing that "Tao is the producer of Heaven and the nurturer of earth,"[36] he was utilizing an agricultural metaphor which Chingiz could easily understand. Chingiz could also empathize with this, for the sentiments are those of the *Secret History of the Mongols*, commissioned during Chingiz's own time.[37] Chingiz was brought up with the the concept of Tengri, to whom his shamans sacrificed, and who was the giver of all life; perhaps this was the very concept that lay behind some of the priest's words, as when Chang drove home his point: "When Tao produced Heaven and Earth, they in turn opened up and produced Man."[38]

Chang Chun warms to his point. Without challenging any deep felt notions which Chingiz may have harbored, Chang introduces subtle but specific differences between "us" and "them," the Chinese/Daoist One and the Mongol Other. One important point is that a life of abstinence is to be preferred, what he terms a "life separated from [one's] family and in the monastic state."[39] Another is that the human being, because "his body grew heavy and his holy light grew dim," developed "appetite and longing."[40] Here we note an espousal of both Zen Buddhism (which Chang's sect had embraced) and an echo of what Arthur Waley has termed "a very Manichean Ring."[41] Suffice it to say that the points being introduced serve to project a version of China that is very different from Confucius's or Lao Tzu's. Chingiz could easily associate the points made with his own experience in foreign lands—certainly with what he knew of Christianity and even of monks and nuns in both the West and the East.

Chang Chun, of course, had to be very diplomatic. He had been "summoned" to the khan's camp and, although his apostle records that every care was taken to ensure his welfare, there was nevertheless a clear power imbalance. But, true to his beliefs and his proseletyzing, Chang must put forth the Word, as he believed it, the Act, as he practised it. So, not much later, the Buddhist element crept in. Having spoken about the human desire for satisfaction of the senses from primordial times, Chang now incorporates the Sinicized Buddhist element to his basic Daoist belief, and states: "Those who study Tao must learn not to desire the things that other men desire."[42] The point is very relevant for a world conqueror, and, at this point in the discourse, roles begin to alter.

Chang relates the yin/yang polarization warning Chingiz, who is, after all, his audience: "But Yin (the imperfect) can quench Yang (the perfect); water conquers fire. Therefore, the Taoist must above all abstain from lust." Surely, by now the point is clear, that the successful conqueror who holds the world in his potential grasp must attempt to live more ethically. The personal pitch now comes:

If common people, who possess only one wife, can ruin themselves by excessive indulgence, what must happen to monarchs, whose palaces are filled with concubines? I learnt recently that Liu Wen had been commissioned to search Peking and other places for women to fill your harem. Now I have read in the *Tao Te Ching* that not to see things which arouse desire keeps the mind free from disorder. Once such things have been seen, it is hard to exercise self-restraint. I would have you bear this in mind.[43]

Thus, on a chilly November day, in the company of a small party, we have the enactment of this most extraordinary scene. Chang is assigning the role of Ultimate Other (indeed of one so far removed from him that he could be termed the Outermost, even Uttermost), to his Mongol lord.

There is never any doubt in *The Travels of an Alchemist* that Chang considers himself a superior person, both as a Daoist and as a Chinese. As the diarist reports, Chingiz as outsider can only express gratitude even at being openly chastized. Supposedly he says: "You have heard the Immortal discourse three times upon the art of nurturing the vital spirit. His [Chang Chun's] words have sunk deeply into my heart." Later, even after Chan returned to China, an emissary brought a message from the khan: "Since you went away, I have not once forgotten you for a single day. I hope you do not forget me. . . I wish your disciples to recite the scriptures continually on my behalf and pray for my longevity." At another stage, Chang even warns this first generation nomad, the khan himself, against hunting. To which, surprisingly, the khan agrees with the words, "In future I shall do exactly as the holy Immortal advises."[44]

The only possible interpretation that can be placed on these words is that they were either a Daoist fabrication or a mistranslation, or that they intentionally represented a desire to portray the Mongol Other as suppliant. We have observed ways in which medieval European chronicles viewed the "Tartar" hordes, and here we note that, even though the "Chinese" were partly conquered and would in time be totally vanquished, there are still definite attempts to assert

Chinese superiority in the face of Mongol inferiority. Thus, it matters little whether every word of the text remembered by a disciple occurred in the way stated; what is more relevant is that it indicates a way of thinking and a frame of mind.

With Chang Chun's journey into the wilderness of the West, beyond his center, we observe that the cultural baggage he bears is quite significant.[45] True, for the first time, he exports aspects of Chinese thought, but he does this within an open structure which had introduced the very belief system he was now returning. There then must be more than a small degree of unintentional irony in Chang's attitude as he seeks to travel with his version of Daoism which itself had already begun to incorporate the larger world. Rightly perceived as a genuine "victim," Chang spoke to the genuine "victor," Chingiz Khan. But some of the ideas he sought to impart from himself as cultural One had already been borrowed from a different barbarian Other, who lived in the wild area to the West, the very region he now traversed as both Savior and supplicant.

HUANG'S *WAITING FOR THE DAWN*

By the time of Huang Zongxi (Huang Tsung-hsi) (1610–1695) and his important work *Ming-i tai-fang lu* or (pinyin, *Mingyi daifang lu*) *Waiting for the Dawn: A Plan for the Prince,*[46] there is clear evidence of the survival of Legalist viewpoints, although the work is Confucian. Basically, Huang's text is a harsh criticism of Chinese despotism, which he sees continuing in the Ming Dynasty (1368–1644), although he dares not say so, since to do this might well have caused the suppression of the work.[47] Basically, to rectify the autocracy of an emperor above reproach, he proposes the restoration of the position of prime minister as a curb to the emperor's power.

Huang's scope is wide; he points out the excesses of the eunuchs and suggests reforms in all branches of education. But Huang is no radical; he is very much in the tradition of Confucius and advocates what he terms "civilized values," which will penetrate "the dark night of barbarian rule." This is perhaps why in his introduction to the English translation, William de Bary not only sees the work as "the most enduring and influential critique of Chinese despotism through the ages," but also notes that the text is "the most powerful affirmation of liberal Confucian political vision in modern times."[48]

De Bary notes the relevance of Huang's text for later reformers, such as Sun Yat-sen, who utilized the work "to promote their own political aims," and thus Huang "was acclaimed by late nineteenth and early twentieth century reformers and revolutionaries as an early champion of native Chinese 'democratic' ideas."[49]

Huang had to be conscious that he lived in the post-Mongol seventeenth century, and that the world of China had been newly defined and was seen anew from abroad. Therefore, although it remains a prescription for ideal Chinese government, *Waiting for the Dawn: A Plan for the Prince,* applies to the new peoples whom the Chinese would have to govern. In a way, it accepts China's hegemony, without catigating the barbarians over whom the emperor must preside.

Hung-lam Chu, in reviewing the work, has noted that he agrees with de Bary in that,

while Confucianism was married to dynastic rule, to equate Confucianism with dynastic tyranny is fallacious because its members were able to be self-critical even of the government institutions that they devised and supplemented. It follows that the "authorization" and "conformist" version of Confucianism is what should be discarded in modern discourse and practice.[50]

Interestingly enough this is what makes Huang's work both relevant for its own time and ours. It employs a wide historical sweep to make generalizations about good government and institutional order which are most relevant for a China that had moved beyond the geographical limitations of Confucius's ideal state and his obsessions with the past.

As de Bary rightly adds, there was a clear discrepancy in the seventeenth century between enthusiastic Jesuit missionary writings about China and the more critical Chinese accounts of the period. Huang attempts to correct the wrongheaded Western viewpoint, seeking, like another famous predecessor, to bring about an "enlightened" prince.[51]

Huang is selective about history, utilizing Mencius, for instance, to ask the important question around which his work will develop: Why is it that since the time of the ancient Sage Kings, China has never known a period of peace and order but only disorders? [52] Therefore, the faraway past is used to rectify the near present. Huang interjects another reference twhich alludes to the dynasties that followed Confucius's death and which had seen no change. Chinese "resurgence in the near future" can come about, but this depends on the welfare of the ordinary people. When Huang deplores a lack of dynastic change, a refusal to see Chinese institutions in a new light, he is criticizing the adamance of the authorities in refusing to move with the flow of history.[53]

Everything then must be altered so that the entire society can restore dignity to the common people. De Bary comments that for Huang "the key for all social evils as well as any hope for improvement lies in the nature and quality of leadership." Weak leadership has failed to respond to the new needs of the people and to understand the manner in which the changed society had departed from the recipes of the Daoists, for instance. De Bary also demonstrates that even though Huang accepts the typical Confucian development of society from primitive to civilized to dynastic, Huang's interpretation does differ. Huang does not hark back to the idyllic time when the "sharing of the world" was undertaken by "all under Heaven in a cooperative community suffused with total unselfish spirit." Thus, the basic undergirding of a perfect age is rejected. There was a primitive time, but then exceptional people sacrificed themselves to the good of all people. Only in this way could one become a prince. Thus, de Bary concludes that Huang in effect challenges the traditional patriarchy.[54]

Daoists and Confucianists had realized that there was a need for rulers, but they had gained selfish and self-seeking ones. It would have been better, Huang argues, had the people themselves selfishly gone about pursuing their own interests. Hence the dire need for radical reform in the law and ministers. Clearly, the fact of the law deprived the ministers of any real power. Here de Bary notes the survival of a bureaucratic type of Legalism, which "took hold and persisted at the imperial court long after Legalism had died out."[55] Therefore Huang's work is an attempt at propelling China into the seventeenth century, indeed, as noted, into the twentieth century, when, free from any useless trammels, the country could truly launch itself as a global power.

In reviewing *Waiting for the Dawn: A Plan for the Prince,* Hung-lam Chu observed its "contemporary relevance" for 1989.[56] But Huang's work goes beyond the occurrences of the political moment; it seems by its very nature to be less about the need to dispose of a Machiavellian prince, and more about the urgent need to erect an idyllic Platonic republic. In this way, it is more concerned with what both Confucianism and Daoism had failed to achieve, in that its impact spread beyond even the contemporary borders of China and it received serious study by Japanese and Korean scholars. Huang's work deserves to be better known in the West since it provides a recipe (albeit ideal) for running a modern state. The Western business world has found emulative points of merit in the *Sun-tzu,* pointing out that many references to warfare could apply equally well to commercial competition. Surely, then, the educational and political segments of Western society could locate in Huang's work specific indicators of the need to limit leadership power and to advance recipes for the solution to bankrupt and defective educational programs.

In this way, Huang's study goes beyond any of the practical concepts of

Confucianism in achieving societal harmony,[57] and moves far away from the mysticism of the Daoists. It is most relevant for a near future, which John King Fairbank shows that by 1755 already had new responsibilities:

the High Qing [1644–1911] rounded out its imperial frontiers far beyond the scope reached by the Ming [1368–1644]. In short, Inner Asia was now taken over by the rulers at Beijing, part of whose success no doubt lay in the fact that as Manchus they were Inner Asians themselves and flexible in ideology. The Qing hegemony over Inner Asia after 1755 began a new era in the perpetual interplay between agrarian China and the tribes of the steppe. China was the nomads' supply house for grain, silk, and other products they wanted. The Chinese and the Inner Asian tribal peoples formed a geopolitical community. In the end the Chinese nation of the twentieth century would have its own version of a colonial empire to deal with in Inner Asia.[58]

Indeed the signs of the presence of this Other, as Owen Latimore shows in *Inner Asian Frontiers of China,* were there from Qin times (221–207 B.C.), before the beginning of the Han that followed in 206 B.C. He indicates that the failure of the steppe "barbarians" and southern "Chinese" to understand one another was that they had refused to compromise—their encounter merely contributed "toward making the Chinese more Chinese."[59] But the lessons of cultivated superiority would later be shattered, at least on two dramatic occasions, by the Mongols and the Manchus.

Huang's work suggests that he had learned from Chinese history more than the moral lesson it supposedly taught to Confucianists. Within the expanded world of a new China, structures had to be erected which went beyond the construction of any mere wall. If the Chinese were to remain in touch with their old past and their new present, Huang adamantly states that they had to go beyond old self-centered views of narrow parochialism to a new, communal embrace of broader proportions. Thus, the "arrogant princes" must not seek "only such people as would be servile" and "indulge themselves," but "serve the world and its people."[60] Huang knows the past, but his gaze is fixed inexorably on a future in which all societal institutions can be perfected.

9

TABOO, TATTOO, AND PACIFIC ENCOUNTERS

Any attempt at considering Chinese/Asian outward expansion ought rightly to begin with the anthropological past. The islands in the South Pacific were themselves both the originator and incubator of a variety of cultures that go back to Asia proper. In noting the connection between Asia and Indonesia, Indonesian novelist Mochtar Lubis has written about the arrivals of early Asians in Java and Timor, and sees this as part of the general expansion into the Pacific:

New men crossed or sailed down the rivers and along the coasts of South Asia into the archipelago, the Land under the Rainbow. What triggered these waves of migration cannot be ascertained. Perhaps it was tribal wars. Or epidemics. Or hunger. Or perhaps, just man's own thirst to look beyond the horizons, to see what was at the feet of the rainbow, to find new lands and start a new life. They came in dug-out canoes with outriggers, and some of them perhaps even crossed the shallow and narrow straits between the islands on rafts to Irian and Australia, and beyond.

These early migrants have been identified as Paleo-melanesoids and Mongoloids, and they spread throughout the archipelago. They were hunters and gatherers of food. Probably they also had started growing certain plants, like tubers. Australian aborigines still put tops of wild yam in the soil and return there to harvest the yam in the next season, as do the people in Irian. Such a practice must have been brought by the migrants to the new land.

The Paleo-melanesoids were dark-skinned, had curly hair, and used oval stone axes. The Mongoloids were light-skinned, had straight hair, and used rectangular stone axes. They claimed tribal territories and lived in small groups, protecting their domain against strangers. They also had to protect themselves against wild animals.[1]

The Pacific Rim, an area spanning almost half the globe, is home to more than half of the population of the world. From the Asian continent, early populations spread to nearby areas like Java and Malaya, later southwest to

tralia, and, of course, across what is now the Bering Strait to the Americas.
Most likely, after this initial period, "island hopping" resulted in the peopling of
"Oceania," "Polynesia," "Micronesia" and "Melanesia"—names which remain
clearly unsatisfactory not only since they stress differences and deemphasize a
cultural continuity, but also because theey serve to emphasize European inventions that have little to do with world reality.

From the latter part of the nineteenth century, when Eugene DuBois un-
earthed an early homo erectus, "Java Man," it became clear that Asia had played
an important part in the evolutionary development of humans who had originated
in Africa.[2] Not only was Java Man declared to be the "missing link," but also the
find suggested incontrovertible evidence of early human development in Asia.
Later on, in the 1920s, "Peking Man" was found in northern China, at Dragon
Bone Hill.[3] This more advanced homo erectus again seemed to confirm, at least
in light of diffusion theory, that early humans had possibly spread from one end
of Asia to the other. At a later stage, anthropological work by the Leakeys and
Donald Johanson suggested differently: that only in Africa did modern humans
emerge. But, more recently, a new theory is being advanced that an early homin-
id could have left Africa and developed independently in Asia.[4]

Whatever may be the final solution locked within the anthropological record,
it is quite clear that Asians did emerge from these early prototypes and that Java
Man and Peking Man were their ancestors, as well as the progenitors of those
who made the ocean crossings of the Pacific as early as forty thousand years
ago.[5]

EARLY VOYAGERS

Early sea journeys were possibly launched on bamboo rafts, originating from
areas in what would now be termed Indonesia. Bamboo stems were light and
buoyant and, lashed together, floated easily. But rafts alone would have been
inadequate for long ocean journeys; these early seafarers must have also
experimented with ships, sails, and outriggers to take advantage of wind and
ocean currents, which would move them on to further islands. Lacking maps and
compasses, they must have been hardy adventurers, since they had set out not
knowing whither they were bound and arrived not knowing what they had
encountered. The very nature of the voyage into unknown and uncharted seas
truly makes them "discoverers" in the most pristine and basic sense.

For long journeys on a seemingly endless ocean waterway, great cooperation
and planning were necessary. Those who embarked on such a journey would have
to decide who else would go, and in what numbers. We can only speculate wildly

at the "push" factors that drove migrants out of Asia in the first place, or even the extent to which Africans might also have engaged in a similar enterprise. Kwang-Chih Chang in *The Archaeology of Ancient China* postulates that from prehistoric times "a Negroid population" traveled first to south China and then "continued on southward into a large part of Southeast Asia."[6] I also suggest further on, despite the prevailing accepted opinion, that one does not have to look too closely to see the extent to which people of a dark complexion with African features, ventured further south to so-called Melanesia and Australia. Could there have been the "negritos" mentioned in ancient Chinese texts, who no longer felt at home in an area that was marginalizing them? I merely pose the question.

One thing is quite certain, namely that we need not speculate too much on these early voyagers. What we see in places as far away as Australia and New Zealand are not artifacts that attest to a past possibility, but living communities that affirm their present actuality. These are the first immigrants who were the first humans in the Pacific islands.

Geologists have shown that these early journeyings were considerably aided by the then closer proximity of land mass as well as lower sea levels. Many of the offshore islands of today, like Japan and Taiwan, were part of present-day China. Malaya, Java, Sumatra, and Borneo formed part of an elongated peninsula, contiguous with the Asian landmass. And further south, Australia, New Zealand, New Guinea, and Tasmania constituted one area. As a result, there were land bridges over which it would have been possible to walk and this obviously helped, though its very ease as a "pull" factor for expanding populations from Asia was not a major factor, since the majority of travelers utilized seacraft.

In addition to the initial planning and choice of passengers and crew required for sea voyages, provisions had to be stored and taken. Furthermore, these ancient seafarers often sought to transplant elements of "home" with them, taking along familiar trees and shrubs (edible and medicinal), as well as domesticated animals, like dogs and pigs.[7] For instance, when Kahu-kura, the god of the Rainbow, arrived in New Zealand, he found Toi-ti-Huatakhi living there. According to the legend:

When Kahu-kura landed in New Zealand he found Toi' and his people living there. The people cooked food for Kahu-kura and his friend, the food consisting of root of the *ti* tree, *ponga* (tree-fern), and *roi* (tree root). Of this they partook, and in return the people of Kahu-kura cooked food which they had brought from Hawaiki. The friend of asked, "What is the name of this food?" Kahu-kura answered, "It is *kumara.*" "Perhaps it can be brought to this land?" said Toi'. Kahu-kura said, "It can be brought here." Pointing to a shed, he asked, "What is that over which a shelter is built to protect it from the sun and rain?" "It is a canoe," said Toi'. "By that the *kumara* can be brought here," said Kahu-kura.

It was at once determined that the canoe, whose name was *Horouta*, should go to Hawaiki for *kumara*. That night the people met; ceremonies were performed and incantations chanted so that the gods might close up the holes out of which the wind blew, and calm the waves of the sea, and attend and guard and uphold the canoe on the voyage, that she might skim swiftly to Hawaiki.[8]

Anthony Albiens in *Legends of the South Seas* states:

No collection of Polynesian oral literature could be called complete without a specimen of one of its principal modes—the migration-and-settlement sequence of legends which explains, in effect, 'How we came here and how the tribes split up the land.' Such legends commonly divide the local literatures in which they are found into two parts, which are though of as quite distinct. The Moriois of the Chatham Islands called the whole of their pre-migration myths Ko Matangi ao—The Wind Clouds'; and all that came afterwards 'Hokorongo tiring'—'The Hearing of the Ears.' New Zealand and Hawaii had this clear division in their literature too, for obvious reasons, and so did Rarotonga. The Marquesans, however, produced no migration stories for collectors—a fact in harmony with the role of dispersal-point now assigned to those islands—and Tahiti lacks the mode. Tonga had no tradition of migration and Samoans [asserted] that *they* originated in Samoa. The dissident Mangaians, too, were firmly of the opinion that their island rose from the World Below with their ancestors already on it. But Easter Island, like Hawaii and New Zealand, took much pride in its tale of 'how we came.'[9]

This often augured well, for when they did arrive at that other point on the horizon,[10] it would take time and effort to learn and understand the environment. Perhaps only through trial and error in the course of generations could they even know what types of local plants and food would be most efficacious and which ones would be clearly inimical to their health and well-being.

Also, having arrived in what was unfamiliar terrain, they would next have to go about two important tasks. First, they would need to utilize the local indigenous trees to provide shelter, and second, they would have to attempt to construct new rituals (perhaps partly recalled from former models left behind) through which they could exist at home with the new environment, in the "navel of the world."

Quite naturally, the all-pervasive sea and its produce provided early archetypes around which they could erect their new codes. Which fish were sacred? To whom should food first be offered? Answers to these laid at the groundwork of a new, relevant belief system which had to be invented. Along with the new gods and priests, they also constructed a hierarchy. Often the "chief," for instance, and aristocracy would be permitted rights that commoners did not have. These included consuming certain scarce items such as pork, and being excused from performing manual labor. Other areas, much to the surprise of later Europeans, recognized no kingship or, at least, had a different version of what a king was.[11] So Jukka Siikala contends that "It was impossible for the Polynesians to believe that the king of England was a real king, if he did not obey the norms attached to the chiefly status and behave like their own chiefs."[12]

Adapting themselves to the new environment, early settlers began to utilize more fully the resources of the sea, at first merely for consumption and later for trade. Those who moved inland took a more intense interest in horticulture, again for food, but also for trade. Indeed, "sea gypsies" (like the Dayak community of Sabah near Borneo) remain as excellent examples of those who, even today, continue to depend on the sea, bartering their excess with others more dependent on the land.[13]

From these early times, there developed at least two distinct economies—one sea-based, the other land-based. Crudely put, the former fished, the latter hunted; both groups remained interdependent because of clear ties involved in trading. In time, the oral narratives of their origins would differ, and people would begin to see each other in a distinct way as One and Other. Language, music, dance, and ceremonies would, in time, also emphasize these distinctions. Marian W. Smith[14] has shown how, with the later advent of colonialism into the area, otherness often developed into a "cult movement," whether that of the Native American Ghost Dance or, in an instance more pertinent to this area, the so-called "Cargo Cults." Thus, although the new response (what we would term their own identification with Otherness) was conscious and deliberate, it nevertheless arose out of social and economic problems and a need, I would add, to rectify the situation.

Even apart from a similar origin, other commonalities are apparent. The first and foremost is the heavy reliance on group, and this sense of communal belonging deemphasized individuality and stressed a sense of new unity. Second, there developed a very functional association so that all art, dance, song, and music shared in community activity and were performed for specific events.[15] Genuine traditional art, therefore, could not be disassociated from public life and could never become part of a private domain. In time, however, Europeans— Dutch, French, British and Germans—would first "discover" the area for themselves and, in the process of settling and administering it, would attempt to impose a new religion that would radically alter the relationships between the group member and his community.[16] This change would also bring about new loyalties, often at variance with previous assumptions of the newly formed group and "tribe."

The most recent archaeological evidence suggests that there were several deliberate waves of immigration from within the area of Oceania itself. The old distinctions, stressing skin coloration in Micronesia, Melanesia and Polynesia possibly derived more from a European conceptualization of race than any actual reality. The earliest settlement was possibly in New Guinea, some twenty-five thousand years ago. By utilizing similarities in language and pottery making (Lapita ware), researchers have shown the established links between New Britain, the New Hebrides, Fiji, and Tonga, the latter two being settled from about 1000 B.C. Modern researchers contend that it is almost impossible to land in Hawaii or New Zealand by accident and, hence, for reasons such as the possible need for "reverse navigation" against the current, many of these early voyagers had perfect conceptualizations of their marine environments, and could judge distances based on the flight of migratory birds.

Sometimes, it makes good sense to fall back on the traditional accounts— Ru's navigation from Raiatea to the Society Islands to Aitutaki in the Cook Islands; Ui-Te-Rangiora's expedition to the Antarctic in 650 A.D.; Kupe's early voyage to New Zealand in 925 A.D., whose directions were followed several generations later by Toi-te-huatahi; Tangiia's, Karika's and Pa'ao's travels from Tahiti to Hawaii, and Mo'ikeha's and Kila'a return journeys from Hawaii to Tahiti; and Laa-mai-kahiki's two return voyages from Tahiti to Hawaii. They all reveal that the early islanders knew their world, and could travel easily across it.[17]

For over a thousand years, indigenous people in the Pacific had existed relatively free from an external "gaze," but this early existence, secure in internal unawareness of, and away from, the gaze, would be shattered. Pacific Islanders would be encountered, found, "discovered." Immediately apparent in this (like all other such mental and physical encounters) is that most people of the area saw themselves as belonging to their island. They possessed hazy legendary memories of a past, but the new rites and rituals that were cultivated bore more resemblance to, and arose from, the actual space they occupied in the Pacific. The far past could be described, as in David Malo's account of Hawaiian origins, to show that they connected themselves with the ancestors of Tahiti who "came from the *lewa*, the firmament, the atmosphere; from the windward or back of the island."[18] The nearer past is often more pragmatic: "The island was pulled up from the sea . . . and on it were found a man plaiting sinnet and a woman making a mat. This pair . . . were the progenitors first of the family of principal gods, and later, through them of men."[19] The legend is concerned with the wonder of place, of a close tie between humans and gods, and of how such a bond may be quite literally Interpreted.

The original Asians who journeyed to these so-called Polynesian islands seemed to begin to hone new skills—fishing, for instance, and acquiring a knowledge of indigenous plants that were both edible and curative. They constructed their rituals around things relevant to the environment, such as the oftentimes sacred dolphin, and gave a high priority to the domestication of animals.

TABOO AND TATTOO

There is no oral or written record that suggests that South Pacific Islanders regarded their locale as "Paradise." In one account from Horne Island, the abode of the gods is called Rulotu, and in the middle of Rulotu grew an immense tree "the leaves of which supplied all wants."[20] But the gods could also be distinctive and localized like the Hawaiian volcano, Pele, who causes men to flee from her fiery wrath.[21] Above all, life evolved around food gathering, the usual traditional rituals that accompanied birth, marriage, and death, and the unending desire to be both caring and cautious of the surrounding ocean.

Differences were, naturally, very evident. First, climatic changes from the area itself distinguished various peoples. Athough possessing a seemingly limitless expanse of forest, the Maori of New Zealand had to make adaptations to endure the different and colder region in which they found themselves. Second, specific areas produced differing products. In New Zealand, for instance, jade was found by the early Maoris and, as "greenstone," was utilized for adzes and weapons of war. Additionally, in turn, greenstone was used to confer status.[22]

Common signs for aiding identification did exist; for instance, water, trees, and rocks provided logical ways in which early inhabitants of the various islands could invent a theology. This supranatural way of "seeing" meant that the environment itself often became the dwelling place of spirits. Some trees were sacred and, for the Maori, could represent an interesting conundrum. For the forest was both provider and god, which meant, in effect, that the abundance of an ancient landscape could provide an excuse for despoliation.

Common to much of the South Pacific were concepts embodied in two words that have been passed onto European languages—"taboo" (from Tonga, "tabu")[23] and "tattoo" (from Tahiti, "tatau").[24] The one forbade excess, whereas the other glorified adornment. Taboos were group sanctioned, foreboding, and often heavy penalties were incurred as a result of their disregard. Tattoos were individually centered and encouraged, and praise could be secured for their very excess. In a way, a type of taboo/tattoo conflict was at the heart of these societies that sought past conformity in group behavior on the one hand (the taboo), while at the same time permitting an excess of present nononformity in individual excess (the tattoo).

War partly arose out of "taboo"—often the need to guard fishing grounds from another group. This, in turn, led to the industry of war, such as the making of weapons and double canoes lashed together for use in battle, as well as to human and animal sacrifice either to appease the gods or express gratitude. Taboos also encouraged conflict, within the group itself, as well as between groups. Since taboos meant that a member of an ethnic group was constrained to adopt a specific kind of behavior, any departure lessened him or her to outsider status. Clearly, in a group-oriented society, this would have been the least likely alternative to be desired.

Since the territory became "sacred," those outside its immediate province became Others. They were at times the enemy, hunted and killed, and this status, in turn, would effect the manner in which domestic group rituals would be conducted. Once the enemy was identified and marginalized, he could hardly be considered a suitor or friend and could certainly never be admitted to the intimacy of male bonding, the *taio,* a homoerotic arrangement by which some societies sought to grant acceptance of homosexuality.[25] As such, relationships became enshrined as the way in which a given group conducted its affairs, by itself, independent of another group.

Europeans recognized that there was a major distinction between a male companion who may have been a *taio* (friend) or an *ari'i* (champion, or protector), and that these terminologies may or may not had homosexual implications.. William Bligh pointed out that:

When Captain Cook was here he was in the same situation [as Bligh]. Tynagh was his friend [*taio*] and Poeeno his Erree [*ari'i*]; and it is from that circumstance that his Picture which he gave to Otoo, now Tynah, is kept by Poeeno, which I have been long in discovering the Cause of. Poeeno is also my Tyo [*taio*] and in his own distrust by his people bears my Name and I his, but everywhere else I have the name of Tynah or Matte which are the two Names he has.[26]

This is of particular interest since it establishes that even after the coming of the Europeans, there was an interchangeability between One and Other. Once Cook and Bligh accepted the local terms of reference, they were defined (however temporarily) in those terms. Note how, at this point, European taboo becomes European license, but is in fact an acceptance of a local norm and not a social deviation at all. A question that may be asked but not answered is the extent to which such associations with European males may or may have conferred status on the "friend." And, additionally, did the tattoo on William Dampier's "Painted Prince," Prince Jeoly, play a part in initial European appeal, and indicate the relationship between Dampier and Prince Jeoly?[27]

Tattoo markings, first a mere beauty aid, came in time to distinguish the One from the Other. Such beauty markings degenerated into "tribal" vaieties of various types of identification, driving people even further apart from each other. Against this paradox of group approved taboo and individually-designed tattoo, interethnic rivalry slowly weakened any attempt at a total group-centered solidarity. When the Europeans arrived in the eighteenth and nineteenth centuries, indigenous people would become conscripted into a new gaze, whereby they would no longer be "perceivers," able to identify the "perceived," but would be forever after lumped together as "natives" and molded into a monolithic whole. They would hitherto function as a new Other created by the European One, solely based on what Gregory Dening has termed "the Europeans' inability to describe what they saw in anything but value judgments, whether moral or aesthetic."[28]

EUROPEAN DISCOVERY AND REDISCOVERY

Often what was observed was clearly wrong. This varied from the usual tendency to impose legends of home on the outside world, to factual misconceptions. For John Keats in "On First Looking into Chapman's Homer," the experience was akin to the discovery of the Pacific by "stout Cortes."[29] The problem was that Keats had got his Europeans slightly mixed up, and if indeed someone had to be singled out as the first "person" (conveniently ignoring the band of Native Americans who led him there) to see the Pacific then, indeed, it would have had to have been Vasco Núñez de Balboa (1475–1519) on September 25, 1513. This indicates only part of the plethora of errors that mark Pacific exploration. Islands like the Solomons are "discovered" and "rediscovered" again and again. Some are "lost," as one adventurer after another attempts the impossible task of placing the European stamp on the unwilling Pacific as decisively as he had done in the New World.

One may rightly assert that the comedy of Pacific discovery was initiated by Balboa himself. Peter Martyr, a contemporary and pro-Spanish enthusiast writes, with no trace of irony, of just how the eventful act took place:

Dismissing the people of Quarequa with some gifts, the Spaniards, under the guidance of the people of Chiapes and accompanied by the cacique himself, made the descent from the mountain-ridge to the much desired ocean in four days. Great was their joy; and in the presence of the natives they took possession, in the name of the King of Castile, of all that sea and the countries bordering on it.[30]

What did the departing Quarequa and the very much present Chiapes make of the spectacle? Surely this represents a supreme instant when European historical effrontery emerges from behind the printed page, when unbeknown to chronicler and "discoverer," the folly of the moment is laid bare for us.

Indeed, did we wish for more written evidence of the uncertainty of "conquest' and "possession," Peter Martyr aids us even further a few pages earlier on, by commenting that when Balboa had his first sight of the Pacific, "a Quarenqua guide showed him a peak from the summit of which the southern ocean is visible."[31] But, as Jeannette Mirsky ironically asserted, Spanish history would recall even these facts more personally: "Balboa had stood on his peak and now he gazed at his ocean." In time, he returned to Darien, in present day Panama, where "he announced the discovery of the Southern sea."[32] In 1517, four years later, he was condemned to death by jealous rivals and beheaded.

The next "discoverer," Ferdinand Magellan, would fare just as badly. On his famous circumnavigation of the world, he would be killed at Mactan Island in the Philippines about 1521. Born in the latter part of the fifteenth century, Magellan had first served the Portuguese, then later the Spanish, much like Columbus himself. Antonio Pigafetta assiduously chronicled Magellan's discoveries and death. Quite early on, Pigafetta (himself Italian) noted that European infighting was part of the voyage. He commented that "he, the captain-general, was Portuguese, and they [the crew] were Spaniards or Castilians, which peoples have long borne ill-will and malevolence toward one another."[33]

Indeed what we note with both Balboa and Magellan is a desire to replicate, sometimes even outdo, Columbus, and thereby accomplish the task of, first, naming the unknown, and second, eliciting and confirming from a distorted observation of the environment monstrous images of the Other which had been invented at home. From Plinian times, there had been constant allusions to ways through which the ultimateness of the most distant Other—the Utter—could be described. One easy way was to note the inhabitants' constant propensity for eating their companions. Columbus, who certainly did not understand the Taínos whom he first encountered, was definitely "told" by them that to their south existed the "Caribs," who were or fierce cannibals.[34] After them, the whole region of the Caribbean was so named. Likewise, Magellan encountered the monsters of medieval European fantasy: Magellan writes of "Patagons" or large giants, as well as cannibals in South America. Hence an entire area is called Patagonia.

Interestingly, other giants are encountered "near" the Antarctic, obviously the very edge of the world, beyond the norm, and where it could be resonably assumed that such monstrosities would indeed reside. What is fascinating about these giants is that, in Pigafetta's words, their weapons "were like the arrows used by the Turks,"then the oriental enemy and obvious candidates for marginalization. Additionally, Pigafetta reveals how extreme Otherness reacts to its Self. After Magellan had given one of the giants a steel mirror, "the giant seeing himself was greatly terrified, leaping back so that he threw four of our men to the ground."[35] Their total divorce from the European norm, the text suggests, is even acceptable to the alien outsider himself; he confirms his own alienation, and thus his need to be controlled and subordinated. So, very much like Columbus, Pigafetta's party gather a few as specimens for the return journey home.

Later on, other Pacific "discoverers" would do likewise: William Dampier would take home a "painted" [tatooed] boy, and Captain James Cook would return to England (before his own final apotheosis and death) with a similar wonder. Home would have the opportunity to inspect the abnormal. And the human monster, so terrified by its own reflection, would be given the chance to understand the aesthetics of the normal. More than anything discussed thus far, this marks the beginning of the colonial encounter, which will be discussed with reference to the South Pacific, and the manner in which a European norm became a substitute for "universality," with the concomittant refusal on the part of the Other to accept his own mirror image.

After Magellan captured his giants and observed their weird behavior, for instance their penchant for eating rats, he seemed to have slowly developed the disposition of an incipient colonial overlord. One unfortunate way that Magellan took to expressing his viewpoint was by burning and pillaging. On one occasion, Pigafetta notes almost matter of factly that "the captain sent some of his men to burn the houses of those people [indigenous to the Philippines] in order to frighten them." If Pigafetta's account is accurate, and not merely the agreed upon version of the crew, this was a grave error on Magellan's part. The locals shot at his leg with a poisoned arrow and, although he fought like "a good captain and a knight," another assailant quickly hurled a bamboo lance at him "whereby he fell face downward. On this all at once rushed him with lances of iron and bamboo and with these javelins, so that they slew our mirror, our light, our comfort and our true guide." This is yet another stage in the "colonial" encounter, and it is no accident that the mirror trope reoccurs; the natives of the Philippines refuse to accept the mirror, look at it, and find themselves askance, and instead destroy it as one of the appurtenances of a civilization they reject. The "giant/cannibal" had looked at himself in the mirror and lived; now the victorious native king made the Europeans withdraw, and as Pigafetta adds in a solemn requiem, "we were constrained to leave there the dead body of our captain-general with our other dead."[36]

Whether Magellan died at the hands of the locals or his own men, the causes of his death lie beyond our purview, since the treachery of the crew is only suggested beneath the layers of Pigafetta's text. What is, however, most apparent is that Magellan's destruction was symbolic, since the European crew, as stated in the text, noted how their own "mirror" was destroyed. Magellan's death merely marked the continuation of European intention to spread the light emanating from the mirror as the light of conquest, civilization, and Christianity.

Next to enter on the scene were the Spanish explorer Álvaro de Mendaña (1541–1595) and two Portuguese travelers, Pedro Fernandez de Quirós and Luis Vaez de Torres (both in the early seventeenth century). Mendaña represents an excellent example of the dubious nature of "discovery": he allegedly "found" the Solomons on his 1567 voyage, but failed to "rediscover" them on his next attempt—he had presumably lost them. With these new "discoveries," the stated purpose had shifted only slightly, and yet remained still closely part of the proto-Columbus quest. Before, Balboa had meekly followed the indigenous people towards his "discovery" of the Pacific and had erected his altars and prayed to Christ and Mary when claiming the entire ocean for his king. Later, Magellan had sought, by traveling round the world, to confirm the oddities of home, something with which Balboa had little truck, for perhaps he had looked into the mirror and recognized himself as Other—he was, after all, married to a Native American woman. But Balboa and Magellan are both part of the Columbus archetype—one was discoverer, the other would-be settler; one, *Christo ferens*, the Christ bearer as Christopher Columbus saw himself, and the other, the conquistador.

With Mendaña, Quirós, and Torres, we are within the mirror image of Columbus: now in the Pacific, they seek Columbus's "otro mondo," the vision of Paradise he discovered on his third voyage. Columbus had written rather rapturously: "I believe that the earthly paradise is there and to it, save by the will of God, no man shall come."[37] Interestingly, therefore, the journey was complete, but no person dared approach the final ascent; Otherness was, in a way, inaccessible and beyond mere humans. "Discovery" had its humbling moments, when the European male discovered the limitations of his purpose. Interestingly though, for Columbus, Mendaña, Quirós, and Torres, Paradise was associated with the equally unattainable beyondness of mortal sexuality, the super-supreme delight in the female, naked and sensuous, as she came to symbolize the tempting glance beyond the immediate, the very gateway to Paradise.

"Terra Australis incognita" became an amorphous metaphor for this unattainable. On various world maps from as early as 1531, Henry Stevens comments in *New Light on the Discovery of Australia*, "the mapmakers of the period began to insert on their maps large tracts of continental land in the Southern Seas, sometimes unnamed, but generally marked 'Terra Incognita,' 'Terra Australis,' or 'Terra Australis nondum cognita,' etc., etc."[38] By 1602, Quirós began to lay his own plans for such a "discovery" before the Spanish King Philip III. Perhaps he sighted the real Australia, perhaps not; but in any event, one can only be certain that he sailed past New Guinea as he made his way back to the Americas. Seemingly, Don Diego de Prado y Tovar first went looking for Quirós and afterwards, with Torres as captain, may have come within sight of the real Australia. But Prado and Torres were such bitter rivals that one cannot be certain that anything mentioned by Prado is true.

What both Prado and Quirós make clear is that they were attempting to locate a phantom, so that even when they came near the reality of the physical southern continent of Australia, they still could not see it, since it was not supposed to be there. Instead, they sought a more southerly continent not yet known, one that perhaps could never be known if we go along with Columbus's viewpoint. Paradoxically, when Prado and Torres came near their quest, they noted that the locals (or "Indians," as they termed them) seemed in dire need of grace. Although Europeans easily identify "chiefs," there is an omnipresent problem shared with Columbus and Crusoe: how does one communicate with the savage? Note the following encounter, which better describes the absurdity of "discoverer" and his "discovered" than could any words of mine:

When they saw that our boats drew near within musket shot of the village, the chief, called in their tongue the Tampitas, came through the water nearly up to the boats and called out loudly. Ha! ha! raising his hand and dropping it he said pu! pu! yac! Captain Luis Baes [Torres] understood perfectly well that he meant to say, Sir, make them put down the arquebuses; he [Torres] answered him [the "chief"] that he likewise should have the arrows put down. [Later on]. . . he went ashore and brought a quantity of bows and arrows and coming to the boat delivered them to Luis Baes, first raising his hands in token of peace and friendship, and he was answered in like manner.[39]

A number of acts here beggar further investigation. First, how could Prado and Torres possibly know that the person to whom they were "talking" was a "chief"? Second, how could Torres so readily translate the sounds he supposedly heard? These actually sound like gibberish and seem only to convey the impression of infantilization on the "discovered." Third, given the absence of an agreed recognition of signs, how could it be said that the "chief" or Torres "understood perfectly" anything that was communicated. Fourth, and most suspicious of all, is the sign on the "chief's" part of "raising his hands to heaven in token of peace." How could he, savage that he was, point so securely and knowingly to Paradise itself?

It turned out that the inhabitants of this island, dubbed Santa Cruz, had already had a most unfortunate encounter with Álvaro de Mendaña, who Prado tells us had already killed one of them on a previous visit. Surely this alone would have predisposed the "chief" against further contact. Additionally, he would be very unlikely to commit so foolish an act as to invite the crew to come ashore, which he did, we are assured, since "he answered with his head in our manner."[40]

This situation of cultural confusion is further compounded the very next day by the arrival of "four Indians" who "were evidently some of the chiefs." Indeed, Prado is preparing us for an early encounter with Noble Savages who instinctively recognize a Christian God, while exhibiting good European table manners and an easy ability to acquire the Latin tongue. Prado assures us that all the "chiefs" "were present at all the masses as if they had been taught," and "when they tasted the wine they made signs that it was good." Furthermore, when Communion had been explained to them "they said Dios, Dios with a bow and reverence to the most holy name of God." Thus, even the savage who spoke in childlike monosyllables could be made to conform and resemble the Discoverer. It was, seemingly, only a question of "civilization," and again, as with Columbus, Prado and his party concluded "they would become

Christians."[41]

Saving heathen souls, all "discoverers" recognized, was a sure way to secure their own monarch's entry to Paradise. So, even as Prado and his party went about the quotidian business of seeking the unknown southern continent, the king could rest assured that his practical progress towards Paradise was being dutifully followed. Part of this quest involved the unwitting native who, seemingly, could always provide directions as, in this case, "pointing to the West he said hu hu hu"—familiar gibberish we almost recognize from before. Now the sign and sound indicated "a very great land having great animals with horns on their heads which are buffaloes, which they worship as gods."[42]

It seems as if the "chief" was sensibly sending the party further on, away from his own base. In the New World, as eager conquistadors sought El Dorado, obliging "Indians" constantly pointed out its mirage beyond every horizon.[43] In the Pacific, Europeans now sought, almost a century after Columbus, a fabled continent where, as Prado wrote about Mexico, they could "build on the side of the river a city to which the name of the New Jerusalem was to be given."[44] In 1606, having met "a native chief, from whom he received much detailed information respecting the existence of islands, and, as was understood, even continental lands to the southward,"[45] Quirós sailed in search of the mythical southern continent. Having "found" an island in the New Hebrides group, "possession having been taken of that land . . . [the place] received the name of the New Jerusalem."[46] He had outmatched Prado and anticipated early settlers to the United States.

Instead of gold, which Columbus had stressed, Quirós found pearls in great abundance. Quirós emphasized this in his 1609 letters to his king, as he importuned him, in terms much like Columbus's, for additional help in finding "Austrialia Incognita." Such efforts had to stress the importance of the "discovery," in order to make the petitioner a worthwhile candidate for receiving the royal aid solicited. Referring to his admiral, Torres, Quirós emphasized the mythical magnitude of his "discoveries":

The greatness of the land newly discovered, judging from what I saw, and from what Captain Don Luis Vaez de Torres, the Admiral under my command, reported to Your Majesty, is well established. Its length is as much as all Europe and Asia Minor as far as the Caspian and Persia, with all the islands of the Mediterranean and the ocean which encompasses, including the two islands of England and Ireland.

That virtually took care of "one-fourth of the world," as Quirós added, without the troublesome problem of having to deal with that specific Other, "Turks or Moors, or others of the nations which are prone to cause disquiet and unrest on their borders."[47] Ironically, when he spoke of the land's "greatness,"he was alluding to what he did not know but which, like Paradise itself, lay beyond the borders of reason.

DUTCH COLONIZATION

Soon the Dutch would enter the scenario. Among these new actors were Willem Cornelzoon Schouten (1580–1625) and Jacob Le Maire (1585–1616). The Dutch had already established a presence in Indonesia, and in his 1615–1616 voyage, Le Maire came from there to "discover" Tonga, among other places. The Dutch were primarily interested in trade, not in a mysterious continent. J. C. Beaglehole comments in *The Exploration of the Pacific* that: "Exploration for forty years was with the Dutch almost a by-product. Out of their voyages, at first like a dim surf-beaten phantom, later with firm and charted distinctness, emerged New Holland—the west and north coasts of Australia and part of the south; not *Terra Australis incognita.*"[48]

Additionally, Abel Janzoon Tasman (c.1603–1659) would journey to the newly seen islands of Tasmania and New Zealand. By his second voyage in 1644, western Australia at least had changed status from "incognita" to "cognita," from the "unknown" to the "great known South Land." Later on, in 1722, the Dutch continued to plod on, and Jacob Roggeveen (1659–1729), for instance, was officially named "discoverer" of Easter Island. Earlier Dutch interest had paved the way for Joris van Speilbergen's voyage round the world between 1614 and 1617.

With Dutch exploration, there is less pretense and more practicality, less spiritual quest for Paradise and more pragmatic searching for trade. Le Maire writes that as he coasted the South Pacific, he too encountered "four Indians," as the nomenclature usually went, who were "quite naked" and, in this instance, "red of colour; with very black and long hair." Their appearance, true enough, was menacing and monstrous, but the Dutch at least admitted to a degree of befuddlement: "we could not understand them nor they us, although we called to them in Spanish, Malay, Javanese, and in our Dutch language."[49] He then departed, after observing that the "Indians" had wisely refused to come aboard.

Joris van Speilbergen's account of his circumnavigation of the world is often more concerned with demonstrating the animosity of locals toward the Spaniards or the antagonism of the Spaniards and Portuguese toward the Dutch than with Dutch confrontations with, or reimaging of, the local people.[50]Indeed, the much feared opprobrium of "cannibal" was bestowed as an alternative name on at least one Dutchman associated with these early adventures—no less a person than the suspected compiler, perhaps even the author, of Speilbergen's journal. He had been called (and this is a profound irony) "Jan Cornelius May, alias Menscheter [Maneater] or Anthropophagus."[51] In such a way are we haunted by our own depictions!—even as the Other assumes our skin and becomes us, and we him. This is the surreal, uncontested space in which an unintended merging takes place, as the colonizer becomes the colonized, the One the Other.

Constantly, even as the Dutch traverse similar routes to those of the Spaniards, they encounter not misshapen dolts but as stated in Speilbergen's journal, "folk of fair intelligence" in Manila, people elsewhere who "have not their equal in the whole land in the art of swimming," or, in another place, inhabitants who "evinced great friendship for us and enmity to the Spaniards."[52] I do not pretend that some of this is not self-serving and intended for local home consumption, but it still reflects a kinder, gentler Other, unheard of in Spanish, Portuguese and British narrative texts.

One reason might be that, as stated, the Dutch were not on a "civilizing" mission. They had a fair amount of experience with alien peoples in Indonesia, and since the Dutch East India Company saw trade as uppermost, it behoved them to be in accord with the locals they met. But another and perhaps more significant reason is that, even though the Dutch were incipient colonialists like the British, Spaniards, and Portuguese, they originated from an area where difference, apartness from Europe, was made most dramatically apparent in Protestantism. Not only had this severed them from the "Mother Church," but also, in many respects, their ideals were more earthbound: even as they awaited the coming of manna, they could go about the business of acquiring their daily bread.

It becomes all the more surprising when the Dutch react like Spaniards or Portuguese, or even the later British. For instance, on December 17, 1642, Dutch explorer Abel Tasman accidently "discovered" this Other in New Zealand. This first act on the part of the Dutch, almost by reflex, was to name this finding after their own home. Their action in demarcating the new land as "Zeelandia Nova" was an exact imitation of Spanish and Portuguese conquistadors of the previous century. The land was "new" because it had never existed before and because it summoned up the image of Eden, Paradise, and a fresh start. It bore the name "Zeelandia" because it had to relate back to a home at the center, since the very nature of "discovery" assumed a large degree of ownership in the image of the owner. The identical way of owning and naming is replicated in Anglo settlement in the present-day United States, beginning with Jamestown and Plymouth.

Tasman's "fierce natives" who inhabited New Zealand also hark back to Columbus's exploits. Both words establish the distance between the perceiver and the perceived, pinpointing the gaze on to the similarity between the strange creatures found here and those in the New World. Also, the word "native" itself emphasizes the disarming simplicity of noncomprehension of a foreign culture, which would be an important feature in European exploitation and colonialism throughout the "discovered" world. Interestingly, Tasman and his crew were so alarmed at what they saw in this "new" "Zealand," that they made all their observations and conclusions from a distance. They actually never set foot on the island, but merely proceeded to fire their cannons in the direction of the painted faces, tattooed bodies, and cries which they saw and heard.[53]

Here the tattoo takes an interesting turn. The tattoo marks the Other as frightful, unappealing, and certainly different. No longer, it seems, does it serve to indicate beauty, strength, or even individual membership in a group. But with a distant gaze (for it can hardly be termed an "encounter," since human contact is absent), the indigenous world in New Zealand begins to recognize the possibility of its own immanent self-destruction. Perhaps new local taboos would come about, seeking to explain the meaning and significance of this external intrusion in 1642. If so, perhaps the new ways of reconciling tattoos, of recognizing congeniality, even consanguinity among groups, lasted a relatively short while. For Tasman's gaze was enough to awaken the European world to tales of more adventures, of further discoveries and appropriations. And if the Maoris went back to business as usual, it would not last very long.

REORDERING THE OTHER: ENTER THE BRITISH

Dutch trade with the East opened up in Macao in 1586 with full Chinese cooperation. Speilbergen observed that trade between Holland and "Japon" (actually he meant China) was brisk.[54] Of course, not unnaturally, the British in the eighteenth century, busily constructing their own "Oriental" empire in India, would envision the Dutch in slightly different terms. British traveler, Samuel Wallis (1728–1795), for instance, meets "the Most Miserable Wretched Creatures of all the Human Race," in the Magellan Straits and points out former Dutch atrocities: "we suppose this was don [sic] when the Dutch was [sic] here: they mention having killed some of this [sic] poor creatures."[55]Wallis tended to develop a rather personalized orthography and grammar.

Issues of violence against indigenous people became part of the entire cycle of "discovery," "recovery," and "rediscovery" of the Pacific. Despite my remarks about the Dutch, there is really no definitive way of isolating any single exploring group as the "good guys," since they all would have agreed (given seventeenth- and even eighteenth-century preoccupations) that they, like Columbus, were indeed encountering "savages." Ironically, though, the savage had altered, or put differently, the European idea of the savage had changed. In the past, in Columbus's time, they were heathens who needed Christian baptism and a heavy work program. By the time of South Sea explorations, Reformation light had outshone the eager righteousness of fifteenth- and sixteenth-century zeal. Now, what was uppermost was to invade these vacant places of the world; the new mandate, sanctioned by the Protestant translations of the Bible, remained "Go forth." For Columbus and the conquistadors, the directive had been different—"Discovery" was mandated by God who would loosen "the barriers of the Ocean Sea."[56]

By the eighteenth century, European exploration of the Pacific had shifted once more, and with this, the interpretation of those encountered. Recall that Spanish quest and conquest had been spurred on by a concept begotten from the lore of Columbus—a search for Paradise. With the Dutch came the more benign desire to trade. For both Spaniards and Dutch, the inhabitants of the islands were all "found," and their supposed lack of history, their "lostness" in time and place could be manipulated into the image-makers' mold, the mirror reflection of the European as either God-bearer or gold-seeker, indeed a type of divine tradesman.

By the time of British interest, the so very European Enlightenment, with its emphasis on the rational and its thrust toward learning, had another indirect effect. William Dampier (1652–1715), former brigadier turned privateer; John Byron (1723–1786), grandfather of Lord Byron; Samuel Wallis (1728–1795) and Philip Carteret (d. 1796) preceded James Cook (1728–1779) in these voyages of "scientific" exploration. The Dutch, under Jacob Roggeveen, and the French, under Louis Antoine de Bougainville (1729–1811) represented aspects of the same spirit of "enquiry" best epitomized by Captain Cook. Their voyages, although allegedly "objective" and "scientific," had the effect of envisioning the local place and person in yet another guise: they could now be studied, much like the eclipse Cook was first to set out to observe, and, if necessary, brought back to Europe for further inspection.

From Tahiti, Bougainville triumphantly bore back to France his Ahutoru, who, on his return to his island, died of smallpox.[57] From Meangis Island in the East Indies, Dampier brought to England the "Painted Prince" Jeoly;[58] and from New Zealand, Cook brought the Maori Omai, supposedly "interpreter" of numerous cultures from Tonga and Tahiti. Prince Jeoly died in Oxford; Omai was returned to his homeland supposedly weeping profusely in Cook's arms, and, later, when he was being sent ashore.

Since none of them left behind their thoughts on England and France or their feelings at being removed from their societies, we must rely on the sentiments of the enlightened European observers. I suspect that Ahutoru, Jeoly, and Omai were not only curious specimens to be investigated and observed, but also objects that were similar to the plant specimens with which Cook returned from his various voyages. For Dampier, Jeoly bore the tattoo markings of wonder, the fascination of the horrible, both in a cultural and physical sense. Dampier remarked that Jeoly told him that there was as much spice on his island as the hairs on his head, and, even more interestingly, that "his Father was Raja of the Island where they lived" and that "there were not above Thirty Men on the Island, and about one Hundred Women: that he himself had five wives and eight children."[59] Obviously, Jeoly had both made himself into the embodiment of the Noble Savage, and provided his island habitation with the lush delights of spices and women, both eagerly sought after.

Jeoly was simply playing back Dampier's own mythologies. Jeoly knew that Dampier sought not gold, but spice, and that Dampier had come from a place where there was a heavy reliance on royalty and its significance. He became (or Dampier had him become) the image in Dampier's own eye—a rich prince ("raja" is an unusual word for Jeoly to use) from a wealthy land. Furthermore, he must have personally known the sexual frustrations of the sailors as they came to port, eyeing whatever moved—child, man or woman. So he increased his own self-worth by laying claim to possessing a semiharem, and existing in a kind of holy whorehouse. Even if Dampier had no way of understanding this, all that Jeoly said would have been sympathetically received by Dampier, unschooled though he was, but nevertheless a European who must have heard tell of the wonders of Marco Polo.[60]

Cook is equally quite eloquent on Omai. Omai had become an excellent mimic or, in different terms, had assumed the image of the master. He became a passable if somewhat comical "European" trader suitably attired for the part:

Our friend Omai got one good thing here for the many good things he gave away, this was a very fine double Sailing Canoe, compleatly equiped Man'd and fit for the Sea. I had made him up a suit of English Colours some time before, but he thought them too good or too Valuable to wear at this time and made up a parcel of Colours, such as flags and pendants to the Number of ten or a dozen which he spread on different parts of his Vessel at the same time and drew together as many people to look at here as a Man of War would dressed in a European port. These Streamers of Omais were a Mixture of English, French, Spanish and Dutch which were all the European colours he had seen.[61]

Omai, it seemed, had wanted to become all of what he had seen—all that was external to himself and his world. Thus, like any good Englishman, his views on the Spanish are interesting. Cook asserts that: "Although we do not think there is a great similarity between our manners & those of the Spaniards, [Omai] did not think this difference great. He only said they seem'd not so friendly[,] & in person they approach'd those of his own country."[62] Omai seems sorely put upon to make a distinction between one White stranger and another! He settles for some tact, downgrading the Spaniards perhaps one notch, but suggesting that his own people (simply by not being on par with the English) obviously achieved equality with the Spaniards.

Omai (like Prince Jeoly) represents the local apart from his habitat and remade into a "native," the Other, an ethnic marker that begins with the "discoverer," quite contrary to what conservative commentators like Rey Chow, author of*Writing Diaspora,* assert.[63] Omai weeps because (like V. S. Naipaul) he cannot stand the sight of his own self; it is disturbing and discomforting. And Cook, like Dampier, can be reassured for much the same reason: the prisoner is now his own warden, content to bide his time, cultivating whatever his owner deems worthy.

Once the new cultural criteria are established and accepted, the "creature" lives by whatever the "creator" deems sacrosanct or scornful, pious or impure, aesthetically refining or repulsive. And if, in coming to terms with his "creator's" polarities, the "creature" must ultimately sacrifice his own tenuous self for the gratification of the alien other, then so be it. Such an act of final debasement must be performed willingly without compunction or regret, but with relish. For such is the final self-effacement that produces the "native."[64]

10

IMAGINING THE PACIFIC

After the "discoverers" came the missionaries and then mariners, penpushers and painters, bums and beachcombers; in the course of time, the Pacific would bear little resemblance to the islands originally inhabited. The image would undergo a drastic alteration, particularly at the hands of European writers, who would return to a theme that had been to a large extent discarded by travelers such as Captain James Cook. I refer here in particular to the constant concern over a newly found Paradise and to how, throughout the nineteenth and twentieth centuries, writers would utilize the islands much like a palimpsest, in order to tell and retell accounts concerned more with European unreality and needs than with Pacific reality and significance.

To a large extent, why some of this is not so prevalent, even in the explorers who preceded Cook and also with Cook himself, lies in the simple fact that most of these men were well traveled had been to Africa, and North America, and usually stopped off in South America on their way to the Pacific. Therefore, although possibly they harbored their own beliefs and prejudices, even suffering more than a little from wishing to become mini-Columbuses, they did not arrive in the South Pacific with too many delusions. The fact that very often they called the inhabitants "Indians" is testament enough to their seeing these people as extensions of Asia and the New World. And in more ways than one, modern anthropology, even without the added but disputed evidence of Thor Heyerdahl, has shown them to have been right.[1]

Cook, for instance, was no novice. Before 1768, the year when the Royal Society in England appointed him commander of the *Endeavour*, he had seen service in the North Sea.[2] Part of his mission was "factual"—namely to observe the transit of the planet Venus in Tahiti. Another part was obviously mythological—that is to "discover" the legendary southern continent of Terra Australis. But, in the course of three successful voyages, Cook would disprove some of the mythical, contribute much to European scientific awareness of the factual, and add his own new store of myth. And since Cook had had a wide experience of the world during his travels, few could question his authority.

COOK'S WORLD

During his first voyage (1768–1771), James Cook charted New Zealand and surveyed the southeastern coast of Australia before returning to Britain via Dja-karta. On his second voyage (1772–1775), he charted Tonga and Easter Island, as well as several other Pacific islands, putting to rest finally the myth of a south-ern continent beyond Australia. And, on his third and last voyage (1776–1779), he again demolished the belief that a northwest passage existed that could take Europeans directly through North America to the fabulous "Orient." In these re-spects, he was certainly a debunker of some of the skewed logic of his day.[3]

Cook had arrived in the Pacific well prepared and adequately sponsored. His visit was not "accidental" but was prompted by British curiosity over the impending eclipse and the urge for settlement. Cook had artists and naturalists with him, as well as a translator from Tahiti. Perhaps Cook was the first to recognize the common kinship between Maori and other Pacific islanders. After all, he was an old hand in that, unlike the conquistadors, he was not unfamiliar with his terrain. His very first voyage had taken him from the Tahitians to the Maori, in what had been really a kind of scientific fishing expedition. Indeed, if we are to glimpse anything of the way in which Pacific islanders see themselves, we have to look through, even beyond, Cook and his party. Certainly, the raw data is included in Cook's journals—Maori agriculture, clothing, food, weapons, even their property rights and burial customs. But beneath the text is Cook's admiration (he was, after all a seaman) for the seafaring skills of the Maori.

Quite often, for instance, Cook mentions Maori canoes. Both he and members of his expedition distinguish between canoes for fishing, for war, and for longer journeys.[4] Cook also notes, in particular, outriggers, which were utilized to stabilize the vessels of islanders in high seas, as well as "double-canoes," which could transport a greater number of people.

As Cook and his party "observe," they, in turn, are "observed." Into the text, therefore, perhaps without conscious intent, there is introduced an interesting aspect of "insiders" registering their own views of "outsiders," thus, in a way, complicating distinctions of outsider/insider separateness. From quite early, we learn that the Maori find their visitors curious, so that "at one time a good many of the people [were] on board and about 170 along side." But the Maori maintained a healthy suspicion, and Cook writes that they were "tollerable [*sic*] friendly but we could not prevale [*sic*] upon them to traffick with us."[5]

Even as Cook debunks prevailing European belief, his presence breeds new European ideas, what Gananath Obeyesekere has termed "ancestral myths of origin" that derive from the Western imagination. Elsewhere, Obeyesekere adds that these become the beliefs of later Western settlers so that even though Cook, as Founder and God, emerges among the recollections of some of his party, the maintenence of these ideas is Western. "There is no Maori voice here: It is a European one imputing to the Maoris a special kind of voice," Obeyesekere concludes.[6]

Therefore, a twofold enterprise is occurring. Cook is, to some extent, "scientifically" exploring the Pacific in order to deconstruct old European beliefs, while at the same time "systematically" constructing new mythologies centered on himelf as person, in the wake of Alexander the Great (and his penchant for deification) and, more recently, Columbus, Hernán Cortés and Francisco Pizarro. European sources would reveal in time that the Cortés/Motecuhzoma and Pizarro/Atahualpa god/servant linkage established a hagiography out of which emerged the idea of Cook as founder, guardian, and civilizer.

As Cook and his accompanying scientists retrieved and categorized the local flora and fauna, the Maori were amazed at the strange actions of visitors who assiduously hunted and gathered, not for sustenance, but for drying their catch in the sun and labeling them. Additionally, it must have seemed to the Maori that Joseph Banks, the naturalist on board, was attempting to accomplish what the ancient Maori had already done—the examining and classifying of the unfamiliar. It could be argued that for the ancient Maori the task had been much more formidable, for their distinctions had to be not only theoretically sound but also absolutely correct, since life and death depended on what could and could not be consumed.

On Cook's voyage, one of the two artists was Sidney Parkinson. He attempted to produce illustrations of the natural scenery and people he had seen. Parkinson produced over a thousand drawings, which would help later European botanists. But his portrayals, not unnaturally, betray the prejudices of his time in that the people who inhabit the landscape do seem at times to conform to pre-set ideas.

One persistent view that partly associates itself with Paradise is assent to the forbidden, an assertion of strange forms and norms in what was supposedly a topsy-turvy world. Here we begin to see the manner in which the area is feminized, beginnng with the nature of these early encounters, of faces fleetingly read and expressions hastily described. When William Brougham Monkhouse, Cook's surgeon on the first voyage, relates an encounter with three young men who became "guests for the night," the third is quickly dismissed as possessing (or representing) "altogether a bad and miserable figure." The second is described as having "an effeminate Voice [and] still less masculine in his figure." The first seemed to be a real favorite, being "well-featured, of a make somewhat delicate," and he becomes the initiator who "presently set about contriving schemes of amusement," among which was an exotic thigh-slapping dance.[7] Side by side with the frivolity, however, lay the "darkness"—the Kurtz-like evil in Conrad that forever lurks in European imaginings of these faraway places. Here, it is dramatically represented by the ever present fear of violence.

On this occasion the frivolity/fear juxtapositioning is presented through the tattoo. The engaging young man of the previous night possessed tattoo marks on his face made from "some cutting tool, which he said he had inflicted upon himself at some mourning ceremony." But with the threat of violence the next day, the suspicious Other is described thusly:

the people in this boat were most ridiculously daubed with patches of red paint on different parts of their face—the nose seemed to be a favourite part—this daubing joined to the black groundwork of tattaou [sic] together with a most savage fierceness thrown into every feature distorted their faces into representations of devils more than Men.[8]

In Paradise, seemingly, both men and monsters live, or in the terminology of the time, the savage was both ignoble and noble. As such, European interpretations of what (s)he represented could change at any moment, since in large measure, the savage, like her/his nobility, was not real, but just a convenient projection that could be altered at will.

In effect, Cook's scouting expedition was hardly as sanguine as it is often represented by historians. He was in fact laying the groundwork for large numbers of settlers who would continue the process of Britain's overseas empire—at first convicts "transported" to Paradise for their sins, and later willing emigrants who would establish a new aristocracy. In Australia, dubbed for a long time "White Australia," White settlers fought desperately to continue their linkage with Europe and to marginalize the "natives," the so-called "Blackfellows." In New Zealand, despite the favorable review accorded race relations by British empire historians, the Maori soon found themselves as second-class citizens. In both these instances, a new "taboo" was established, namely race mixing, which carried attendant consequences, and the new half-One/ half-Other bore a specific "tattoo," namely a different skin color, as his new definition of super-subaltern status.

Therefore, the taboo/tattoo polarity was extended in ways the indigenous people never expected. The taboo/tattoo syndrome continued to redefine hierarchy in its largest possible sense. Social hierarchy was bolstered by the European social, legal, and cultural system, the church, education, and all the other appurtenances of the West. Above all, the West established a new apartheid and separateness, both taboo and tattoo, in prioritizing, indeed privileging, its system of rewards to recipients through language and social abilities.[9]

Because Cook became the official British "discoverer" of Australia, New Zealand, and Tasmania, English assumed preponderance as the sole and proper medium of speech. This had the effect of further stressing how the new taboo and tattoo operated. The "taboo" showed now that "native" "dialect" was somehow bad speech, and when locals attempted a compromise, it was dismissed, as elsewhere, as an amusing childlike "pidgin." One obvious result was that "class" became redefined, even among European rejects, since normative speech was very closely modeled on a British pattern. Anything else was "taboo." Those who lacked the appropriate "tattoo" (even the "native" in theory) could achieve modified success by copying certain speech styles and might, in the course of time, approximate more closely those who bore the accepted "tattoo." In Hawaii, "ceded" to Britain 1843, the kings from the time of Kamehameha the Great (born c. 1737) to the four successors who bore his name all utilized various devices to accommodate themselves to the Western presence. For instance, before Kamehameha died in 1819, he had incorporated the British Union Jack into the Hawaiian standard. Later, monarchs abolished the ancient religion, ended the segregation of men and women, gave themselves and their children English names, and even set up royal courts complete with palace, crown, scepter, coronation pavilion, and royal band. This attempt at assimilative mimickry hardly helped the luckless Queen Liliuokalani, a direct descendant of Kamehameha; she was overthrown with official United States complicity on January 17, 1793. Two hundred years later, on November 23 1993, President Bill Clinton at last managed to extend a formal apology to the Hawaiian people from the government and Congress of the United States. But it was too little too late; Hawaii had already been conscripted into statehood.

LANGUAGE AND ALIENATION

Language (particularly English) imposition and the manner in which the new speech began to define a new "class" has, unfortunately, not received the attention it deserves. Earlier studies of the 1960s, through which I suspect the

British were desperately attempting to hang on to some shred of a fading "empire," were dubbed "Commonwealth Studies." These works tended to stress that the texts bore merit because they made "a distinctive contribution to our common heritage,"[10] as the Australian critic A. Norman Jeffares has asserted. But by the time, modern American and "postcolonial" scholars of the eighties began their work, they were hardly so complimentary.

The earlier period had, however, laid the groundwork for a degree of globalism, very much part of the later studies. For instance, Bruce King, a noteworthy American scholar, who, during the sixties and seventies was a professor at Ahmadu Bello University in Nigeria, was willing to grant that emphasis had moved away from texts concerned with "national vitality" to those which could establish a canon of "important authors of enduring values"[11] in Australia. And in *Awakened Conscience*, C. D. Narasimhaiah, himself an Indian, could mourn how an Australian poet in "Nigger's Leap: New England" bemoaned the Oriental Japanese terror which, during the Second World War, was "threatening to overrun Western society in Australia."[12]

Under the general rubric of the Commonwealth, writers and critical scholars were all extending their purviews; literature in English was in the process of loosening its insular bonds and becoming un-English, non-English, what some critics have called "english." Not until the late 1980s was there the kind of a-political, yet very politicized agenda, that would permit any attempt at serious discussion of indigenous representations. By 1989, when *The Empire Writes Back* appeared, it could and did relate language and hierarchy in a new way. Its editors faulted earlier colonial writers since they sought an "alternative authenticity . . . endorsed by a centre to which they did not belong."[13] They note, as did D.E.S. Maxwell, an Irish scholar and onetime professor at the University of Ibadan in Nigeria, now a professor in Canada, that language imposition followed a political model. According to Maxwell, in "settler" countries (like Australia and New Zealand), the writer brought "his own language," whereas elsewhere, in New Guinea, for example, "the writer brings an alien language." Maxwell contends that both approaches share a fundamental kinship, namely, "to subdue the experience to the language, the exotic life to the imported tongue."[14] About this same time, Malaysian scholar Edwin Thumboo noted in his introduction to an anthology of poetry from Singapore and Malaysia that Japan's phenomenal successes in the early years of the Second World War and India's postwar independence had begun to whittle away at this comfortable distinction since, as he puts it, "the demission of colonial power had begun in earnest,"[15] but with it, one might add, came the ascendancy of English as an international language for writers.

On the other hand, it is not until the viewpoint of the "settler" is made irrelevant and demonstrated to be distorted that there can be a replacement of one model with another. Not until English is "un-Englished," and constructed anew by indigenous people, can there occur a different "construction" of "place"— meaning society and one's position in it, as well as environment.

There are two relatively new important studies that focus on indigenous work—Terry Goldie's excellent cross-cultural study, *Fear and Temptation: The Image of the Indigene in Canadian, Australian and New Zealand Literatures,* and, the Australian Aboriginal, Mudrooroo Narogin's *Writing from the Fringe: A Study of Modern Aboriginal Literature.*[16] They mark different beginnings that seek (and must attempt) to differentiate between "natives," so that there can emerge what Diane Bell terms new concepts of "self, humanity or race." For, as she continues,

Aborigines may have lived in relative isolation for millennia, but they were certainly not lacking in fascination with certain sorts of new experiences. Aborigines were not the passive by-standers they appear to be in the "Discovery of Australia" genre of literature as they provide case material for the systematizing of sons of the Enlightenment. Aboriginal experiences of other did inform their subsequent behavior, but it was not in a comparative global classification: There were those who could be incorporated and those who should be excluded. While Europe expanded its horizons and encompassed all men, Aborigines built understandings of outsiders. They responded on the basis of these encounters, partial though they were.

In short, Aboriginal interpretative frames for the accommodation of outsiders were diametrically opposed to that of the expanding European consciousness. Theirs was not a land discovered by sea, mapped from the outside in, but one pioneered by the ancestral heroes who in the founding era, glossed the "Dreamtime," marked out the land.[17]

The beginning of their culture in the faraway Dreamtime of the distant past had prepared Aborigines for their new roles as hosts and guardians. This is their novel *Weltanschauung,* that must always be recalled, as the Dreamtime becomes the reality of the near presence and the projection of the faraway future.

European language, particularly English and French, became the accepted norm of European and indigenous achievement, so that even though the Pacific islands never became settler colonies, Cook and his followers "acquired" place through the enforcement of language—their very appearance the new tattoo mark; their behavior the new taboo. Thus, in the words of Greg Dening, the years between 1767, when Wallis first visited Tahiti, and 1797, when the missionaries arrived, became a "season of observing," not without a certain theatricality, when

the nations of Europe and the Americas saw themselves acting out their scientific, humanistic selves. Government-sponsored expeditions from England, France and Spain followed one another, self-righteously conscious of their obligations to observe, describe and publish, to be humane and to contribute to the civilizing process of natives out of their superior arts and greater material wealth. It was a time of intensive theater of the civilized to the native, but of even more intense theater of the civilized to one another.[18]

Dening suggests that more than a small degree of self-consciousness is at work here. Cook and his ilk are replaying Columbus with newer and more dangerous assurances; they are concerned with dominating the globe and extending imperial sway.

Cook's name and exploits are also associated with Tahiti. There, the situation was a little different. Mainly because of the climate, a different kind of gaze was projected on the island—one in which Tahiti was seen as the representation of an idyllic lifestyle. The stories recounted about Tahiti fed an eager Romantic appetite, and the depictions of the place outlasted Wallis, Cook, and their crew. Tahiti truly became the epitome of the Paradise which the entire South Pacific supposedly represented. In the case of Cook's men, the idea of Paradise was considerably increased by the barter of ship's nails for sexual favors, but somewhat diminished by the transmission of sexual diseases.[19]

NATIVE BOYS

More important for our purposes, and a reason why we should be surprised at the prevailing mythology of the Pacific islands as Paradise, was Cook's intimate knowledge of the people of the area. I have already mentioned Omai, part human exhibition, part savage exhibitionist. But long before Cook's time, these distant people from far away had already forced themselves on to the European historical record. Ready examples come to mind, such as Ahmed Ibn Masdjid al Din,[20] without whose skills as a pilot Vasco da Gama would have been stuck in Zanzibar once he rounded the Cape. Another, even more relevant at this point of our discussion, is Enrique of Molucca—the name by which he became known in Antonio Pigafetta's account.[21]

Before discussing him, I wish to say a little more about Portuguese exploration[22] and to assert quite categorically that it would have been impossible without assistance from Africans and the numberless Others who themselves lived in Portugal, often as slaves. King Alfonso V had appointed his son John II with the responsibility of exploring the coast of western Africa. He had embarked as early as 1481, with Diogo Cão, reaching the Congo, where he zealously implanted his *padrões* (stone markers), as religious/proprietorial symbols.[23] By the time that Bartolomew Dias sailed, probably 1487–1488, the Portuguese sought not only proprietorial rights but also Ogané (a new name for Prester John, the mythical priest-king of the East). He would assist Christians in opening up the East and thwarting Muslim expansionist plans.

When Dias sailed, he was able to carry with him the very Blacks who had been earlier imported into Portugal. True, few around the Cape could understand them—they were after all from West Africa. But it presumably helped to have indigenous Africans on board in that, although the locals are said to have fled before returning to attack Dias, at least they would not have assumed that these seemingly similar Others (or at least no chronicler could have claimed this) were like Columbus's "men from Heaven," or Cortés, Pizarro, or even Cook as latter-day gods.

I wish to suggest that the presence of native peoples on board European ships was a practical, sensible move and was in the diplomatic interest of the Portuguese and Spaniards. They represented early symbols of assimilation, incorporation into the grand designs of Empire, before empire had been even officially conceived. Obviously, the Europeans had learned from these early explorations, and they would later put these lessons to very practical use.

This is why Ibn Masdjid's participation was no accident for Vasco da Gama. Before Dias, the Portuguese had stumbled like blind men in search of the East; first Pêro da Cavilhã, and later on, Afonso Paiva, utilizing the African land route in a vain search of the elusive "East." In a way, they must have made rather comical figures, as they imported into Africa their very own personal concept of landownership. It is no accident that several centuries later, Dias's own *padrões* would be discovered offshore. What could Africans possibly have made of signs that were worthless and totally alien to them?

One effect of all this marine meandering was that Pedro Álvarez Cabral accidentally bumped into Brazil, thus continuing the notion of the benighted savage and establishing the belief that on the other side of the world land was available for all Portuguese willing to take to sea.[24] Between 1497 and 1499, some nine years after Dias, Vasco da Gama successfully rounded the Cape of Good Hope, and finally made it to India; however, little official credit was given to the navigational skills of those who accompanied him. As I have suggested, this had been official Portuguese policy for some time.[25]Indeed, it should not be forgotten that Africans and Arabs had plied the waters of the Indian Ocean off the east African coast for centuries. Arab geographers had even divided up the East African coast into the land of the "Barbar," the land of the "Zanj," and "Sofala" somewhere to the south. Even further south lay "Wak-Wak," where there existed "brisk trade [between]. . . the Zanj countries [and those] around the Indian Ocean."[26] Arab historian and geographer Al-Idrisi described some of the political structures (such as kingship), and economic wealth (such as gold) that helped establish the area as a stable society.

Our problem, therefore, is that satiated with a Eurocentric version of history, we often fail to comprehend the simple fact that the world existed before Europeans saw it and, furthermore, that European exploration of the New World, of the "East," and of the Pacific would have been extremely difficult, if not impossible, without a great deal of local assistance. Therefore, although da Gama's vessels, sailing between 1497 and 1499, also carried *padrões*, the stone markers which signified Portuguese overlordship, what was more significant was that his symbol of ownership was unintentionally mitigated by the presence of at least two pilots, and later one, offered him by the Sultan of Mombasa. The one who guided da Gama safely to India was the aforementioned Ibn Masdjid.

Pacific exploration had initiated this very kind of cooperative enterprise. Between 1506 and 1516, Magellan had visited Africa, India, and the East. Before his circumnavigation of the globe and his death in the Philippines in 1522, he had been in the employ of the Portuguese and must have mastered a little of their technique. Now, in 1518, at the head of a Spanish expedition, he made sure that he first located the same nameless, anonymous "native" guides that dot the pages of Conquest. Antonio Pigafetta kept a record of the voyage, marvels and all, but not too far beneath the text is the degree of Indonesian/"Eastern" achievement. Here, Enrique is depicted as an interpreter,[27]intermediary, patriotic royalist, and fervent Christian, and even though sometimes lost in the text, he remains a person without whose assistance Magellan's circumnavigation would have been impossible.[28]

As if these roles were not enough, Enrique had obviously preceded Magellan, Pigafetta, and their entire party as circumnavigator. After all, as Simon Winchester, writing in the *Smithsonian,* so ably concluded, Enrique was a person who had also circumnavigated the "linguistic globe." He was, Winchester asserts:

A man who had originated in these parts [the Moluccas in Indonesia], had traveled across Asia and around Africa as a slave, and had now returned home by the Americas and the Pacific. Enrique de Molucca may well have been, strictly speaking, the first of humankind to circumnavigate the world: he was never to be honored for so doing.[29]

Therefore, despite his semi-slave status, this Other (rendered only by a single name) forces himself off the pages of Pigafetta's text. But the very hierarchical Subject power structure in the ship is quick to remind him of his stature as Object. For instance, on one occasion, when the crew imagine that he is feigning illness, he is "told in a loud voice that, although the captain his master was dead, he would not be set free or released, but that, when [they] reached Spain, he would still be the slave of Madame Beatrix, the wife of the deceased captain-general."[30]

Through Richard Eden's sixteenth century *First Three English Books on America,* the very insular English had learned about the need to utilize the foreign languages of the areas in which they found themselves. Not unnaturally, communication became a major reason why English accounts are also heavily overlaid with an indigenous presence. Through non-English eyes, Dampier and Cook gleaned a little understanding of Otherness (which, true, they still considered inferior), but at least their accounts were not as totally unrepresentative and inaccurate as Sir Walter Raleigh's fables regarding a golden city tucked away in South America.[31] I am aware that in Dampier and Cook we are dealing with people who were a trifle more "sophisticated" than their predecessors, but therein can lie an enormous problem. Even as these new "Discoverers" display their enlightened pride, there nevertheless occurs the "conquest" of a man, a woman, a place, a people.

Dening has added this about the "Discoverers" of the Pacific, even as they mediate between order and disorder, Christian and savage: "it is not otherness that attracts the attention of a wider public. It is the experiencing of otherness, the ethnographer mediating the strangeness. Then there is recognition that the native is not different, only worse, somehow deformed morally, aesthetically, physically. The other is self writ comically."[32] These are the Others I now wish to examine briefly at this stage, noting that they are active participants in the voyages, but that their "otherness" is defined as curiously odd, something to be gawked at, possessing the fascination of the monstrous, and yet still Self, often desired as a sex object for personal pleasure and later public display at the kind of forum the later P. T. Barnum would have relished.

Let us now briefly look at the parts played by the "boys," as companions who could help with knowledge of local customs, as translators, Noble Savages, diplomats, and often not too far beneath the textual embellishments, lovers, as already observed with Cook and Omai. For instance, earlier on during his voyages between 1595 and 1606, Quirós understood that indigenous people possessed much useful knowledge of the sea, wind and currents and that it bode well to ensure that segments of the indigenous population sided with the Europeans. Malope, said to have been a chief of fine presence and a tawny-colored skin, was courted by Quirós for much the same initial reasons. Malope even goes through the friendship ritual of name exchange with Álvaro de Mendaña, thus becoming the *taio* (companion) to one/One (an)Other.

Writing of this custom and the relationship that developed between boy and man, the mastered and his master, Quirós comments that "when anyone called him Malope he said No, that his name was Mendaña; and pointing with his finger to the Adelanto [Mendaña], he said that was Malope."[33]The formal nature of the ceremony seems to indicate not only an exchange of names, but also of personalities, so that the native Other could see himself as belonging to the European. There is some disagreement among experts regarding the extent to which the arrangement was purely homosexual, but clearly the homoerotic nature of the realtionship also broke down gender barriers.

This name exchange is also partly an assuming on the part of the *taio*. indigenous name-sharer of the totality of the world of his namesake. In this way, it became incumbent on him to undertake the tasks of an intermediary, well beyond those even vaguely imagined by his European peer. First, the taio all learned a new language, speaking it with varying degrees of conformity. Second, they tried to master the new equipment of Western seacraft, applying their own ancient knowledge of the science. Third, as intermediaries, they acted in important ways as agents of cultural transfer.

Very often through their eyes Europeans were able to visualize the Other side On a subsequent voyage, information about Malope was passed on to a new would-be intermediary, Tumai. Malope had been shot and killed, Tumai is told. Another side to the need for full cooperation is now stressed—European arquebuses had the power to destroy and kill. When Quirós questions Tumai, Tumai responds with much-needed information regarding the extent to which Spanish national interests were secure. Quirós is most curious: "The Captain asked Tumai whether he had seen ships or people like us. He gave it to be understood that he had not, but that he had received reports about them."[34]

More significantly, Tumai (like a host of others) also helped speed the "discoverers" on to their "discoveries." Witness this entry:

The Captain further asked Tumai whether he knew of other lands far or near, inhabited or uninhabited. For this he [Tumai] pointed to his island, then to the sea, then to various points of the horizon, and having explained by these signs, he began counting on his fingers as many as sixty islands, and a very large land, which he called "Manicolo." The Captain wrote down the names.[35]

As Europeans continued their "discoveries" of the area, more and more did local people, often unnamed, become the real driving forces of their enterprises.

Dampier mentions encountering a "Moskito Indian" in 1684, had existed alone for three years on the Juan Fernández Islands. There he had lived the life of a "natural" savage, hunting for goats, and making and hammering out his own weapons. He fished, built a house, and went about quite naked.[36] Dampier is anxious to make two points in keeping with received opinion of his day. First, man in a "state of nature" can exist quite satisfactorily, although Dampier's argument is somewhat spoiled by the fact that the castaway had taken with him some basics from the "civilized" world. Second, and this is perhaps more important, he is greeted by a kinsman who was a member of Dampier's crew and whose name was Robin. Obviously, when Daniel Defoe recreated the adventure of Alexander Selkirk in 1719, he based Crusoe's first name and some of his adventures on this incident. Thus, the South Pacific returns to the West the very hauntings of our own imaginings, and we savour and retain them, as they pass from lore to language, as old fiction becomes factualized into new and accepted misperceptions and misinterpretations of the world out there.

Dampier's second point is definitely worth stressing. Savages, it seems, can demonstrate affection, and he remarks on the "tenderness and solemnity of this Interview, which was exceedingly affectionate on both sides." Furthermore, although these men were capable of showing love and although Robin's friend, Will, had been able to survive in the natural state, they would obviously still have been visualized as non-humans, were it not for European intervention. For instance, Dampier comments on the names Will and Robin: "Those were names given to them by the English, for they had no Names among themselves; and they take it as a great favour to be named by any of us; and will complain for want of it, if we do not appoint them some name when they are with us: saying of themselves they are poor Men, and have no Name."[37]

Evidently Dampier had got his regions slightly confused. As noted before, the mutual exchange of names was common among certain Pacific islanders, but the Mosquito, who live on islands just off the west coast of Honduras and Nicaragua, were not known for this custom. In any event, the adoption of another person's name did not connote (and I am sure Dampier knew this) the absence of one's own name; instead, it reflected a degree of closeness with the one whose name one assumed.

Will and Robin establish quite early in the historical record the living presence of real "savages," capable of affection, and even adaptability, but existing in a hopeless condition. This leaves open the possibility of the "state of nature" being a little like a tabula rasa because European "civilization" and "culture" had as yet made no impact. Although Europeanization could be transferred and doled out to a deserving few who might well be mocked—the WOG or Western Oriental Gentleman is a case in point—therein lies an obvious concomitant to the danger of what seems, at first, like mere harmless theorizing. The Noble Savage could only prove himself both "noble" and no longer "savage," if he could be brought to the West. As noted, Columbus and subsequent explorers did just that. Their Indians were basic curiosities, meant to be loaned out to the inquisitive, and put back in their boxes—Dampier's Prince Jeoly was such a curiosity, as were Cook's own finds.

Others continued to be represented as creatures in some space inhabited by the subhuman, apart from European attestations to the contrary. Tupaia in the Cook narratives (sometimes called Tobia or Tupia) was of princely stock (he is called an *arii*) from Raiatea, a real place, but at the same time, as Alpers points out "a legendary homeland known to nearly all of them by the same name."[38] Tupaia is doubly important: he is supposedly "noble" (like Cook's Omai), but his existence hints at ancestral linkage, even deification—a neat departure from the usual explorers' fantasies in which they picture themselves as gods—in what was perhaps an early hint of Cook's own apotheosis.

Tupaia emerges as a seasoned seaman. Cook attests to his skill as a pilot, for he can read the winds and currents.[39] He is an excellent interpreter and linguist, for he is able to make himself understood to the Maori. Indeed, he is mainly responsible for rescuing Cook's party in 1769, after about a hundred Maori had brandished their weapons and executed a war dance. Later on, he demonstrates his diplomatic skill in dealing with Australian Aborigines; as intermediary, he "prevailed upon them to lay down their arms and come and set down by him, after which more of us went to them." This despite the fact that at Botany Bay communication was impossible, for as Cook points out, "neither us nor Tupia [Tupaia] could understand one word they said."[40]

Tupaia has to be commended for his bravery, for the people of New Zealand and Australia were as alien an Other to him as they were to Cook and his men—particularly so since he himself had begun to assume a somewhat hurried attempt at appearing different. He learned English, expressed an appropriate aversion to cannibalism, and above all, between April and August 1769, drew a navigational chart, a copy of which was apparently made by Cook.[41] The latter was no mean accomplishment, and one can only regret that Tupaia's original has not survived.

Not surprisingly we read of da Gama, but never of Ibn Masdjid; of Magellan, but never of Enrique of Molucca; of Defoe's Robinson, but never of Robin himself; and of Cook, but never of Tupaia. The reasons are not difficult to comprehend. After all, if "Discoverers" and "Conquerors" are supposedly bringing the enlightened fruits of "civilization" to a barren wilderness, then they could hardly admit to conscripting the "savages" as their cohorts. Yet despite what the narratives point toward (and they are always indicative of European triumphalism), there exist subterranean voices that whisper beneath the texts, asking, indeed demanding to be heard, above the officially encoded English text.

11

PACIFIC FICTIONS

Europe had already exported one of its phantoms to Paradise. Perhaps some of the other issues could be viewed as insignificant when considered side by side with a disease for which there was no cure. The sexual taboo of interracial relationships was now made concretely manifest. The Other it seemed could kill the One, or at least brand him for life, with tattoo-like permanence, as one who had dabbled with this ultimate taboo. Or perhaps it was the other way round.

The West found a new dimension for the taboo/tattoo enigma. Now it became quite clear, in view of any evidence to the contrary, that the Ultimate Other had ultimate power over life and death. The One, male, White, lustful, equipped with a penis and a battery of the latest gadgetry of warfare devices, could be outmaneuvered, even undone, by the Other, female, brown, sexually beguiling, possessing a vagina with the power to kill in the midst of love.

Ironically, this weapon of the Other had been borne to the South Pacific, as to the New World, by the One—by early sailors, castaways, pirates, settlers, missionaries, and traders. It resulted, as it had in the Americas, in wholesale and widespread death and destruction. What had not been achieved by Tasman's early warning shots had been just as quickly realized by the impact of smallpox, tuberculosis, and venereal disease. On many islands the population was ravaged, oftentimes reduced to as many as half the total number. Yet, despite the genocide (intentional or not), there continued to exist aspects of a most perverse Romanticism—one quite in keeping with the times. Native inhabitants had moved through various stages, ranging from simplistic, idle dwellers needing hard work to lustful inhabitants craving good sex, and finally to empty souls desperate for Christianity. Tied in with this total misunderstanding was the dire necessity to comprehend exactly where indigenous people fit into the scheme of things.[1]

A VIEW OF THE SAVAGE

John Byron (Lord Byron's grandfather) was shipwrecked off South America in 1768. Lord Byron would afterwards alter the locale in "Don Juan," which was published between 1819 and 1824.[2] True enough, the poem is satiric, but Lord Byron does transfer some of his grandfather's real "adventures" to the Mediterranean. In the poem there are retained the elements of the natural and the macabre that so delighted the Romantics. For instance, Don Juan's spaniel and his tutor are eaten by the crew, and he is himself rescued by a beautiful maiden, Haidée. The poem is unfinished, and no doubt Byron had intended it to be a major derisory thrust against some of his contemporaries, but interestingly, it nevertheless preserves (even if only in the form of humor) what was by then the commonly accepted views of the behavior of non-Europeans—they eat one another and make violent love.

Attempts at engineering the Noble Savage from the Wild Man are slow, but I am suggesting that they are noted in explorers' accounts before they are validated by armchair fictionalizers. In the older Byron's account, there is a throwaway line about Indians resembling monkeys,[3] in which we can see how the man/savage equation becomes centered on a specificity. By 1767, when Samuel Wallis and Philip Carteret sail into the Pacific, even as they, respectively, "discover" Tahiti and Pitcairn, the mythology takes firmer root. John Hawkesworth's earliest versions of Wallis's and Cook's voyages, as Hugh Carrington points out in *The Discovery of Tahiti*, "substantially contributed to the sentimental conception of an innocent primitive society, upon which the most significant social theory of the later eighteenth century was founded."[4]

Of course, not everyone bought into the idyllic picture depicted, especially when it often conflicted with basic standards of decency which the British felt that at least they personified. For instance, Horace Walpole rightly laughed at Hawkesworth's mistaken notion of gallantry in depicting "an old black gentlewoman of forty [as she] carries Captain Wallis across a river when he was too weak to walk."[5] Walpole was particularly bemused that Hawkesworth had envisioned this as his own update of Dido and Aeneas.

Hawkesworth was very much a creature of his time. He had fallen in love with the unknown, unseen "Orient" and, by 1761, had produced *Almoran and Hamlet*. Interestingly, Almoran is not restricted by time or space and can assume whatever temporal or spatial dimension he wishes as he pursues villains. By the time Hawkesworth came to "edit" Cook and Carteret in 1773, the results were already anticipated in his own head. The Pacific islanders would be gentle and innocent, catering to prurient public interests, in Hawkesworth"s effortless display of the blind leading the truly blind.

New versions of savagery enter into mainstream European media at first through the distortions of the travelers themselves, then via the elaborate inventions of the editors, who manufacture what this newly encountered savage was like. In the process, there is much intentional gender confusion, as already seen, although Philip Carteret does add on his 1766–1769 voyage that, "The men and women are clothed, so that it requires a little attention to distinguish the sex."[6] Their "feminization," Carteret suggests, for us to ponder today, is a result of their own willfullness in confounding the Europeans. No European could be blamed for seeking out such "friendships," when the locals themselves took such scant care in distinguishing one gender from another.

By the time of Pacific exploration, imaginative European literature had already hinted at the possibility of exotica. Even though, the display of "Indians" (Africans, Indians from India, Native Americans, South East Asians, and Pacific Islanders) had become a commonplace, Hanke reminds us that "few Europeans had ever seen an Indian in the flesh."[7] The color of the non-European could be reason for romantic excess, as in Shakespeare's sonnets where the so-called Dark Lady could often be presented as a goddess. Or in *The Tempest* where, even as Caliban bemoans the loss of his island, he still acknowledges the deformed nature of his appearance and speech—reason enough perhaps for his disinheritance.[8]

THE SAVAGE CONSTRUCTED

Anxieties and tensions resulted from contact, and harsh lines had to be drawn between the European and non-European. In the process the "non" became a curious mixture of peoples, unified mainly by their comical and tragical emotionalism, stupidity and overcleverness, but, in any event, demarcated as very, very different from the norm. Since European mastery was taken for granted, all non-European ethnicity had to be subjugated to its direction. Eldred Jones in *Othello's Countrymen*, examining English masques between the latter part of the sixteenth century and the 1630s, comments that "figures from Africa frequently contributed to the splendour and strangeness of both the spectacle and the policy of the masque."[9] He utilized several examples of British obsessions long before imperialism had become a political reality.

I am intentionally utilizing the European conceptualization of "Africa" as a way of illustrating that there was in European literature scant differentiation between African and Indian peoples of the period. In neither Christopher Marlowe's *Tamburlaine the Great* (written around 1587) nor Ben Jonson's *Masque of Blackness* (of 1605) did the characters bear any resemblance to a real

Other. The character of Tamburlaine (supposedly the Persian, Timur) confuses us with his sweeping references to Turkey, Egypt, Babylon, and Jerusalem. Likewise, Jonson had simply created his masque to satisfy Queen Anne's wish to play the part of a Black woman.[10]

What is intriguing in both dramas (and other instances could be cited) is that the Black figures of Marlowe's *Tamburlaine* and Jonson's *Masque* are defeated by the very fact of being different. Niger terms them in Jonson's *Masque*—"black with black despair."[11] Marlowe's *Tamburaline* is a cruel and vicious overlord whose end must justly be marked by death. Jonson's daughters of the Nile discover that they are not really beautiful at all, but, in actuality, disfigured by the sun. So, on the one hand, Tamburlane is defeated by the inner callouses of morality, and the female Aethiops, on the other, by the outer horrors of their deformed physicality.

As I have suggested the "barbarian" can also be good, saintly, the envy of Europe—which is, of course, merely another flip of the same coin of misrepresentation. Michel de Montaigne, who was fascinated with what he had heard of the New World, had even witnessed some of the indigenous people in 1560, at a coming of age celebration in honor of Charles IX. Montaigne's "On the Cannibals" places Brazil and its natives within the national context of "discovery" by a Frenchman in 1537, and as part of the remembering of heritage, Montaigne summons up Plato and the myth of Atlantis, as well as Aristotle, quite early in his text. Although their "myths" are dismissed as irrelevant to the New World experience, they nevertheless are significant enough to be mentioned.

Then Montaigne turns the argument on its head by declaring that the people of this land are "barbarous only in that they have been hardly fashioned by the mind of man," existing in a land so bountiful that "it is rare to find any one ill there." In this place of fulfillment, "husbands have several wives." All this Montaigne claims (as Thomas More would afterward) that he learned from a well-traveled and authoritative source. Above all, the inhabitants live in a reality in which concern for one another is most manifest. The Indians who Montaigne saw at Rouen commented on the lack of egalitarian principles in Europe: "they had noticed that there were among us men fully bloated with all sorts of comforts while their halves were begging at their doors."[12] He does not not tell us how he understood this.

Eating people, Montaigne suggests, is not really all that bad. After all, Europeans, he opines, had made a regular habit of it. What the essay does stress is that Europeans, particularly the French, could learn much from the cannibals.

Montaigne is, of course, only half serious here. What he is actually doing is arguing against the initial demonization of the Other (true enough), but his far more sincere purpose is to satirize sixteenth century French customs, habits, and beliefs.

Montaigne's cannibals continue the monolithization of non-Europeans in that this interpretation meant that "Indians" were depicted as gentle people living in a harmonious society at one with Nature. Although we cannot yet utilize the term Noble Savage, it is in Montaigne that we begin to see its ramifications from the earliest times. In the age of Cook, notions regarding the savage would come to fruition, and consolidate into serious beliefs in his "noble" nature, in the display of living exhibits like Prince Jeoly and Omai. As I have already suggested, they did have a life, but no one knew; for Europeans, they were merely objects to be gawked at.

Confusion comes full circle with Aphra Behn's creation of her hero in *Oroonoko* (c. 1688). The name of this supposed enslaved African prince is itself taken from of all places, the Orinoco River. Like Montaigne's witness, Behn also has her credentials: "I have often seen and conversed with this great man, and been a witness to many of his mighty actions," the narrator tells us.[13] Authenticity, or its appearance, is thus established quite early in the narrative, so we are not surprised to learn of Oroonoko as a kind of physical and cultural mulatto— "Oriental" and "African" all combine into the making of a kind of ideal European copycat.

For instance, in the presence of women, Oroonoko displays "the best grace in the world." More importantly:

His face was not of that brown, rusty black which most of that nation are, but of a perfect ebony, or polished jet. . . His nose was rising and Roman, instead of African and flat. His mouth, the finest shaped that would be seen from those great turned lips, which are so natural to the rest of the Negroes. . . His hair came down to his shoulders. [14]

His appearance suggests that he is African, but the reference to the Roman nose, lips, and long hair introduce if not an "Oriental," then certainly a very non-African element. If Behn was not confused, since her brief stay in Surinam may well vouch for a degree of veracity, then at least her readers would be.[15] Blackamoor, Moor, Indian, Native American, African, Oriental, and Egyptian all became delightfully jumbled up.

The very popularity of *Oroonoko* ensured the continuation of this confusion.

Not only was the work soon translated into French, Dutch, and German, but additionally in 1696, it was made into a very popular play by Thomas Southerne. The 1690s also saw a revival of *The Indian Queen* (written since 1664) by John Dryden and Robert Howard, which Behn herself alludes to in setting up her credentials as an "authentic" narrator.[16] But how genuine is she? Given the most recent attacks that have been launched against the author, one is loathe to regard *Oroonoko* as anything other than fantasy. Moira Ferguson denounces what she terms its "constant misrepresentation and romanticizing of African reality." Ferguson is particularly critical of the famous speech that Oroonoko delivers to the slaves in Surinam urging them to revolt; in his oratory, she contends, "Behn affirms an abolitionist and emancipationist perspective," but in the development of the novel's events, Behn intensifies her own "Eurocentric attitudes toward Africans, [by] bolstering the colonial status quo."[17]

The supermix of non-European "native," aloof, westernized, English-speaking, European-looking, and definitely procolonialist, has never really vanished from the fictionalizing narratives of the British and their subjected Others. In a way, the very unrepresentational omnipresence of such a "native" accounts for the armchair theorizing that makes up the invention of the Noble Savage, which included the "real" "savages" of Dampier and Cook. They were *da unten* (down there) somewhere apart over there yonder waiting to be "discovered," as they would be time and time again in the European narratives of those who sailed away, and the cogitations of those who sat at home. The "evidence" of this wannabe European was so entrenched in the minds of Eurocentric writers that it became an important aspect of the policy of colonial education. When the colonials, in turn, began writing, very often much of their work would be used in the easy vilification of their own personal Other that they hated most, and in the tender embrace of the Mother Country's very own Self that they adored most deeply.

Arbitrariness of place meant that any alien background could always assign clues of an artificial homogeneity to these Other cultures. Daniel Defoe vaguely gave Crusoe's whereabouts, which up to now suggest to those who pander to tourists that Trinidad's sister island of Tobago was a viable site. The larger point to *Robinson Crusoe* (1719) is not the inverse of the savage in civilized climes, although it does depict a resourceful European male as conqueror and subduer. Although the origins of Crusoe may have been in Will's adventures in the Juan Fernández Islands, it was, most likely, the rescue of the Scotsman Alexander Selkirk from the uninhabited Más a Tierra Island in the Juan Fernández chain that stimulated public interest in Defoe's recreation. In a way, then, only when the public recognized its Self in the Other did it take notice.

Again, as with Montaigne and Behn, care is taken to establish the appearance of authenticity. Captain Edward Cooke in *A Voyage to the South Sea in and Round the World,* published in 1712, was the first to record Selkirk's rescue the year before. His report is brief and laconic

All this Day had a clear Ship, hoping to get some Purchase, but saw no Vessel, only one Man ashore, with a white Ensign, which made us conclude that some Men had been left there by some Ship, because the Island is not inhabited. The *Duke's* Boat went ashore, and found one Alexander Selkirk, who had been formerly Master of the Cinque Ports Galley, an English Privateer in those Parts; and having some Difference with the Captain of the said Ship, and she being leaky, he left the said Capt. Stradling, going ashore on this Island, where he continu'd four Years and four Months, living on Goats and Cabbages that grow on Trees, Turnips, Parsnips, &c. He told us a Spanish Ship or two which touch'd there had like to have taken him, and fir'd some Shot at him. He was cloath'd in a Goat's Skin Jacket, Breeches, and Cap, sew'd together with Thongs of the same. He tam'd some wild Goats and Cats, whereof there are great Numbers.[18]

Edward Cooke had sailed under Captain Woodes Rogers, and Rogers was the second to recount Selkirk's adventures in *A Cruising Voyage Round the World,* also published in 1712. His version is much longer and includes expanded details as to how Selkirk lived, presumably as semi-savage:

He had with him his Clothes and Bedding, with a Firelock, some Powder, Bullets, and Tobacco, a Hatchet, a Knife, a Kettle, a Bible, some practical Pieces and his Mathematical Instruments and Books. He diverted and provided for himself as well as he could; but for the first eight months had much ado to bear up against Melancholy and the Terror of being left alone in such a desolate place. He built two Hutts with Piemento [*sic*] Trees, cover'd them with long Grass, and lin'd them with the skins of Goats, which he kill'd with his Gun as he wanted, so long as his Powder lasted, which was but a pound; and being near spent, he got fire by rubbing two sticks of Piemento Wood together upon his knee. In the lesser Hutt, at some distance from the other, he dress'd his Victuals, and in the larger he slept, and employ'd himself in reading, singing Psalms, and praying; so that he said he was a better Christian while in this Solitude than ever he was before, or than, he was afraid, he should ever be again.[19]

By the time Richard Steele (who, in 1711, had cofounded *The Spectator* with Joseph Addison) had taken up the account, it possessed a novelistic ring, complete with a typical moralistic eighteenth-century ending:

The Man frequently bewailed his Return to the World, which could not, he said, with all its Enjoyments, restore him to the Tranquility of his Solitude. Though I had frequently conversed with him, after a few Months Absence he met me in the Street, and though he spoke to me, I could not recollect that I had seen him; familiar Converse in this Town had taken off the Loneliness of his Aspect, and quite altered the Air of his Face.[20]

In addition to being a very practical survivor, an individualist who willed himself into being, Selkirk became (for Steele) a man who loved solitude and sought to shun the artifices of society.

These differences are not merely stylistic. They show how, from Edward Cooke to Richard Steele, the idea of the Noble Savage (as European, not Indian) had grown and expanded. By Steele's time, Selkirk was hardly like the morose testifiers of Montaigne's Indians, but had become a loquacious crowdpleaser, ill at ease in the very society that produced him, not at all at home at Home, but sullen, lost, and unhappy. This is not a view that is fiercely promoted because I suspect that one could not very well argue for instant exodus to another utopia.

WHAT BOY FRIDAY LEARNED

The idea, most persistent in the Crusoe myth, is that European Man overcomes all obstacles, teaches the natives to pray and to speak (among Friday's first words is "Master"), and guides life, even in unfamiliar terrains, toward a smooth and agreeable culmination. Crusoe, it turns out, like Columbus, Cortés, and James Cook, is good for native life. He is educator and civilizer, linguist and god. The travel chronicles had said as much; *Crusoe* merely confirmed the ascendancy of the male and the European in the global structure. It is no accident that this particular male European was also English. Like the later Jungle Jim or Tarzan, he realizes that it is incumbent on him to take up the "White Man's Burden."

Even if we cannot be certain *where* Crusoe lives or, for that matter, *who* or *what* Friday stands for, the fact that the Juan Fernández Islands in the Pacific and Tobago in the Caribbean can both satisfactorily represent Crusoe's abode is fascinating in itself. First, because it confirms that the naming of place and the extension of myth, once validated by the authoritative metropolitan center, become perfectly acceptable ways of understanding and accepting subject/Other relationships. Second, and this goes back to Ben Jonson's *Masque of Blackness*, to Montaigne and to Behn. Their travel fictions about the Other had all confirmed the reality of a single, uniform type termed "savage,"who that could be redeemed, but only through the means that *Crusoe* suggests—traveling to the center of European maleness and/or the European metropolis, and being incorporated in it. After all, it is there that Ben Jonson's "negros" found their center and discovered that they were no longer hideous but acceptable because their physical attributes had now been confirmed by Britain itself. A few did challenge this, not Montaigne whose "models" were in Europe, but Jonathan Swift, for instance, who made fun of European ignorance, especially of things African. Swift ironically commented that very often mapmakers would gloss over unknown and uninhabited areas by sketching elephants in the place of towns they did not know.

Thus, in the literature a remote place, a non-Europe, is being invented. There macabre fantasies can be enacted, since the setting provides a mere backdrop for European activity. So, even when, by the eighteenth century, a better understanding of the geography of place and the mode of custom have been fairly well recognized, there remains a tendency to treat "over there" as a specific locus, with certain commonalities directly opposed to the metropolitan norm. Essentially, this is how the "native" construct comes about. To use Werner Sollors's phrase, this "invention of ethnicity" is not merely self-generated; it arises, in no small measure, from the external mapping of the constitution of the "native" in a colonial world.[21]

Reducing the variety of the world and downsizing it in terms of "native" obviously made it more manageable, more easily understood, and more easily controlled. But this is an artificial device that strips the Other of ancestral lineage and language, indeed every element of personality, and merely enables the new colonial supervisors to travel with the lightest of cultural baggage. It is also a delusion, but one that the very people, from wherever, on whom the new label is implanted will begin to wear it under new guises, it is true, but display it none the less.

Hence Friday, much like Oroonoko, only *resembles*, but does not *personify*, African, Indian, or Pacific Islander. Indeed, he is a kind of conglomerate species, invented for one purpose alone, as a contrast to Crusoe's own known circumscribed ethnicity. Quite early in their encounter, Crusoe notes, much the same as Behn's narrator, that Friday's "hair was long and black . . . the colour of his skin was not quite black," not at all resembling "the Brazilians and Virginians, and

other Natives of America." Again, as with Behn, his semi-European appearance
is noted, namely that "his nose [was] small, not flat like the negroes," and he
possessed "a very good mouth, thin lips." Friday is a Europeanized composite of
an invented "native," representing everyone and no one, and, at the same time,
suggesting the possibility of physical alteration that could more closely ally him
with the European. As Crusoe notes, "he had all the sweetness and softness of an
European in his countenance." One of the first acts that Friday performs is that
of worship. Instinctively, like Columbus' Taínos, Cortés's Aztecs, Pizarro's
Incas and Cook's Hawaiians, he recognizes in the European, the presence of an
incoming god. Crusoe describes their first encounter:

I beckon'd him again to come to me, and gave him all the signs of encouragement
that I could think of and he came nearer and nearer, kneeling down every ten or twelve
steps in token of acknowledgement for my saving his life . . . [I] beckon'd to him to
come still nearer; at length he came close to me, and then he kneel'd down again,
kiss'd the Ground, and laid his head upon the ground, and taking me by the foot, set
my foot upon his head; this it seems was in token of swearing to be my slave
forever.[22]

Crusoe's culture, from which the materials he had salvaged are symbolic
evidence enough, had, it seemed, placed him in this supreme regal position. As
for Friday, he possessed nothing; no language, no clothes, no god, no morality.
All of the anxieties of the Other are reposed in Friday: he is savage, cannibal,
and completely at the mercy of Crusoe, an altruistic European who, true enough,
had to kill off some of Friday's kinsmen, but nevertheless retains his own
Christian moral purpose.

Defoe has taken Will's account of exile as a Mosquito Indian on a Pacific
island and turned it around. At center stage is not the Noble Savage, but instead
the Christian European who, in enduring his time on the island, proves his
superiority once and for all. Indeed, very often in his private musings, Crusoe
can even exhibit "liberal" feelings (perhaps he can afford to), as for instance
when he ponders (Montaigne-like but without any satire) on the similarities
between savages and Christians.[23]

SYNTHETIC SAVAGES

Just as it is impossible to pinpoint Friday's ethnicity, many texts follow
utilize this same cultural chaos in order to develop themes unrelated to the chosen regions, but definitely connected with European yearnings, needs, and even

aspirations. Note that there is scant difference between the "invention" of the world in imaginative literary outpourings and actual descriptions of the world in travel texts. Both seek reassurances of the stability of Home, apart from the distant and what Ishmael in *Moby-Dick* (1851) contrasts as "the watery part of the world."[24]

With Voltaire's *Candide* (1759), we are back in the world of Montaigne. The faraway place beyond, where mores are turned upside down, might well be France. But although most of the work is good French farce, even in the laughter of the anonymous place beyond Europe, the legends persist. In this "unknown country," there are naked women, sexually agressive monkeys, and cannibalism, which much upset Candide who, after all, rightly refuses to believe that this is the best of all possible worlds. Cacambo rises to the occasion. Like a Noble Savage, he suffers from the burden of being an eternal linguist out of love with local custom, but able to speak the lingo and to rectify any untoward occurrence. He reasons with the "naked Otellions, armed with arrows, clubs and stone hatchets,"[25] all intent on consuming a Jesuit. After he preaches, he kindly proffers Candide and himself for their sustenance, but his point—that the Jesuits are not really enemies—is proven and he and Candide are soon unbound, uneaten, and provided with women and refreshment.

Despite the hilarity of this scene the old mythologies are very much apparent, as I have suggested, particularly in the sacrifice of Cacambo's life for the Jesuit priest's. But Voltaire's world outside the Europe he knew is a confusing one of Blacks, Whites, Egyptians, Muslims, and Chinese. Although Voltaire was a veritable pioneer in his studies of history in moving away from a purely ethnocentric view of Europe, the locale of his satires constitutes too much of a mishmash.

In this respect, Voltaire's creations are not unlike Dr. Johnson's prince in *Rasselas* (1759). *Rasselas* is *Candide* without the wit, set in an unrecognizable "Egypt" (the "Orient") to which the prince must journey if he seeks to escape the rigidity of the "happy valley." Voltaire's hero, Candide, concluded that there was no simplistic answer or explanation to life, so he takes up gardening—a trifle Swiftian when Gulliver forsook the company of humans for horses. Johnson's hero, Rasselas, returns to Abyssinia—happiness is not out there, in another place, but within. Imlac, the philosopher who accompanies Rasselas, also turns to nature, not as in the strong words of Wordsworth, "Let nature be your teacher," or even as in Shelley's firm mandate for the poet to be one of the world's unacknowledged legislators in his *The Defence of Poetry*. Instead, the return is a kind of surrender, not to philosophy, but to the same simple "Nature" of Candide's garden. Romanticism would introduce a new way in which the "savage" would be represented.

I observe four stages in the West's conceptualizing of the Other. First, there is the Wild Man, African, Native American, fabricated from Plinian lore and reassembled in the New World.[26] Second, in the Americas, the "Red Man," the "Injun" comes into being. Again, he exists solely as a response to European invention, in this case the villain of the post Lewis and Clark incursions into the west. Third, the myth comes from Europe; it partly co-exists with the second type as the Noble Savage, but is never totally accepted in the United States, although Thomas Jefferson (like any good European), seriously toyed with the idea.[27] Finally, today, there is what I should like to term the "Environmental Indian," latter day spokespersons on ecology. These are all western creations and have little to do with Native American realities.

I mention this at this point of our discussion, since I note in Rousseau's *Emile* (1762), for instance, the manner in which the Noble Savage comes to fruition, but *within* Europe, *within* the context of European Romanticism. In other words, the portrait of the exotic Other alters in direct response to Europe's own internal evolution, totally independent of any "objective" external reality, and in the process, and he is changed into a White male. This becomes the basis for intellectual and cultural notions that are exported to all parts of the world by travelers, and their texts exhibit as high a degree of the "fictionalized" as the versions of those who never journeyed. This is all part of a European cultural imposing of Self on the Other, and it matters little that some of the writers were personally familiar with the reality of the Other—at least to a limited extent. The mythology remained so indispensably cumbersome that it was well nigh impossible to describe the faraway in any other but unreal terms.

The "real" became the substitution of nearby fantasy arising from national expectation, far more important than any attempt at a true depiction of the faraway. As a result, the inevitable collision of these projections—what was real and what was needed—forced the dislocated polarities of "subject" toward "object," of "Self" toward "Other." At first, it was not merely an exercise in power (although power was involved), but a basic desire to translate new experiences into understandable, recognizable European terms. Readers of a text should not feel dislodged from ordinary expectations of life within their control. They should know that their world and its expansion did not threaten their existence, for control was in the hands of not mortal men but human gods. It mattered very little how reality looked close up; the European metropolis manipulated the images.

Take Dr. Johnson, for instance. He had adopted Francis Barber soon after Barber arrived in England from Africa in 1750. Johnson had sent him to school and encouraged him to learn Latin and perfect his English. With Johnson's typical injunction in a letter of September 25, 1770, "You can never be wise unless you love reading,"[28] he encouraged Barber to pursue the Classics. Indeed, at least according to James Boswell, Johnson had "all along treated [Barber] truly as an humble friend." Johnson's will allowed Barber to retire in relative opulence, even though at least one of Johnson's critics did suggest "a caveat against ostentatious bounty and favour to negroes."[29] So much for the enlightenment of the Enlightenment.

Yet Johnson's personal knowledge of Barber scarcely aided him in his projection of Rasselas, who is a prince of an unreal world. His language is not intended to convey the real but the surreal; his journey from Ethiopia to Egypt is meant only in a metaphorical sense to conjure up ideas of the need for challenges that go beyond the everyday satisfaction of senses toward a search for soul. Johnson's book is a parable, an allegory, an extended metaphor that cannot be taken to represent anything beyond the imposition of mythology. No one has ever seriously suggested that Rasselas was based on Frances Barber. Rasselas is far removed from the world of humdrum reality to realms where his own physical appurtenances and those of his companions count for far less than what was beginning to be seen as their inner selves, but was in fact a self introspection of Europeans by themselves.

THE MIND OF THE SAVAGE

Since the famous 1560 debate between Juan Ginés de Sepulvéda and Bartolomé de las Casas, there had been doubt about whether native peoples had souls, about whether their inner nature could actually be altered. By the time of Johnson and Jean-Jacques Rousseau, intellectuals had provided the answer. Wealthier patrons, such as the Duke of Montagu, were able to put the experiment to its most severe test with the accuracy of a scientist at work on laboratory rats. Francis Williams was sent to Cambridge, where he studied mathematics, before going back to Jamaica to teach.[30] Ignatius Sancho, a Black grocer in Westminster, was often loaned books by the Duke of Montagu and, after the duke's death, became a butler at Montagu House until he retired in 1773.[31] In Germany, Duke Anton Ulrich von Braunschweig-Wolfenbüttel was engaged in a similar experiment. He had adopted a man to whom he gave the names of his son and himself, calling him Anton Wilhelm Amo, an unlikely appellation for someone originally from Axim, Ghana. Both dukes were really engaged in attempting to show that the Noble Savage could be housetrained and domesticated.

However, it would be fair to conclude that these attempts—crude, but well-intentioned given the times—all failed. Francis Williams did return to Jamaica, but according to a contemporary writer, described himself as a "white man acting under a black skin."[32] Johannes Capitein, another experimental subject adopted in Holland, in turn, distinguished himself by composing a "thesis" in Latin and Dutch proving that slavery was not contrary to the laws of God.[33] Such instances may be multiplied,[34] but suffice it to say that these noble experiments only proved that the Noble Savage could be Europeanized and rendered harmless and nonthreatening. He could be schooled in a manner beyond his own self-worth so that eventually he came to despise himself and his origins. This was the purpose of the more sinister later U.S. experiments in taking the Indian out of the Indian at educational institutions such as the infamous Carlisle Indian School, founded in Carlisle, Pennsylvania in 1879.[35]

Dr. Johnson's Rasselas does not have to be westernized. He comes from Ethiopia, "a country where the sciences first dawned that illuminate the world" before which "all European magnificence in confessed to fade away." However, both Rasselas and his tutor, Imlac, accept European superiority as evident. In answer to Rasselas's question, "By what means . . . are the Europeans thus powerful?" Imlac, responds, "They are more powerful, Sir, than we. . . because they are wiser; knowledge will always predominate over ignorance, as man governs the other animals. But why their knowledge is more than ours, I know not what reason can be given, but the unsearchable will of the Supreme Being."[36] This is the kind of heady stuff we have encountered before. And the words are particularly significant because Imlac expresses them. But they had always existed as part of the national subconscious that we found before, in *Crusoe,* and, indeed, could be located in both supposedly realistic travel and imaginative literature much earlier on. In *The Tempest,* one reason why Caliban always fascinates me is that he is a worshipper without a deity, ever seeking to implant a godliness on all Europeans with whom he comes into contact, even two bizarre figures, Stephano (an intoxicated butler) and Trinculo (a clown).

This fervent, ever-present wish on the part of the "native" to worship and adore Columbus, Cortés, Pizarro, Crusoe, Cook, and so on is symptomatic not of the Other's imbalance, but of European arrogance. The heartfelt need to be deified and addressed as god represents the supreme hierarchial triumph whereby the Discoverer/Conqueror transcends his own mortality and lays claim to a significance beyond that of his own mortal prince or emperor. It positioned the adventurer beyond the pale of the ordinary, placing him almost outside the basic everyday concerns of his lackluster world and elevating him to the beyondness of heroism and humanhood, to godhead itself.

THE SELF AND THE SAVAGE

Apart from its pointed political irony, Jonathan Swift's *Gulliver's Travels* (1726) may be viewed on one level as an exercise in world domination. In the work, subtitled "Travels into Several Remote Nations of the World in Four Parts," Lemuel Gulliver, like Crusoe, is shipwrecked in Lilliput, but his superior strength, intelligence, and ability are all apparent, even obnoxious, especially when he extinguishes a fire by urinating on it. In Brobdingnag, where the inhabitants are gigantic, or in Laput, where no one seems earthbound, or even among the Houyhnhnms, the horselike people, Gulliver is always the same. He is the distant, witty observer of the habits of Others (grantedly supposedly connected to Self). And the observed are odd, strange, macabre, because Swift is utilizing the tall tales of the travel narratives of Dampier, Cook, and even Crusoe to demonstrate an important point: Gulliver is English, and as an Englishman, with the God asserted by Crusoe and Imlac by his side, he cannot possibly go wrong. However, Gulliver is humbled enough to forsake the follies of the European Self. On Gulliver's return home, Swift noted, Gulliver gave up human companionship for the intellectual stimulation of his horse, spending his time thereafter in his stable.

Once Oliver Goldsmith left the deserted village, empty because of the Industrial Revolution, his English insularity became very apparent. For instance, in *An History of the Earth and Animated Nature* (1774), the cultural confusion which we observed earlier, is once more manifest. The external environment becomes narrowed to accommodate everyone and everything. According to Goldsmith, there were, for instance, tigers in Canada and migratory squirrels in Lapland. But his heart was in the right place, even if his head might not always have been. He was an anti-imperialist at a time of great optimism for Empire, often seeing and noting the contradictions of so-called civilization. He pointed out in "The Traveller" how the force that drove the slave economy was often self-generating, with funds "Pillaged from slaves to purchase slaves at home."[37]

This is the period, after all, for seeking some kind of perfection —the selfsame physical State of Bliss which had eluded the biblical Adam expelled from Eden, and every traveler from Columbus onward. Certainly, it was the idyllic that had eluded Crusoe, Candide, and Rasselas, but kept them alive, always searching. Out there, in some unnamed place, must lie perfection, and this hope for Paradise motivated the European mindset, even softening it toward an easier acceptability of colonization. "Possession" came to mean that at least little pieces of the ideal or gruesome world could be borne back Home—masks, sculpture, paintings, ebony heads, ivory, baskets, tapestry, skulls, painted gourds—the fragmented paraphernalia of the culture proffering shallow assortments for display. Within the space of the London Crystal Palace, Anne McClintock alluded to the "commodity spectacle" or " the illusion of marshaling all the globe's cultures into a single, visual pedigree of world time. . .global progress consumed visually in a single image."[38] And, as she adds, contained by, and controlled from, the metropolitan center.

In a way, "possession" was a realization of the temporary nature of trying to grasp both heaven and earth, for the "possessor" did not embrace, incorporate, unify—he merely took over. There is no forever timespan involved, and one reading of Montaigne is that "the solution he would advocate is an attempt to regenerate society along more wholesome lines, as a person contained in the present."[39] Similarly, as with Crusoe, the presence of Home is always in the present, whether in his thoughts, his language in the journal, the artifacts he salvages from the vessel, his Christianity, or, ultimately, his dramatic "rescue," his return Home, away from the non-Home, non-place, and non-people of the island—but, most importantly, bearing with him the logbook, the supreme artifact and artifice that represented the world for the European reader.

I suspect this link with Home is a major reason why Jean Jacques Rousseau has his young pupil in *Émile* (1762) in only a *temporary* state of withdrawal from European society. The important caveat is phrased almost negatively— namely that the chief function of Émile's tutor is to make sure that nothing outside of Nature unduly influences the boy. Untrammeled by Western society and its harmful influences, the child develops in response to the environment. *Émile* does hint at Montaigne's society of perfection, but for the same reason that Montaigne does—it is a state removed, apart, different, and unattainable for Western man.

Rousseau did not merely agree with the theoretical suggestions of armchair thinkers regarding this state of Nature. It was to be found, he most assuredly tells us, in the Americas.[40] Yet a major problem remains, in that the "ideal" Rousseau enthusiastically paints is indeed the "nightmare" of the Other. For instance, Rousseau cites lovemaking as one of the benefits that results from existing in this peaceful state of nature. He asserts that people are so blissfully content in the Caribbean that a European bureaucrat would look slightly silly. He argues that those who go about naked obviously want nothing and therefore can hardly be controlled, and so on. The points are more relevant for France and Europe and have little, if anything, to do with Caribbean/New World fact. It is the point of view of the privileged observer seeing the unprivileged observed as happy in their sexual activity, deprivation of social order, and lack of basic material means of sustenance. Rousseau's supposed "positives" for the Caribbean and its inhabitants are actually "negatives" in context. All day sex doth not a culture make, and lolling around in the buff scarcely constitutes a required building block for societal advancement.

For Rousseau, as well as for many of his contemporaries, the "native" is merely representational even ornamental, and, as seen, equals the Indian (from India or the Americas), equals the African, equals the Asian, equals the South Pacific Islander. If, as Fairchild argues, Rousseau "seized upon the Indian as an example of certain abstract principles he had evolved," then certainly the reality of Native American life and experience continues to be obscured by European theory. All that we can say with any assurance is that the "native" experience is only meaningful for the West when they can image and manage it, convert it into a simile, make of it a metaphor, digress about it in terms of allegorical ramifications, or literally master the trope. All of its significance must relate back to the West, or the "native" can have no place in the discourse.

Most scholars therefore would agree with Gaile McGregor that the newly constructed savage had to possess a global commonality and nationality, that "he might appear as a subtle Persian, a sardonic Turk living in Paris and reporting on the curious customs of the natives, an ageless wise Chinese, a simple and upright Huron."[41] So even when the virtues applied are supposedly "positive," they only serve to distance Western "readers" further away from the non-Western "read." The effect is cumulative, as explorers to the South Pacific, for instance, simply bear along with them the database of these earlier inputs. For the new adventurers, it would be a simple matter to recall these mistaken assumptions when confronted by a different reality and to apply them willy-nilly, thus validating anew the longevity of myth.

12

EAST IS WEST

By the nineteenth century, the United States had officially "claimed" and entered the Pacific. Reasons for this may be found as early as the 1840s, when "Manifest Destiny" (first articulated by John L. O'Sullivan in a magazine article)[1] expressed the God-given mission of Anglo-Americans to move and expand in an ever-increasing burst of territorial aggrandizement. Sullivan was referring to Texas, but Manifest Destiny soon became a rallying cry for both political parties in efforts to legitimately sanction the move west.

Earlier, in 1803, President Thomas Jefferson had dispatched Meriwether Lewis and William Clark and their "Corps of Discovery" on what proved to be the beginning of a legitimized westward movement. By 1805, the group had crossed the Rockies and descended the Columbia River to the Pacific.[2] Like Cook, Lewis and Clark also considered their journey as "scientific," but in addition to spying out the land, the people, and their customs, the party was also laying claim to U.S. "possession," for instance, of Oregon. By their action, Albert Furtwangler comments, "the Corps of Discovery was unwittingly [?] anticipating what later generations would develop into a creed called Manifest Destiny."[3]

The 1850s pell-mell rush for land and gold saw large numbers heading for Arizona, California, Colorado, Nevada, and Utah. Just as the "Pilgrims" had "opened up" the East, the "Pioneers" would now "develop" the West. Land was cheap and available since, apparently, it belonged to no one. As the "frontier" shifted, it bore along with it the exportation of the much cultivated mythologies of individualism, free enterprise, liberty, faith in the future, and more than a small degree of machismo. Frederick Jackson Turner's later romanticized concept of the frontier in American history lent an academic imprimatur to expansionism.[4]

Actually, it was not so much the frontier that was extended, as the idea of "wilderness." The Pilgrim concept of a barbaric no man's land was simply adapted by the Pioneer to the new concept of place. Both, of course, explained away the Native American as "wild," part of the wilderness, "heathen," in dire need of Christianization, and "uncivilized," as standing in the way of progress. But as one historian succinctly suggests, Native American presence was only a temporary setback, and the invention of the West as a nursery for civilization, indeed a New Eden, was more than ably reinforced by the print media, long after the "military campaigns had practically ceased and the western country was no longer possessed of the mystery and romance which interested the literary traveler."[5]

REORDERING OTHERNESS AS ODD/OUTER/UTTERMOST

During the actual period in which the journey west took place, migration was sanctioned thrice—by expediency (and the pragmatic lure of land and gold), by officialdom (as articulated in the legal fiction of "Manifest Destiny"), and by holy writ. The latter is particularly evident among the Mormons. Ironically, the founder of the Mormons, Joseph Smith, had stated that he owed his own heavenly manifestations to divine words engraved on golden tablets by an ancient Native American prophet. But this was in the 1820s; once Mormons, under Brigham Young,[6] began their push west to present-day Utah, what irked the federal government was not the Mormons' firm conviction that Blacks were cursed or that the Native American Lamanites had killed off the original occupants of the land, but the Mormon insistence on polygamy and the role of the Mormon Church in politics and business.

The Book of Mormon, the most sacred text of the church, does express views that quite definitely fit in with nineteenth century American expansionism. Certain Native Americans are termed "Lamanites," "a remnant of the House of Israel."[7] They are descendants of the unruly Laman and, indeed, the term stands for "any person who rejects the gospel."[8] Contrasted with the bloodthirsty, idolatrous, *red-skinned* Lamanites are the peaceful, God-fearing, *fair-skinned* Nephites. The Lamanite/Nephite polarity is not just a delusion of the founders of the Mormon Church, but also a very pragmatic approach to rendering, depicting, visualizing, and verbalizing the nature of the Other.

Mormons further clearly demonstrate for us the European/Euro-American perception of the time, one we have already noted, in representing everyone else as odd and strange, but yet all alike, only different from Europeans. We read in *The Book of Mormon* that the "skin of blackness" was placed on the Lamanites as a curse. The words of infliction occur in the second chapter and state as follows:

And he [the Lord] had caused the cursing to come upon them, yea, even a sore cursing, because of their iniquity, for behold, they had hardened their hearts against him, that they had become like unto a flint; wherefore, as they were white, and exceedingly fair and delightsome, that they might not be enticing unto any people the Lord did cause a skin of blackness to come upon them.[9]

The meaning remains clear enough, latter-day revisions not withstanding; the Mormons effectively state in religious terms the total alienation of the Black Other, thus articulating a widely accepted view of the time. Even as they made their own separatist Salt Lake Trail west, Mormons considered non-Mormon Whites on the Oregon Trail as mainly "Odd," Blacks as belonging to the "Outer," and some Native Americans to the "Uttermost" realm of the Mormon norm, as the Mormons went about their business of reordering Otherness. But Mormons merely represented a microcosm of Euro-American society.

The confrontations that Joseph Smith had feared were played out in the Indian Wars between 1865 and 1880. Even the alienated Mormons, like the very European Americans, continued to seek European approval for their action as they moved westward. John Taylor, Brigham Young's right-hand man, complained bitterly to Count Leonetto Cipriani, who had followed in the steps of Lewis and Clark, visiting California in 1853. Taylor said that he and the Mormons felt ill-used, entreating "We ask for nothing more than that a European may know us personally."[10] Cipriani interviewed Brigham Young himself and had a brief correspondence with him. On the whole, I suppose because most of his information comes from Brigham Young, Cipriani describes the Mormons in the most positive terms, although he admits to finding their polygyny a trifle discomfiting. I can only surmise that the Italian count came to the Mormons unmarked by any mythical scars from their holy book, or their experience of the West.

Even as internal forces were pushing Euro-Americans westward, toward land or gold, Europeans were themselves witness to this expansion. Clearly, neither the Prussian Prince Alexander Philipp Maximilian (who traveled in 1833–1834)[11] nor the Italian Count Leonetto Cipriani (who traveled in 1853) had any vested national interest in North America or its expansion westward, but their European presence and contacts seemed to validate the idea of expansion as international credo. Spain was, of course, different in that its foothold in the Americas (in a period of proprietorship) went back centuries. The Spanish-American War may have been "splendid" and "little," as John Hay had described it to President Theodore Roosevelt, but it finally bridged the last permanent geographical boundary to the west—the Pacific Ocean. How much farther west was West? The United States had now achieved hegemonic status on par with Europe.

WEST OF THE WEST

Hawaii had been formally "annexed" by Congress on August 12, 1898. Despite internal machinations on the part of U.S. powerbrokers who sought control of the island's sugar industry, the new Queen Liliuokalani in 1891 had nevertheless attempted to mount serious opposition to control. But no less a figure than Sanford B. Dole established himself as president. Hawaii's commercialization had begun, as Daniel Boorstin adds, like its contemporary hula dances, neither "real ritual" nor "real festival."[12]

By the time that Americans physically established their presence in the Pacific, two factors were evident. One, brought from Europe, coincides with the idea of "flight from" and "journey toward"—in biblical language, from the land of Egypt to the Promised Land; in Pioneer language, from the continent of Europe to the New World. The second refers to the (again European) penchant for the transference of real place into trope, so that the American trek west across the Pacific (and to Hawaii especially) became a journey to Paradise, a name by which Hawaii continues to be referred. Therefore, the "westward" movement may be seen, with its mandates and wars, movement of peoples and Eurocentrism, as one that inexorably led to the Pacific, and inevitably to Pearl Harbor, the defense of territory in the Pacific islands, and even conflicts in Korea and Vietnam.

Looked at a little differently, in more ways than one, American interest in the Pacific seemed to be derived from a wish to go to the farthest place in the world. White American history had been one of constant movement, away from Europe, away from the East Coast, now away from the West, to seek out further places of perfection. In a way, it became a national preoccupation to search for a personal utopia, whether it be the present-day flight to suburbia away from the inner city, or the historical reaching out toward an ever moving horizon. R.W.B. Lewis phrased it best when he wrote in *The American Adam*:

The American myth saw life and history as just beginning. It described the world as starting up again under fresh initiative, in a divinely granted second chance for the human race, after the first chance had been so disastrously fumbled in the darkening old world. It introduced a new kind of hero . . . an individual emancipated from history, happily bereft of ancestry, untouched and undefiled by the usual inheritance of family and race. . . . The world and history all lay before him.[13]

A major problem with this conclusion lies in the assumption that the world was empty and that "the human race" excluded Native Americans and African Americans.

Despite her own racial misgivings, perhaps this is why Cora Munro in James Fenimore Cooper's *Last of the Mohicans* (1826) can see an Adam in Natty Bumppo, but only a localized Noble Savage in Chingachgook. Perhaps this is also why a servant in Cooper's *Redskins* (1846) can suggest that whereas "The nigger grows uglier and uglier every year . . . the Indian grows 'andsomer and 'andsomer."[14] If, after all, "the human race" meant the same as "all people [who] are created equal," then, obviously, such humans must be White and male and, as such, may establish distinctions among the Other, however arbitrary or even ridiculous these might seem. Cooper, in fact, had argued in *The American Democrat* (1838) that humans could not possibly have been created equal.[15]

AMERICANS AND THE *BOUNTY*

One powerful way through which the South Pacific enters into the imagination and conceptualization of the West is through the incident of the *Bounty*. Under the command of Captain William Bligh, the ship had been dispatched to Tahiti to collect breadfruit saplings. The intention was to replant them in the West Indies, where it was expected it would provide a cheap source of food for slaves. But having left Tahiti, bound for the Cape of Good Hope, the famous mutiny occurred; on April 28, 1789, Fletcher Christian and other crew members seized Bligh and set him adrift with eighteen members of his crew, having allotted them basic provisions. Somehow Bligh, perhaps because he was a skilled seafarer, made it to Timor, now part of Indonesia. The *Bounty,* with twenty-five crew members, first sailed back to Tahiti, where Bligh would later charge that the sailors had become totally intoxicated with the sensuous pleasures of its women. Sixteen men were left in Tahiti, and they were later arrested and charged. But on their way back to England, the HMS *Pandora,* in which they were being transported, sank, and most of them lost their lives. Fletcher Christian and eight others, in addition to a company of Tahitian men and women, had sailed further on, founding a colony on Pitcairn Island. There they remained for several years without being found. Present in the narrative, occurring so soon after the American Revolution and in the year of the French Revolution, were all the elements that would attract a loyal following of readers. Fletcher Christian was seen as a hero who had refused to accept the dictates of a tyrannical overlord. Not only had he not compromised, but he had sailed away into the unknown, never to be found, to some other Paradise on the edge of the earth, where dreams of liberty, equality, and fraternity could be perhaps truly realized. In any event, the bare bones of the story were intriguing, and a host of writers would attempt to imagine the Pacific against the background of these events. I shall now look at William Bligh, Sir John Barrow, and Charles Nordhoff and James Norman Hall

First, Bligh himself made two attempts. The first account, *Narrative of the Mutiny on Board His Majesty's Ship Bounty,* was rushed into print, appearing in London in 1790. Later, in 1792, in *A Voyage to the South Sea,* Bligh retold his story, adding new material, and positioning himself as the misunderstood and wronged party.

Second, Sir John Barrow, citing Bligh's writing, had also used his own access to the Admiralty Office in Britain to read the records of the *Bounty.* In 1831 he published his first of three versions,*The Mutiny and Piratical Seizure of HMS Bounty.* Barrow's book was reedited and published in 1900 under a different title, *The Eventful History of the Mutiny and Piratical Seizure of H.M.S. Bounty* , when some material was omitted. The basic text was once more republished in 1972 as *A Description of Pitcairn's Island and its Inhabitants with an Authentic Account of the Mutiny of the Ship Bounty,* again with some minor editorial alterations. The title changes and editorial revisions are testament to the longevity of the 1789 mutiny in the minds of the English-speaking public, and how again and again its construct became representative of events beyond the Pacific per se, having more to do with European needs and aspirations.

Supposedly anonymous, since Barrow said "he presumes not to write Author,"[16] the account was fairly chronological. It began with the "discovery" of Otaheité island by Wallis, then described the crew, the mutiny, Bligh's problems as a result of having been set adrift, the court martial, and the pardon, closing with an account of those living on Pitcairn Island.

Barrow's account is fairly dry—Cook features in the early part, and Barrow quotes Bligh's two accounts of 1790 and 1792, as he sought to whet his readers' appetites for sea yarns, while seeking a degree of self-mitigation. Bligh argues that the reason for revolt was not any undue harshness on his part, "but the promise of Paradise on the island," to utilize his own words from the 1790 account. Bligh adds:

It will very naturally be asked, what could be the reason for such a revolt? In answer to which, I can only conjecture that the mutineers had flattered themselves with the hopes of a more happy life among the Otaheitans than they could possibly enjoy in

England; and this, joined to some female connections, most probably occasioned the whole transaction. The women at Otaheite are handsome, mild, and cheerful in their manners and conversation, possessed of great sensibility, and have sufficient delicacy to make them admired and beloved. The chiefs were so much attached to our people that they rather encouraged their stay among them than otherwise, and even made them promises of large possessions. Under these, and many other attendant circumstances equally desirable, it is now perhaps not so much to be wondered at, though scarcely possible to have been foreseen, that a set of sailors, most of them void of connections, should be led away; especially when, in addition to such powerful inducements, they imagined it in their power to fix themselves in the midst of plenty, on one of the finest islands in the world, where they need not labor, and where the allurements of dissipation are beyond anything that can be conceived.[17]

This is a veritable Paradise, away from the humdrum cares of the workaday world. The island offers hopes of a "happy life" among beautiful women. Furthermore, the men had high hopes of becoming members of a propertied class, no mean achievement in rigid, caste-ridden, eighteenth-century England. Finally, the place is a virtual cornucopia, "in the midst of plenty," Bligh asserts, an Edenic existence is assured, for "they need not labor." I am only surprised that Bligh did not personally take up the opportunity of committing the act of mutiny against himself. The rewards seem so tantalizingly satisfying when compared with the mundane labor of ferrying breadfruit trees from Tahiti to the Caribbean.

Fletcher Christian offered readers the vision of life more abundant, free from physical restraints. His appeal must have been instantaneous, not only for Europeans, but also for Americans, in particular, who could see in the mutiny and Christian's escape a microcosm of two wars they had themselves fought, one for independence against the British, and the other in part for the liberty of slaves. Christian and his band represented small people battling against the might of the British Admiralty, Captain Bligh, and indeed the hostile world itself. Pitcairn, uninhabited and remote in an idyllic Pacific, would have seemed perfect, far removed from the rancor of social altercations.

Third, after Bligh and Barrow, two American expatriates living in Paris, Charles Nordhoff and James Norman Hall, composed a trilogy about the event. The first volume was published in 1932, and the second and third in 1934. Additionally, three American movies were made on the subject of the mutiny: One as early as 1935, with Charles Laughton, won an Oscar. Another followed in 1962, with Marlon Brando as Fletcher Christian, and yet another, "The

Bounty" as late as 1984. To this should be added the host of documentaries which constantly make the *Bounty* experience a trope for the Western experience of the entire Pacific—a place of total abandonment, where humans can pursue carefree lives, unencumbered by the demands of any hierarchy, and away from the prying eyes of the world

Barrow's work had emphasized Hall's connection with the South Pacific and the *Bounty,* and both connections enter into American awareness through a European intermediary. Hall had picked up an edition of Barrow's book while browsing in a Paris bookstore. He later visited the South Pacific and, with Nordhoff, composed their trilogy which continues to fascinate Americans.

In the Nordhoff/Hall reenactment, the entire account is visualized through the eyes of 1930s American authors living in Paris as expatriates. The narrative has an air of authenticity; for instance, there is a reference to Cook's charts, and Joseph Banks (who had sailed with Cook) is a character, although he seems a trifle too stiff and virtuous. Their account does not put Fletcher Christian in a bad light and sticks fairly closely (without Barrow's plodding approach) to the details of the case. It relates the mutiny, the men who were set adrift with Bligh, Fletcher Christian's later departure, and the fictionalized Roger Byam's stay in Tahiti—Byam is one of the sailors through whom the story is recounted. Nordhoff and Hall report in their text on what is important and relevant for Byam, much as if he were an American in the 1930s.

A strong homoerotic theme runs through the account. The farewell scene between Fletcher Christian and Byam almost resembles one between lovers. But what Nordhoff and Hall exploit are not only homoerotic concerns but misogynic issues as well. There is, for instance, more than a small degree of chauvinistic complacency in the following observation:

the Indians believe that Man was sky-descended, and Woman earth-born. Man *raa,* or holy; Woman *noa,* or common. Women were not permitted to set foot in the temples of the greater gods, and among all classes of society it was forbidden—unthinkable in fact—for the two sexes to sit down to a meal together. I was surprised to find that Hitihiti and I sat down alone to our dinner, and that no woman had a hand either in the cooking or in the serving of the meal.

We sat facing each other across the cloth of fresh green leaves. A pleasant breeze blew freely through the unwalled house, and the breakers on the distant reef made a murmuring undertone of sound. [18]

The ease, security, and suggestion of homosexual enticement have added another, yet older, sometimes misunderstood dimension to Pacific exploration. Hitihiti is the *taio*—a term we have already encountered—of Roger Byam, the narrator. But here, as elsewhere, the homosexual nature of the relationship is played up so that once more the veracity of the Pacific friendship pact eludes us. Additionally, the islanders even seem more than a little misanthropic.

Nordhoff and Hall also fall back on appeasing their readers. Cook is evoked by Hitihiti as a remembered god when Hitihiti first introduces himself to Byam. Constantly the scene of happy natives forever frolicking is introduced to us— such a lifestyle represents, after all, what we expect of "a people given over to levity, passionately devoted to pleasure, and incapable of those burdens of the white man."[19] This is more than a little disingenuous, for the clear implication is that "the white man" must therefore annex, control, rule, bring order. Indeed, apart from Hitihiti, most locals seem rather oafish and quite satisfied with this assigned role.

Apart from the sexual feelings that Byam has toward Hitihiti, there is another troubling side to Hitihiti's attraction—Hitihiti is different, odd and outer, like that really Noble Savage Oronooko; he speaks English, and he is taller and "lighter-skinned that the run of his countrymen."[20] Race, therefore, that supreme American preoccupation, is introduced as a measure of beauty, although grantedly it is in part a legacy from the first fictionalized encounters of Europeans in the New World.

Quite naturally the happy savages are addicted to sacrifice and cannibalism. Among such simple people, it is very easy for Byam to make "rapid progress" in acquiring Tahitian. Again, in this very unnatural of natural worlds, it is logical for Byam to marry one of the most beautiful women, amidst the barbaric splendor of Conradian Kurtz-like ancestral skulls and white sheets smeared with blood.[21]

I do not feel that any author must reproduce with the accuracy of a polaroid shot the people and landscape he encounters. I am merely attempting to show that some of the issues here, as with any earlier "nonfictitious" documentation, suffer more from the prejudices and needs of the observer than from the realities of the observed. Particularly because the *Bounty* mutiny is narrated several decades after it occurs, it is Americanized (much as earlier encounters had been Europeanized), and signs are still not understood, and at times are even intentionally misread. Byam lives among Noble Savages, but Nordhoff and Hall must not be faulted too much. This is their twentieth century perception of the Pacific based on earlier European versions.

LOVE IN THE TROPICS

J. H. Bernardin St.-Pierre's *Paul and Virginia* (1789),[22] written on the eve of the French Revolution, the romanticization of Wordsworth's "Lucy," Coleridge's Ethiopian maid and de Quincey's "Malay" in his essays, all dictated ways of visualizing the Orient. From Romanticism, Emerson and Thoreau invented their own "Orientalism"—a mixture of holy Indian writ, plus "Chinoiserie" and "Japonaiserie" or "Japonisme." In 1889, the Universal Exposition of Paris had validated the entire cultural mishmash: the worlds of the Pacific, "French" Indo China, India, and Africa were all equally tantalizing.[23] Effectively, Otherness was introduced to the 32 million visitors to the Fair as one delightful potpourri, and it was accredited as existence on the fringe, in the remote areas of the world, *da unten*, where all Others were allied in their own non-ness.

Interestingly, Paul and Virginia in the pastoral novel of the same name had continued Rousseau's *whitening* of the Noble Savage. Now they no longer just looked White, like Oroonoko or Rasselas but, in this instance, were actually French. I suppose that by the 1780s the intellectual and political freedom of the American and French revolutions was far more important than the mere physical freedom of Will, Crusoe, or the early Noble Savage. Paul and Virginia, of French parentage, grow up in Mauritius, then called the Île de France, which is presented as an idyllic setting where religious, social, and political egalitarianism is the norm.

There they can empathize with escaped slaves, the Maroons (a terrible word derived from the Spanish-American word *cimarrón,* meaning a runaway animal). But note that even these "innocent" little children are recognized for their intrinsic goodness and given a godlike reception. The chief of the Maroons acknowledges them as "good little white people" and then, on his orders, "four of the strongest negroes immediately formed a sort of litter with the branches of trees and llanas, in which having situated Paul and Virginia, they placed it upon their shoulders."[24] The interpretation is clear: even though (like Crusoe) they have joined the barbarians, they have, nevertheless, retained the civilizing elements of Europe which the savages themselves laud.

Paul and Virginia were not just Rousseau's creatures of Nature. They were stand-ins for the anti-slavery crusade, so that the representation of the Noble Savage (Indian, African, and so on) shifted focus: she/he now represented the "unfree" who could be liberated by enlightened and concerned European benevolence. The British, Wylie Sypher says, particularly would have loved the book's reference to Britain as the place where none could be enslaved. Add to this the intentional confusion of references to the "Indian Seas" and to Virginia "clad in the blue cloth of Bengal,"[25] and the world of Africa plus India, helps to bolster the illusory heterogeneity of the accepted and fanciful globalism of the time.

THE ORIENT COMES HOME

Since there was thought to exist some binding commonality among the inhabitants of "beyond," fairs and expositions were to import this paradoxical world to the general public of Europe and America. Frederick Douglass had objected to Black exclusion at the Chicago World's Fair of 1893 by decrying the fact that this was because "we are outside of the church and largely outside of the state."[26] Even as Douglass decried *exclusion* on the basis of difference, there continued to exist *inclusion* on the grounds of supposed similarity. From the Universal Exposition of Paris in 1889, where the true showpiece was the Eiffel Tower, through the Chicago World's Fair of 1893, the Paris exposition of 1900 (where French sculptor Auguste Rodin had his own pavilion containing 150 of his sculptures and drawings), and the New York World's Fair of 1939 and 1940, this much is evident: sponsors elevate the West and its accomplishments and add a cosmopolitan mixture of "Third World" Otherness almost as an afterthought, certainly as a mere exotic backdrop.

At the 1893 Chicago World's Fair, despite Douglass's complaint, the Other was resplendent in all its homogeneous splendor, as represented by India, China, Dahomey (lately "subdued with such great difficulty by France"), Turkey (represented as both a "building" and a "village"), and Egypt. There on "A Street in Cairo," an attraction that had been very popular in Paris, were available "camel and donkey rides, bazaars—and girls who did the *danse du ventre*. The most famous of them [the dancers] was 'Little Egypt'. . . and it is with her that we associate a tune that has become part and parcel of the American consciousness, the 'hootchy-cootchy' dance."[27] The Other had been popularized into a genre, miniaturized into a comical sameness that would become its hallmark—a construct, despite its unreality, that hereafter would be eternally affixed on the non-European world.

Exhibitions and fairs did not invent this supposed sameness, but certainly popularized accepted concepts whereby the non-European, non-Western world would be seen as quaint and odd, but certainly recognizable. By extending and validating these stereotypes of the non-European world, popular expositions, with government support and approval, not only gave authenticity to the symbols, but also officially accorded the representations a degree of validity and popular acceptance which travel books and novels had not been able to achieve.

Consider, for example, the limited appeal of Wordsworthian Romanticism, or its American counterpart, partly noted in Transcendentalism. Readership would have been restricted both through illiteracy, and the genre of the poem or the essay, so that even as Wordsworth inveighed in poetry against the city ways that brought his poor Michael to a bad end, not everyone (certainly not his own contemporary John Clare, who was an actual farmer and poet) could have empathized. To visualize Michael as "primitive" or to see the animal spirits of the young boy in "Tintern Abbey" as apart from the civilized world is, to my mind, a little strained. Michael is an English farmer; the young boy is the older Wordsworth recalling his youth. There are certainly elements of a yearning for "freedom" in the Romantics, but liberty associates itself more with the urban aspirations of the American and French revolutions than with vague conceptualizations of a distant savage.

Coleridge is little different in "The Rime of the Ancient Mariner." The narrator in reality does venture out beyond the familiar, precisely because the poem begins and ends on the sure footing of Home. Thus, we are confident that his adventures among strange and different people (truly other worldly), will bring the mariner safely back. And, despite the fictionalized confusion of "Kubla Khan," with its elaborate mazelike river and (almost in the same breath) the nubile Ethiopian maid, we should not be unduly harsh. Coleridge's reading of Samuel Purchas, successor to Richard Hakluyt (and both fervent propagators of English maritime accomplishments and subsequent imperial rights), helped with the blending of heterogeneous Others into single monolithic oddities.[28]

Coleridge's "Kubla Khan" is therefore a map of the era in that (whatever may have been the truth of Coleridge's poem having been interrupted by a visitor from Porlock) the prevailing confusion of images represents a reflection of the time. Likewise, when Ralph Waldo Emerson and Henry David Thoreau threw Indian and Chinese theology, Free Religion, communitarian experiments at Brook Farm and Fruitlands, and abolitionism into the same mix, such a variety represented the cultural plethora of geographical odds and ends that had been passed on from Europe.[29] This is what the expositions and fairs inherited and popularized.

I certainly do not wish to assert in any absolute sense that the Romantics on both sides of the Atlantic did not understand the true boundaries of the real world outside their own, but I should like to suggest that in their conceptualization, more so their evocation of it, they continued to introduce a multiplicity of unconnected ideas and beliefs, associated more with them and their needs than those of the foreign societies toward which they turned. And if their conceptualizations and evocations sounded familiar, it was because they were replicating similar European endeavors, as Europeans also attempted to play up their own external world.

One should not expect to find too great an ethnic difference, therefore, between the Odd Hindus who inform Emerson's "Illusions," the freed Outer Blacks in his "Boston Hymn," or the ultimate, Uttermost nomads who inhabit his "Hamatreya," "Saadi," and "Maia." Similarly, Thoreau's pro- and anti-Abolitionist stances, his nature poem "To the Maiden in the East" (partly about a personal experience of unfulfilled love), and his interest in the "Orient" (mainly in Indian theology) all exhibit the same reductionism to rather elemental factors. Lost in such a creations is any realistic fidelity to the realm of fact. Instead, Romantic writers conjure up an all-purpose evocation of a Thinking Man's Other that will presumably act as a foil to the innumerable problems of Europe and the United States. Frederick Ives Carpenter categorically states that Emerson largely disagreed with Islam,[30] and Edward Said seems to feel that even though American Transcendentalists often associated their way of thinking with the Orient, yet "there was no deeply invested tradition of Orientalism [in the United States], and consequently in the United States knowledge of the Orient never passed through the reforming and reticulating and reconstructing processes that it went through in Europe."[31] I suspect that this was in part due to the same prejudicial forces that made the Noble Negro into "nigger," the Noble Indian into "injun," and the "Oriental," into the "heathen Chinee/Chinaman." For example, rampant anti-Chinese feeling had contributed largely to U.S. failure to accept a less European Oriental, and to perceive and recognize the true reality present in the United States itself at the time. The Chinese Exclusion Acts from 1882 officially ended Chinese immigration to the United States for twenty years.[32] This was at the domestic level. In foreign affairs, the new hegemonic thrust of the United States officially put forward an "Open Door" policy from before 1900 to guarantee its commercial trading interests, and permit the United States free access to Chinese markets. At home, in the United States, the Chinese were excluded; abroad, in China, the United States was included. One wonders to what extent the relationship has altered today, even as China is constantly threatened with "favored" nation status, and once more, even as Hong Kong recedes, the Taiwan problem looms large.

13

PARADISE CONQUERED

In the works of Herman Melville, Mark Twain, Robert Louis Stevenson and Henry Adams, the "Orient" came to be realized by the authors' very presence in, and writings about, the South Pacific. Recall that this was the period that marked the beginning of American expansionism, and while I do not wish to imply that they were mere apologists for Empire, I do insist that they saw themselves as inheritors of the European legacy of hegemony. In 1841, Melville had shipped out on a whaler; he deserted and spent a month in the Marquesas, later the raw material of *Typee* (1846). In 1842, he lived in Tahiti, the experiences there later giving rise to *Omoo* (1847), a kind of sequel to *Typee*. Perhaps his best work is *Moby-Dick* (1851); by the time he wrote it, he had purged himself of most of the European-derived romanticism of the islands.

MELVILLE'S WATERY PLACES

In *Typee,* Melville takes the predictable stance of relating life as idyllic among a faraway people, the supposedly savage Taipis of the Marquesas. The novel's success was guaranteed: cannibals existed in Eden. Melville described these ever-present carnivores with their robust appetite for human flesh, although later in his life he insisted on believing that he had existed in the last Eden of the world. In *Typee*, all the other familiar symbols that Europe had placed in far-off places were present: the beauty of the Marquesas, both landscape and people, side by side with the terror that existed there. Melville writes that "the word 'Typee' in the Marquesa dialect signifies a lover of human flesh." But these are a people who "retain their original primitive character, remaining very nearly in the same state of nature in which they were first beheld by white men."[1] Clearly, we are back in the well-mapped world of Rousseau, which Paul Gauguin would inherit in the late nineteenth and early twentieth century. In Melville's construction of the Marquesas any real personal experience is subsumed beneath European legendary concoctions.

Not unnaturally, at the center of the description of lush landscape and beautiful people is situated the exquisite Fayaway, whose name suggests the personification of all that is faraway, remote, inacessible, perhaps even a trifle forbidding. Melville describes her in this manner:

Her free pliant figure was the very perfection of female grace and beauty. Her complexion was a rich and mantling olive, and when watching the glow upon her cheeks I could almost swear that beneath the transparent medium there lurked the blushes of a faint vermilion. The face of the girl was a rounded oval, and each feature so perfectly formed as the heart or imagination of man could desire. Her full lips, when parted with a smile, disclosed teeth of a dazzling whiteness. [2]

The technicolored maiden almost seems ill, but whether he realized it or not, Melville was playing the race card. In mid-nineteenth-century America, with slavery still rampant and "miscegenation" illegal in many states, the coupling of Fayaway and the young American had an obvious power to titillate. Interestingly enough, she bears a tattoo mark, and one wonders if this is not Melville's way of having his hero branded also through the sex act as a temporary, honorary, "native" Other.

On the subject of "taboo," Melville concludes that, although there were religious ceremonies and "I saw everything, but could comprehend nothing," yet "I am inclined to believe that the islanders in the Pacific have no fixed and definite ideas whatever on the subject of religion." The real Melville had spent but a few weeks in the Marquesas, and it seems strange that he could come to such a conclusion, were it not for the presuppositions that previous European texts had implanted. Earlier on, there is a different note, when he dispenses with his European guides. For instance, just before he describes the "Taboo Groves" where, although he represents that "the idols were quite as harmless as any other logs of wood," he yet infers that "however ignorant man may be, he still feels within him his immortal spirit yearning after the unknown future."[3] Yet later on, when the place is recalled in a poem "To Ned," the persistent European images remain there. Melville alludes in this poem (dedicated to his former companion, Toby Greene) to the "Pantheistic Ports," "Authentic Edens in a Pagan Sea," "primeval balm," and a Paradise[4] they had together shared as younger men.

It mattered little what had *actually* existed in the Marquesas; it had already been constructed for writers and, indeed, visualized in a specific way. Therefore, when D. H. Lawrence later wrote on Melville in his *Studies in Classic American*

Literature, he waxed quite eloquent, falling back on Wordsworth as he conjured up Melville's Pacific:

So he finds himself in the middle of the Pacific. Truly over a horizon. In another world. In another epoch. Back, far back, in the days of palm trees and lizards and stone implements. The sunny stone age.

Samoa, Tahiti, Rarotonga, Nukuheva: the very names are a sleep and a forgetting. The sleep-forgotten past magnificence of human history. "Trailing clouds of glory."

Lawrence argues that Melville yearned for "Home and Mother" (Lawrence's words), but could never really reclaim either. The South Seas, the nostalgia for the faraway, remains only that, Lawrence asserts. You may, Lawrence suggests with his typical Fascist exuberance, "Turn to your first negro," but, in reality, "we can't go back." Lawrence suggests (at least here) that a dash of the Primitive is good for the White man's soul and body, but only in small doses, once he understands that the Female Other is equally savage "with her knotted hair and her dark, inchoate, slightly sardonic eyes [with] soft warm flesh, like warm mud . . . *Noli me tangere.*"[5]

Lawrence's verdict on *Omoo* is virtually the same. He argues that Melville cared too much about European culture and civilization to abide the idea of becoming a renegade. Lawrence expounds, "He always cared. He always cared enough to hate missionaries, and to be touched by a real act of kindness." Then Lawrence is back on to the racial theme: "When he [Melville] saw a white man really 'gone savage,' a white man with a blue shark tattooed over his brow, gone over to the savages, then Herman's whole being revolted. He couldn't bear it."[6] How could Lawrence possibly have known this?

True enough, there is an assumption in both *Typee* and *Omoo* that Home lies at the center, but the point about the novels is that the White characters merge with the locals during the time that they remain on the islands. In other words, artificial though it may be, there is a temporary breakdown of the One/Other relationship. Thus, in *Omoo,* in a Tahiti setting, the reader can no longer be sure. The narrator, Nukuheva, is no East Coast American, and he is portrayed with a different voice, on alien shores and amidst people scarcely recognizable. The action resembles that of *Moby-Dick*, which, to my way of thinking, is about the ultimate demise of a very *sane* and purposeful Captain Ahab, as well as the ethnic global microcosm he already controls on board. *Moby-Dick* is a novel of attempted Conquest, world conquest, over the ubiquitous whale of a world.

Melville's *Moby-Dick* utilizes the Pacific as mere background in order to relate Captain Ahab's relentless pursuit of the whale/world. The *Pequod* is not so much made up of the "world," as it is comprised of every "native" who had ever guided or sailed on European ships. But these Others are often presented in monstrous ways; for instance, through Ishmael's eyes, Queequeg's oddities are frightening, particularly his general appearance, his tattoo, his one leftover shrunken human head, which he is attempting to peddle, and his macabre wish to have his coffin made. Various different Others add to the complement of the crew—Tashtego, an Indian; Daggoo, an African; Fedallah, a Parsi; and Pip, the young African American cabin boy—all reconstructions of a menacing miniworld completely under Ahab's power and control.

Tashtego's appearance—his eyes are "Oriental in their largeness" —hints at the origin of Native Americans, as well as their role in America itself, for he was "an inheritor of the unvitiated blood of those proud warrior hunters." Daggoo is described as "a gigantic, coal-black negro-savage, with a lion-like tread."[7] Between Tashtego and Daggoo there is the Oriental/African link we noted before. They are "noble," they are "savage," and, along with Queequeg, they constitute a trio of degrees of Otherness. Tashtego is the Odd, Daggoo represents the Outer, and Queequeg stands for the Uttermost forms of human degredation.

This is meant to contrast sharply with the White officers, American born, who are the supervisors of the enterprise, as they were in charge of most other activities. Ishmael himself comments:

As for the residue of the Pequod's company, be it said, that at the present day not one in two of the many thousand men before the mast employed in the American whale fishery, are Americans born, though pretty nearly all the officers are. Herein it is the same with the American whale fishery as with the American army and military merchant navies, and the engineering forces employed in the construction of the American Canals and Railroads. The same, I say, because in all these cases the native American [White American male] literally provides the brains, the rest of the world as generously supplying the muscles.[8]

For Ishmael, this is a very ordered world, recognizable and representative as it existed in 1851, secure under the control and guidance of a wise male patriarchy.

White Americans were moving ever westward, following the Gold Rush of 1849, and the country was "expanding" thanks to the credo of Manifest Destiny and the creation of "Indian Territory." Overseas, Empire held full sway; the British, French, Portuguese, Spaniards, Belgians, Germans, and Dutch were in the process of carving up the world into their own spheres of influence at the famous Berlin Conference. By 1890, Alfred T. Mahan, in *The Influence of Sea Power Upon History*, would urge the United States to build a navy and assume its destiny as a global power.

Token representatives of the Other world merely assist the ship of state, the *Pequod*, embark on its global mission from the United States, across the Atlantic, round Africa, and into the Pacific, as it encompasses the world. The appearance of the Columbus/Crusoe figure Ahab is delayed until the twenty-seventh chapter. Ishmael sees him as godlike and legendary with

no sign of common bodily illness about him. He looked like a man cut away from the stake, when the fire has overrunningly wasted all the limbs without consuming them, or taking away one particle from their compacted aged robustness. His whole high, broad form, seemed made of solid bronze, and shaped in an unalterable mould.

True, he is a "moody striken Ahab," but Christlike with, "a crucifixion in his face," and because all his officers understand his awesomeness "by their minutest gestures and expressions, they plainly showed the uneasy, if not painful, consciousness of being under a troubled master-eye."[9]

Ishmael only faintly understands that this is no ordinary whaling voyage, but one of Conquest, to discover and subdue one of the last places in the world. There is an early hint that this might well be one of "the longest of all voyages now or ever made by man." And, in the process, we note how Captain Ahab assumes the role of a kind of god-king, with a macabre ability to manipulate and terrorize people through speech:

he sometimes masked himself; incidentally making use of them for other and more private ends than they were legitimately intended to subserve. That certain sultanism of his brain, which had otherwise in good degree remained unmanifested; through those forms that same sultanism became incarnate in an irresistible dictatorship.

It is, Ishmael reasons, because of this "incarnate" "sultanism" that "God's true prince of the Empire" becomes known. And although Ishmael asserts that "this episode touching Emperors and Kings . . . [has nothing] to do with a poor old whale-hunter like him,"[10] the point is richly evident. Ahab is the resuscitated god of the travel narrative, a latter-day Cook bent on world domination, even though Ishmael pretends to a certain coyness about this knowledge.

Melville continues the depiction of Ahab as deity and leader—a construction that Ishmael in the earlier chapel scene had refused to admit openly. But presently Ahab passes round a measure in communion with his crew, appointing three of them as his "three pagan kinsmen,"[11] rather like some unholy Trinity. And, as they swear death to Moby-Dick, they are indeed vowing to use all might to crush any force that seeks to withstand them. This demonstrates neither an idealism nor a faith which Starbuck, Ahab's first mate, is quick to assert that he does not share.

Ahab cannot defeat his whale. He is no knight, no crusader, but a "grey-headed, ungodly old man; chasing with curses Job's whale round the world." The reference here takes us back to Father Mapple's sermon about Jonah, who was saved at a time of deepest despair because he was humble and believing, unlike Ahab. The futile nature of Empire is noted by Ishmael in the chapter on the albatross, for even as Ahab shouts "keep her off round the world," Ishmael muses: "Round the world! There is much in that sound to inspire proud feelings; but where does all that circumnavigation conduct? Only through numberless perils to the very point whence we started." There is no point to the journey, for the very monsters we pursue "either lead us on in barren mazes or midway leave us whelmed."[12] Ishmael understands this; only he accomplishes a little by surviving.

Perhaps the world cannot be possessed, or perhaps Ahab/Melville has set himself too tremendous a task. For even when Melville reduces the globe to the microcosm of the *Pequod*, he is often too conscious of the crew's otherness to humanize them. One particular example is that little is done with Tashtego's Indianness. When, in chapter 22, an entire section is given to him, it is merely for him to mutter, as any savage might, the monosyllables "Um, um, um," and go on to describe his fear of thunder and his love of rum.

Pip is also not really developed until toward the end of the novel, and then only in relationship to Ahab. Earlier on, he had appeared merely full of youthful zeal and incomprehension as he tried to play his musical instrument to what was presumably a dying Queequeg. But by Chapter 125, in response to his own loneliness, Ahab moves Pip into his cabin, an act and proclivity well in keeping with the narratives of the soujourners thus far examined. Melville takes the occasion here, in the South Pacific (but, as I am arguing, it could be anywhere), to deal with that peculiar American problem—race. Pip cries out that he wants to "Rivet these two hands together, the black one with the white, for I will not let this go," and Ahab responds, "Come then to my cabin . . . Come! I feel prouder leading thee by thy black hand, than though I grasped an Emperor's!" But here again, Pip is mishandled by Melville, for there is no ostensible reason for such a sentiment—we have simply not been prepared for this emotional outburst. In a scene a few chapters later, when Ahab hints at his impending end, their exchange is typical of a mismatched relationship. Ahab can only proffer Pip the chance to play at captain, "Do thou abide below here, where they shall serve thee, as if thou wert the captain." In turn, Pip can only increase his servant's role as tool and appendage, as "another screw." He entreats Ahab, "do you but use poor me for your one lost leg; only tread upon me, sir, I ask no more, so I remain a part of ye."[13] The imagery suggests a Black longing for debasement.

In the Pacific, the crew on the *Pequod* remain apart from the seascape, existing in a vacuum, having brought with them American versions of the problems of the world. Perhaps, in the final analysis, Moby-Dick wins and most of the crew die because none of them realized that the battle they sought was the one deep within each person's heart, fought alone with all polarities reconciled. Ishmael had pursued a supreme paradox, "the watery part of the world," where nothing was assured. He had found himself eventually, after everyone else had died, "gaining that vital centre" floating through a shark-infested sea on a "coffin life-buoy."[14] At that moment, some of the contradictions seem realized—perhaps Ishmael managed to achieve a measure of self-conquest, even as he floated at the mercy of the elements, an orphan, alone, awaiting the miracle of a rescue beyond his control.

At the center of Melville's novel was Ahab, who had sought to conquer the whale, the whole world. More importantly, the "native," whether noble or savage, had been effectively rendered neutral. One may argue that this process began with the first European incursions, when Dampier, Cook, and the other "discoverers" effectively, through the written script in English, had displaced the "native" oral word. At the center of the narration now was the White male with his *fact of "civilization"* and his absurd, often incomprehensible, *fiction of "possession,"* acts which Dening calls "cultural sets of possession rituals, as sods were turned, trees carved, flags raised, crowns toasted and blessed, bottles buried, sand thrown." As Dening asserts (and this is what the new American "discoverers" continued in their imaginative accounts):

those now historicized places were mapped in all the complex dimensions of that word—set in relation to some center-point, related to some model of diplomacy, military strategy or economic system, abstracted from the praxis of travelling, of wind and water, into some simplified model of a world encompased so that men of power or men craving power could see crossroads, high-ways, toll-stations on the ocean. All this possessing, naming, mapping was done with little or no reference to those possessed named or mapped.[15]

BRITISH VERSIONS

It little mattered what those who were being described felt or thought. Let me cite two examples outside the United States to demonstrate how the central, controling idea of fixed homogeneity flourished despite place. One excellent example is from Thomas de Quincey's *Confessions of an English Opium-Eater* (1821). He relates the visit of what I shall term a "real" Malay to his cottage: in his "turban and loose trousers of dingy white," his "sallow and bilious skin" contrasted with "the beautiful English face" of de Quincey's maid, who was quite startled to see him. Later, under the influence of de Quincey's opium stupor, an "imaginary" Malay is bred: he is "a fearful enemy, the seat of awful images and associations," a presence that de Quincey associates with "Southern Asia, in general," with the "capricious superstitions of Africa, or of savage tribes elsewhere," with "Asiatic things," China, and "Oriental imagery" on the whole. But the "imaginary" Malay (so much like the "real") also conjures up the Crusoe/Cook image of the White male as god: "I was the idol, I was the priest; I was worshipped; I was sacrificed."[16]

John Barrell in *The Infection of Thomas de Quincey* has pointed out the possible implications of de Quincey's encounter with the "real" Malay. During the visit, de Quincey had given the Malay an enormous amount of opium, which the Malay had apparently ingested in one mouthful. De Quincey cheerfully assures us that he had expected the man to die from this, and had indeed awaited news of his demise. Barrell feels that the incident points to something much larger, namely that de Quincey saw the Malay as a threat, as someone from whom he needed protection, and from whom he needed to safeguard the members of his household. But there is an even greater issue, Barrell contends, whereby the Malay as Ultimate Other, the Uttermost, could well exhibit emotions beyond the Malay's control and "run amock," or go uncontrollably mad and attempt to commit murder. They were known for this and, therefore, de Quincey's gesture of trying to kill the Malay is almost humanitarian. As Barrell suggests:

De Quincey's gift of opium was to be read as a (more or less symbolic) attempt to procure the death of the Malay so as to prevent him killing the little child [in de Quincey's house]. This interest in large-scale and more or less indiscriminate revenge, however, puts a large question mark against either de Quincey's motives or his choice of toxin. Malays in the eighteenth and early nineteenth century had a 'character' for violence; they were known by all East India hands as the most terrifying orientals of all.[17]

Therefore, for the Malay the enormous burden of being so totally removed, Kunlun fashion, from de Quincey's English norms carried with it the imposition of a heavy burden. The irrational qualities which the "real" Malay possessed were transferred to the "imaginary" Malay who does run amuck. The Malay, representing the disorder from without, has to be contained by whatever means, and if in the process he is destroyed, then this becomes the adage by which the colonial world has to be managed. De Quincey's Malay, the Uttermost Other, must not be allowed to threaten order, as apparently his mere appearance did. Out of the subconscious of the British mind, the need for instant rectification comes about, so that "balance," actually ethnocentric certainty, is maintained. Therefore, the "real" and the "imaginary" are actually the same—composite creations, not so much of an excess of opium, but of the multifarious associations which the East conjured up for Europe.

A second instance may be found in John Stuart Mill. Much as de Quincey could develop his ideas of the "Orient" independent of fact, John Stuart Mill saw little relationship between his ideas on liberty or women's rights and his experience in India House. Surely the wellknown dictum of Jeremy Bentham, who influenced him enormously, and who wrote on the need for the greatest happiness for the greatest number, ought to have impacted on Mill's views concerning colonial India. Indeed, in a recent review, Bhiku Parekle found Mill's sojourn in India House in the 1850s almost irrelevant, rendering Mill "so insensitive to Indian feelings, aspirations and modes of thought that he was unable to grasp the moral problems raised during his time there."[18]

For both de Quincey and Mill, the actuality of the East was irrelevant to their preoccupations. The East was phantomlike, wanting tactility. Whatever was proclaimed must be done outside the irrelevance of the Orient Other, for it lacked (as they saw it) the necessary human dimension necessary to make it relatable to them as a real focal point for their own interests. Malaya and India were merely names possessing little or no inherent reality, and even for the most libertarian, had no relevance for writers concerned with the near, relevant, and meaningful.

THE WORLD ACCORDING TO MARK TWAIN (SAMUEL CLEMENS)

Since they were in search of their own version of Paradise, few Americans or Europeans cared about the role and subsequent fall of the monarchy in Hawaii, followed bu U.S. "annexation." When Samuel Clemens first arrived in Hawaii in 1866, he was more interested in the "adventures" of those Americans who had suffered misfortunes. For instance, he chronicled the story of Captain Josiah Mitchell and his crew of fourteen who had limped into Hawaii after their ship had burned. The story was first published in the Sacramento *Union* of July 21, 1866, and later rewritten as two separate pieces: "Forty-three Days in an Open Boat," in *Harper's* of December 1866, and "My Debut as a Literary Person" in *The Man That Corrupted Hadleyburg and Other Stories and Sketches* (1900).[19] Therefore, quite independent of whatever Hawaii may or may not have been, Clemens, like any other "European" writer, simply claims it, converting all action to what existed within his own controlling purview.

As Clemens travels the world, he finds most foreign things ironical, funny, or comical, although I grant he is adamantly opposed to colonialism. He writes about how, "in our day land-robbery, claim-jumping, is become a European governmental frenzy. Some have been hard at it in the borders of China, in Burma, in Siam, and the islands of the sea; and all have been at it in Africa." Fortunately, Clemens is also aware that he comes upon the world "second-hand" as "a thing which you fortunately did not think of or it might have made you doubtful of what you imagined were your own." [20] He says this about the Taj Mahal, as he attempts to strip away the accumulation of mythologies that have been applied by the West.

At times Clemens can be very, very reverential and honest; a good example is to be found in his description of the holy Hindu festival of Kumbh Mela at Allahabad on the Ganges. Humbly, he can often plead his own inability as outsider to comprehend the insider:

Reverence for one's own sacred thing—parents, religion, flag, laws, and respect for one's own beliefs—these are feelings which we cannot even help . . . But the reverence which is difficult, and which has personal merit in it, is the respect you pay, without compulsion, to the political or religious attitude of a man whose beliefs are not yours.[21]

This, he argues, is the more difficult and the truly humbling, particularly because it is so difficult. This is not something that D. H. Lawrence bothered to understand when he considered Melville.

Twain's *Roughing It* (1872) has recently been made available in a new edition.[22] Stephen Fender, in a 1994 review, claims that what distinguishes Twain, at his most cynical, from his European counterparts, is that "Even the most confident aspirations for the American future . . . were constructed in contradiction to Europe."[23] And yet, the memories of old Europe are there in the description of journeying once again to "a Paradise which I had been longing all those years to see again," a place where the king is described as "a remarkable man for a savage," and where "savages are eager to learn from the white man any new way to kill each other, but it is not their habit to seize with avidity and apply with energy the larger and nobler ideas which he offers them."[24] Therefore, despite his anti-colonialist leanings, which I think are personally and deeply felt, an element of Eurocentrism constantly seems to betray a personal bias in Clemens. At least he admits to prejudice and does not attempt to pawn it off as enlightened experience through travel.

Perhaps Blacks in South Africa come off worse for one reason only: Twain thinks he knows them—they are merely copies of African Americans or, as he says in one context, exactly "like the negroes of our Southern States." He then establishes his supposed authenticity to judge the Other and describes them: "round faces, flat noses, good-natured, and easy laughers." Thus a whole people are dismissed as strange, odd, well meaning, but empty-headed. In yet another instance, he compares them with Blacks whom, "I had seen so often at home." Twain then makes fun of the women's apparel as a "showy mixture of assorted colors." Indeed, he goes further, in suggesting that *his* fantasy is both correct and appropriate: South African Blacks are not just *like* but indeed *are* "precise counterparts of our American Blacks." What spoils the mirage are the missionary-inspired clothes of South African Blacks, who, when they appear thus clad, would "spoil it all, making the thing a grating discord, half African and half American."[25] There is little about the horrendous condition in which they lived under Afrikaaner and British control, with the controls of apartheid in the making, although not yet officially sanctioned by law.

HENRY ADAMS VISITS ROBERT LOUIS STEVENSON

By 1894, Robert Louis Stevenson was dead and the era of romantic evocations of the East was almost ending. Strangely, for someone who had lived in Samoa with his family since 1888, there is little in his published work that comes over as positively beautiful or even negatively "exotic," and we should recall that even the marooned pirate Ben Gunn, in *Treasure Island* (1883), was visualized through Defoe's eyes, long before Stevenson had gone to the South Pacific.

Stevenson's correspondence has been collected in *The Letters.*[26] Most recently the volumes which relate to Stevenson's Pacific home have been published,

and they help convey something of the urgency he felt about the rights of indigenous people, and how he began to see Yailima, the village in Samoa where he
lived, as home. This new centering is intriguing, if only because for the first
time it seems that a European (grantedly one who had made a profession out of
writing adventure stories about the remote) could look with cool assurance at the
local. Furthermore, Stevenson, following his well-known visit to Father Dami-
en, who had died in 1889, took up Fr Damien's cause and that of the leper colony at Molokai. But all this refocusing took time. Earlier on, for instance, *In the
South Seas* (1890),[27] Stevenson's sketch of King Tembinoka of Apemama, is
devoid of any empathy. It is a laughable portrait of a corpulent scoundrel. Stevenson has the king use pidgin to make him seem utterly foolish. Irony is particularly vicious, especially when the "joke" is lost on the "jokester," when Stevenson's humor is private, solely meant for consumption in Britain. The Other
merely represents the butt of the joke.

Of course, Britain was about the very serious business of Empire. American
writers were really not expected to be spokespersons for government policy,
drawn as they were from the hurly-burly, ragtag arenas of ordinary folk. Not
unnaturally, even as inveterate a traveler as Henry Adams, who met Stevenson in
1890, would be expected to see the world with less laconic irony and distaste
than Stevenson had expressed. Between 1890 and 1891, Henry Adams had
traveled with a friend to Hawaii, Samoa, Tahiti, Fiji, Australia and the then
Dutch East Indies. In Adam's letters, the "natives" are not funny, but courteous
and polite, friendly and charming. Naturally, behind every door lurks a beautiful
damsel, in this case Princess Wakea and her sister Siva. But I wonder, does he
detect something of his own removed presence when he suggests that a woman
named Faaiuro was probably Fayaway? Is Adams hinting that his "true" account
produces a larger than life replica of a "fictionalized" Melville? That, perhaps, it
is impossible to visualize the "reality" of place without falling back on the
"fable"? And so, like Clemens, is he admitting to a jaundiced view?

When Adams met Stevenson on October 16, 1890, he was far less generous
to Stevenson than to the locals. Adams wrote that the hut in which Stevenson
lived was dirty and that Stevenson himself looked ill (he was). Adams admired
Stevenson's knowledge of the islands, but he was cautious about Stevenson's
conclusion that Tahitians were finer people than Samoans. Their meeting is of
particular interest, especially as one was a representative of New World
aristocracy and the other a scion of the English meritocracy, both men of letters.
They stood on Stevenson's balcony together observing the scenery below, both
strangers looking out at the incomprehended.

Certainly, at this point, roles might have changed. Adams who had argued that the dynamo at the 1900 World's Fair was the symbol of the twentieth century, must have visualized what he saw in terms of the landscape below, as submitting itself inevitably to the power of machine—the European machine, that had already begun to convert the islands into sugar plantations. On the other hand, Stevenson, old world scion or not, was a popular novelist who could afford a certain liberalism and honesty, as witnessed in his later South Sea novellas *The Beach of Falesá* (1893) and (with his stepson) *The Ebb Tide* (1894), both of which were condemnatory of European imperialism. Indeed, the former was considered too radical for Stevenson's Victorian public and was only published in full book form in 1984.

Adams was a tourist, Stevenson a resident. But Stevenson had come to the South Pacific via the New World. And even though, for Stevenson, there were causes he could champion, and for Adams, a stargazer's paradise he could later convert into journalistic material, both men saw the area in the same way. For both of them the Pacific was a refuge. Adams had gone there, following his wife's suicide, and his disenchantment with life in America. He would return again to the South Pacific, and then attempt such fictions as *Marau Taaroa, Last Queen of Tahiti* (1893), which was intended to bring home to the American public the life of Queen Liliuokalani and the official annexation of Hawaii on February 1 of the year of the book's publication.

Stevenson's poor health had likewise driven him round the world, from Europe to America, and finally, to Samoa where he purchased his estate,Valima. More than Adams, Stevenson became incensed at the iniquities that European missionaries and administrators had introduced. He was very active, on Polynesian behalf, as he championed the cause of colonial exploitation. Stevenson might have felt freer to do this, since his letters to *The Times* in London were clearly intended to strike a blow against "Yankee" imperialism. But at least he spoke up, unlike de Quincey and Mill. Perhaps, as a Scotsman, he may also have understood more deeply and intrinsically the horrific nature of the colonial agent as a kind of official ponce.

In their letters and novels, both Adams and Stevenson had to relate the South Pacific in terms of its pathetic condition, in order to elicit the sympathetic response they both sought. The problem with this is that, however noble the intentions of the authors, their agendas forced them into a degree of misrepresentation, even of intentionally constructing the pitiful, if they hoped to achieve any empathy. Therefore, once more the indigenous people are positioned, differently it is true and detached, it is true, to a much greater degree of the romanticism of the past, but still relegated to acting out postures that could not possibly hope to confer on them any holistic reality.

GAUGUIN: PLAYING THE SAVAGE

Before Paul Gauguin embarked for Tahiti, the landscape of the Pacific had already been prepared. Gauguin himself was an artist in search of the "primitive," for, although born in Paris, he was of French/Peruvian "creole" stock. Perhaps, in a way, this had already demarcated his Otherness. A recent exhibition at the Indianapolis Museum of Art, "Gauguin and the School of Pont-Aven," demonstrated his early search for the "primitives"in Pont-Aven, a small Breton village.[28] This was during the late 1880s. Later, he would seek further, in Martinique in 1887, for the sensuous, the primitive, the "natural" life. Finally, from 1891 to 1893 and from 1895 and1901, he lived in Tahiti, and he moved to the Marquesas in 1901, and died there in 1903.

Noa Noa (1920),[29] probably written by Gauguin's onetime friend, Charles Morice, attempts to strip away the legend of the haunted man in search of Paradise. Gauguin is a European artist responding to European urges—as he puts it, "to get away from the European centre." Once he arrives in Tahiti, he begins to "read" the European beliefs into the landscape, "a whole Oriental vocabulary." The act is Crusoesque all over again; on the one hand, he observes of the Tahitians: "These black people, these cannibal teeth." On the other, he reverses the norm of the mode, admitting with some relish, "I was the savage."[30]

Again the land of *Noa Noa* is one of abandonment, of naked people, carefree days, forbidden homoeroticism:

We went naked, both of us, except for the loincloth, and axe in hand, crossing the river many a time . . .—Complete silence,—only the noise of water crying against rock, monotonous as the silence. And two we certainly were, two friends, he a quite young man and I almost an old man in body and soul, in civilized vices: in lost illusions. His lithe animal body had graceful contours, he walked in front of me sexless.[31]

Gauguin's young companion is the resuscitation of Oroonoko/Friday. Are we not also reminded of Nordhoff and Hall's Byam and Hitihiti? The Noble Savage female seems now specially prescribed as medication to cure the problems of the older European male seeking the exotic. Now Gauguin went one step further to a stage of total abandonment, a script without rules. The sight of the young man ahead of him has the effect of instantaneous conversion: "Savages both of us,"

Gauguin exults.

After they had felled a tree, Gauguin felt "the pleasure of sating one's brutality and of destroying something . . . I returned at peace, feeling myself thencefoward a different man, a Maori."[32] Personally, I do not understand this. What is clearly wrong with the image is that there is an assumption that brutality accompanied by liberal amounts of blood make a Maori, a savage, and that the European merely has to playact in order to revert and claim the status. We recall Lawrence's caveat almost with a degree of relief now—the return to the "savage" state is hardly possible.

After a young boy, *Noa Noa* seems to ask, what next? The answer is soon forthcoming, for after a few preliminary questions, matters are sealed and a young girl of thirteen, having laid out some food for him, "enchanted me and scared me: what was going on in her soul?" He again confesses, "I, nearly an old man"—he was forty three. Soon he marries Tehamana, who not too long after is giving him detailed instructions on how he should "beat me, strike me hard."[33] She was presumably still thirteen.

Up till now we can definitely affirm that the Pacific is one of the most accomodating places on earth: It stands for anything a *man*'s heart desires; it becomes anything—man, woman, child. It is Eden before the Fall, Paradise after death. It is every man's soft porn, disguised as reality. Even if *Noa Noa* were the work of Charles Morice,[34] and not Gauguin himself, the text is still representative of Europe, in general, and France, in particular, especially as it positions itself in relationship to the external Other. Charles Morice himself had written, especially when controversy over the book's authorship erupted, "Here then is Tahiti, *faithfully imagined.*"[35]

Were it not for Gauguin's artistic depictions of life in this distant place, *Noa Noa* would qualify as little more than empathetic storytelling, tasteless at best, because it comes at the dawn of the twentieth century, when, supposedly, we had moved past the stage of the Noble Savage, and when, presumably, more sophisticated issues made claims on our attention. But it is as a painter, a "synthesist" (a term he preferred) or "primitivist" that we recall Gauguin. Apart from this, there is little that he, or Morice, adds to the reality of place in *Noa Noa*.

PACIFIC SPACE EXPLORED

Encounter from the beginning up to the twentieth century shows how the Pacific was "discovered," conquered, mapped, organized, mythologized and fantasized.[36] Instead of seventeenth- and eighteenth-century "Chinoiserie" yielding to nineteenth-century "Japonaiserie," one would have hoped to see reproduced in European and American ornamentation not mere simulacra, but genuine representations of the "East," "the Orient," and whatever was meant by that. But with the twentieth century the illusion continued, for instance in the interior decorations of the lavish homes built by some of the new American millionaires.

Joseph Conrad's *Lord Jim* (1900) begins the century with an elaborate ruse: in the case of Tuan Jim (the word "Tuan" meant just "Mr." not "Lord"), Patusan is where a person may hide. Jim is driven there, good Englishman that he is ("one of us," someone calls him), because he forces a form of expiation on himself after the drowning of some pilgrims bound for Mecca on the *Patna*. Jim's attempt at living a life of partial anonymity, and his rise to the important role of "tuan" among the locals, actually show for me that the Englishman will thrive to rule, even given the most enormous odds. Indeed, Jim's undoing at the hands of the local chief, comes about as a direct result of his honor, the Englishman's word, which he is bound to keep, even if the debacle was not his fault, and even if he has to lose his life in the process.

In Somerset Maugham's instance, the facts are again manipulated to situate European problems on the center stage of the Pacific. Maugham had visited Tahiti in 1917, but his portrayals of the locale merely showed Europeans attempting to work out their problems against the background of the islands. In *The Moon and Sixpence* (1919), Charles Strickland is a Gauguin-like individual, who gives up everything for art; in Maugham's short story "Miss Sadie Thompson," Maugham again represents the Pacific as a place of refuge for hidden lust. Sadie is the means through which the beast surfaces in the Scottish missionary, Davidson, leading to rape and his ultimate suicide.

Seemingly, then, it is not possible for Western writers to construct the Pacific in terms that distance Pacific space from the an all-encircling Eurocentric sentimentality and melodrama imposed on it. How else, therefore, could Margaret Mead have conceptualized her local "informants" in *Coming of Age in Samoa* (1928) but as oversexed, "deviant," even "delinquent"? Why else would a young Thor Heyerdahl and his wife take off for the "marvels" of Fau Hiva to play at Adam and Eve? The area had been drawn in a certain manner, and secreted in the Western mind as a place of refuge and repose, both revolting and revolutionary, constantly revived and resuscitated to pander to personal hopes and expectations.

Quite naturally, James Michener returns to the area in *Tales of the South Pacific* (1947). Because the South Pacific (the East, or the Orient, or by any other name), just mirrors the heart, it offers no solutions, except the ones you choose to take. When Michener's book was made into the Rogers and Hammerstein musical *South Pacific* in 1958, the story and songs were about the United States and its racial problems in Little Rock, ARK, as the song went, and not about (of all places) Bali. And, more recently, when the "East" was conjured up in films like *Heaven and Earth* (1993), the images have more to do with Asian, in this case Vietnamese, feminism (perhaps even a Western-perceived need for it), and American preoccupation with the Vietnam War, than with Asia, or Vietnam, itself. The instances may be multiplied to include even authentic, modern Chinese films which very often seem more concerned with satisfying a Western concern, in choosing such themes as homosexuality and feminism, than in reproducing the reality of China. So, once again, for different reasons, we note a dangerous development by which the East might well be revising, refashioning and reconstructing itself in terms of the West, the Other remaking itself in the reflected image of the One.

A final point must be made, and this is that we have an unfortunate tendency to see the world through a single eye. Very often we seem precluded from being able to enter into any experience within its own terms, having left our own presumptions and presuppositions at home in the West. And the foreign, the alien, continues to affront us. Nevertheless, we have to find ways in which we can divorce ourselves from our unreal constructs and, with a new, great leap of the mind, reclaim different human realities. Therein, and only there, lies our sovereign validity for the possibility of coexistence in tomorrow's world.

AFTERWORD

In the instances of China, the Pacific, Africa, and Native America, one overall theme is pervasive: the extent to which differing indigenous cultures were, to a greater or lesser extent, influenced by European norms. Although patterns vary, what is uppermost in all instances is that with the arrival of Europeans, all Others become reduced to familiar patterns through European ways of visualizing the world.

Particularly in reference to the Pacific Islands and Africa, the imposition of European languages distorted the image of place. Europeans had firm concepts regarding their belief in their "travel" in China, their "discovery" of the New World and the Pacific, and their "exploration" of Africa. Part of their new way of understanding the concept of space meant that all "discovered" areas became defined and adjusted to new constructions of the European world—its language, religion, and norms. Even when European influence did not penetrate far into these areas, the local environments were nevertheless perceived, described, and related from the standpoint of core European cultural beliefs, as matters outside the Self, language, and the world itself. This was what was meant by being "native," "savage," or even "colonial," and it to this assumption that degrees of difference, of Otherness, were applied, varying from the Odd/Out to the Odder/Outer and, finally, the Oddest/Outermost/Uttermost, unreachable and beyond redemption. We noted that the Chinese had much earlier on mastered this art of differentiation.

One obvious reason is that travel had consolidated Europeans into a unified group experience for their time; they could easily agree on the mythologies of a given period. Thus, they could neither know nor comprehend the disparity and difference they encountered. To make the varied people understandable, Europeans had to do one of two things: render them remote as "heathen" or "dark," or claim them as "neighbors," "natives," and extensions of Self. Colonial policy thus identified the uncivilized and the civilized, the bushman and the *évolué*—the one unwesternized, the other schooled with the credentials of a good colonial upbringing.

This attempt to "know" without knowing, in reality to "understand" without understanding, often meant that those foreign environments, once conscripted either as "alien" or "domestic," and once "named," were, in fact, then dominated. Such an act of triumphalism on the part of Europeans meant that a justification had to be established whereby foreign realities, once conscripted, could then be downgraded. As such, the "heathen" and the "native," no longer mythological, became factual (perceptions which those affected often shared), and with the wide acceptance of this status, it was easy to categorize the societies as abnormal, base, primitive, and inferior, often with indigenous compliance. In turn, the margins fed back their sense of isolation to the center, and thereby gave a new concept to what the metropole stood for and how it was represented.

As suggested, there were varying degrees to the control. In certain instances, societies and groups in Asia and Africa erected cultural bulwarks that could fend off these intrusions. In other words, possessed of their own intrinsic Self, they saw no need to accept and adhere to mysterious impositions of Otherness. Other societies in the South Pacific were not so fortunate and, in the process of contact, collapsed and became extensions of Europe. On the one hand, China stands as an excellent example of a society that, in general, successfully resisted Europeanization. On the other hand, the South Pacific and Latin America are perfect cases of societies that, in general, failed to counter Europeanization.

One should therefore ask, particularly in this century, now that there are so many caveats against ethnocentrism, whether this former model of a super European/American domination continues to hold? The counter thrust toward a global identity would seem to indicate a new possibility for the recognition of difference. But there is an equally strong traditional and powerful conservative movement in the United States that points back to a past in which secure archetypes had presumably existed.

These assumptions about the world that attempt historical backtracking are basically invalid, for they rely on the invention of a mythological past that never really existed. Hence, the many Chinese today who still refer to themselves as "Han" are as legendary as constructions such as European, African, Asian, Native American or Black and White people, since there never existed a time, even in the remote past, when such monolithic conceptions were possible. All that had occurred was that people with larger guns forced a specific view on the world, a vision that was termed righteous, God-fearing, and civilized. This was certainly efficacious, but hardly an objective viewpoint, and merely one in which the powerful situated everything they encountered within the purview of their own cultural boundaries. Hence, both objectivity and universality seem to be relative, dependent solely on the wielder of the more powerful weapons.

Such imposed "universalism" begins and ends with its own home-based and homegrown notions about the Other world. The Other becomes rendered as only relative and relevant to the mores, beliefs, culture and language of the One. The assumption of "universalism" is directed away from real global concerns toward the narrow, parochial limitations of the power wielder, reduced to his viewpoint, and pinpointed in his direction. Any intellectual growth that results from this radiates from the thinking of the supreme authority figure. Within such a context, no true dialogue is possible, or if it does take place, it occurs in one direction, much like a command or an order.

As noted, the wielders of European/American authority and power subscribe to an elitism born out of their own cultural formats. This is why "Mandarins" in China, "Maharajahs" in India, some "kings" and many "chiefs" in Africa, as well as "chiefs" in the New World and Pacific exist. They are largely created out of an imperial wish to see its Self and its norms reflected, but, even more pragmatically, to establish dialogues with "leaders" who are "educated." In other words, these representatives were fashioned after British, French, Spanish, and Portuguese imaginings, provided with a title and basic perks of office, in exchange for their compliance. The system worked well into the era of "independence," for by then the leaders of Asia and Africa were hardly "indigenous" people, but curious hybrids constructed from the imperial system.

Since indigenous communities had been largely invalidated, they themselves began to question the significance of their own communal structures. Certainly their "Native Government" (a term the British liked to use for a recognized and approved but meaningless indigenous bureaucracy), "superstition," "Native schools," and so forth were all weak and ineffective. Ironically, therefore, the very support of alien norms by local people had facilitated their journeys to, and occupation of, the European metropolitan centers. In effect, they had definitely established that somewhere, far away, was "Home" (a place to which expatriates traveled every few years), and here, nearby in their own countries, was "away." The home/away syndrome had the deleterious effect of total societal disintegration for the subject/colonial who accepted the polarity. Believe me, I know—I lived through this, and the effects remain with us.

I am stressing that without indigenous cooperation, the collapse of local cultures could not have occurred on such a worldwide scale. Such an acceptance of a new coda meant that in the Americas (North, Central, and South), in Africa, in the South Pacific, and only to a lesser extent in Asia, indigenous peoples and their leaders accepted their own Third Worldism, actually a politically updated version of monolithization. Such a belief, despite its rhetoric, meant that there was a supposedly unstated, assumed commonality about the subjugated, based solely on the subordination of their assumptions and beliefs about the world, derived solely from their reaction to imperialism. Of course, such a response was clearly nonsensical, for it ignores the very multiculturalism that its adherents advocate. What the European powers had done was to erect their own belief system as paramount and specific and to deny any other kind of consciousness anywhere else in the world. To suggest that this vacuity or supposed emptiness itself constituted a common basis for identification—La France d'Outre-mer, the British Commonwealth, overseas Holland, or the American "territories"—was, in reality, to accept an "unfree" condition as associative, endemically "native," total, and yet devoutly desired.

Colonialism and ghettoism, particularly through the paramountcy of Language, helped construct a new "reality" and different "mythology" above and beyond the older ones. This fake hierarchy was established as a cultural uniform, a reality that was immutable and absolute, and well worth aspiring to—after all its physical and monetary rewards were self-evident. Pretensions to a new elitism by colonial subjects advanced the acceptance of an artificial unity that put forward the colonizer's "Self" and "Language" as exemplary models beyond "Otherness" and "dialect." It suggested that somewhere beyond the borders of local geography was situated the Ideal Archetype. As such, it was easily able to conscript residual, even emerging discourses, into its own dominant voice, establishing its own legitimately sanctioned echo. Further, it could and did blindfold everything, directing all toward its own Supreme Self. Non-European entities were not supposed to exist because they were denied their own realities; "tribe" was out, "nation" was in.

Yet these new places were "Paradise," "Eden"—Marco Polo, Columbus, and Vespucci first testified to this, and Pilgrims and Pioneers in the United States would continue this affirmation; and in such a "new" Eden, a "new" World, all things became possible. The assumption yet again maintains that the world had not been traveled, explored, or "discovered," that it did not really exist until Europeans arrived. Time begins with European encounter; for there existed no history prior to this, and as such, the conquered were out of time. The Pacific and the New World share that much in common—they are both removed from geography and history, existing outside the reality of "place" or people. Hence they were "East," "West," or "South," providing a fascinating lack of direction, that even suggested that their very place was not fixed or secure.

If indigenous "past" itself was capricious, by definition it was also unnecessary, ambiguous, and oppressive. As such, it must be rejected, to make way for a European "present" that is fixed, relevant, meaningful, and liberating. However, this "present" which points toward the "future" is complicated not by old indigenous mythologies, but by the new externally imposed ones, like Eden and Paradise, which survived the journeys to China, Africa, and the South Pacific. This new conceptualization of time and place totally ignored the locals, since this New World, New Eden, Paradise were not created for them; they were merely patient watchers, awaiting the coming of the rightful dwellers. But, as Benedict Anderson warns us in *Imagined Communities*, the view of the overlord is incomplete, for each person knows of the image of the elastic boundaries of community, beyond which exist other communities.

Much as Europeans sought an indigenous social hierarchy, they also looked for "nations." When these seemingly did not exist, Europeans simply carved up the land, regardless of language ties or blood groups. Both Asia and Africa present examples which we have noted. The Pacific area is a little different, in that the geography of islands helped demarcate their borders, if not their new names.

Another major problem lay in the European concept of contiguity and nationhood, for such self-manufactured concepts had nothing to do with Other-related beliefs. Thus, the very countries in Asia and Africa that guard their borders so zealously today continue the foolish and mistaken mythologies first implanted there. Of course, it remains quite evident that territorial boundaries possess no intrinsic significance, but often merely validate the mistaken follies of colonialism.

Images of nebulousness are at the core of the callous disregard of "place" and "people." How could anyone be certain of these realities when Asia, Africa, and the South Pacific lay beyond the mapmakers' constructs? Strictly speaking, these areas were not supposed to be there, and not only did their presence challenge cherished illusions about the world, but also their very existence presupposed the existence of otherworldliness, of Columbus'*otro mundo*. Therefore, they became "territories," "possessions," "dependencies," "colonies," where names could be arbitrarily assigned, relating to the names of their "discoverers" or their kings, the "saints" of the Catholic church, the day of the week, the month of the year, or the nature of trade. All in all, the names affixed the identity of the external gaze on countries in Africa and the Pacific. China was mercifully spared from this, although English approximations continued to dilute the Chinese language.

In "naming," more often than not, the wrong "sign" (the obvious external landmarker say) is what defines a country, a people. Larzer Ziff, in *Literary Democracy,* adds that humans can only have the dominion of Adam if they can assign words to a representative reality. European encounters largely ignored internal conceptions of things—local names, languages, ideas. They substituted instead the beliefs and language of the One for those of the Other and, in so doing, very often merely succeeded in defining what supposedly was, by what had never been. The missionaries in Hawaii, for instance, ran into a real dilemma: how to translate "sin" when there was no local equivalent.

However, one major aspect of Europe's encounter with China is that, in reality "One" meets "One," not the Other. The European One and the Chinese One then go about delineating varieties of Otherness to all else. In both the European One and the Chinese One, the degrees of Otherness vary in direct relationship to space and distance, as well by traits and and resemblance. Again, in both instances, Odd(er), Out(er), and Utter(most) become fixed ways in which Europeans situated Chinese, and Chinese affixed Europeans, as well as those Other peoples beyond their center.

For Chinese, clearly the Odd would be defined purely in terms of traditional frames of reference. There was no doubt that as "barbarians" all Europeans belonged to some degree of Otherness; the Odd would be those who inhabited perhaps the outer rims of recognizable dimensions, just within the area allocated to thieves and strangers. These would perhaps have included the earliest peoples encountered by the Chinese on the eastern rim of the Roman Empire.

As the Chinese moved further away from their own center, indeed even from the limits of their own extreme periphery, they began to see people of whom they had no previous knowledge. No wonder the earliest explorer turned back, probably at the region of the Persian Sea. Those he encountered, European and non-European alike, would have been a little more removed from the norm of the periphery, less recognizable, less contiguous in terms of space, and thus even further Outer.

Beyond all this for the Chinese was a dim region heard about, but never ever encountered by them until just before the time of Zheng He. Even though they would later see this Uttermost in Africa to their south, their own West was only partly explored by them. When their West arrived, particularly during the time of the Mongol invasions, it came from far beyond the fringes of the norm, representing extremes that no ancient text had ever described. Its emissaries and conquerors, much like the African "Kunlun," represented the Utter, since they lay beyond the demarcations of known boundaries, beyond recognizable space and time, beyond sanity itself, and obviously seemed alien and inhuman.

The Utterness of the Africans made them irrelevant to the Chinese, especially following the cessation of their maritime explorations. But not the Utterness of Europeans; Europeans came into the Chinese center as travelers and missionaries and, from the nineteenth until the twentieth century, established themselves on the frontiers of China, at Shanghai, Canton, Hong Kong, and Macau. There is the important difference—power—between the Chinese assignation of Utterness to Africans and to Europeans. The African Kunlun were distant, remote, and ineffective; the European barbarians were near, present, and powerful.

The encounter between China and the West must be seen not only in terms of the manner in which the Other is subdivided into degrees of Otherness, but also as means through which as the European/Chinese One confronts the Chinese/European One, the European/Chinese One subdivides its supposed opposite Chinese/European Other into sections of "familiarity." Those closest to the One were obviously more acceptable than those more removed. Granted these were mere "perceptions," but they indicated very real ways by which Europe looked at China, and China at Europe. For the Chinese, the Portuguese seemed to be less distant, extreme, and opposite, not closer to the Chinese norm, but certainly nearer at least to the extremities within that norm. Unlike some of the indigenous people of the South Pacific, the Chinese quite early made the distinction between any One European nation (closer to them) and an Other (farther removed).

Likewise, Europeans also identified their closer Asian Other, which I have termed the Odd. Always in search of a familiar hierarchy, the Europeans envisioned a process in the land whereby "mandarins" (i.e. local "chiefs," spokesperson, bandits, royal representatives) could be identified as intermediaries. The word "mandarin" (to command) is itself from Portuguese, modified from the Hindi *mantri* or "minister of state." In English, it came to represent everything from a dialect to a type of orange or a style of dress. At its most detractive it meant a pompous person. It is easy to see how the term was arbitrarily borrowed from the "East," passed through Portuguese and Hindi misappropriations, and then irrelevantly and irreverently applied to Chinese bureaucrats. In any event, this was the way in which Europe could interpret its intermediaries. The Portuguese gave Europe its Chinese mandarins, and the Chinese accepted the Portuguese as their typical Europeans. Both Ones had identified the leaders of their Uttermost parameters.

The idea of conscripting the Other to accept this requires both confidence and power. But it helps a minority group withstand undue pressure if it is partly cut off from external interactions, and if its own mutual influences can be reinforced by a prevailing adherence to common norms. Thus, it became much easier for the Chinese (although, as I have tried to show, China as an idea is itself an invention) to withstand not merely Western military pressure, but Western influence in any wholesale manner. It was more difficult for South Sea islanders; they were relatively few in number and were beset on all sides by a variety of European intrusions and enticements which had gone on since the days of early contact.

Within the context of the Pacific Islands, although grantedly there exists a culture (indeed several cultures), it took so little to convince the inhabitants that they were "wrong"—that their gods were misnamed, that the hula was immoral, that their language was malformed, and, in general, that they lacked a culture. Perhaps, after a while, they too began to believe that they lived in Paradise—it is pretty heady stuff to reject! And therein lies the greatest danger, for if this were perfection, here, on this island, on this beach, why strive toward anything else? There would be little need to try to establish the perfect governance, or to refine the arts, or even to keep the gods alive, if indigenous people became truly convinced that their world was perfect, lacking only in a few easy refinements which a little European tinkering could easily accomplish.

Unconvertible change thus came about mainly through the introduction of religion. Much as the European languages had banished indigenous speech, religion not only exiled the local spirits, but expanded the acceptable, even required, "taboo" into new and completely unforeseen directions. Faced with the new Christianity of the One exhorting its followers about sin and hellfire, the old religions of the Other retreated. In many ways, this is understandable, since these were often pragmatic theologies dependent on a certain accepted, even acceptable, state of well-being in relationship to the environment. When "being" was redefined, out of the context of the old taboos and within the meaning of the new Christian religion, the past could not hold. It seemed irrelevant, almost accidental, and of little value. The future, not the present, was what counted, and it presented an interesting conundrum; a chance for the saved to be redeemed in Paradise itself was a message that New England missionaries took to Hawaii.

Yet according to standard European mythologizing, Paradise was here. It is to these areas that the mutinous crew of the *Bounty* had fled, and where Fletcher Christian sought his refuge. It is in these very islands that a very real Will/ Alexander Selkirk and their fictionalized alter ego, Robinson Crusoe, learned how to revert to the truly primordial. It is within this very real space that the fictions of Herman Melville's *Typee* and *Omoo,* Joseph Conrad's *Lord Jim,* and Somerset Maugham's *The Moon and Sixpence* were located. It is where Robert Louis Stevenson and Paul Gauguin sought refuge. So, within European myth-making, there occurs a type of contrapuntal arrangement: They acknowledge the presence of Paradise, while contending that the "natives" did not seem part of it, even though they lived there.

Furthermore, it seems very odd that Paradise, once found, had to be dramatically altered. Throughout the entire region, Europeans have unrelentingly continued the deforestation began by earlier settlers, but on a much grander scale. They introduced all the accouterments of Home, but these were often inimical to the welfare of the environment. For instance, quite early when Europeans introduced cattle, horses, and sheep, these had the effect, through grazing, of wearing away the fragile topsoil. Often the introduction of livestock had little to do even with the satisfaction of basic food needs. A case in point is the introduction of sheep into nineteenth century New Zealand by the British, mainly for the purpose of exporting wool; another example is the introduction of sugar into Hawaii, now thankfully giving way to sustainable ecotourism.

With the advent of the Industrial Revolution in England and its export to the far-flung outposts of Empire, the taboo/tattoo syndrome moved to a different scenario. Land was now the major agent of change, as sheep grazing on areas owned by settlers altered the old (even limited) concept of land and water rights and attendant taboos. Land, as the North American Indians also found out, was no longer community held, but could be bought and sold to individuals. These were frightening and disturbing concepts that could not be easily understood. They did serve to emphasize the primacy of the "tattoo" of the skin color of the new settlers. The indigenous became wage earners and were, by reason of economic disparity and language, effectively locked out from official public discourse and decision making.

As a way of literally transferring the gardens of Home, British newcomers also brought with them their own plants. Contemporary New Zealand thus bears little resemblance, even in this one instance, to what was encountered by the scientists on board Cook's *Endeavour.* The simulation of Home also effectively confirmed the idea of permanency for residents, and with a dwindling indigenous population, settler paramountcy became assured, even as the death of the one last Tasmanian indigene dramatically demonstrated. The effect of transporting "Little England" to the Pacific, the Caribbean, and the Americas therefore profoundly alienated the indigenous people from their own familiar terrain. In time, there would be little that was recognizable. They became estranged in their own "home," even buying into the idea that "home" was located elsewhere, overseas, in Britain or France, any European metropolitan center that the new education had made recognizable.

As stated, alteration of landscape was nearly always done in the name of progress, but actually because of selfish efforts to enrich the powerful few. As in the Caribbean (with sugar), and in the southern states of the United States (with cotton), Hawaii became a sugar-bowl to help satisfy the European sweet tooth. Hawaii's narrative should occupy an entire volume, but suffice it to say that the expanding faith of Manifest Destiny did not pause on the western coast of the United States. Not until Hawaii was "annexed," and then converted into a state did Paradise (so long sought by early East Coast settlers), finally became a part of Home. But the center simply strangled its new Eden into its own conformity. Today, the Hawaiian Islands have become the supreme showcase for sun and surf, constantly evoked in the hellish recollections of Pearl Harbor. Truthfully, the oft quoted "Aloha Oe" composed by Queen Emma Kaleleonalani, wife of King Kamehameha IV, recalls with a kind of sad, prophetic irony, a time before grass-skirted tourists, when it was one of the early settlements of a simple Asian people who sought not Paradise but a haven.

Modern Honolulu with its expressways, skyscrapers, and traffic jams bears little resemblance to the Paradise that the Europeans "discovered." Its palm trees almost seem irrelevant side by side with double traffic lanes, noise, and pollution. In a way, mainland America has simply imprinted its own version of "Home," complete with inner-city problems and crime, on what was once a lush landscape. Perhaps, in a way, the urban sprawl, the chaos at Waikiki Beach, the tourist shops, and the jet planes all exist as continuous loud declamations against Europe's intrusion, so many centuries ago. For it was here in one part of this unspoilt Paradise that Cook was killed.

Even if, Europeans seem to say, the Shangri-La of James Hilton's *Lost Horizon* (1933) did not exist in Tibet, or El Dorado in the New World, or even Marco Polo's vision of a benign autocracy in China, the world could be remade again. Perhaps, in some strange and undefined way, this speaks to an unfailing European optimism that Eden was never really lost, and that a determined search would finally reveal it in all its splendor. Perhaps, particularly in the New World context, this is what each Utopian venture is about. Perhaps, in another way, the quest also addresses European dissatisfaction with its own present, at any time, which did not hold out the tantalizing possibility of hope in this life. Christianity, for its believers, could take care of those in the next world, but the pragmatists seemed to ask—what of the here and now?

If we, like Coleridge's Mariner, Tennyson's Lotus Eaters, or even T. S. Eliot's Magi, pursue the dream on the hardest journey of the world, will we be rewarded with a sustaining vision? If we look to European and American culture for answers, we need not ponder too long, for the response is most assuredly not located there. Joseph Campbell sought and found the "Bliss," the spiritual upliftment to divine peace, in many of the world's religions. Campbell, in looking *outward*, is like any discoverer, conqueror, empire ruler, adventurer. Beyond the limitations imposed by the West, out there stands the shining city of St Augustine.

Now, toward the end of the twentieth century, Pacific islanders are beginning to reinvest in their past. Maori elders have adapted their ancient tree ceremonies to embrace global conservationism. In the Cook Islands, at the "Festival of Pacific Arts," Polynesians celebrated their newfound pride, that they alone had conquered and discovered the Pacific. They demonstrated, through newly built crafts modeled on the old, how they had learned to traverse the ocean, guided only by stars, sun, wave currents, birds, and the hope of a nearby island. To a recent festival at Rarotonga, indigenous people came from all over the Pacific Rim, from Tahiti and the Marquesas, Samoa and Tonga, Easter Island and Fiji, as well as New Zealand. This was the very first time that people, so long divided by the impositions of a foreign "taboo" and "tattoo" had cast aside differences in a new alliance that superimposed itself beyond acceptance of being mere native or Other.

There they were no longer French, British, or American "natives," or indigenous Australians or New Zealanders, but instead a replication of what they had once been—Pacific islanders from Southeast Asia, voyagers across a vast ocean, who had engaged in noble and virtuous acts of discovery. In a way, they were introducing themselves to one another for the first time, since they had been divided from each other, oceans apart, generations ago. There, at least for a brief moment, they could sing and dance in their own old languages, confident that the gaze was not from the curious observer/tourist to the observed/performer. For this had been their immediate past, ever since the French, Dutch, and British fought over their little pieces of Paradise. Now they could evoke the possibility of a future as their own agents.

Even as they interacted, they gave birth to a new past. But they could also take part in guarding the future, indeed a global future, from further recidivism into the hell that followed their own earlier demarcation of One and Other, and subsequent European conquest, which shifted the emphasis away from any decision-making power on their part. In song and dance, they reclaimed language, and when they did this, untroubled by the eye of the spectator, they revived new possibilities for themselves as a people, long silenced by the imposition of an alien will.

Now they were engaged in a final act of discovery that took them past separate islands, obviated ancient and modern "taboos," and imprinted a new "tattoo." Perhaps this is how history must be written; even as a similar European One had defined its own indigenous Other, a new indigenous One isolates the older Others into one single homogeneous One/Other. In turn, this new local One/Other, accepting its status, seeks and finds renewed possibilities of identification as it appropriates its old past, beyond the romanticizing and mythologizing formerly imposed. Thus, ancient tattoos develop into new taboos, no longer restrictive but now descriptive.

In this study, I have attempted to show how the Western imposition of its own fantasy served to dislocate location and to replace place. I have argued that in many respects this is not a suitable way to envision the world, especially when Western power in all its enormity often offers illusions of participation to indigenous people, of allowing them to enact the mirage that is really a distorted image of their own self-destruction. But purely from a Western ethnocentric standpoint, the vision beyond Home, even given the construct of monsters and marvels and the coopting of the "native" as willing burden bearer for the fantasy, has served the West very well. For even today, as people in the West look beyond the circumscription of their languages, their nations, and their peoplehood, even as the "rest" perplexes, it nevertheless provides important antidotes for the West. In an era that lacks faith, perhaps the mystery of the Other will continue to add an old and yet novel dimension to the age, as it searches for the very revelations which science has failed to reveal. And perhaps, even as the West continues to discover mystery and magic and wonder in the Other, it may reclaim its former Self, the hybridity that Homi Bhapha stresses time and time again, as the true repose of culture. It must of needs do this as the world comes "Home"—Turks to Germany, Pakistanis to Britain, Algerians to France, Asians to Anglo-America. For the next century, an urgent issue remains: how does the fictional One speak, live, act, and coexist with the fictionalized Outermost/Uttermost in this new global village? Are they not in a very real sense conjoined twins?

NOTES

CHAPTER 1

1. *Encyclopaedia Britannica* (Micropaedia), 15th ed., s.v. "China."

2. J. Ki-Zerbo, ed., *Methodology and African Prehistory*, vol. 1 of 8 *UNESCO General History of Africa* (Berkeley: University of California Press, 1981), 1.

3. Summarized by Geo. C. Hurlbut in his rebuttal,"The Origin of the Name 'America,'" *Journal of the American Geographical Society of New York*, 20 (1888): 183–196. Jules Marcou wrote extensively on this topic. See especially his "Sur L'Origine du Nom d'Amérique," *Bulletin de la Société de Géographie* (Paris) 9, 6th Series (1875): 587–97, and "Nouvelles Recherches sur L'Origine du Nom d'Amérique," *Bulletin de la Société de Géographie* (Paris) 9, 7th Series (1888): 480–520. Also see Jan Carew's article "The Caribbean Writer and Exile," in *Fulcrums of Change* (Trenton, NJ: Africa World Press, 1988), 91–114, in which he argues strongly in favor of Marcou, making the point that both the Mayan holy book, *Popul Vuh*, and Miguel Asturias's novel, *Strong Wind*, identify Nicaragua as a credible location.

4. J. M. Roberts, *The Triumph of the West* (London: British Broadcasting Corporation, 1985), 38.

5. See Tom McArthur, ed., *The Oxford Companion to the English Language* (Oxford: Oxford University Press, 1992), 212, 213.

6. Michael Crowder, ed., *West African Resistance* (New York: Africana Publishing, 1971), 4.

7. Confucius, *The Analects,* trans. D. C. Lau (London: Penguin, 1979), 79.

8. Güyük Khan's reply to the pope makes delightful reading. There are Latin versions and a supposedly "original" Persian version. See I. de Rachewiltz, *Papal Envoys to the Great Khans* (London: Faber and Faber, 1971), 104 in which there is a translation from the Persian. In the letter, the khan admonishes the pope, warning

him that since he could not prove that he was God's representative on earth, the pope should make his way to China and pay suitable homage to the khan. At least Khan Güyük did not seem to have any doubts about his own place in the scheme of things.

9. Stephen Greenblatt, *Marvelous Possessions: The Wonder of the New World* (Chicago: University of Chicago Press, 1991), 103, 104.

10. "The Journey of Friar John," in *Contemporaries of Marco Polo,* ed. Manuel Komroff (New York: Dorset, 1989), 34.

11. "The Journal of Friar William," in Ibid., 119.

12. Milton Rugoff, ed., *The Travels of Marco Polo* (New York: New American Library, 1961), 71–72.

13. Even the name "Boxer" is a misnomer, indicating once again a complete failure to understand a complex civilization. The "I-He-Chuan" were the "righteous-uniting-*band*" that sought foreign overthrow in 1900. It was wrongly translated as "righteous-uniting-*fists*," hence "boxer," which was clearly meant to be derogatory.

The Opium Wars, between 1839 and 1842, first pitted Chinese against British, and next, between 1856 and 1860, forced Chinese to fight British and French, all for the sake of keeping British Indian opium out. This was the precursor of the anti-imperial struggle, which saw its messianic highpoint in the colorful Taiping Rebellion, in which, under Hong Xiuquan (Hung Hsiu-ch'üan), a Christ-figure emerged to proclaim the Heavenly Kingdom of Great Peace in 1851. The power and influence of Hong's radicalism officially ended in 1864, but his early reforms have been heralded by both the mainland Communist and Tawain capitalist governments as the origins of modern Chinese nationalism. The Boxer Rebellion was a logical anti-imperialist struggle, drawing its strength from ancient Chinese rituals and openly battling the church of the European Christians as a visible symbol of oppression. The end of the struggle offered carte blanche to European allies, as well as Russian and Japanese forces, preparing the way for the long struggle that culminated in final post-World War II independence for China and Taiwan.

14. Peter Worsley, *The Three Worlds: Culture and World Development* (Chicago: University of Chicago Press, 1984), 252.

15. Fray Bernardino de Sahagún, *Florentine Codex, General History of the Things of New Spain* ed. Arthur J. O. Anderson and Charles Dibble. 12 vols. (Salt Lake City: School of American Research and University of Utah, 1950–1982),12: 6.

16. Tzvetan Todorov, *The Conquest of America: The Question of the Other* (New York: Harper & Row, 1984), 76.

17. George Orwell, "Marrakesh," in *A Collection of Essays* (New York: Doubleday Anchor, 1954), 187.

18. See a small book by J.J.L. Duyvendak, *China's Discovery of Africa* (London:

Probsthain, 1949), and also Philip Snow, *Star Raft: China's Encounter with Africa* (Ithaca: Cornell University Press, 1988), 21–36.

19. See Frederick Hodge and Theodore Lewis, eds. *Spanish Explorers in the Southern United States* (New York: Barnes and Noble, 1907), 59, 65, 71, 73, 78, 80, 95n., 102, 107, 112, 113, 126, 275, 288–90.

20. A good source for the Taiping Revolution is Theodore Hamberg, *The Vision of Hung-siu-Tshuen and the Origin of the Kwang-si Insurrection* (Hong Kong: n.p. 1854). More general information is given in C. P. Fitzgerald, *China: A Short Cultural History* (London: Cresset, 1986), 577–83; Jacques Gernet, *A History of Chinese Civilization* (Cambridge: Cambridge University Press, 1982), 545–54; and Ssu-yü Teng, *New Light on the History of the T'ai-p'ing Rebellion* (Cambridge: Harvard University Press, 1950).

21. See A. A. Boahen, ed., *Africa Under Foreign Domination, 1800–1935,* vol. 7 of 8, *UNESCO General History of Africa* (Berkeley: University of California Press, 1993), 19–44 and 782–809. Also see Ali Mazrui, *The Africans* (Boston: Little, Brown, 1986), 107–8 for a discussion of the pros and cons of European division of Africa.

22. The language debate is quite old in Africa. See Gerald Moore, *The Chosen Tongue* (London: Longmans, 1969), ix–xxiii and 133–212, in which the use of English is taken for granted and almost a point for commendation; and Oyekan Owomoyela, *A History of Twentieth-Century African Literature* (Lincoln: University of Nebraska Press, 1993), especially 347–68.

23. Kwame Appiah, *In My Father's House* (London: Oxford University Press, 1992).

24. Taban lo Liyong, "Negroes are not Africans," *The Last Word* (Nairobi: East African Publishing House, 1969), 83–97.

25. For background information on Amo, Capitein, and Williams, see Janheinz Jahn, *A History of Neo-African Literature* (London: Faber and Faber, 1966), 34–41.

26. Ibid., 35.

27. Edward Long, *A History of Jamaica* (London: Printed for T. Lowndes, 1774), 478.

28. "The Meaning of Africa," under the late Dividson Nichol's pen name, Abioseh Nicol, has been widely anthologized. See John Reed and Clive Wake, *A Book of African Verse* (London: Heinemann, 1964), 42–46.

29. See C. H. Fyle, *The History of Sierra Leone* (London: Evans Brothers, 1988) for Sierra Leone Creoles and their difficulties with adjusting, their demonization of the locals as "natives," and conflicts that still persist into the present. Fyle is himself a Creole.

30. President Tubman's speech is cited in E. R. Townsend, ed., *President Tubman of Liberia Speaks* (London: Consolidated Company, 1959), 98–99.

31. Countee Cullen, "Heritage" in *Color* (New York: Harper & Brothers, 1925), 36–38.

32. Winston Churchill, *My African Journey* (1908; reprint, London: Octopus, 1989), in which like the hunter, the British overlord must always be in charge of the African "a naked and unconscious philosopher." Churchill continues (truly in the vein of Rudyard Kipling's "White Man's Burden") by sounding a note a little reminiscent of God in the Old Testament: "The white man shall do the rest. He shall preserve the peace, that the tribes may prosper and multiply" (p. 41).

33. Theodore Roosevelt, *African Game Trails* (New York: Charles Scribner's Sons, 1910) who also sees the advantages of British imperialism. About Uganda he wrote, "For their good fortune, England has established a protectorate over them . . . and the chief task of the officials of the intrusive and masterful race must be to bring forward the natives" (pp. 430–31).

34. Ernest Hemingway, *The Green Hills of Africa* (1935; reprint New York: Permabooks, 1954), 49.

35. Ibid., 50.

36. Ngugi wa Thiong'o, *Homecoming* (London: Heinemann, 1972), 85.

37. Chinua Achebe, *Hopes and Impediments* (New York: Doubleday, 1989), 12.

38. Alice Walker, *Possessing the Secret of Joy* (New York: Harcourt Brace Jovanovich, 1972), 10.

39. See Luciano Formisano, *Letters from the New World: Amerigo Vespucci's Discovery of America* (New York: Marsilio, 1992). See Letter [*Mundus Novus*] 3–18 and also the editor's discussion of the "unknown land" of "Mundus Novus" on p. xx.

40. The appearance of the "Noble Savage" in literature is treated exhaustively, if somewhat laboriously, in Hoxie Neale Fairchild, *The Noble Savage* (New York: Columbia University Press, 1928), 80–89; 121–39; 328–31; 404–7. A more recent study looks at the topic from a Black standpoint; see Edward Scobie, *Black Britannia* (Chicago: Johnson Publishing, 1972), 37–47.

41. Rodney W. Shirley, *The Mapping of the World* (London: Holland Press Cartographica, 1984), 28–29. Waldsemüller's map is reproduced in Jay A. Levinson, *Circa 1492* (Washington: National Gallery of Art, 1991), 232–33. Emerson lamented that the New World had neen named after a thief.

42. References to Columbus will be mainly drawn from Cecil Jane, ed., *The Four Voyages of Columbus* (New York: Dover, 1988) which is a reprint of the Hakluyt Society Series, vol. LXV (1930) and vol. LXX (1933). Some corrections have been made in the Dover edition. This work will be listed as Columbus, *Four Voyages*.

43. For Samuel de Champlain, I used *Voyages of Samuel de Champlain* ed. W. L. Grant (New York: Barnes & Noble, 1967).

44. For complete historical treatment of travel, see Samuel Eliot Morison, *The European Discovery of America: The Northern Voyages, A.D. 500–1600* (New York: Oxford University Press, 1971) and *The European Discovery of America: The Southern Voyages, A.D. 1492–1616* (New York: Oxford University Press, 1974). I am deeply indebted to these volumes for the factual information provided.

45. See Germán Arciniegas, *Germans in the Conquest of America* (New York: Macmillan, 1943).

46. Champlain, *Voyages*, 121–71.

47. Frank Bergon, Introduction to *The Journals of Lewis and Clark* (London: Penguin, 1989), ix.

48. Stephen Greenblatt, *Marvelous Possessions: The Wonder of the New World* (Chicago: University of Chicago Press, 1991), 130–32; 136–37; 138–39.

49. There are three translations I compared and used: *Hernan Cortés: Letters from Mexico,* trans. and ed. A. R. Pagden (New York: Grossman, 1971); *Fernando Cortés: Five Letters, 1519–1526,* trans. J. Baynard Morris (New York: W. W. Norton, 1969); and *His Five Letters of Relation to the Emperor Charles V, 1519–1526,* introduced by John Greenway, trans. and ed. Francis Augustus MacNutt (Glorieta, NM: Rio Grande Press, 1977).

50. For a discussion of the shield of Emperor Charles V, see John Block Friedman, *The Monstrous Races in Medieval Art and Thought* (Cambridge: Harvard University Press, 1981), 201.

51. I have consulted Bernal Díaz del Castillo, *The True History of the Conquest of New Spain* [1632] trans. by Alfred Percival Maudslay, 5 vols. (London: Hakluyt Society, 1908–1916). There are two other editions I found useful. The more complete is *The Discovery and Conquest of New Mexico, 1517–1521,* [1632], shortened from Maudslay's longer version, ed. Irving A. Leonard (New York: Farrar, Strauss & Giroux, 1956). The shorter and handier is *The Conquest of New Spain,* [1632], trans. J. M. Cohen (London: Penguin, 1963). My references here will be to the latter, abbreviated Diaz, *Conquest,* ed. Cohen.

52. As indicated, this is *not* a complete list, but most of the known "codices." See another partial listing in David Carrasco, *Quetazlcoatl and the Ironies of Empire* (Chicago: University of Chicago Press, 1982), 18, 21, 24, 26, 29–31, 32–33, 42–48, 157–59, 161–64. Also see Miguel Léon-Portilla, *Pre-Columbian Literatures of Mexico* (Norman: University of Oklahoma Press, 1969), 177–78.

53. Zelia Nuttall, ed., *Codex Nuttall* (1902; reprint, New York: Dover Books, 1975).

54. Patricia Rieff Anwalt and Frances F. Berdan, "The Codex Mendoza," *Scientific American* 266, no. 6 (1992): 41. A new edition of the *Codex Mendoza* is edited by Frances F. Berdan and Patricia Rieff Anawalt. 4 vols. (Berkeley: University of California Press, 1992).

55. Jill Leslie Furst, ed., *Codex Vindobonensis Mexicanus I: A Commentary* (Albany: State University of New York, Institute for Mesoamerican Studies Publication 4, 1978), 7.

56. José Rabasa, "Dialogue as Conquest: Mapping Spaces for Counter Discourse," in *The Nature and Context of Minority Discourse,* ed. Abdul R. JanMohammed and David Lloyd (Oxford: Oxford University Press, 1990), 209.

57. Details may be found also in William H. Prescott, *The Complete and Unexpurgated History of the Conquest of Mexico and History of the Conquest of Peru* (New York: Random House, n.d.), 210–220.

58. See John Greenway, Introduction to *Cortés: Five Letters,* ed. Macnutt, 1: 17.

59. Irving Rouse, *The Taínos: Rise & Decline of the People Who Greeted Columbus* (New Haven: Yale University Press, 1992), 142.

60. Greenblatt, *Marvelous Possessions,* 88.

61. Ibid., 99.

62. Marianna Torgovnick, *Gone Primitive: Savage Intellects; Modern Lives* (Chicago: University of Chicago Press, 1990), 4.

63. *Cortés: Five Letters,* ed. Macnutt, 1: 233.

64. Ibid., 234–35.

CHAPTER 2

1. J. C. Cooper, *Chinese Alchemy: The Taoist Quest for Immortality* (New York: Sterling, 1990), 42. Also see Huang Di, *The Yellow Emperor's Book of Medicine* trans. Maoshing Ni (Boston: Shambhala,1995). The work, attributed to the legendary Yellow Emperor, takes the form of a discourse between the emperor and his ministers.

2. C. P. Fitzgerald *China: A Short Cultural History* (London: Cresset, 1986), 231.

3. See "The Annals of the Bamboo Books," in James Legge, *The Shoo King, or the Book of Historical Documents,* vol. 3 of *The Chinese Classics* (Hong Kong: Hong Kong University Press,1960) 3: 150–51, separate pagination. If pagination is not continuous and/or is duplicated, I shall indicate by the term "separate pagination."

4. Legge, *Shoo King, Chinese Classics,* 3: 150–5, separate pagination.

5. Irene M. Franck and David M. Brownstone, *The Silk Road* (New York: Facts on File, 1986), 34.

6. Ibid., 34.

7. Ibid., 35.

8. Wing-Tsit Chan, *A Source Book in Chinese Philosophy* (Princeton: Princeton University Press, 1963), 5 n. 6.

9. Burton Watson, trans., *The Tso Chuan* (New York: Columbia University Press, 1989), 166.

10. Cooper, *Chinese Alchemy*, 42.

11. James Legge, *Confucian Analects, Great Learning, Doctrine of the Mean*, vol 1 of 5 of *The Chinese Classics* (Hong Kong: University of Hong Kong Press, 1960), "Texts," 245, n. 1–3.

12. Chuang Tsu, *Inner Chapters*, trans. Gia-Fu Feng and Jane English (New York: Vintage, 1974), 125.

13. Quoted in Kenneth Dean, *Taoist Ritual and Popular Cults of Southeast China* (Princeton: Princeton University Press, 1993), 71.

14. Michael Loewe, *Ways to Paradise: The Chinese Quest for Immortality* (London: George Allen & Unwin, 1979) discusses the Chinese *spiritual* interest in alchemy as opposed to the western *material* concern for the manufacture of gold.

15. *Chinese History* (Beijing: China Reconstructs Press, 1988), 131–32. I have used dates from this text, as well as C. P. Fitzgerald's.

16. Poem by He Shanyan, quoted in Dean, *Taoist Ritual*, 80.

17. Ssu-ma Chien [pinyin, Sima Qian], *Records of the Grand Historian of China*, trans. Burton Watson (New York: Columbia University Press, 1961), 2:155–92.

18. Ibid., 2: 155.

19. Ibid., 2: 192.

20. Ibid., 2: 155. See 2: 182–83 for a good example of Xiongnu [Hsiung-nu] battle tactics.

21. Suntzu, *The Art of War*, trans. Samuel B. Griffith (London: Oxford University Press, 1963), 80.

22. Ssu-ma Chien, *Records*, 2: 158 n. 3.

23. See Li Yu-Ning, ed., *The First Emperor of China* (White Plains, NY: International Arts and Sciences Press, 1974).

24. See map in Paul H. Clyde and Burton F. Beers, *The Far East: A History of Western Impact and Eastern Response* (New York: Prentice Hall, 1966).

25. Ssu-ma Chien, *Records*, 2: 166–67.

26. Arthur Waley, introduction to *One Hundred and Seventy Chinese Poems* (London: Constable & Co., 1918), 4–5.

27. Ibid., "Lament of Hsi-Chün," 53.

28. Ssu-ma Chien, *Records,* 2: 169–70.

29. Confucius, *The Analects,* trans. D. C. Lau (London: Penguin, 1979), 67.

30. Information concerning Zhang Qian may be found in the primary source Ssu-ma Chien, *Records* 2: 264–274. In addition, also see n.a. *Chinese History*, 45–46; 51–52 and Jacques Gernet, *A History of Chinese Civilization* (Cambridge: Cambridge University Press, 1982), 117–128.

31. Ssu-ma Chien, *Records,* 2: 268.

32. Ibid.

33. Ibid.

34. Ibid.

35. Details found in Hugh B. O'Neill, *Companion to Chinese History* (New York: Facts on File, 1987), 160, 286, 369, 372–73.

36. *Mencius,* trans. D. C. Lau (London: Penguin, 1970), 114.

37. Ssu-ma Chien, *Records,* 2: 268.

38. Franck and Brownstone, 96.

39. Ssu-ma Chien, *Records,* 2: 266.

40. Ssu-ma Chien, *Records,* 2: 274.

41. Ssu-ma Chien, *Records,* 2: 269. There is some debate as to whether "Shen-tu" could have meant India proper or a was a "general literary designation" for an entire area, including north India. See Thomas Watters, ed., *On Yuan Chwang's Travels in India* (New Delhi: Munshiram Manoharlal Publishers, 1973), 132–38.

42. Ssu-ma Chien, *Records,* 2: 273–74.

43. *Chinese History,* 45.

44. Ibid., 46.

45. Ibid., 44.

46. See *The I Ching,* trans. James Legge (New York: Dover, 1963), introduction, 1–55. As noted, Legge has done a great deal of translating on which the nonexpert must rely. Unfortunately, he has his own distinctive orthography, in addition to interpretations that are often turgid, long winded, and very Western oriented (oftentimes with a very Christian slant).

47. Ssu-ma Chien, *Records,* 2: 274–75.

48. Ibid., 2, 285.

49. Ibid., 2, 285.

50. Quoted in Franck and Brownstone, *Silk Road,* 110.

51. Legge, *Shoo King, Chinese Classics,* 3:142–151.

52. Ibid., 3: 147.

53. Ibid., 3: 150.

54. Ssu-ma Chien, *Records,* 2: 268–69.

55. Arthur Waley, "The Heavenly Horses of Ferghana: A New View," *History Today* 5, no. 2 (1950), 96–97. See also another reference to a horse immortalized in a Chinese hymn, 99.

CHAPTER 3

1. For historical background, consult Pan Ku [Ban Gu], *The History of the Former Han Dynasty,* ed. Homer Dubs (Baltimore: Waverly Press, 1955), 3:125–461 and selections from Pan Ku [Ban Gu], *Courtier and Commoner in Ancient China,* trans. Burton Watson (New York: Columbia University Press, 1974), 233, 246, 267.

2. Fitzgerald, *China,* 194–201, 217. For a note on the family, see Wm. Theodore de Bary et al., ed., *Sources of Chinese Tradition* 2 vols. (New York: Columbia University Press, 1960), 1: 237–38.

3. For details of Ban Chao, see Ibid., 194–96, for Bau Gu and Ban Zhao, see Gernet, *Chinese Civilization,* 167.

4. See Legge, *Shoo King, Chinese Classics,* 3: 141–51.

5. See Watson's introduction in Pan Ku [Ban Gu], *Courtier and Commoner,* 5.

6. For the official Han version of the Xiongnu, see Ssu-ma Chien, *Records,* 2: 155–92.

7. Reference to this letter is made in Franck and Brownstone, *Silk Road,* 125. Ban Gu wrote to his brother, "I now send 300 pieces of white silk, which I want you to trade for Bactrian horses, storax [an aromatic], and rugs."

8. See the discussion of the "Mandate of Heaven" in Wing-Tsit Chan, *Source Book,* 6–8, 22–23, 45, 62, 78, 93, 225. Also, as advanced by Neo-Confucianists, see 528, 599, 699. The term is first mentioned in Ode no. 235, cited in Chan, 67, which states that "Heaven's mandate is not constant."

9. Huang Tsung-Hsi, *Waiting for the Dawn: A Plan for the Prince,* trans. Wm. Theodore de Bary (New York: Columbia University Press, 1993). See especially 91–93. As he compares the past with the present, Huang states, "In ancient times all-under-Heaven were considered the master, and the prince was the tenant. . . . Now the prince is master, and all-under-Heaven are tenants"(p. 92).

10. Fitzgerald, *China,* 197–98; Franck and Brownstone, *Silk Road,* 126–29.

11. Gernet, *Chinese Civilization,* 133.

12. As quoted by Fitzgerald, *China,* 197. Also see Franck and Brownstone, *Silk Road,* 127.

13. See Confucius, *Analects,* 68–69, and for Mencius's detailed instructions on

filial obligations toward a mother, see *Mencius*, 89–90.

14. Fitzgerald, *China*, 198.

15. Ibid., 198–200. Here Fitzgerald translates and quotes a lengthy passage from the *Hou Han Shu*.

16. Fitzgerald, *China*, 199; Franck and Brownstone, *Silk Road*, 129–30.

17. Fitzgerald, *China*, 200.

18. See Pliny, *Natural History*, ed. H. Rackham et al. 10 vols. (Cambridge: Harvard University Press, 1938–1967). Perhaps we should not be too hard on Pliny. Around 425 B.C., he categorically wrote that "Asia is inhabited as far as India; farther east the country is uninhabited, and nobody knows what it is like." Also see Herodotus, *The Histories*, trans. Aubrey de Sélincourt (London: Penguin, 1954), 283.

19. Pliny, *Natural History*, 2: Book VI, 279.

20. Ibid., 2: Book VI, 379.

21. As quoted in Franck and Brownstone, *Silk Road*, 132.

22. Pliny, *Natural History*, 2: Book VI, 379.

23. Pliny as translated by Franck and Brownstone, *Silk Road*, 132.

24. Pliny, *Natural History*, 2: Book VI, 379.

25. Hugh B. O'Neill, *Companion to Chinese History* (New York: Facts on File, 1987), 260–61.

26. Consult Wing-Tsit Chan, *Source Book*, 336–342, for good treatment of early Buddhism in China; and for various schools of Buddhism, including the Ideation Only School of Xuanzang, 370–95; and for Zen, 425–49.

27. See Aurel Stein, *Innermost Asia* (Oxford: Clarendon University Press, 1928): 1: 232; 243–44, and, more importantly, his *Ruins of Desert Cathay* (New York: Benjamin Bloom, 1912), 1:274, 283, 469 and 2: 227, 252, 369. Also see L. Augustus Waddell, *Lhasa and Its Mysteries* (New York: E.P. Dutton, 1905). Since many of these turn-of-the-century explorer/travelers had their own agendas, which consisted mainly of contrasting British might with any other culture, one has to approach them warily.

28. Richard Stoneman, ed., *The Great Alexander Romance*, (London: Penguin, 1991), 186.

29. Matthew Paris, for instance, argued that they were a "monstrous and inhuman race [who] had burst forth from the northern mountains." He punned on "Tartar" and "Tartarus." See Matthew Paris's 1238 entry in James Bruce Ross and Mary Martin McLaughlin, eds., *The Portable Medieval Reader* (London: Penguin, 1955), 465. William of Rubruck actually visited the mythical area. See also Manuel Komroff, ed., *Contemporaries of Marco Polo* (New York: Dorset, 1989), 198.

30. See Arrian, *The Campaigns of Alexander* (London: Penguin, 1971) 179–86,

and Peter Green, *Alexander of Macedon* (Berkeley: University of California Press, 1991), 282–95 and 297–349.

31. William H. Willets, *Chinese Art*. 2 vols. (Harmondsworth, UK: Penguin, 1958), 1: 324 in which the author argues that "the Buddha image was invented at Mathura and not in Gandhara." He places Gandharan art well into the second and third centuries A.D. On the other hand, Kenneth Ch'en, in *Buddhism in China* (Princeton: Princeton University Press, 1964), 77 points out that at least two Chinese pilgrims would have seen and admired Gandhara. René Grousset in his free adaptation of both of Xuanzang's accounts, *In the Footsteps of the Buddha* (New York: Grossman, 1971), 948, notes that the pilgrims would have seen "these profiles of positively Appolonian purity" when they looked "at the first images which the hand of man had made of the apostle of their religion."

32. Willetts, *Chinese Art.*, 1: 325–39 especially Figs 49, 50, 51, 52, 53, and 54.

33. Ibid., 339. Willetts notes "a new lease of life" in Chinese depictions and suggests that these may be traceable to early models brought to China by Kumarajiva, who is discussed further on.

34. The historical Buddha's life is recounted in the *Buddha-Karita of Asvaghosha* in *Buddhist Mahayana Texts,* ed., E. B. Cowell et al (New York: Dover, 1969), Part 1, 1–201 (of 2 Parts, individually numbered). Also see Sir Edwin Arnold, *The Light of Asia* (London: Kegan Paul, Trench, Trübner & Co., 1906), which is important since it demonstrates European curiosity about the East.

35. Fitzgerald, *China,* 277.

36. Gernet, *Chinese Civilization,* 215–16.

37. The Chinese called the Kushans the "Great Yüeh-chih" (pinyin, Yuezhi) See Ssu-ma Chien, *Records,* 2:267–68. Also see Xuanzang's praise for him in Samuel Beal, ed., *Si-yu-ki: Buddhist Records of the Western World.* 2 vols. (London: Trubner & Co., 1884) 1: 117.

38. For detailed information on these early Buddhist Indian monks, consult Wing-Tsit Chan, *Source Vook,* 370–71, and He Zhaowu et al., *An Intellectual History of China* (Beijing: Foreign Language Press, 1991), 213–17.

39. Gernet, *Chinese Civilization,* 218–19.

40. For general background, I consulted the following: Kenneth K. S. Ch'en, *Buddhism in China* (Princeton: Princeton University Press, 1964); Edward Conze, trans., *Buddhist Scriptures* (London: Penguin, 1959); Caroline A.F. Rhys Davids ed., *Stories of the Buddha* (New York: Dover Publications, 1989); Wm. Theodore de Bary, ed., *The Buddhist Tradition* (New York: Vintage Books, 1972); *The Dhammapada,* trans. Juan Mascaró (London: Penguin, 1973); and D. T. Susuki, *Manual of Zen Buddhism* (New York: Grove Press, 1960). Specifically, some discussion of the

Mahayana and Theravada schools may be found in Ch'en, 11–14. The proper term for "Theravada" is "Hinayana" which gets rid of the troublesome reference to the "Lesser Vehicle."

41. Concerning Ch'an, see Kenneth Ch'en, *Buddhism in China,* 357–364.

42. De Bary, *Sources,* 1: 348.

43. Gernet, *Chinese Civilization,* 225.

44. Ibid., 222–25. Also see Map 12, p 224 and I-Ching's account in Latika Lahiri, *Chinese Monks in India* (Delhi: Motilal Banarsidass, 1986).

45. Samuel Beal, trans., *Travels of Fah-hian and Sung-yun* (New York: Augustus M. Kelley, 1969), 1: 54.

46. Grousset, *In the Footsteps,* 126.

47. Faxian, *A Record of Buddhistic Kingdoms,* trans. James Legge (New Delhi: Munshiram Manoharlal Publishers, 1991), 12.

48. Grousset, *In the Footsteps,* 36.

49. For Xuanzang, I have used the following and made reference where relevant: Beal ed., *Si-yu-ki* ; Grousset, *In the Footsteps*; Watters, *Yuan Chwang's Travels,* and Arthur Waley, *The Real Tripitaka* (London: George Allen & Unwin, 1952).

50. Grousset, *In the Footsteps,* 30.

51. Ibid., 29.

52. Ibid., 189.

53. Beal, *Si-yu-ki,* 1: 99.

54. See, for instance, Edwin O. Reischauer, trans., *Ennin's Diary* (New York: Ronald Press, 1955). Ennin was sent by the Japanese imperial court to the Tang between 838 and 847. During this time, there was a period of persecution against Buddhists in China. Also see Philip B. Yampolsky, ed., *Selected Writings of Nichiren* (New York: Columbia University Press, 1990) for another important Japanese missionary. Nichiren (1222–1282) began the only Buddhist school to originate in Japan.

55. Wu Ch'eng-en, *The Journey to the West,* trans. Anthony C. Yu, 4 vols. (Chicago: University of Chicago Press, 1977–1983).

56. Preface by Chang Yueh in Beal, *Si-yu-ki,* 1: 5.

57. Beal, *Travels of Fah-hian and Sung-yun,* 184.

58. Beal, *Si-yu-ki,* 1:15.

59. Faxian, *A Record of Buddhistic Kingdoms,* 102–103.

60. Grousset, *In the Footsteps,* 191. Compare with Watters, *Yuan Chwang's Travels,* 349. Contemporary Chinese scientific achievements are discussed in He Zhaowu, *Intellectual History,* 192–96, 277–78.

61. Grousset, *In the Footsteps,* 66.

62. Beal, *Travels of Fah-hian and Sung-yun*, 186–88. Also see Grousset, *In the*

Footsteps, 60 n.1.

63. Compare, for instance, William of Rubruck and the description of Batu Khan in Komroff, *Contemporaries*, 131–32.

64. See a short study by Helen Kanitkar and Hemant Kanitkar, *Asoka and Indian Culture*, ed., Malcolm Yapp (San Diego: Greenhaven, 1980), or a more detailed study by Radhakumund Mookerji, *Asoka* (New Delhi: Motilal Banarsidass, 1986).

65. Ch'en, *Buddhism in China*, 338–50 adds that the concept was ably spread by "paintings and illustrations of the joys of the Western Paradise and the miseries of hell." (p. 349) He also mentions Li Bai and Du Fu, poets who were both impressed with Buddhist art work (p. 350). Also see Jean Pierre Drège and Emil M. Bührer, *The Silk Road Saga* (New York: Facts on File, 1946), 62–79, on "Dunhaung, The Sacred Oasis."

66. Bunyiu Nanjio, in Cowell et al, *Mahayana Texts*, 73 n.

67. In addition to Ch'en, *Buddhism in China* cited before, consult *The Smaller Sukhavati-Vyuha* in Cowell et al., *Mahayana Texts* 89–103. In addition, see *The Larger Sukhavati-Vyuha* also in Cowell et al., 1–72.

68. Ch'en, *Buddhism in China*, 341 traces the origin of Kuan-yin's (pinyin Guanyin) mercy to *The Lotus Sutra*. See Burton Watson, ed., *The Lotus Sutra* (New York: Columbia University Press, 1993), 298–306.

69. See *The Diamond Sutra & the Sutra of Hui-neng*, trans A. F. Price and Wong Mou-lam (Boston: Shambala, 1990) as follows: *Diamond Sutra*, 17–53 and *Sutra of Hui-neng*, 67–154.

70. *Diamond Sutra*, 70.

71. The Eightfold Path to Righteousness was expounded by Lord Buddha in his First Sermon. It consists of right understanding, right thought, right speech, right action, right livelihood, right effort, right awareness, and right meditation. Through correct observation of these, the believer may be freed from suffering and thus achieve Nirvana. See Paul Thomas Welty, *The Asians: Their Heritage and Their Destiny* (Philadelphia: J. P. Lippincott, 1970), 73–77.

72. I am using *The Diamond Sutra & The Sutra of Hui-neng*, previously cited. Hui-neng is called a "barbarian" because he comes from another part of China. Also see some background information on the manuscript of the *Sutra of Hui-neng* in Wing-Tsit Chan, *Source Book,* 430, n.17. He seems to agree that the work is not "autobiographical" and was probably written by an eighth-century monk.

73. *Sutra of Hui-neng*, 74.

74. Faxian, *A Record of Buddhistic Kingdoms,* 105.

CHAPTER 4

1. For background information on the Mongols, see R. P. Lister, *The Secret History of Genghis Khan* (London: Peter Davies, 1969); Robert Marshall, *Storm from the East* (Berkeley: University of California Press, 1993) and the four part television series of the same name; and David Morgan, *The Mongols* (Oxford: Blackwell, 1986). Above all, Herbert Franke and Denis Twitchett, eds., *The Cambridge History of China* (Cambridge: Cambridge University Press, 1994) was particularly informative. I am indebted to all these sources for background information.

2. For biographical information on Yeh-lü Ch'u-ts'ai (pinyin, Yelü Chucai) see O'Neill, *Companion,* 370–71. For more details concerning the role he played in government, particularly his reforms, fall from power and death, see Franke and Twitchett, *Cambridge History of China,* 364,375–81, 402, 636.

3. On Mongol achievement, especially canal construction, see N.A. *Ancient China's Technology and Science* (Beijing: Foreign Languages Press, 1983), 246–47. For a quick review of Chinese technical contributions to the world, see Gernet, *Chinese Civilization,* 378, Table 16, and for Mongol achievements in particular, see Gernet 364–68.

4. See A. C. Scott, *Traditional Chinese Plays,* 3 vols. (Madison: University of Wisconsin Press, 1967–1973) as follows: vol. I (1967); vol. 2 (1969); vol. 3 (1973). Also consult the introduction by Liu Jung-en, ed., *Six Yüan Plays* (London: Penguin, 1972), 7–35. Details concerning the first hexagram may be found in "The Khien Hexagram," which states "Khien (represents) what is great and originating, penetrating, advantageous, correct and firm." See Legge, *I Ching,* 57. Also see John D. Langlois, *China Under Mongol Rule* (Princeton: Princeton University Press, 1981), 4 including n.2 and n.3. About the importance of the term "Yüan," Tung Chung-Shu (c. 179–c.104 BC) has commented:

It is only the Sage who can relate the myriad things to the One and tie it to the origin. If the source is not traced and the development from it followed, nothing can be accomplished. Therefore in the *Spring and Autumn Annals* the first year is changed to be called the year of *yüan* (origin). The origin is the same as source (*yüan*). It means that it accompanies the beginning and end of Heaven and Earth. Therefore if man in his life has a beginning and end like this, he does not have to respond to the changes of the four seasons. Therefore the origin is the source of all things, and the origin of man is found in it. How does it exist? It exists before Heaven and Earth.

Cited in Wing-Tsit Chan, *Source Book,* 285. Obviously, the Mongols had learned how to utilize their Sinicization to their own advantage. Their name itself was a bold, propagandistic initiative, what we would laud today as good public relations strategy.

See commentary by Langlois, *China Under Mongol Rule*, introduction, 3–7.

5. Gernet, *Chinese Civilization,* 374.

6. Marshall, *Storm from the East,* 217.

7. See Francis Woodman Cleaves, *The Secret History of the Mongols* (Cambridge: Harvard University Press, 1982), introduction,xvii–lxv.

8. Cleaves, *Secret History,* i. See variant readings in Cleaves's introduction, xxv–xxvi, in which the wolf's color is sometimes rendered as "blue-white."

9. Serge A. Zenkovsky, ed., *Medieval Russia's Epics, Chronicles and Tales* (New York: Penguin, 1963), 197.

10. Ibid., 199–200.

11. Ibid., 202.

12. Ibid., 208.

13. *The Hungarian Illuminated Chronicle* (Budapest: Corvina Press, 1969), 140. It should be noted that an entirely different picture of the Huns is painted in the *Chronica Picta* (1358–1370; reprint Budapest: Helikan Publishing House, 1991), which is an anonymous fourteenth-century codex in the Hungarian National Library. There, the Huns are not seen as even remotely connected with the Mongols. As such, the continuity of good government from the time of Atilla himself not only confirmed divine right, but additionally showed that a God-fearing ruler would always be the victorious leader of a prosperous people.

14. *The Hungarian Illuminated Chronicle,* 141.

15. Richard Vaughan, ed., *The Illustrated Chronicles of Matthew Paris* (Cambridge, UK: Alan Sutton, 1993), 14.

16. Ibid., 78.

17. James Bruce Ross and Mary Martin McLaughlin, *The Portable Medieval Reader* (London: Penguin, 1949), 465.

18. See Ch'ang Ch'un, *The Travels of an Alchemist,* trans. Arthur Waley (Taiwan; SMC Publishing, 1991). As in the text, I will refer to him here as Changchun.

19. In Ibid., 96, Changchun says rather curtly, "My diet . . . consists of rice, meal and vegetables. Please convey this fact to the Khan's son." Chang was expressing his apprehensions about the long journey to the Hindu Kush, where he had been just told Chingiz had gone, and the food of a "civilized" Chinese aesthete.

20. Waley translates much of the sermon to Chingiz in his introduction to Changchun, *Travels of an Alchemist,* 21.

21. Ibid., 22.

22. Ibid., 23.

23. Waley's introduction in Ibid., 8.

24. "The Journey of William of Rubruck," in Christopher Dawson, ed., *Mission to*

Asia (Toronto: University of Toronto Press, 1980), 187–194.

25. Waley's introduction to Changchun, *Travels of an Alchemist,* 32.

26. See John of Plano Carpini's "History of the Mongols," in Dawson, *Mission to Asia,* 6.

27. Ibid., 11–12.

28. Cleaves, *Secret History,* 162.

29. Reprinted and trans. in Dawson, *Mission to Asia,* 73–76.

30. Ibid., 75.

31. Ibid., 86. The translation of the entire letter is on pages 85–86.

32. Ibid., 86.

33. Ibid., 93.

34. Ibid., 106.

35. Ibid., 92, 128–9, 152, 154, 206.

36. Of course, William of Rubruck was familiar with areas outside his own "center." He seems to have been specially chosen by King Louis because of his experience in eastern Europe. Dawson points out in his introduction to *Mission to Asia* that William of Rubruck began his journey from Acre, "was in touch with Armenians, Syrians and Greeks," and did not go to the East via Russia, but via "the old highway to Central Asia through Constantinople and the Crimea." (xxii)

37. For more on this, see T. W. Arnold, "Arab Travellers and Merchants: A.D. 1000–1500," in Arthur Percival Newton, ed., *Travel and Travellers of the Middle Ages* (London: Routledge & Kegan Paul, 1926), 88–103. Also see Ibn Battuta, *The Adventures of Ibn Battuta,* ed. Ross E Dunn (Berkeley: University of California Press, 1986), 213–14, 222, 225, 250, 259, 271.

38. Dawson, *Mission to Asia,* 128–9.

39. For information about Jewish travelers, see Elkan Nathan Adler, ed., *Jewish Travellers in the Middle Ages* (Mineola, NY: Dover, 1987), and for African travelers, see in particular, Thomas J. Abercrombie, "Ibn Battuta: Prince of Travelers," *National Geographic* 180, no.6 (1991): 2–49.

40. I deal with this in my book *Imagining the World: Mythical Belief versus Reality in Global Encounters* (Westport, CT: Bergin & Garvey, 1994). See 81–94 and 117–128.

41. John Block Friedman, *The Monstrous Races in Medieval Art and Thought* (Cambridge: Harvard University Press, 1981), 9–21.

42. See Columbus, *Four Voyages,* vol 1: 28, 30–32, 34, 36.

43. See James E. Bruson "African Presence in Early China," in Ivan Van Sertima and Runoko Rashdi, eds., *African Presence in Early Asia* (New Brunswick: Transaction Publishers, 1988), 120–137.

44. For Matteo Ricci, see Vincent Cronin, *The Wise Man from the West* (New York: E. P. Dutton, 1955), and George H. Dunne, *Generation of Giants* (Notre Dame: University of Notre Dame Press, 1962).

CHAPTER 5

1. For a discussion of Chinese achievements in maritime navigation, see *Ancient China's Technology and Science*, 494–503. On the compass and its part in seafaring, see Ibid., 152–65.

2. Regarding Islam in China, consult Gernet, *China Civilization;* 287 and 380–2 as well as Marshall, *Storm from the East;* Broomhall, *Islam in China: A Neglected Problem* (1910; reprint, New York: Paragon, 1966); Toby E. Huff, *The Rise of Early Modern Science: Islam, China, and the West* (Cambridge: Cambridge University Press, 1993); and Raphael Israeli, *Islam in China: A Critical Biography* (Westport, CT: Greenwood, 1994).

3. Chau Ju-Kua (pinyin, Zhao Rugua) *Chu-fan-chi* , trans. Frederick Hirth and W. W. Rockhill (New York: Paragon, 1966), 275. I will indicate the actual names of translated sources of relevant works in the text, but in most instances, simply list them as part of the notes or introduction of this important work.

4. Ssu-ma Chien, *Records,* 2: 278 and 288.

5. Legge, *Shoo King, Chinese Classics,* 3: 147–149.

6. Confucius, *Analects*, 139.

7. *Mencius,* 151.

8. Ssu-ma Chien, *Records,* 2:278.

9. Ibid., 2: 288.

10. Ibid., 2: 289.

11. I have retained the chronology, facts, and some translation of Snow, *Star Raft,* 21–36.

12. Faxian, *A Record of Buddhistic Kingdoms,* 101.

13. For details of Cosmas's life and work, see Cosmas Indicopleustes, *The Christian Topography of Cosmas, an Egyptian Monk,* trans. and ed. T. W. Crindle (London: Hakluyt Society, 1897, Old Series Number 98), 47.

14. Ibid., 365.

15. Snow, *Star Raft,* 3.

16. Ibn Khaldun, as translated from the French, by J. Devisse and S. Labib, in "Africa in Inter-Continental Relations," in *UNESCO General History,* 4:637 n.5. Also see Ibn Khaldun, *The Muqadimah: An Introduction to History* , trans. Franz

Rosenthal (1377; reprint, Princeton: Princeton University Press, 1967), 58–59, 63, 117.

17.   Zhao Rugua, *Chu-fan-chi*, 9.

18.   Ibid., 18.

19.   I. Hrbek, "Africa in the Context of World History," in *UNESCO General History of Africa*, 3: 23.

20.   Zhao Rugua, *Chu-fan-chi*, 15–19.

21.   Ibid., 20.

22.   F. T. Masao and H. W. Mutoro, "The East African Coast and the Comoro Islands," in *UNESCO General History of Africa*, 3: 612.

23.   Marco Polo, *The Description of the World* eds. A. C. Moule and Paul Pelliot. 2 vols. (London: George Routledge & Sons, 1938), 1: 416.

24.   Snow, *Star Raft*, 5.

25.   Zhao Rugua, *Chu-fan-chi*, 126.

26.   Ibid., 127.

27.   Scott, *Traditional Chinese Plays*, 9.

28.   *Ancient China's Technology and Science*, 257.

29.   Mandeville is useful because he synthesized the wild beliefs of earlier European travels. See *Mandeville's Travels*, trans. Malcolm Letts (London: Hakluyt Society, 1953), 1:117.

30.   Zhao Rugua, *Chu-fan-chi*, 151.

31.   Ibid., 151.

32.   Ibid., 149.

33.   Ibid., 149.

34.   Ibid., 130–31.

35.   Ibid., 149.

36.   Ibid., 128; also see 129 n.6 and 7.

37.   Jan Knappert, *A Choice of Flowers* (London: Heinemann, 1972), 2.

38.   Lyndon Harries, *Swahili Poetry* (Oxford: Clarendon Press, 1962), 3.

39.   Masao and Mutoro, in *UNESCO General History of Africa* , 3: 615.

40.   For biographical information on Zheng He (Cheng Ho), I have used L. C. Goodrich and Chaoying Fang, eds., *Dictionary of Ming Biography: 1368–1644* (New York: Columbia University Press, 1976).

41.   *Cambridge History of China*, 7: 232.

42.   J.J.L. Duyvendak, *China's Discovery of Africa* (London: Arthur Probsthain, 1949), 14.

43.   In Chan Ju-kua, *Chu-fan-chi* 128.

44.   Ibid., 130–31. Also see n.1 on these pages.

45. Ibid., 149.

46. Duyvendak, *China's Discovery of Africa,* 23.

47. Philip Snow gives an interesting account in which he says that, as late as the 1960s in the midst of Mao's great experiment in international coexistence, rather startled African students were greeted by "Hallo, uncle black man [*hei ren*]," *Star Raft,* 198. For 1980s update, see Snow, 186–212. Indeed, all foreigners come in for a dose of Chinese ethnocentrism, being addressed as *laowai* (old foreigner).

48. "The Annals of the Bamboo Books," in Legge, *Chinese Classics,* 3:150–51, separate pagination.

49. *P'ing-chóu-k'o-t'an* (pinyin, *Pingchouketan*) in Zhao Rugua, *Chu-fan-chi,* 31–32 n.2.

50. Duyvendak, *China's Discovery of Africa,* 22.

CHAPTER 6

1. Albert Chan, *The Glory and Fall of the Ming Dynasty*. (Norman: University of Oklahoma Press, 1982), 18–116.

2. Ibid., 117–119.

3. *Cambridge History of China,* 7: 232–39, including Map 11. See also the detailed account in Ma Huan, *Ying-yai Sheng-lan: The Overall Survey of the Ocean's Shores* [1433]. Trans. by J.V.G. Mills (Cambridge: The University Press, Hakluyt Second Series, 1970), 8–19. For a careful reconstruction of Zheng He's (Cheng Ho) dates of travel, see J.J.L. Duyvendak, "The True Dates of the Chinese Maritime Expeditions in the Early Fifteenth Century," *T'oung Pao,* 34 (1938), 395.

4. Albert Chan, *The Glory and Fall,* xxii.

5. J.V.G. Mills, introduction to Ma Huan, *Ying-yai Sheng-lan,* 55–64.

6. Ma Huan, *Ying-yai Sheng-lan,* 69.

7. Mills introduction to Ma Huan, *Ying-yai Sheng-lan,* 34–37 contains what little is known of Ma Huan.

8. Ibid., 37–41.

9. For the foreword of 1416 by Ma Huan, see Ma Huan, *Ying-yai Sheng-lan,* 69–70. For poem see Ibid., 73–75. The poem was also found in a 1597 novel, for it apparently appealed to the fantastic. See Mills's note 1 of Ibid., 73. For Ma Ching's foreword of 1444, see Ibid., 71–72.

10. Ma Ching, foreword to Ma Huan, *Ying-yai Sheng-lan,* 71–72.

11. Ma Huan, *Ying-yai Sheng-lan,* 73.

12. See Duyvendak, *China's Discovery of Africa,* 27, for one possible explanation.

13. Ma Huan, *Ying-yai Sheng-lan,* 83.

14. Ibid., 93.

15. Ibid., 104.

16. For more on Plinian Wife-Givers, and other monsters, see Friedman, *Monstrous Races,* 9–21. This was replicated in the "discoveries" of Odoric, Marco Polo, and, of course, Mandeville and resurfaced in the New World in the accounts of Columbus and the conquistadors.

17. Ma Huan, *Ying-yai Sheng-lan,* 127.

18. See J.V.G. Mills comment in note 1, Ibid., 127.

19. See the account of the arrival of the giraffe in Duyvendak, *China's Discovery of Africa,* 32–35, including a laudatory poem composed in its honor. On the cover of Duyvendak's book, he reproduces one of the two paintings its arrival inspired.

20. Ibid., 33–34.

21. Ibid., 33.

22. Confucius in *Mencius,* 121.

23. *Mencius,* 120.

24. Ma Huan, *Ying-yai Sheng-lan,* 159.

25. Ibid., 123.

26. Ma Huan's foreword to Ma Huan, *Ying-yai Sheng-lan,* 70. Also see Mills's note 3 on the same page, concerning Chinese attitudes to barbarians and the emperor's obligations.

27. Mills, introduction to Ma Huan, *Ying-yai Sheng-lan,* 13.

28. Edward Dreyer, *Early Ming China: A Political History, 1355–1435* (Stanford: Stanford University Press, 1982), 195.

29. Yap Yong and Arthur Cotterell, *The Early Civilization of China* (New York: G. P. Putnam's Sons, 1975), 112. Vasco da Gama (b. circa 1460–1524) made three voyages around the Cape of Good Hope: the first in 1497–1499, the second in 1502–1503, and the third in 1524, when he was appointed Viceroy of India. On the first voyage, he had to rely on Arab/African help to get to India, showing just how familiar East Africans and Arabs were with navigational skills. The name of the pilot was Ibn Masdjid al-Din Ahmad. For publication of his maps, first published with an Arab text in 1490, see G. R. Tibbetts, *Arab Navigation in the Indian Ocean Before the Coming of the Portuguese* (London: Royal Asiatic Society of Great Britain and Ireland, 1971). Also see *UNESCO General History of Africa,* 4: 659.

30. Yap and Cotterell, *Early Civilization of China,* 264.

31. Niane, *UNESCO General History,* 4: 657, Plate 26.1.

32. Ibid., 4: 659.

33. The navigational charts have been published by G. Fernand, *Instructions*

nautiques et routiers arabes et portugais des 15e et 16e siècles, 3 vols. (Paris: Geuthner, 1921–1928).

34. *UNESCO General History of Africa,* 4: 655.

35. Daniel Boorstin, *The Discoverers* (New York: Vintage Books, 1983), 190.

36. For a translation of Fei Xin (Fei Hsin) see W. W. Rockhill, "Notes on the Relations and Trade of China with the Eastern Archipelago and the Coasts of the Indian Ocean During the Fourteenth Century, Ormuz, Coast of Arabia and Africa," Part 1, *T'oung Pao,* 15 (1915), 419–447; Part 2, *T'oung Pao,* 16 (1915), 61–159, 236–71, 374–92, 435–67, 604–26.

37. Duyvendak, *China's Discovery of Africa,* 31.

38. Mills suggests four expeditions between 1409 and 1433. See his introduction to Ma Huan, *Ying-yai Sheng-lan,* 62.

39. Ibid., 61.

40. As translated in Duyvendak, *China's Discovery of Africa,* 30.

41. Ibid.

42. Ibid., 31.

43. Details regarding Mao Kun's life and his cartographical work may be found in Mills's Appendix 2 in Ma Huan, *Ying-yai Sheng-lan,* 236–302, 329–30, 346–48. My information is mainly taken from here, unless otherwise cited. One map is reproduced on pp. 290–91.

44. As translated in Duyvendak, *China's Discovery of Africa,* 31.

45. Mills, Appendix 2 in Ma Huan, *Ying-yai Sheng-lan,* 241.

46. Ibid., 302, n.5, 47. Mills mentions that the delineation of the East African coast on the map is about 4.6 inches for 990 miles. Ibid., Appendix 2, 247.

48. N.A. *Ancient China's Technology and Science,* 250–257.

49. Mills in Ma Huan, *Ying-yai Sheng-lan,* Appendix 2, 253.

50. Snow, *Star Raft,* 15.

51. Ibid., 10.

CHAPTER 7

1. Concerning Faxian's journey home by sea, consult Faxian, *A Record of Buddhistic Kingdoms,* 111–114.

2. Ibid., 111–112.

3. Ibid., 112.

4. Ibid., 113.

5. Ibid., 114.

6. I am indebted to Marshall Broomhall, *Islam in China: A Neglected Problem*

(1910; reprint New York: Paragon, 1966) for some of the factual information reprinted here; see 5–8.

7. Emil Bretschneider, *On the Knowledge Possessed by the Ancient Chinese of the Arab and Arabian Colonies*, 1871 pamphlet, quoted in Broomhall, *Islam in China*, 15.

8. Quoted in Fitzgerald, *China*, 339.

9. Ibid., 340.

10. For background information on Arabs in China, I consulted G. F. Hourani, ed., *Arab Seafaring in the Indian Ocean in Ancient and Medieval Times* (Princeton: Princeton University Press, 1981). Also see "China's Islam," in *Beijing Review*, 3, no. 28 (July 9, 1990), 29.

11. Information on An's revolt against the Tang is found in Howard S. Levy, trans. *Biography of An Lu-shan* (Berkeley: University of California Press, 1960), and E. G. Pulleybank, *The Background of the Rebellion of An Lu-shan* (London: Oxford University Press, 1955).

12. T. W. Arnold, "Arab Travellers and Merchants," 88–103.

13. Nafis Ahmad, *Muslim Contribution to Geography* (Lahore: Sh. Muhammad Ashraf, 1972), 18.

14. Ahmad Zaki Validi, "Muslim Geography," *Islamic Culture* 8 (1934), 514. For information on Buzurg ibn Shahriyar, see Hourani, *Arab Seafaring*, 65–6, 76–82, 98–100; and for al-Maqdisi, see 69–70, 79–80, and 107–8.

15. Quoted by T.W. Arnold, "Arab Travellers and Merchants," 96.

16. Ibid., 97.

17. Ibid., 95.

18. The account given is that Ibn Jubayr was determined to make the pilgrimage to Mecca after the Prince of Granada had forced him to drink seven cups of wine. He then was rewarded with seven cups of gold. He vowed to spend his new wealth, partly in expiation for this, by making the pilgrimage to Mecca. See Arnold, "Arab Travellers and Merchants," 98, Muhammad ibn Ahmad ibn Jubayr, and *Travels of Ibn Jubayr* ed. W. Wright and M. J. De Goeje (Leyden: Brill, 1907), 97, 325. William Wright's earlier first edition was published in 1852 and contained the Arab text. A more accessible text is *The Travels of Ibn Jubayr Being the Chronicle of a Medieval Spanish Moor,* trans. and ed. R.J.C. Broadhurst (London: Jonathan Cape, 1952).

19. Ibn Battuta, *Travels in Asia and Africa:1325–54,* ed. H.A.R. Gibb (New York: Robert A. McBride & Company, 1929), 283.

20. Gibb, introduction to Battuta, *Travels in Asia and Africa,* 11–12.

21. Ibid., 11.

22. Bernard Lewis, "What Went Wrong? Some Reflections on Arab History," *The*

American Scholar 62, no. 4 (1993), 601–2.

23. Battuta, *Travels in Asia and Africa,* 290.

24. See *Koran,* trans. N. J. Dawood (London: Penguin, 1990) 18:84 to 18:99, 302.

25. Ibn Khaldun, *Muqadimah,* 61, 63, 30, 51.

26. Battuta, *Travels in Asia and Africa,* 319. His description of his travels to West Africa appear on pp. 317–39.

27. Ibid., 292.

28. Ibid.

29. Odoric, *The Voyage and Travayle of Syr John Mandeville Knight with the Journall of Frier Odoricus* (London: J. M. Dent, 1887), 247.

30. Marco Polo, *Description of the World,* 2: 231.

31. For the Latin, Italian, and English versions of Toscanelli's letter, see John Boyd Thacher, *Christopher Columbus: His Life, His Work, His Remains,* 3 vols. (New York: G. P. Putnam's Sons, 1903), 1: 312–16.

32. Battuta, *Travels in Asia and Africa,* 297–98.

33. Ibid., 299.

34. Ibid., 372–73, n.29 and n.32–35, where the editor condenses some of the frustration he felt in trying to reconcile fact and fancy.

CHAPTER 8

1. Benedict Anderson, *Imagined Communities* (London: Verso, 1983). Anderson's major thesis demonstrates that more often than not, "community" arises as a direct effect of colonialism. He notes that: "At some stage in the antiresistance phase of nationalism there is a sort of dependence between the two sides of the contest" for "the cultural horizons of nationalism are fatally limited by the common history of colonizer and colonized" (p. 74). He applies this particularly to twentieth-century China; see pp. 1–2, 41–42, 69–70, 125–6, 155–6,158–61.

2. Xi Wangmu's incarnation as Daoist Immortal probably goes back to the fourth century revelations of the Mao Shan hills, located southeast of Nanking, where a young writer, Yang Xi (Yang Hsi) (c. 364 and 376 AD) was presented with a number of classical texts that were supposedly divine in origin. In turn, this gave rise to secular works such as the sixth century account of Emperor Wu's life. See de Bary et al., *Sources of Chinese Tradition,* 1: 256–61.

3. "The Annals of the Bamboo Books," in Legge, *Shoo King, Chinese Classics,* 3: 150, separate pagination.

4. James Brunson, "African Presence in Early China" in Van Sertima and

Rashidi, eds., *African Presence in Early Asia*, 132.

5.   An additional problem with this approach is that many of the assertions about early African presence in China have been advocated by writers who have tended to be more Afrocentric than academic. See, for instance, Chancellor Williams, *The Destruction of Black Civilization* (Chicago: Third World Press, 1974), 44. On the other hand, researchers such as Cheikh Anta Diop have been more scrupulous and avoided hasty conclusions. See Cheikh Anta Diop, *The African Origin of Civilization* (New York: Lawrence Hill, 1974), 280–1 and *passim*.

6.   Roger Fry, *Vision and Design* (New York: Brentano's, 1920), 103.

7.   Mariana Torgovnick, *Gone Primitive: Savage Intellects, Modern Lives* (Chicago: University of Chicago Press, 1990), 96.

8.   P'ing-chóu-k'o-t'an [sic] in Zhao Rugua, *Chu-fan-chi*, 31–32, n2.

9.   Perhaps even afterward as well. See a new book by Li Zhisui, *The Private Life of Chairman Mao* (London: Chatto and Windus, 1994), which points out the extent to which Mao's private and public image differed. Rather than reading Marx, Mao indulged fully in matters of the "spirit" as the answer to problems of a changing world. Apparently, in his later years, Mao even conceded that Buddhism made sense. Thus, he too was concerned with the past.

10.   In the post-Mao period, Zhou Enlai laid down the "Four Modernizations" in 1975, and they were officially adopted as policy in 1978. They referred to modernizing industry, agriculture, science, and technology. They also included attacking "the ideas of the exploiting classes," satisfying "spiritual needs," educating "new socialist youth," and increasing the "ideologized, cultural, and moral levels of the entire society." Deng Xiaoping then listed thirteen ways through which writers could help achieve this utopia. Cited in Michael S. Duke, *Blooming and Contending* (Bloomington: Indiana University Press, 1985), 8. Also see Mao Zedong, *Mao Tse-tung on Literature and Art* (Beijing: Foreign Language Press, 1987). Even more interestingly, see T. A. Hsia in "Heroes and Hero-Worship in Chinese Communist Fiction," in Cyril Birch, ed., *Chinese Communist Literature* (New York: Praeger, 1963), in which "fiction" becomes the means of approving a perfect present.

11.   Owen Lattimore, *Inner Asian Encounters of China* (Boston: Beacon Press, 1962), although somewhat dated, shows one aspect of how a new concept of China occurred. Lattimore stresses that an interaction between "the agriculture of China and the pastoral nomadism" of the steppe brought about a mutual dependency between Chinese and Other. (p. 382)

12.   Most contemporary critics exhibit these same reservations. See de Bary et al., *Sources of Chinese Tradition*, 1: 4. See also Burton Watson's introduction to *The Tso Chuan* (pinyin, *Zuo Zhuan*) (New York: Columbia University Press, 1989), where he

argues that it is "uncertain whether he [Confucius] had anything at all to do with the work" (p. xii).

13. See Legge, *Ch'un Ts'eu with the Tso Chuen, Chinese Classics,* vol. 5. The *Ch'un Ch'iu* or *Spring and Autumn Annals* is reprinted on pp.1–837, and the commentary on pp.838–864, both separate paginations independent of the preceding text. Burton Watson finds that the original work is "brief and laconic"; see Watson, *Tso Chuan,* xii.

14. Although much of this folk belief is no longer on the surface, I saw it present in various facets on a recent visit to China. I noted the survivals of customs, like the New Year ceremonies, that clearly predate Confucius since they bear more resemblance to nature "mythology" than to any formally constructed school of thought. Of course, as stated before, much of the "folk belief" was absorbed into later Confucianism, Daoism and Buddhism. Today, in Taiwan for instance, much of the ceremony and paraphernalia associated with folk ancestor exaltation has now become part of "temple" worship, perhaps even the way in which former leaders are revered. For background, see H. A. Giles, *Religions of Ancient China* (1906; reprint, Chicago: Open Court, 1918). Also consult Huang Di, *The Yellow Emperor's Book of Medicine.*

15. For instance, see *Mencius,* 80 and 102–4.

16. Ibid., 114.

17. David Bonavia, *The Chinese* (London: Penguin, 1980), 114.

18. He Zhaowu et al., *An Intellectual History of China* (Beijing: Foreign Languages Press, 1991), 6.

19. See D. C. Lau's introduction to *Mencius,* 12.

20. James Legge, trans., *The Texts of Taoism:The Tao Te Ching of Lao Tzu, The Writings of Chuang Tzu,* 2 vols. (New York: Dover Publications, 1962), 1: 35.

20. De Bary adds that it was difficult for both Confucius and Mencius, given the internal problems of the time, to gain a hearing even at home. "The rulers of the day," he notes, "were less than ever interested in hearing sermons on the efficacy of virtue and the wise ways of the ancients," De Bary et al. eds., *Sources of Chinese Tradition,* 1: 86.

21. Arthur Waley argues quite convincingly that there was a need for the expanse of vocabulary as new territories became incorporated. Also, because of Chinese knowledge of India through merchants and Buddhist missionaries, Waley contends that "the literature of the 3rd century is full of geographic and mythological elements derived from India." See Arthur Waley, *The Way and Its Power: A Study of the Tao Te Ching* (New York: Grove Weidenfeld, 1958), 114.

23. References will be from Ch'ang-ch'un (pinyin,Changchun), *The Travels of an Alchemist,* trans. Arthur Waley, and cited as Changchun. In the case of Waley's

introduction to the work, references will so indicate.

24. Waley, *Three Ways of Thought in Ancient China* (London: Allen & Unwin, 1939), 119.

25. Wing-Tsit Chan, *Source Book,* 211.

26. Quoted in Waley, *Three Ways,* 231.

27. Paul Thomas Welty, *The Asians* (Philadelphia: J.B.Lippincott, 1970), 168–9; 168.

28. See Wing-Tsit Chan, *Source Book,* 252.

29. For the translation used, see J.J.L. Duyvendak, *The Book of Lord Shang* (London: Probsthain, 1928).

30. Burton Watson, trans. *Basic Writings of Mo Tzu, Hsün Tzu, and Han Fei Tzu* (New York: Columbia University Press, 1963), 35. This edition utilizes separate pagination for each writer.

31. See Waley, *Three Ways,* 202–3, in which he writes that "Even in the mystical doctrine of *wu-wei*, the Non Activity of the ruler by which everything is activated, finds a non-mystical counterpart in [Legalism]" (pp. 202–3). Once the Ruler embodies his wishes in law, as with Daoism, "everything will happen of its own accord" (p. 203).

32. Watson, *Basic Writings,* 100.

33. Ibid., 97–99.

34. Some would and do argue that Legalism in modern form lies at the basis of much "authoritarianism" which the West constantly criticizes in modern China. See Yu-lan Fung and Derek Bodde, trans., *A History of Chinese Philosophy* (Princeton: Princeton University Press, 1952), and Li Yu-ning ed., *The First Emperor of China: The Politics of Historiography* (White Plains, NY: International Arts and Sciences Press, 1974).

35. Changchun, *Travels of an Alchemist,* 19.

36. Ibid., quoted by Waley in his introduction, 21.

37. As shown in Cleaves, introduction to *Secret History,* xvii–lxv.

38. Changchun's sermon translated in part by Waley, introduction to Changchun, *Travels of an Alchemist,* 21.

39. Ibid., Changchun's sermon.

40. Ibid., Changchun's sermon, Waley, 22.

41. Ibid., Waley, "Introduction," 22, n.1. Manichaeism, as taught by the Persian Mani (also known as Manichaeans), was significant between the third and seventh centuries, AD. Manichaeism was itself a synthesis of the doctrines preached by Zoroaster (Zarathustra), Gnostic Christianity, and folk beliefs. It stressed the principle of two contending forces, namely, light, which came from God and the soul,

as opposed to darkness, which represented Satan and the body.

42. Changchun's sermon, Waley, introduction to Changchun, *Travels of an Alchemist,* 22.

43. Changchun's sermon, Waley, Introduction to Changchun, 22.

44. Ibid., 113, 135, 118.

45. Perhaps Changchun was too successful for his own good and that of his sect. Although his sect was much favored for a while, by 1281 Khubilai Khan became quite tired of the constant strife between Daoists and Muslims (Waley, introduction to Changchun, *Travels of an Alchemist,* 32). After a huge disputation held at Shen-tu in 1258 had failed to bring these hostilities to an end, Khubilai decreed the destruction of all Daoist books. It should be added that this had been prevented at an earlier stage through the help of Yeh-lu Ch'uts'ai (1190–1244), a trusted Chinese who served the Mongols for thirty years. See Waley, introduction to Changchun (27–28). Yeh-lu had known Changchun personally and had even been personally sympathetic towards the Buddhist sect. But by 1222, whether for pragmatic political reasons or simple self-survival, he began to distance himself from it.

46. As mentioned before, Huang Zongxi (Huang Tsung-hsi),*Waiting for the Dawn: A Plan for the Prince* has been translated by Wm. Theodore de Bary (New York: Columbia University Press, 1993). References to the "Preface" will be cited as "de Bary," and to the Introduction and text as "Huang," where De Bary is citing Huang, or where de Bary directly quotes Huang.

47. Huang, *Waiting for the Dawn,* 7.

48. Ibid., 8, 85.

49. Ibid., De Bary, xi–xii.

50. Hung-lam Chu, review of *Waiting for the Dawn,* in *Journal of Asian Studies* 53, no. 2 (May 1994), 534.

51. Huang, *Waiting for the Dawn,* 6.

52. Ibid., 9. This is actually de Bary's synopsis of Huang.

53. Ibid., 10.

54. Ibid., 11, 13.

55. Ibid., 25.

56. Hung-lam Chu, review of *Waiting for the Dawn,* 533.

57. In de Bary et al., *Sources of Chinese Tradition,* the editors note that Huang "re-examined some of the age-old prejudices of the Confucian literati and came to his own conclusions." (1: 531)

58. John King Fairbank, *China: A New History* (Cambridge: Belknap Press of Harvard University Press, 1992), 153.

59. Owen Lattimore, *Inner Asian Frontiers of China* (Boston: Beacon Press,

1951), 431.

60. Huang, *Waiting for the Dawn*, 95.

CHAPTER 9

1. Mochtar Lubis, *Indonesia: Land Under the Rainbow* (Singapore: Oxford University Press, 1987), 1–2. This was translated from the Dutch in 1979 by A. W. Sisthoff. In addition to this and other sources cited, I wish to acknowledge my debt to the PBS series *Nomads of the Seas*, 1994, as well as *Pacific Origins* broadcast by the Discovery Channel during 1994.

2. Lubis, *Indonesia*, xv–xvii.

3. For instance, W. W. Howells, in "Origins of the Chinese People: Interpretations of Recent Evidence," argues for "genetic continuity from Peking man to modern Mongoloids on the basis of common cranial and dental features," thus helping to make "East Asiatic continuity a logical hypothesis," in David W. Keightley, *The Origins of Chinese Civilization* (Berkeley: University of California Press, 1983), 297–98. For archaeological information on Peking Man, see Kwang-Chih Chang, *The Archaeology of Ancient China* (New Haven: Yale University Pres, 1963), 29–32.

4. See *Time*, 143 no. 11 (March 14, 1994), 80–87 where it is argued that new fossil dates suggest that the first humans may have left Africa over a million years earlier than previously thought, and may have independently evolved in various parts of the world. Also see *Newsweek*, cxxiii, no.15 (April 11, 1994), 84.

5. There is still a great deal of debate about this date. Much of it has been centered round physical anthropology, some archaeology, and linguistics. See Robert C. Suggs, *The Island Civilization of Polynesia* (New York: Mentor, 1960) for a handy, popular reference. For more detailed research, consult Genevieve A. Highland, R. W. Force et al. eds., *Polynesian Culture History: Essays in Honour of Kenneth P. Emory* (Honolulu: Bishop Museum Press, 1967 [Bishop Museum Special Publication No 56]); D. J. Mulvaney, *The PreHistory of Australia* (New York: Frederick A. Praeger, 1969), 153, which describes use of radiocarbon dating to establish a site in Koonalda Cave in Australia as between 20,000 and 30,000 years old; and I. Yawata and Y. H. Sinoto eds., 1967), *Prehistoric Culture in Oceania* (Honolulu: Bishop Museum Press, 1968) [Eleventh Pacific Science Congress, Tokyo 1966].

6. The "African" presence does not seem to have been dealt with in any depth, except with reference to justifying "Melanesia" as an area of darker-skinned people. Kwang-Chih Chang does refer to the"Oceanic Negroid," but only in passing. See also Chang, *Archaeology of Ancient China*, 33, 43, 46, 129, 229.

7. See Johannes C. Anderson, *Myths and Legends of the Polynesians* (Routland, VT: Charles E. Tuttle, 1969), for the supportive base for this, see particularly 29–46, 55–56. For a well-researched anthropological study, see Jukka Siikala, *Cultural Conflict in Tropical Polynesia* (Helsinki: Suomalainen Tredeakatemia Academia Scientiarum Fennica [The Finnish Academy of Science and Letters], 1982), 94.

8. Andersen, *Myths and Legends,* 424–25.

9. Anthony Alpers, *Legends of the South Seas* (New York: Thomas Y. Crowell, 1970), 382–83.

10. Ibid., 236. Métraux argues that "navel of the world" is a mistranslation and thar the term merely means "land's end." See Alfred Métraux, *Easter Island* (New York: Oxford University Press, 1957), 36.

11. An indigenous Hawaiian who wrote in Hawaiian spoke of how "the king was appointed . . . so long, however, as he did right." David Malo, *Hawaiian Antiquities,* trans. by Nathaniel R. Emerson (1898; reprint Honolulu: Bernice P. Bishop Museum, 1951), 53. Malo's dates are c. 1793–1853, and although he writes from the viewpoint of a good missionary fledgling, he is at least reliable once he avoids comparing Christianity and Hawaiian religions.

12. Siikala, *Cultural Conflict,* 134–35. Not all areas had "kings" or chiefs, but the colonial powers did not allow this to handicap them and simply appointed persons whom they thought possessed "leadership" qualities. See also Siikala, 112–27, in which he discusses rank and power, conflict, religion, and the role of the "divine" king.

13. Although Indonesian novelist Mochtar Lubis in *Indonesia: Island under the Rainbow* does not deal to any large extent with "boat people," he writes extensively in two chapters about Indonesia as a kind of marine culture; see pp. 1–56 and note his use of Chinese sources. Of some passing interest are the Hong Kong "Boat people." The tour guides confidently assure visitors that that theirs is the last generation.

14. Marian W. Smith, "Towards a Classification of Cult Movements," *Man,* 59, no. 2 (Jan 1959), 12. Fred W.Voget notes these reactions and new types of identifications, so-called natavistic movements being, at least in the instance of the Cargo Cults, an attempt that was "economic-incooperative" and intended "to restore individuating social and appetitive gradients disorganized by cessation of economic surpluses introduced from outside." See Voget, "Shorter Notes Towards a Classification of Cult Movements: Some Further Contributions II," *Man,* 59, no. 26 (February 1959), 26–28; see 27, Table 1.

15. See, for instance, Alpers, previously cited. But note also that even in earlier collections, although this point is never made by the collector, there is obviously a very practical raison d' être for all oral narrative. See also Peter H. Buck, *Vikings of*

the Sunrise (New York: Frederick A. Stokes, 1938), in which the accounts (unfortunately interspersed by Buck's "interpretations") have much to do with shipbuilding, travel, exploration, settling, and, of course, the so-called grander issues of creation peculiar to all cultures.

16. A good, discursive account of early European exploration may be found in J. C. Beaglehole, *The Explorations of the Pacific* (1934; reprint, Stanford: Stanford University Press, 1966).

17. For various theories concerning Polynesian origin, see Alan Howard, "Polynesian Origins and Migrations" in Highland et al., *Polynesian Culture History*, 45–101. He gives a summary of arguments, some clearly outlandish, but offers no conclusion. Also see Alpers, 2–5 including unnumbered illustration on p. 2.

18. Malo, *Hawaiian Antiquities,* 7.

19. Raymond Firth, *Tikopia Ritual and Belief* (Boston: Beacon Press, 1967), 28.

20. Andersen, *Myths and Legends,* 419. The concept of "Heaven" and of "one God" often came from Christian missionaries. See Dorothy B. Barriere, "Revisions and Adulterations in Polynesian Creation Myths," in Highland et al., *Polynesian Culture History,* 103–119.

21. See Alpers, "The Eruption of Pele's Anger," 253–56, which is, of course, an etiological narrative that explains a volcanic eruption. Also see Andersen, *Myths and Legends,* 267–87 and note that Alpers adds in his notes that "Pele seems to have been created in Hawaii *in her own image"* (emphasis added), 385.

22. Contrast adze making in New Zealand with Australian burren adze-flakes and fula adzes found on many sites. See Mulvaney, *The PreHistory of Australia,* 73–74, 113–18, 257–58. Of some limited use is the older, *Literature of the Aborigine* by J. J. Healy (St Lucia, Australia: University of Queensland Press, 1978). See the introduction to the 1989 edition of the book, ix–xxi, and the conclusion 291–4. I, however, find that *The Speaking Land: Myth and Story in Aboriginal Australia,* by Ronald M. Berndt and Catherine H. Berndt (Rochester, VT: Inner Traditions International, 1994) is especially insightful and very relevant to a contemporary understanding of native Australians; note particularly 15–72, 126–75, and 408–27.

23. David Malo, an indigenous Hawaiian, cites one particularly horrific example of a taboo against women, whereby "during the days of religious tabu, when the gods were specially worshipped, many women were put to death by reason of infraction of some tabu." Malo, *Hawaiian Antiquities,* 28. As I said before, Malo, although homegrown, is oftentimes a Christian apologist and may thus overstate the case of indigenous "barbarism."

24. In *Easter Island,* Métraux finds that tatooing was a substitute for "personal vanity" (p. 76). In his opinion, the Marquesans and Maori "have carried this art to a

high degree of perfection" (78).

25. See Douglas Oliver for an interesting study, "Friendship Pacts in Ancient Tahiti," in Highland et al., *Polynesian Culture History,* 447, n.14, in which he argues that one male often assumed the identity of the other, even foregoing female sexual contact. I discuss this with reference to possible "homosexual" imputations on the part of Western interpreters.

26. William Bligh, *The Log of the Bounty* (London: Golden Cockerel Press, 1937), 1: 6.

27. William Dampier, *Dampier's Voyages.* 2 vols. (London: E. Grant Richards, 1906), 1: 499–500 and editor's note 539–40. Prince Jeoly was born around 1661 and died around 1731. Captain James Cook "possessed" a similar "specimen Negro" from the world beyond, a Pacific Islander named Omai, but he was returned by Cook on another voyage. Dampier kept Prince Jeoly on permanent exhibition as the "painted or stained" wonder of the age, until he died in Cambridge. I am not sure which account is more comforting. For more information on Dampier's Prince Jeoly as possible lover to Dampier, consult B. R. Burg, *Sodomy and the Pirate Tradition* (New York: New York University Press, 1984), 123.

28. Gregory Dening, "Ethnohistory in Polynesia: The Value of Ethnohistorical Evidence," *The Journal of Pacific History* [Canberra, Australia], 1 (1966), 36.

29. John Keats, "On First Looking Into Chapman's Homer," in John Keats, *The Poetical Works,* ed. H. Buxton Foreman (London: Oxford University Press, 1908), 39.

30. Peter Martyr, *De Orbe Novo,* trans. Francis Augustus MacNutt. 2 vols. (New York: Burt Franklin, 1912), 2: 288.

31. Ibid., 286.

32. Jeanette Mirsky, *The Westward Crossings* (New York: Alfred A. Knopf, 1946). Also see an abstract from *Westward Crossings* entitled, "Silent Upon a Peak in Darien—Balboa discovers the Pacific," more easily available in Helen Wright and Samuel Rapport, *The Great Explorers* (New York: Harper & Brothers, 1958), 256, 257.

33. Antonio Pigafetta, *Magellan's Voyage,* trans. and ed. R.A. Skelton. 2 vols (New Haven: Yale University Press, 1969), 1: 38.

34. Columbus, *Four Voyages,* 1: 27.

35. Pigafetta, *Magellan's Voyage,* 1: 47.

36. Ibid., 88. Compare the more succinct version of Richard Eden, *The First Three English Books on America,* 258 in which a brave Magellan battles against "Barbarians."

37. Columbus, *Four Voyages,* 2: 36.

38. Henry N. Stevens and George F. Barwick, eds., Introduction to *New Light on the Discovery of Australia as Revealed by the Journal of Captain Don Diego De Prado y Tovar* (London: Hakluyt Society, 1930), 15.

39. Ibid., 109.

40. Ibid.

41. Ibid., 111.

42. Ibid.

43. Concerning how El Dorado was shifted and repositioned, see my discussion in *Imagining the World*, 10–12.

44. Stevens and Barwick, *New Light,* 123.

45. Introduction by Clements Markham to Pedro Fernandez de Quirós, *The Voyages:1539–1606,* trans. and ed. Clements Markham (Cambridge: Hakluyt Society, 1906; reprint, Nendeln, Liechtenstein: Kraus Reprint, 1967), xxiv.

46. Quirós, *The Voyages,* 253.

47. "Memorials of Quirós" in Quirós, *The Voyages,* 478.

48. Beaglehole, *Explorations of the Pacific,* 112.

49. Jakob Le Maire, "The Australian Adventures of Jakob Le Maire," in *The East and West Indian Mirror,* trans. J.A.J. de Villiers (London: Hakluyt Society, 1906; reprint, Nendeln, Liechtenstein: Kraus Reprint, 1967), 192, 193.

50. See two examples in "Speilbergen's Journal" in *East and West Indian Mirror,* 25–29 and 74–77.

51. De Villiers, introduction to *East and West Indian Mirror,* xxiv, n.1.

52. "Speilbergen's Journal" in *East and West Indian Mirror,* 117, 115, 126.

53. Beaglehole, *Explorations of the Pacific,* 147–48, quotes Tasman as reflecting that, from his distant survey "there can be no doubt there must be men here of extraordinary stature." Despite apparently good Dutch intentions, seventeenth century Maori were branded with the same Plinian misnomer as the "Patagons" of Chile, as constructed by Magellan.

54. "Speilbergen's Journal" in *East and West Indian Mirror,* 150.

55. George Robertson, *The Discovery of Tahiti,* ed. Hugh Carrington (London: Hakluyt Society, 1948), 62. Robertson was captain of the H.M.S. *Dolphin* during its circumnavigation of the world in 1766–1768. It was under the command of Samuel Wallis.

56. On his Fourth Voyage, Columbus combined his knowledge of Seneca and the Bible. See Seneca, *Selections,* ed. Umberto Moricca (Turin, Italy: I. B. Paravia, 1947), 258–61, and Columbus, *Four Voyages,* 2: 92. Also see the biblical references Columbus cited in *Libro de las profecías,* trans. Delno West and August King (Gainesville: University of Florida Press, 1991), 3, 5, 16, 22–23, 58–59, 87–88,

90–92.

57. J. C. Beaglehole, *The Life of Captain James Cook* (London: The Hakluyt Society; Stanford: Stanford University Press, 1974), 309; also see 267, 345.

58. William Dampier, *A New Voyage Round the World* (1927; reprint New York: Dover, 1968), 238, 329, 342–44, 366. Dampier had the good sense to purchase Prince Jeoly's mother as well, since he had earlier heard the frantic cries of a mulata Other. Seemingly, one Captain Swan, obviously smitten by another one of her children, unceremoniously "kept" him. According to Dampier, he was "a very pretty boy about seven or eight" (p. 174).

59. Ibid.

60. For just two examples, see Marco Polo's updating of the Plinian Wife-Givers, in which the host's generosity accorded each visitor his wife for the duration of his stay. Even Khubilai Khan, having dutifully banished prostitution to the outer demarcations of his city, requires\d that the captains who organized the women should supply all his guests with suitable comfort. See Marco Polo, *The Description of the World,* 1: 21 and 236.

61. J. C. Beaglehole, ed., *The Journals of Captain Cook on his Voyage of Discovery* (Cambridge: Hakluyt, 1955–1974), 3: Part 1: *The Voyage of the Resolution and Discovery:1776–1780* (published 1967), 219–20. A more convenient, but less scholarly selections with the editor's comments may be found in A. Greenfell Price ed., *The Explorations of Captain James Cook in the Pacific* (New York: Dover Publications, 1971).

61. Ibid

62. Beaglehole, *Cook's Journals,* 3: Part 2: *The Life of Captain James Cook* (published 1974), 734.

63. Rey Chow, *Writing Diaspora: Tactics of Intervention in Contemporary Cultural Studies* (Bloomington: Indiana University Press, 1993), 6. Her contention is that academics who posit attitudes that support a view of the Other as repressed and oppressed perhaps become the instruments of a new kind of power; see also pp. 17 and 103, concerning manipulation in Chinese letters.

64. Some post-colonial critics have reclaimed the use of the word "native," not as a monolithic construct, but as one that best describes a shared colonial experience for disparate peoples. See Elleke Boehmer, *Colonial and Postcolonial Literature* (Oxford: Oxford University Press, 1995) 8–9, 111–17. For a contrasting view, see Homi K. Bhabha, *The Location of Culture* (London: Routledge, 1994), especially 19–39 for what he calls the "Third Space" which Bhabha terms a pre-condition for setting cultural distinctiveness.

CHAPTER 10

1. I am referring here in particular to Thor Heyerdahl's early attempts, with his wife, to establish Paradise in Polynesia. In Thor Heyerdahl and Christopher Ralling, *Kon-Tiki Man* (San Francisco: Chamick Books, 1991), Heyerdahl and his wife are conscious that they are following in the footsteps of Gauguin. Thor wrote that,"Adam and Even, when God drove them out of the Garden of Eden, must have felt the very opposite of us as we started our walk into the lush valley of Omoa at sunrise next morning. They left, we were returning" (p. 43). Here they can "strip off the clothes which the white man from cool countries was now imposing on the tropical islanders" (p. 50). But very soon he would realize, "One can't buy a ticket to Paradise" (p. 76). Also see Tim Severin, *The China Voyage* (Boston: Little, Brown, 1994). In 1993, Severin set out from Vietnam on a bamboo raft. He argues that he was following in the wake of a Chinese sailor of 218 B.C. who had journeyed to America. At least Severin established that such a journey was possible.

2. For details on Cook's life, I have used Beaglehole, *Life of Captain James Cook*.

3. For a handy reference work on early circumnavigators, see Derek Wilson, *The Circumnavigators* (New York: M. Evans & Company, 1989). Cook's contributions to demythologizing the beliefs of his time are considered, 171–191.

4. See, for instance, "W. B. Monkhouse's Journal," in appendix IV of Beaglehole, *Cook's Journals,* 1: 573–74.

5. Beaglehole, *Cook's Journals,* 1: 170, 212.

6. Gananath Obeyesekere, *The Apotheosis of Captain Cook: European Mythmaking in the Pacific* (Princeton: Princeton University Press, 1992), 225 n. 62, 136. Even a relatively "conservative" evaluation, such as A. Grenfell Price's explanatory commentaries, suggests that Cook's willing acceptance of scarce food supplies and the Chief's generosity may have overstrained the resources of the island (p. 261). A rebuttal to Obeyesekere appears in Marshall Sahlins, *How "Natives" Think About Captain Cook, for Example* (Chicago: University of Chicago Press, 1995).

7. Beaglehole, *Cook's Journals,* 1: 574. Note that even the visual depictions are feminized. For instance, William Hodges drew both Omai and Odiddy with long hair, full seductive lips, arched eyebrows, and sensuous features. Both are draped in white gowns with the loose upper part suggesting the presence of breasts. See Beaglehole, *Life of Captain Cook*, Figs. 25a and 25b between pages 432 and 433. On the other hand, William Dampier is depicted in a National Gallery portrait by T. Murray as stern, almost menacing, emerging from a dark background. A staff, at the bottom,

left-hand corner of the portrait suggests a kind of phallic virility. See William
Dampier, *A New Voyage Round the World* (1927; reprint, New York: Dover, 1968),
xliv.

8. Beaglehole, *Cook's Journals,* 1, 574, 576. In a slightly different context,
Anne McClintock stresses the use of the woman as icon, or what she terms the
"persistent gendering of the imperial unknown." She observes how, as "European
men crossed the dangerous thresholds of their known worlds, they ritualistically
feminized borders and boundaries" (p.24) in Anne McClintock, *Imperial Leather:
Race, Gender and Sexuality in the Colonial Context* (New York: Routledge, 1995).

9. Peter Buck, in *Vikings of the Sunrise* (New York: Frederick A. Stokes, 1938),
142–43, gives an amusing example of how the European administration frequently
had to contend with the signals it was sending. As a government medical officer in
1912, he was required to stamp the pass cards of laborers. He was surprised to learn
that this was not enough; the workers required official stamps on their hands, cheeks,
and forehead, and, according to Buck, "no man would attempt to wash off his badge of
honor."

10. A. Norman Jeffares, introduction to John Press, ed., *Commonwealth Literature:
Unity and Diversity in a Common Culture* (London: Heinemann, 1965), xiii.

11. Introduction to Bruce King, ed., *Literatures of the World in English* (London:
Routledge & Kegan Paul, 1974), 7.

12. C. D. Narasimhaiah, ed., *Awakened Conscience: Studies in Commonwealth
Literature* (Atlantic Highlands, NJ: Humanities Press, 1978), 6. I should add that from
the late 1960s more and more indigenous literature began to appear in the West. Ulli
Beier had began to edit and publish writing from New Guinea, but this remained
limited in readership owing to distribution problems. Also see Ulli Beier ed., *Voices
of Independence: New Black Writing from Papua New Guinea* (St. Lucia, Australia:
University of Queensland Press, 1980).

13. Ashcroft et al., *Empire Writes Back,* 41.

14. D.E.S. Maxwell, "Landscape and Theme," in Press, *Commonwealth Literature,*
82–83.

15. Edwin Thumboo ed., *The Second Tongue* (Singapore: Heinemann Educational
Books (Asia), 1976), xiii.

16. I selected these because they deal in part with our immediate area of study. Terry
Goldie, *Fear and Temptation: The Image of the Indigene in Canadian, Australian and
New Zealand Literatures* (Montreal: McGill-Queen's University Press, 1989) is still
an external gaze, but it is a less distant look and a more intense examination. I
particularly liked Mudrooroo Narogin, *Writing from the Fringe: A Study of Modern
Aboriginal Literature* (Melbourne: Hyland House, 1990) because it is an unabashed

view from within, a forward-looking, unapologetic assumption of his own indigeneity. He is, of course, a well-known novelist.

17. Diane Bell, "An Accidental Australian Tourist: Or a Feminist Anthropologist at Sea and on Land," in Stuart B. Schwartz, ed., *Implicit Understandings* (New York: Cambridge University Press, 1994), 506–7.

18. Greg Dening, "The Theatricality of Observing and Being Observed: Eighteenth Century Europe 'discovers' the ? Century 'Pacific,'" in Schwartz, *Implicit Understandings*, 452.

19. Cook alludes to venereal disease, known as "kaokao," but during his 1778 voyage near Maui, his reference that "these people had got amongst [them] the venereal distemper" almost suggests that venereal disease was self-generating (Beaglehole, *Cook's Journals*, 4: Part 1, 474). He assumed that the indigenous women were the bearers. On the other hand, Edward Riou, midshipman on the *Discovery*, noting that the crew were shortly to be examined by a surgeon, blames this "horrible disease" inflicted on "poor harmless and innocent people" by the Spaniards (Beaglehole, *Cook's Journals*, 3: Part 1, 474–75, n. 5). In October 1778, David Samwell, surgeon on the *Discovery*, seems to return to Cook's point, without Riou's self-serving empathy (Beaglehole, *Cook's Journals*, 3: Part 2, 1150 and 1151).

20. See T. W. Arnold, "Arab Travellers and Merchants" in Newton, *Travel and Travellers*, 95. Also see *UNESCO General History of Africa*, 4: 659. Also see the discussion of Arab travel and the part played by Ibn Masdjid in G. Ferrard, *Instructions nautiques et routiers arabs et portugais de 15e et 16e siècles* (Paris: Geuthner, 1921–1928), 3 vols. As noted before, see Tibbets, *Arab Navigation in the Indian Ocean*.

21. With reference to Enrique, see Simon Winchester, "After Dire Straits, An Agonizing Haul across the Pacific," *Smithsonian*, 22, no. 1 (April 1991), especially pages 86 and 92.

22. For background information on early Portuguese travel in Africa, consult Samuel Eliot Morison, *Portuguese Voyages to America in the Fifteenth Century* (Cambridge: Harvard University Press, 1940).

23. See Rebecca Catz, *Christopher Columbus and the Portuguese* (Westport, CT: Greenwood, 1993), 13, 15–16, 20 n. 42.

24. For a good survey of early Brazil contact, see John Hemmings, *Red Gold: The Conquest of the Brazilian Indians* (Cambridge: Harvard University Press, 1978). An early work of interest is the 1556 account of a young Protestant missionary, Jean de Léry, *History of a Voyage to the Land of Brazil* [1578] trans. Janet Whatley (Berkeley: University of California Press, 1990).

25. See, for instance, Fred F. Kravath, *Christopher Columbus, Cosmographer*

(Rancho Cordova, CA: Landmark Enterprises, 1987), 269, in which Vasco da Gama is heroized beyond measure and given sole credit for sailing to India.

26. Sometimes the inhabitants are referred to as "Black Berbers" to distinguish them from the Berbers of North Africa. The area probably ran as far south as Somali. The term was utilized in this way by Ptolemy in the *Periplus of the Erytheaen Sea*; and by Cosmas Indicopleustes in *The Christian Topography*. See also *UNESCO General History of Africa*, 3: 600–3, 712.

27. Anthony Reid, in "Early Southeast Asian Categorizations of Europeans," in Schwartz, *Implicit Understandings*, 272, points out that: "The most valuable lingua franca was however Malay, which foreign traders including the Europeans were quick to pick up."

28. See references in, Richard Eden, *The First Three English Books on America [?1511]–1555 A.D.*, ed. Edward Arber (Birmingham, UK: n.p., 1885), 255, 256, 258. I used this edition quite intentionally at this stage, since this is how the English would have first heard of world travel. Eden translated and summarized many texts that were unavailable at the time to the mass public.

29. Winchester, "After Dire Straits," 91. Also see Jan Carew, *Rape of Paradise* (New York: A & B Books, 1994), 126–27.

30. See the modern text of Antonio Pigafetta, *Magellan's Voyage,* trans. and ed., R. A. Skelton. 2 vols. (New Haven: Yale University Press, 1986), 1: 89.

31. See Walter Raleigh, *The Discoverie of the Large, Rich, and Beautiful Empyre of Guiana* (1506; reprint, Amsterdam: De Capo Press, 1968). Raleigh had inherited the El Dorado concept from gold-crazed Spaniards with overfertile imaginations.

32. Dening in Schwartz, *Implicit Understandings,* 477.

33. Markham, *Voyages of Quirós*, 1:41.

34. Ibid., 2:226.

35. Ibid., 2:227.

36. Dampier, *A New Voyage,* 66–67.

37. Ibid., 64.

38. Alpers, *Legends of the South Seas,* 10. He also points out that Hawaii, "[i]n the form Hava'i . . . was an old name for Ra'iatea, near Tahiti."

39. Evidently, there is some intentional? misunderstanding here, on the part of Cook and his crew. Tupaia is rather romantically described as "praying" to the wind. See Beaglehole, *Cook's Journals,* 1: 140 n. 6.

40. Ibid., 1: 169, 357, 305.

41. Ibid., 1: 291–93; also see 293 n. 1 and 294 n. 1. The chart is reproduced by Andrew David, ed., *The Charts & Coastal Views of Captain Cook's Voyages* (London: Hakluyt Society, 1988), 1: 130; also see the editorial note on 131.

CHAPTER 11

1. An Australian Aborigine gives a recent account as follows, based on European misunderstanding regarding the nature of communal property:
The encounter between the bubu qujin [traditional people] and the crew of the *Endeavour* was not entirely peaceful. Incidents arose out of conflicting notions of reciprocity. The Gung u Yimithirr [traditional owners] had offered fish to the voyagers and couldn't understand why the Europeans refused to share one of the many turtles on the deck of the *Endeavour*.
See Noel Pearson, "A Troubling Inheritance," *Race & Class*, 35, no. 4 (April–June 1954), 2.

2. See Lord Byron, *The Poetical Works* (London: Oxford University Press, 1945), especially Canto II.

3. Robert E. Gallagher, ed., *Byron's Journal of His Circumnavigation, 1764–1766* (Cambridge: Hakluyt Society, 1964), 112.

4. Hugh Carrington, ed., *The Discovery of Tahiti* (London: Hakluyt Society, 1948), 281. Carrington's work is an edited version of an account by George Robertson, master of H.M.S. *Dolphin* under Wallis's command from 1766–68.

5. See Paget Toynbee, ed., *Letters of Horace Walpole* 16 vols. (Oxford: Clarendon Press, 1903–1905), 8: 292–93. Also see Hoxie Neale Fairchild, *The Noble Savage: A Study in Romantic Naturalism* (New York: Columbia University Press, 1928), 111, for a discussion of John Hawkesworth.

6. Helen Wallis, ed., *Carteret's Voyage Round the World: 1766–1769*. 2 vols. (Cambridge: Hakluyt Society, 1965), 2: 318.

7. Lewis Hanke, *Aristotle and the American Indian: A Study in Race Prejudice in the Modern World* (Bloomington: Indiana University Press, 1959), 50.

8. Between April and June 1991, the European Community mounted an exhibition termed "Le Noir du Blanc" in Brussels. Over 2,000 illustrations and hundreds of pieces drawn from popular culture were displayed. The exhibition was accompanied by a collection of essays by fifteen writers. One writer, Jeanne Remacle, in "'Le Noir du Blanc': An Exhibition of Clichés and Racial Stereotypes," wondered whether modern Europe had inherited this legacy of hatred from its textbooks and ethnocentric documents. *The Courier*, no. 130 (Nov–Dec, 1991), 91–93.

9. Eldred Jones, *Othello's Countrymen* (London: Oxford University Press, 1965), 27.

10. See ibid., 31–32.

11. Ben Jonson, "The Masque of Blackness," in Ben Jonson, *The Works*, ed. William Gifford (London: Edward Moxon, 1853), 545.

12. Michel de Montaigne, *The Essays,* trans. and ed. M. A. Screech (London: Allen Lane, Penguin, 1987) 232, 233, 239, 240–41. Also see treatment of longevity (113–14), Edenic nakedness and sex (202–5), and other such topics in Jean Delumeau, *History of Paradise* (New York: Continuum, 1995).

13. Aphra Behn, *Oroonoko, the Rover and Other Works,* ed. Janet Todd (London: Penguin, 1992), 80.

14. Ibid., 80–81.

15. See a study by Frederick M. Link, *Aphra Behn* (New York: Twayne, 1968), 20. Also note references to the Inkle-Yarico myth in the theme of the New World as tryst, in which separated lovers are reunited. See Richard Steele's version of the legend in the *Spectator,* No. 11 (March 3, 1711). For a list of poems and plays, see Lawrence M. Price, *Inkle and Yarico Album* (Berkeley: University of California Press, 1937), 155–59. See especially, George Colman the Younger's light "opera," *Inkle and Yarico* (London: Printed for T. Cadell, 1787), based the *Spectator* version, and containing the libretto only. A handier reference may be found in *Plays of George Colman the Younger and Thomas Morton,* ed. Barry Sutcliffe (Cambridge: Cambridge University Press, 1983).

16. Behn, *Oroonoko,* 356–57; notes by Janet Todd.

17. Moira Ferguson, "*Oroonoko*: Birth of a Paradigm," *New Literary History,* 23, no. 2 (Spring 1992), 346, 356. Also see Stephanie Athey and Daniel Cooper Alarcon, "*Oroonoko's* Gendered Economies of Honor/Horror: Reframing Discourse Studies in the Americas," *American Literature* 55, no. 3 (1993), 415–43.

18. Edward Cooke, *A Voyage to the South Sea, and Round the World* (1712; reprint, New York: De Capo Press, 1969.), 36–37.

19. Woodes Rogers, *A Cruising Voyage Round the World* (1712; reprint, London: Longmans, Green & Co., 1928), 121–31.

20. Richard Steele, *The Englishman,* No. 26, Dec 3, 1713.

21. Werner Sollors, ed., *The Invention of Ethnicity* (New York: Oxford University Press, 1989), ix–xx.

22. Daniel Defoe, *Robinson Crusoe,* ed., Michael Shinael (New York: W. W. Norton, 1975), 160, 159.

23. Wylie Sypher suggests quite generously that in *Robinson Crusoe,* as well as some of Defoe's other novels, "the Negro, or savage in general, is a fellow-being." See Wylie Sypher, *Guinea's Captive Kings* (Chapel Hill: University of North Carolina Press, 1942), 259–64. This is not a point of view with which I can agree. I feel that Crusoe/Defoe mouths the pious platitudes of his time, but never really acts out of any true Christian egalitarian impulse.

24. Herman Melville, *Moby-Dick, or, The Whale* (1851; reprint, Norwalk, CT:

Eaton Press, 1977), 3.

25. Voltaire, *Candide* [1759] (New York: Literary Guild, 1929), 48, 50.

26. See Friedman, *Monstrous Races,* 9–21. Also see Hanke, *Aristotle and the American Indians,* 4, in which he shows that the Wild Man was a European invention of the Middle Ages.

27. Thomas Jefferson, "Notes on the State of Virginia," [1784] in *The Portable Thomas Jefferson* ed., Merrill D. Peterson (London: Penguin, 1975), 192.

28. See James Boswell, *The Life of Samuel Johnson.* 3 vols (London: Swan Sonnenschein, Lowrey & Co., 1888), 1, 388. Dr Johnson's letters to Samuel Barber are all in 1:352, 388–9. Also see other references in 1: 145, 212, 352 and 3: 161–64.

29. Ibid., 3: 162–64.

30. Long, *History of Jamaica,* 475–85.

31. See *Letters of the Late Ignatius Sancho* [1782], ed. Paul Edwards (London: Dawsons of Pall Mall, 1968).

32. This is according to Edward Long, who, in all fairness, it must be stated was no fervent admirer of Williams. See Long, *History of Jamaica,* 478.

33. Janheinz Jahn, *A History of Neo-African Literature* (London: Faber and Faber, 1966), 35. More recent scholars tend to avoid discussing this troublesome aspect of Capitein. See, for instance, Keith A. Sandiford, *Measuring the Moment: Strategies of Protest in Eighteenth Century Writing* (Cranbury, NJ: Associated University Presses, 1988), 31–32.

34. See the following studies by Blacks in eighteenth-century Britain: Kenneth Little, *Negroes in Britain: A Study of Racial Relations in English Society* (London: Kegan Paul, 1947); N. V. McCullough, *The Negro in English Literature* (Ilfracombe, UK: Stockwell, 1962); Edward Scobie, *Black Britannia* (Chicago: Johnson Publishing, 1972); Folarin Shyllon, *Black People in Britain* (London: Oxford University Press, 1977); and Sypher, *Guinea's Captive Kings.*

35. Interestingly, we find the idea of monolithization here. General Richard H. Pratt found that the "assimilationist" model of institutions like the Hampton Agricultural School for Negroes was ideal for Native Americans. In Utley's caustic words, "as the Negro had been civilized, so could the Indian be civilized." Robert Utley, ed., *Battlefield and Classroom: Four Decades with the American Indian, the Memoirs of Richard H. Pratt* (New Haven: Yale University Press, 1964), xiv.

36. Samuel Johnson, *The History of Rasselas Prince of Abissinia* [1759], ed., J. P. Hardy (Oxford: Oxford University Press, 1988), 73, 28–29.

37. Oliver Goldsmith, *The Miscellaneous Works* (Edinburgh: William P Nimmo, 1801), 102. I should, however, add that the traveler to the "remote places" of Swift's satire journeyed among "savage nations," among people like the "brown Indian

[who] marks with murd'rous aim." The poem, in essence, is not so much "anti-imperial" as "antiemigration."

38. McClintock, *Imperial Leather,* 58.

39. Gaile McGregor, *The Noble Savage in the New World Garden: Notes Toward the Syntactics of Place* (Toronto: University of Toronto Press, 1988), 17.

40. For a brief discussion of Rousseau's debt to the literature of exploration, see Fairchild, *Noble Savage,* 128–29. For Rousseau's "State of Nature" and Paradise, see Delumeau, *History of Paradise,* 226–28. For more information consult O. R. Dathorne, *In Europe's Image: The Need for American Multiculturalism* (Westport, CT: Bergin & Garvey, 1994), 23–24.

40. McGregor, *Noble Savage,* 16.

CHAPTER   12

1. John O'Sullivan, *United States Magazine and Democratic Review,* July-August, 1845. O'Sullivan had argued that it was"our manifest destiny to overspread the continent allotted by Providence for the free development of our yearly multiplying millions," as quoted by Eric Foner and John A. Garraty, eds., *The Reader's Companion to American History* (Boston: Houghton Mifflin, 1991), 697–98. Thus, in a few words, God had been divinely yoked to untrameled population growth and the vagaries of Empire. O'Sullivan's words would be immortalized by Congress, quoted, and requoted, until they provided a heavenly mandate for widespread invasion. The irony was that he had been refering to Texas.

2. For a handy account, consult the edition compiled by Frank Bergon, ed., *The Journals of Lewis and Clark* (New York: Penguin, 1989).

3. See Albert Furtwangler, *Acts of Discovery: Visions of America in the Lewis and Clark Journals* (Urbana: University of Illinois Press, 1993), 11. Also see Mirsky, *Westward Crossings,* 238–360, in which the author places the Lewis/Clark expedition within the context of similar incursions by Balboa and representatives of other European powers.

4. See Frederick Jackson Turner, "The Significance of the Frontier in American History," in *America: One Land, One People,* ed. Robert C. Baron (Golden, CO: Fulcrum, 1987),   245–77. Originally, this began as a paper, read at the July 12, 1893 meeting of the American Historical Association; it was printed in the association's publication and was later developed into other papers and finally a book. However, Max Lerner rightly argues that even as Turner delivered and later wrote this romanticized account, the old West had died. See Max Lerner, *America as a Civilization* (New York: Henry Holt, 1957), 34–35.

5. Roscoe Carlyle Buley, "New Homes in the West," in Baron, *America: One Land, One People*, 165.

6. For a review of the Mormons, consult Leonard J. Arrington and Davis Betton, *The Mormon Experience: History of the Latter-day Saints* (New York: Knopf, 1979).

7. See *The Book of Mormon* (Salt Lake City: Corporation of the President of the Church of Jesus Christ of Latter-day Saints, 1981). I am utilizing this edition, since it omits some of Joseph Smith's works like the *Book of Abraham*, which most scholars rightly agree is plagarized from an Egyptian funerary text. See mention of Lamanites on frontispiece and *passim*.

8. Ibid., 652.

9. Ibid., 66.

10. As stated by a visiting Italian count, Leonetto Cipriani, *California and Overland Diaries* (Portland, OR: Cambridge Press, 1962). Count Cipriani traveled west in 1853.

11. Between 1833 and 1834, Prince Alexander Philipp Maximilian, a Prussian prince, had followed a route similar to that of Lewis and Clark. He published his narrative in Europe between 1839 and 1843, in German, French, and English editions (in condensed form). The Joslyn Art Museum in Omaha, in conjunction with the University of Nebraska Press, is translating and publishing a four volume version. I wish to thank David C. Hunt of the Joslyn Art Museum for providing me with useful information. Also see David Thomas and Karin Ronnefeldt, eds., *People of the First Man: Life Among the Plain Indians in Their Final Days of Glory* (New York: E. P. Dutton, 1976).

12. Daniel J. Boorstin, *The Image: A Guide to Pseudo-Events in America* (New York: Atheneum, 1980), 108. For the Hawaiian perspective, see Queen Liliuokalani's personal and unimbittered account in Liliuokalani, *Hawaii's Story by Hawaii's Queen* (1891; reprinted, Honolulu: Mutual Publishers, 1990), especially pages 239–299.

13. R.W.B. Lewis, *The American Adam: Innocence, Tragedy, and Tradition in the Nineteenth Century* (Chicago: University of Chicago Press, 1955).

14. James Fenimore Cooper, *The Redskins* (1846; reprint, New York: G. P. Putnam's, n.d.), 307.

15. James Fenimore Cooper, *The American Democrat; or, Hints on the Focal and Civil Relations of the United States of America* (Cooperstown: H. & E. Phinney, 1838), 4.

16. John Barrow, *A Description of Pitcairn's Island and its Inhabitants* (1900; reprint New York: Haskell House, 1972).

17. William Bligh, *Narrative of the Mutiny on Board His Majesty's Ship Bounty* (London: George Nicol, 1790), in Carl Stroven and A. Grove Day, *The Spell of the*

Pacific (New York: Macmillan, 1949), 6. Also see an update on the *Bounty* descendants and how they left Pitcairn to find work in New Zealand. Indeed, there was an earlier departure from Pitcairn in 1856, when the island had become too crowded for all the descendants and some had gone to live in the Australian Norfolk Island. See Ed Howard, "Pitcairn and Norfolk: the Saga of Bounty's Children," in *National Geographic* 164, no. 4 (1983), 510–541.

18. Charles Nordhoff and James Norman Hall, *The Bounty Trilogy* (Boston: Little, Brown, 1985), 67–68.

19. Ibid., 82.

20. Ibid., 62.

21. Ibid., 155, for the sacrifice, and p. 69, for Byam's ease with the language. The wedding is on pp. 147–48.

22. See J. H. Bernardin de St.-Pierre, *Paul and Virginia,* trans. Helen Maria Williams [1796] (Oxford: Woodstock Books, 1989).

23. For detailed information on expositions, consult *The Books of the Fairs: A Collection of World's Fair Publications, 1834–1915* available in microform through Research Publications, 17 Lunar Drive, Drawer AB, Woodbridge, CT 06525. I have found "Les colonies Françaises" for the 1889 Paris exposition, with its descriptions of the "French" Pacific, "French" Indochina, and "French" Africa to be particularly indicative of the near colonial period of ownership and domination.

24. Bernardin de St.-Pierre, *Paul and Virginia,* 51–52.

25. Ibid., 103, 119.

26. Frederick Douglass, cited in "Honor to Their Race," *Chicago's Daily Inter Ocean*, 26 August, 1893, 2.

27. Stanley Appelbaum, *The Chicago World's Fair of 1893* (New York: Dover, 1980); see 2, 77, 80, 96, 97, 103, 104, 106, and Fig 98. A fascinating point is that Wordsworth seems to have decided what part the Ancient Mariner should play in Coleridge's poem. He suggested that the Ancient Mariner should kill the bird "on entering the South Sea, and that the tutelary Spirit of those regions take upon them to avenge the crime." All Wordsworth's advice was dispatched from the safety of his Lake District retreat, I should add. See reference in J. B. Owen, ed., *Lyrical Ballads 1798* (London: Oxford University Press, 1969), 135. The reference is taken from notes dictated by Wordsworth to Isabella Fenwick in 1843.

28. Thomas Hakluyt (1552–1616) devoted his life to collecting accounts of British explorations, as a way of justifying British colonial claims to territorial acquisition. It was a little like a child's game. The basic logic was "I saw it first—it's mine." In Hakluyt's accounts, John Cabot's journey to North America, Frances Drake's to the Caribbean, John Hawkins's to West Africa, and Martin Frobisher's and

Walter Raleigh's to North and South America not only highlighted their personal achievements, but laid down firm British claims to possession and "Empire." See Richard Hakluyt, *Principall Navigations, Voiages, and Discoveries of the English Nation.* 2 vols. (1589; reprint, Cambridge: Hakluyt Society, 1965). When Samuel Purchas (1577?–1626) took up the task in 1613, he was similarly motivated by patriotic intentions. The first section of his 1625 work reproduced accounts of British travel to China, Japan, India, and Africa, whereas the second section dealt with attempts to find a North-West Passage, as well as descriptions of the Caribbean and Florida. See Samuel Purchas, *Hakluytus Posthuumus, or Purchas his Pilgrimes, contayning a History of the World in Sea Voyages and Land Travell by Englishmen and Others.* 20 vols. (1625; reprint, Glasgow: James MacLehose & Sons, 1905).

29. See the "orientalizing" of the "Orient" in Edward Said, *Orientalism* (New York: Vintage, 1979), 5–6, 65–67, 325.

30. Frederick Ives Carpenter, *Emerson and Asia* (Cambridge: Harvard University Press, 1930), 215.

31. Said, *Orientalism,* 290. Said adds that, with the exception of Melville, Twain and the Transcendentalists, very few American writers displayed much interest in the East. Their border, he adds was west, not east. I would argue that Americans do nevertheless enter the East via their west, and also inherit the East in terms of ostentatious European imitation, especially during the post-Civil War period, when moneyed men began to construct elaborate mansions.

32. Incidentally, Chinese in 1882 comprised a mere .002 percent of the population, yet seemed to deserve to have an Exclusion Act all their own. By 1902, Chinese immigration was illegal on a permanent basis, and Chinese could not apply for citizenship until 1943. Others had their turn: those from the Middle East, India, and Japan. See Robert McClellan, *The Heathen Chinee* (Columbus: Ohio State University Press, 1971), especially 85–86, 183–84, 192–93, 208–10, 221, 228–38, 247–49. See also Chinese compared with Blacks, 58–59; with Japanese, 117–18.

CHAPTER 13

1. Herman Melville, *Typee* (New York: Dodd, Mead , n.d. 1846?), 19, 8.

2. Ibid., 86. Also, note how, in her description, the old clichés like her seminakedness reemerge. Further on, Melville writes, "for the most part [she] clung to the primitive and summer garb of Eden" (p. 88).

3. Ibid., 193, 188.

4. See Herman Melville, "To Ned," in *John Marr and Other Sailors, with Some Sea Pieces* (New York: DeVinne Press, 1888), 75-76.

5. D. H. Lawrence, *Classic American Literature* (1923; reprint, London: Penguin, 1971), 142, 144, 145.

6. Ibid., 149.

7. Melville, *Moby-Dick,* 127.

8. Ibid.,128.

9. Ibid., 132.

10. Ibid., 156.

11. Ibid., 176.

12. Ibid., 253.

13. Ibid., 457, 558, 570.

14. Ibid., 3, 615.

15. Dening, "The Theatricality of Observing" in Schwartz, *Implicit Understandings,* 476–77.

16. Thomas de Quincey, *Confessions of an English Opium-Eater, together with Selections from the Autobiography* (London: the Cresset Press, 1950), 314, 332–33. The description, particularly of dress, bears no relationship to any Malayan living or dead. Thus both de Quincey's Malayan and Coleridge's South Seas become domestic inventions of the exotic.

17. John Barrell, *The Infection of Thomas de Quincey: A Psychopathology of Imperialism* (New Haven: Yale University Press, 1991), 128

18. See Bhikhu Parekh, "Incurious Mill" [review of Lyn Zastoupil, *John Stuart Mill and India]* in London *Times Literary Supplement,* November 11, 1994 (No. 4780), 23. Also see Lynn Zastoupil, *John Stuart Mill and India* (Stanford: Stanford University Press, 1994), in a recent book that argues this point concerning Mill's total unconcern with the aspirations of the Indian subcontinent.

19. Details may be found in Stroven and Day, *Spell of the Pacific,* 69–70.

20. Mark Twain, *Following the Equator,* 624, 508.

21. Ibid., 514; see also his more sympathetic descriptions of Benares and his warm understanding of an important Hindu festival, although the accounts still contain some of the usual annoying witticisms, 496–506. Also, in slightly different form, see the English edition of Mark Twain, *More Tramps Abroad* (London: Chatto & Windus, 1898), 341–49.

22. See *The Works of Mark Twain,* ed., Harriet Elinor Smith and Edgar Marquess Branch. 2 vols. as of 1995 (Berkeley: University of California Press, 1994). Vol. 2 contains *Roughing It.*

23. Stephen Fender, "The West as Test," in London *Times Literary Supplement,*

June 3, 1994 (No. 4757), 25, citing Washington Irving and Frederick Jackson Turner, who both claimed that a visit to the American West would reveal not an
"effeminate" old Europe but a "new product that is American." Another point worth
noting is that even if Twain could reject Europe in favor of an indigenous (White?)
America, Black writers had no such luxury. Even as early as 1855 (long before the
1920s, when it was "acceptable"), Black writers like William Wells Brown contrasted
their unfree status in America with what they encountered in Europe. "I was recognized
as a man and an equal," Brown says. See William Wells Brown, *The American Fugitive in Europe: Sketches of Places and People Abroad* (Boston: John P. Jewett,
1855), 18; also see 40–47, 60–61, 140, 313, 314–15. William W. Stowe contends
in *Going Abroad: European Travel in Nineteenth Century American Culture*
(Princeton: Princeton University Press, 1994), 71–72 that Brown "was not ready to
reject European-American culture or to criticize the class structure of British and
American society." Brown did wish to appropriate European culture for himself to
gain his own self-respect. Thus, Black and White writers saw Europe in totally different ways. Whites claimed that they wanted to be liberated *from* Europe; Blacks wanted
to be freed *within* a European framework.

24. Twain, *Following the Equator*, 48, 51.

25. Ibid., 638, 693, 638, 693, 692, 693.

26. *The Collected Letters of Robert Louis Stevenson.* 8 vols. Ed. Bradford A. Booth
and Ernest Mehew (New Haven: Yale University Press, from 1994–1995). Vols. 7 and
8 are relevant for the South Seas. Also see William Maxwell "Stevenson Revealed,"
review of *The Collected Letters of Robert Louis Stevenson* ed. Booth and Mehew, *The
New Yorker,* LXX (December 26, 1994), 134–41.

27. Robert Louis Stevenson, *In the South Seas* (New York: Charles Scribner's
Sons, 1890). The account of Stevenson's encounter with the king actually took place
in 1889, after he, his wife, and stepson sought permission to disembark on the island
of Apemama. In order to do this, they had to seek permission from King Tembinoka.
Also see Stevenson's *Island Night's Entertainment* (New York: Charles Scribner's
Sons, 1893), in which the short story "The Bottle Imp" appears; parts of it were
originally composed in Hawaii and later translated into Samoan and published in that
language, before being printed in English.

28. "Gauguin and the School of Pont-Aven," *France Magazine* 32 (fall 1994), 48.

29. Nicholas Wadley, ed., *Noa Noa: Gauguin's Tahiti* (Salem, NH: Salem House,
1985). Gauguin's authorship is in dispute.

30. Ibid., 14, 17, 20.

31. Ibid., 25.

32. Ibid., 28.

33. Ibid., 33.

34. See Appendix II, "The Collaboration with Morice," ibid., 102.

35. See Appendix III, "Maori Mythology: Tehamana and Moerenhout," ibid., 108. Editor Nicholas Wadley points out that Gauguin knew that much of the "primitive" he sought in Tahiti had already vanished. Seemingly, the author of the text utilized a book by a Belgian consul of the 1820s and 1830s to work elements of the ancient Paradise theme into *Noa Noa.* Wadley cites J. A. Moerenhout's two volume account published in 1837, entitled *Voyages aux Îles du Grand Océan,* as the source. See Wadley, *Noa Noa,* 109.

36. See Paul Theroux, *The Happy Isles of Oceania* (New York: G. P. Putnam's Sons, 1992) as he journeys from New Zealand, Australia, New Guinea, Solomon Islands, Vanuatu, Fiji, and Tonga. He does what a twentieth-century American would be expected to do—he meets a king, lives like Crusoe on a desert island, then moves on to the Paradise of Tahiti, the Marquesas, Easter Island and Hawaii, which he says is "full of marvels." Theroux, who lived in East Africa in the 1960s, has written travel books of his worldwide sojourns, and is no gawky soujourner, is, nevertheless, still a great believer in the mythologies of the Pacific. Before he cites Defoe, Melville, Conrad, Swift, and Shakespeare, he confesses, "Anything can happen on an island" (p. 502). But, by contrast, note his unsentimentalized portrayal of Singapore, where he had lived and taught, in his seemingly factual short story,"Poetry Lesson," in *The New Yorker* LXXI, no. 18 (1995), 153–65.

BIBLIOGRAPHY

Abercrombie, Thomas J. "Ibn Battuta: Prince of Travelers." *National Geographic* 180: no.6 (December 1991): 2–49.

Abimbola, Wande. *Ifa: An Exposition of Ifa Literary Corpus*. Ibadan, Nigeria: Oxford University Press, 1976.

———. ed. *Yoruba Oral Tradition*. Ife, Nigeria: University of Ife, 1975.

Abrahams, Roger. *Deep Down in the Jungle*. New York: Aldine, 1970.

Achebe, Chinua. *Hopes and Impediments*. New York: Doubleday, 1989.

Adler, Elkan Nathan, ed. *Jewish Travellers in the Middle Ages*. Mineola, NY: Dover, 1987.

Ahmad, Nafis. *Muslim Contribution to Geography*. Lahore, Pakistan: Sh. Muhamad Ashraf, 1972.

Allan, Sarah. *The Shape of the Turtle: Myth, Art, and Cosmos in Early China*. Albany: State University of New York Press, 1991.

Alpers, Anthony. *Legends of the South Seas*. New York: Thomas Y. Crowell, 1970.

Anawalt, Patricia Rieff, and Frances F. Berdan."The Codex Mendoza." *Scientific American,* 266, no. 6 (June 1992): 40–49.

Ancient China's Technology and Science. Beijing: Foreign Languages Press, 1983.

Anderson, Benedict. *Imagined Communities*. London: Verso, 1983.

Anderson, Johannes. *Myths and Legends of the Polynesians*. Routland, VT: Charles E. Tuttle, 1969.

Appelbaum, Stanley. *The Chicago World's Fair of 1893*. New York: Dover, 1980.

Appiah, Kwame. *In My Father's House*. London: Oxford University Press, 1992.

Arciniegas, Germán. *Germans in the Conquest of America*. New York: Macmillan, 1943.

Arnold, Sir Edwin. *The Light of Asia*. London: Kegan Paul, Trench, Trübner,

1906.

Arnold, T. W. "Arab Travellers and Merchants," in *Travel and Travellers of the Middle Ages,* edited by Arthur Percival Newton. London: Routledge & Kegan Paul, 1926.

Arrian. *The Campaigns of Alexander.* London: Penguin, 1971.

Arrington, Leonard J., and Davis Betton, *The Mormon Experience: History of the Latter-day Saints.* New York: Knopf, 1979.

Ashcroft, Bill, Gareth Griffiths, and Helen Triffin. *The Empire Writes Back: Theory and Practice in Post-Colonial Literature.* London and New York: Routledge, 1989.

————. eds. *The Post-Colonial Studies Reader.* London and New York: Routledge, 1995.

Athey, Stephanie and Daniel Cooper Alarcon. *"Oroonoko's* Gendered Economics of Honor/Horror: Reframing Discourse Studies in the Americas." *American Literature,* 55 no. 3 (September 1993): 415–43.

Ban Gu, see Pan Ku.

Baron, Robert C., ed. *America: One Land One People.* Golden, CO: Fulcrum, 1987.

Barrell, John. *The Infection of Thomas de Quincey: A Psychopathology of Imperialism.* New Haven, Yale University Press, 1991.

Barriere, Dorothy B. "Revisions and Adulterations in Polynesian Creation Myths." In *Polynesian Culture History: Essays in Honour of Kenneth P. Emory,* edited by Genevieve A. Highland et al. Honolulu: Bishop Museum Press, 1967.

Barrow, John. *A Description of Pitcairn's Island and its Inhabitants.* 1900. Reprint, New York: Haskell House, 1972.

Barthes, Roland. *S/Z.* Translated by Richard Miller. New York: Hill and Wang, 1974.

Bascom, William. *Shango in the New World.* Austin: University of Texas, African and Afro-American Research Institute, 1972.

————. *Sixteen Cowries: Yoruba Divination from Africa to the New World.* Bloomington: Indiana University Press, 1980.

Beaglehole, J. C. *The Explorations of the Pacific.* 1934. Reprint, Stanford: Stanford University Press, 1966.

————. ed. *The Journals of Captain Cook on his Voyage of Discovery.* 3 vols, as follows: *The Voyage of the Endeavour: 1768–1771* (Cambridge: Hakluyt, 1955) vol 1; *The Voyage of the Resolution and Adventure:1772–1775* (Cambridge: Hakluyt, 1961) vol 2; *The Voyage of the Resolution and Discovery: 1776–1780* (Cambridge: Hakluyt, 1967) vol 3, Part 1; *The Voyage of the Resolution and*

Discovery:1776–1780 (Cambridge: Hakluyt, 1967), vol. 3, Part 2.

———. *The Life of Captain James Cook.* London: The Hakluyt Society; Stanford: Stanford University Press, 1974.

Beal, Samuel, ed. and trans. *Si-yu-ki: Buddhist Records of the Western World.* New Delhi: Munshiram Manoharlal Publishers, 1983

———. *Travels of Fah-hian and Sung-yuan.* 2 vols. New York: Augustus M. Kelley, 1969.

Behn, Aphra. *Oroonoko, the Rover and Other Works.* Edited by Janet Todd. London: Penguin, 1992.

Beier, Ulli, ed. *Voices of Independence: New Black Writing from Papua New Guinea.* St. Lucia, Australia: University of Queensland Press, 1980.

Bell, Diane. "An Accidental Australian Tourist: Or a Feminist Anthropologist at Sea and on Land." In *Implicit Understandings,* edited by Stuart B. Schwartz. New York: Cambridge University Press, 1994, 502–55.

Bellegarde-Smith, Patrick, ed. *Traditional Spirituality in the African Diaspora.* Lexington, KY: Association of Caribbean Studies, 1994.

Berdan, Frances F., and Patricia Rieff Anawalt, eds. *The Codex Mendoza.* 4 vols. Berkeley: University of California Press, 1992.

Bergon, Frank, ed. *The Journals of Lewis and Clark.* London: Penguin, 1989.

Berndt, Ronald M., and Catherine H. Berndt. *The Speaking Land: Myth and Story in Aboriginal Australia.* Rochester, VT: Inner Traditions International, 1994.

Bhabha, Homi K. *The Location of Culture.* London: Routledge, 1994.

Birch, Cyril, ed. *Chinese Communist Literature.* New York: Praeger, 1963.

Blassingame, John. *Black New Orleans.* Chicago: University of Chicago Press, 1973.

Bligh, William. *The Log of the Bounty.* 2 vols. London: Golden Cockerel Press, 1937.

———. *Narrative of the Mutiny on Board His Majesty's Ship Bounty.* London: George Nicol, 1790.

Boehmer, Elleke. *Colonial and Postcolonial Literature.* Oxford: Oxford University Press, 1995.

Bonavia, David. *The Chinese.* London: Penguin, 1980.

The Book of Mormon. Salt Lake City: Corporation of the President of the Church of Jesus Christ of Latter-Day Saints, 1981.

The Books of the Fairs: A Collection of World's Fair Publications, 1834–1915. Woodbridge, CT: Research Publications, 1989–1990. Microform.

Boorstin, Daniel. *The Discoverers.* New York: Vintage Books, 1983.

———. *The Image: A Guide to Pseudo-Events in America.* New York: Atheneum,

1980.

Boswell, James. *The Life of Samuel Johnson*. 3 vols. London: Swan   Sonnenschein, Lowrey & Co., 1888.

Bretschneider, Emil. *On the Knowledge Possessed by the Ancient Chinese of the Arab and Arabian Colonies*. Pamphlet, 1871.

Broomhall, Marshall. *Islam in China: A Neglected Problem*. 1910. Reprint New York: Paragon, 1966.

Brown, William Wells. *The American Fugitive in Europe: Sketches of Places and People Abroad*. Boston: John P. Jewett, 1855.

Bruson, James E. "African Presence in Early China." In *African Presence in Early Asia,* edited by Ivan Van Sertima and Runoko Rashdi. New Brunswick, NJ: Transaction Publishers, 1988. 120–37.

Buck, Peter H. *Vikings of the Sunrise*. New York: Frederick A. Stokes, 1938.

Buley, Roscoe Carlyle. "New Homes in the West." In *America: One Land One People,* edited by Robert C. Baron. *America: One Land One People*. Golden, CO: Fulcrum, 1987.

Burg, B. R. *Sodomy and the Pirate Tradition*. New York: New York University Press, 1984.

Byron, Lord. *The Poetical Works*. London: Oxford University Press, 1945.

Cabrera, Lydia. *El Monte*. 1954. Reprint, Miami: Ediciones Universal, 1975.

The Cambridge History of China, see Twitchett and Fairbank.

Campbell, Mary. *The Witness and the Other World*. Ithaca: Cornell University Press, 1988.

Carew, Jan. *Fulcrums of Change*. Trenton, NJ: African World Press, 1988.

———. *Rape of Paradise*. New York: A & B Books, 1994.

Carpenter, Frederick Ives. *Emerson and Asia*. Cambridge: Harvard University Press, 1930.

Carpini, John. "The Journey of Friar John of Pian de Carpini." In *Contemporaries of Marco Polo,* edited by Manuel Komroff. New York: Dorset Press, 1989.

Carrasco, David. *Quetzlcoatl and the Ironies of Empire*. Chicago: University of Chicago Press, 1982.

Carril, Pepe. *Shango de Ima, a Yoruba Mystery Play*. Garden City, NY: Doubleday, 1969.

Carrington, Hugh, ed. *The Discovery of Tahiti*. London: Hakluyt Society, 1948.

Castillo, J. M. *Ifa en Tierra de Ifa*. Miami: privately printed, 1976.

Catz, Rebecca. *Christopher Columbus and the Portuguese*. Westport, CT: Greenwood, 1993.

Chan, Albert. *The Glory and Fall of the Ming Dynasty*. Norman: University of

Oklahoma Press, 1982.

Chan, Wing-Tsit. *A Source Book in Chinese Philosophy*. Princeton: Princeton University Press, 1963.

Chanchun, see Ch'ang-Ch'un.

Chang, Kwang-Chih. *The Archaeology of Ancient China*. New Haven: Yale University Press, 1963.

Ch'ang-Ch'un [pinyin Chanchun]. *The Travels of an Alchemist*. Translated Arthur Waley. Taiwan: SMC Publishing, 1991.

Chau Ju-kua [pinyin, Zhao Rugua]. *Chu-fan-chi*. Translated Friedrich Hirth and W. W. Rockhill. New York: Paragon, 1966.

Ch'en, Kenneth. *Buddhism in China*. Princeton: Princeton University Press, 1964.

"China's Islam." *Beijing Review* 3, no. 28 (July 9, 1990): 29.

Chinese History. Beijing: China Reconstructs Press, 1988.

Chow, Rey. *Writing Diaspora: Tactics of Intervention in Contemporary Cultural Studies*. Bloomington: Indiana University Press, 1993.

Chronica Picta. 1358–1370. Reprint, Budapest: Helikon Publishing House, 1991.

Chuang Tsu. *Inner Chapters*. Translated by Gia-Fu Feng and Jane English. New York: Vintage, 1974.

Churchill, Winston. *My African Journey*. 1908. Reprint, London: Octopus, 1989.

Cipriani, Leonetto. *California and Overland Diaries*. Portland, OR: Cambridge Press, 1962.

Cleaves, Francis Woodman, trans. *The Secret History of the Mongols*. Cambridge: Harvard University Press, 1982.

Clyde, Paul H., and Burton F. Beers. *The Far East: A History of Western Impact and Eastern Response*. New York: Prentice Hall, 1966.

Codex Borgia, see Díaz and Rodgers.

Codex Florentine, see Sahagún.

Codex Mendoza, see Berdan and Anawalt.

Codex Nuttall, see Nuttall.

Codex Vindobonensis Mexicanus I: A Commentary, see Furst.

Colman, George the Younger, *Inkle and Yarico*. London: Printed for T. Cadell, 1787.

Colman, George the Younger, and Thomas Morton. *Plays by George Colman the Younger and Thomas Morton*. Edited by Barry Sutcliffe. Cambridge: Cambridge University Press, 1983.

Columbus, Christopher. *The Four Voyages of Christopher Columbus*, see Jane.

———. *Libro de las profecías*. Translated by Delno West and August King. Gainesville: University of Florida Press, 1991.

Confucius. *The Analects*. Translated by D. C. Lau. London: Penguin, 1979.

Conrad, Joseph. *Lord Jim*. 1900. Reprint, edited by Thomas C. Moser. New York W. W. Norton, 1968.

Conze, Edward, trans. *Buddhist Scriptures*. London: Penguin, 1959.

Cook, James, see Beaglehole.

Cooke, Edward. *A Voyage to the South Sea, and Round the World*. 1712. Reprint, New York: De Capo, 1969.

Cooper, J. C. *Chinese Alchemy: The Taoist Quest for Immortality*. New York: Sterling, 1990.

Cooper, James Fenimore. *The American Democrat; or, Hints on the Focal and Civil Relations of the United States of America*. Cooperstown: H. & E. Phinney, 1838.

———. *The Redskins*. 1846. New York: G. P. Putnam's, n.d.

Cortés, Fernando. *Fernando Cortés: Five Letters, 1519–1526*. Translated by J. Baynard Morris. New York: W. W. Norton, 1969.

———. *Hernan Cortés: Letters from Mexico*. Translated and edited by A. R. Pagden. New York: Grossman, 1971.

———. *His Five Letters of Relation to the Emperor Charles V, 1519–1526*. Translated and edited by Francis Augustus MacNutt. Introductory essay by John Greenway. 2 vols. Glorieta, NM: Rio Grande Press, 1977.

Cosmas Indicopleustes. *The Christian Topography of Cosmas, an Egyptian Monk*. Translated and edited by T. W. Crindle. Old Series No. 98. London: Hakluyt Society, 1897.

Cowell, E. B. et al., eds. *Buddhist Mahayana Texts*. New York: Dover, 1969.

Cronin, Vincent. *The Wise Man from the West*. New York: E. P. Dutton, 1955.

Crowder, Michael, ed. *West African Resistance*. New York: Africana Publishing, 1971.

Cullen, Countee. *Color*. New York: Harper & Brothers, 1925.

Culler, Jonathan, ed. *Framing the Sign: Criticism and Its Institutions*. Oxford: Basil Blackwell, 1988.

Dampier, William. *Dampier's Voyages*. 2 vols. London: E. Grant Richards, 1906.

———. *A New Voyage Round the World*. 1927. New York: Dover, 1968.

Dathorne, O. R., ed. *African Poetry*. London: Macmillan, 1969.

———. *Imagining the World: Mythical Belief versus Reality in Global Encounters*. Westport, CT: Bergin & Garvey, 1994.

———. *In Europe's Image: The Need for American Multiculturalism*. Westport, CT: Bergin & Garvey, 1994.

David, Andrew, ed. *The Charts and Coastal Views of Captain Cook's Voyages*. 2

vols. London: Hakluyt Society, 1988.

Davids, Caroline A.F. Rhys, trans. *Stories of the Buddha.* New York: Dover, 1989.

Davis, Wade. *The Serpent and the Rainbow.* New York: Warner Books, 1985.

Dawson, Christopher, ed. *Mission to Asia.* Toronto: University of Toronto Press, 1980.

Dean, Kenneth. *Taoist Ritual and Popular Cults of Southeast China.* Princeton: Princeton University Press, 1993.

De Bary, Wm. Theodore, ed. *The Buddhist Tradition.* New York: Vintage, 1972.

De Bary, Wm. Theodore, Wing-tsit Chan, and Burton Watson, eds., *Sources of Chinese Tradition.* 2 vols. New York: Columbia University Press, 1960.

Defoe, Daniel. *Robinson Crusoe.* Edited by Michael Shinagel. New York: W. W. Norton, 1975.

Delumeau, Jean. *History of Paradise.* New York: Continuum, 1995.

Dening, Gregory. "Ethnohistory in Polynesia: The Value of Ethnohistorical Evidence." *The Journal of Pacific History* (Canberra, Australia), 1 (1966).

———. "The Theatricality of Observing and Being Observed: Eighteenth Century Europe 'discovers' the ? Century 'Pacific.' " In *Implicit Understandings,* edited by Stuart B. Schwartz. New York: Cambridge University Press, 1994, 451–83.

De Quincey, Thomas. *Confessions of an English Opium-Eater, Together with Selections from the Autobiography.* London: Cresset, 1950.

Derrida, Jacques. *Margins of Philosophy.* Translated by Alan Bass. Chicago: University of Chicago Press, 1982.

De Villiers, J.A.J., ed. *East and West Indian Mirror.* London: Hakluyt Society, 1906.

The Dhammapada. Translated by Juan Mascaró. London: Penguin, 1973.

The Diamond Sutra and the Sutra of Hui-neng. Translated by A. F. Price and Wong Mou-lam. Boston: Shambala, 1990.

Díaz del Castillo, Bernal. *The Conquest of New Spain.* 1632. Translated and edited by J. M. Cohen. Harmondsworth, UK: Penguin, 1965. Abbreviated version with editor's summaries for omitted parts.

———. *The Discovery and Conquest of Mexico, 1517–1521.* 1632. Translated by A. P. Maudslay and edited by Irving A. Leonard. New York: Farrar, Straus & Giroux, 1956.

———. *The True History of the Conquest of New Spain.* 1632. Translated by Alfred Maudslay and edited by Genaro García. 5 vols. London: Hakluyt Society, 1908– 1916.

Díaz, Gisele, and Alan Rodgers, eds. *Codex Borgia.* New York: Dover, 1993.

Diop, Cheikh Anta. *The African Origin of Civilization.* New York: Lawrence Hill, 1974.

Douglass, Frederick. Cited in "Honor to Their Race," *Chicago's Daily Inter Ocean*, August 26, 1893.

Drège, Jean Pierre, and Emil M. Bührer. *The Silk Road Saga*. New York: Facts on File, 1946.

Dreyer, Edward. *Early Ming China: A Political History, 1355–1435*. Stanford: Stanford University Press, 1982.

Duke, Michael S. *Blooming and Contending*. Bloomington: Indiana University Press,1985.

Dunn, Ross, ed. *The Adventures of Ibn Battuta*. Berkeley: University of California Press, 1986.

Dunne, George H. *Generation of Giants*. Notre Dame: University of Notre Dame Press, 1962.

Duyvendak, J.J.L. *The Book of Lord Shang*. London: Probsthain, 1928.

———. *China's Discovery of Africa*. London: Probsthain, 1949.

———. "The True Dates of the Chinese Maritime Expeditions in the Early Fifteenth Century." *T'oung Pao* 34 (1938): 341–412.

Eden, Richard. *The First Three English Books on America, [?1511–1555 A.D.]*. Edited by Edward Arber. Birmingham, UK: n.p., 1885.

El Inca, see Garcilaso de la Vega.

Elliott, J. H. introduction to *Hernan Cortés: Letters from Mexico*. Translated and edited by A. R. Pagden. New York: Grossman, 1971.

Fairbank, John King. *China: A New History*. Cambridge: Belknap Press of Harvard University Press, 1992.

Fairchild, Hoxie Neale. *The Noble Savage: A Study in Romantic Naturalism*. New York: Columbia University Press, 1928.

Faxian. *A Record of Buddhistic Kingdoms*. Translated by James Legge. New Delhi: Munshiram Manoharlal Publishers, 1991. (Also see Beal, Watters).

Fender, Stephen. "The West as Test." London *Times Literary Supplement*, June 3, 1994 (no. 4757), 25.

Ferguson, Moira. "*Oroonoko*: Birth of a Paradigm." *New Literary History* 23, no. 2 (spring 1992): 339–59.

Ferrand, G. *Instructions nautiques et routiers arabes et portugais des 15e et 16e siècles*. 3 vols. Paris: Geuthner, 1921–1928.

Feserman, Steven. "African Histories and the Dissolution of World History." In *Africa and the Disciplines,* edited by Robert H. Bates, V. Y. Mudimbe, and Jean O'Barr. Chicago: University of Chicago Press, 1993.

Fiedler, Leslie, and Houston A. Baker, Jr., eds. *English Literature: Opening up the Canon*. Baltimore: John Hopkins University Press, 1981.

Finnegan, Ruth. *Oral Literature in Africa.* Oxford: Clarendon Press, 1970.

Firth, Raymond. *Tikopia Ritual and Belief.* Boston: Beacon Press, 1967.

Fitzgerald, C. P. *China: A Short Cultural History.* London: Cresset, 1986.

Florescano, Enrique. *Memory, Myth and Time in Mexico: From the Aztecs to Independence.* Austin: University of Texas Press, 1994.

Foner, Eric, and John A. Garraty, eds. *The Reader's Companion to American History.* Boston: Houghton Mifflin, 1991

Formisano, Luciano. *Letters from the New World: Amerigo Vespucci's Discovery of America.* New York: Marsilio, 1992.

Franck, Irene M., and David Brownstone. *The Silk Road.* New York: Facts on File, 1986.

Friedman, John Block. *The Monstrous Races in Medieval Art and Thought.* Cambridge: Harvard University Press, 1981.

Fry, Roger. *Vision and Design.* New York: Brentano's, 1920.

Fung, Yu-lan and Derek Bodde, trans. and eds. *A History of Chinese Philosophy.* Princeton: Princeton University Press, 1952.

Furst, Jill Leslie, ed. *Codex Vindobonensis Mexicanus: A Commentary.* Albany: State University of New York, Institute for Mesoamerican Studies Publication 4, 1978.

Furtwangler, Albert. *Acts of Discovery: Visions of America in the Lewis and Clark Journals.* Urbana: University of Illinois Press, 1993.

Fyle, C. H. *The History of Sierra Leone.* London: Evans Brothers, 1988.

Gallagher, Robert F., ed., *Byron's Journal of His Circumnavigation, 1764–1766.* Cambridge: Hakluyt Society, 1964.

Garcilaso de la Vega (known as El Inca). *The Florida of the Inca.* 1605. Edited and translated by John and Jeannette Verner. Austin: University of Texas Press, 1951.

———. *Royal Commentaries of the Incas* [1609] *and General History of Peru* [1616–17]. Translated by Harold V. Livermore. Austin: University of Texas Press, 1966.

Gates, Henry Louis. *The Signifying Monkey: A Theory of African American Literary Criticism.* Oxford: Oxford University Press, 1988.

"Gauguin and the School of Pont-Aven." *France Magazine* 32 (fall 1994), 48.

Gernet, Jacques. *A History of Chinese Civilization.* Cambridge: Cambridge University Press, 1982.

Giles, H. A. *Religions of Ancient China.* 1906. Chicago: Open Court, 1918.

Goldie, Terry. *Fear and Temptation: The Image of the Indigene in Canadian, Australian and New Zealand Literature.* Montreal: McGill-Queen's University

Press, 1989.

Goldsmith, Oliver. *The Miscellaneous Works*. Edinburgh: William P. Nimmo, 1801.

Gómara, Francisco López de. *Historia de la Conquista de México*. 1553. Translated as *Cortés: The Life of the Conqueror by His Secretary*. Translated and edited by Lesley Byrd Simpson. Berkeley: University of California Press, 1964.

Goodrich, L. C. and Chaoying Fang, eds. *Dictionary of Ming Biography: 1368–1644*. New York: Columbia University Press, 1976.

Green, Peter. *Alexander of Macedon*. Berkeley: University of California Press, 1991.

Greenberg, Joseph H. *Languages of West Africa*. The Hague: Mouton, 1966.

———. *Universals of Language*. Cambridge: M.I.T. Press, 1963.

Greenblatt, Stephen. *Marvelous Possessions: The Wonder of the New World*. Chicago: University of Chicago Press, 1991.

Greenway, John. Introduction to Fernando Cortés, *His Five Letters of Relation to the Emperor Charles V, 1519–1526*, translated and edited by Francis Augustus MacNutt. 2 vols. Glorieta, NM: Rio Grande Press, 1977. Greenway's introduction is entitled "New Front Matter," and numbered 11–104.

Grousset, René. *In the Footsteps of the Buddha*. New York: Grossman, 1971.

Hakluyt, Richard. *Hakluyt's Voyages: The Principal New Voyages, Traffiques, and Discoveries of the English Nation*. 1589. Selected and edited [and modernized] by Irwin R. Blacker. New York: Viking, 1965.

———. *Principall Navigations, Voiages, and Discoveries of the English Nation*. 1589. 2 vols. Reprint, Cambridge: Hakluyt Society, 1965.

Hamberg, Theodore. *The Vision of Hung-siu-Tshuen and the Origin of the Kwang-si Insurrection*. Hong Kong: n. p. 1854.

Hanke, Lewis. *All Mankind is One*. De Kalb: Northern Illinois University Press, 1974.

———. *Aristotle and the American Indians: A Study in Race Prejudice in the Modern World*. Bloomington: Indiana University Press, 1959.

Harries, Lyndon. *Swahili Poetry*. Oxford: Clarendon Press, 1962.

Healy, J. J. *Literature of the Aborigine*. 1978. St. Lucia, Australia: University of Queensland Press, 1989.

He Zhaowu, ed. *An Intellectual History of China*. Beijing: Foreign Languages Press, 1991.

Hemingway, Ernest. *The Green Hills of Africa*. 1935. Reprint, New York: Permabooks, 1954.

Hemmings, John. *Red Gold: The Conquest of the Brazilian Indians*. Cambridge: Harvard University Press, 1978.

Herodotus, *The Histories*. Translated by Aubrey de Sélincourt. London: Penguin,

1954.

Herskovits, Melville. *The Myth of the Negro Past.* 1941. Boston: Beacon Press, 1990.

Heyerdahl, Thor, and Christopher Ralling. *Kon-Tiki Man.* San Francisco: Chronicle Books, 1991.

Highland, Genevieve A., R. W. Force et al., eds. *Polynesian Culture History: Essays in Honour of Kenneth P. Emory.* Honolulu: Bishop Museum Press, 1967.

Hill, Donald R. *Calypso Calaloo: Early Carnival Music in Trinidad.* Gainesville: University Press of Florida, 1993.

Hill, Errol. *The Jamaican Stage.* Amherst: University of Massachussetts Press, 1992.

Hodge, Frederick, and Theodore Lewis, eds. *Spanish Explorers in the Southern United States.* New York: Barnes and Noble, 1907.

Holloway, Joseph E., ed. *Africanisms in American Culture.* Bloomington: Indiana University Press, 1991.

Holloway, Joseph E., and Winifred K. Vass. *The African Heritage of American English.* Bloomington: Indiana University Press, 1993.

Hourani, G. F., ed. *Arab Seafaring in the Indian Ocean in Ancient and Medieval Times.* Princeton: Princeton University Press, 1981.

Howard, Alan. "Polynesian Origins and Migrations." In *Polynesian Culture History: Essays in Honour of Kenneth P. Emory,* edited by Genevieve A. Highland et al. Honolulu: Bishop Museum Press, 1967, 45–101.

Howard, Ed. "Pitcairn and Norfolk: the Saga of Bounty's Children." *National Geographic,* 164, no. 4 (October 1983): 510–41.

Howells, W. W. "Origins of the Chinese People: Interpretations of Recent Evidence." In *The Origins of Chinese Civilization.* Edited by David W. Keightley. Berkeley: University of California Press, 1983.

Hrbek, I. "Africa in the Context of World History." In *UNESCO General History of Africa.* Berkeley: University of California Press, 1988. Vol. 3, 1–30.

Hsia, T. A. "Heroes and Hero-Worship in Chinese Communist Fiction." In *Chinese Communist Literature,* edited by Cyril Birch. New York: Praeger, 1963.

Huang Tsung-hsi [pinyin, Huang Zongxi]. *Waiting for the Dawn: A Plan for the Prince.* Translated by Wm. Theodore de Bary. New York: Columbia University Press, 1993.

Huang Zongxi, see Huang Tsung-hsi.

Huff, Toby E. *The Rise of Early Modern Science: Islam, China, and the West.* Cambridge: Cambridge University Press, 1993.

The Hungarian Illuminated Chronicle: Chronica de Gestis Hungarorum [1358]

Budapest: Corvina Press, 1969.

Hughes, Langston and Arna Bontemps. *The Book of Negro Folklore.* New York: Dodd, Mead, 1958.

Hung-lam Chu. Review of Huang Tsung-hsi, *Waiting for the Dawn,* trans. Wm. Theodore de Bary. In *Journal of Asian Studies* 53, no. 2 (May 1994). 533–34.

Hurlbut, Geo. C. "The Origin of the Name 'America.'"*Journal of the American Geographical Society of New York* 20 (1888): 183–96.

Ibn Battuta. *The Adventures of Ibn Battuta,* see Dunn, Ross.

———. *Travels in Asia and Africa: 1325–54.* Edited by H.A.R. Gibb. New York: Robert A. McBride, 1929.

Ibn Jubayr, Muhammad ibn Ahmad. *The Travels of Ibn Jubayr, Being the Chronicle of a Medieval Spanish Moor.* Translated and edited by R.J.C. Broadhurst. London: Jonathan Cape, 1952.

———. *The Travels of Ibn Jubayr.* Translated and edited by W. Wright and M. J. DeGoeje. Leyden: Brill, 1907.

Ibn Khaldun. *The Muqadimah: An Introduction to History.* 1377. Translated by Franz Rosenthal. Princeton: Princeton University Press, 1967.

Idown, E. Bolaji. *Olódùmaré: God in Yoruba Belief.* London: Longmans, 1962.

Israeli, Raphael. *Islam in China: A Critical Biography.* Westport, CT: Greenwood, 1994.

Jahn, Janheinz. *A History of Neo-African Literature.* London: Faber and Faber, 1966.

Jane, Cecil, ed. *The Four Voyages of Christopher Columbus.* Cambridge: Hakluyt, 1930–1933; reprint (2 vols. in 1, each with separate pagination) New York: Dover, 1988.

JanMohammed, Abdul R., and David Lloyd. *The Nature and Context of Minority Discourse.* Oxford: Oxford University Press, 1990.

Jefferson, Thomas. "Notes on the State of Virginia." 1784. In *The Portable Thomas Jefferson.* Edited by Merrill D. Peterson. London: Penguin, 1975.

Johnson, Samuel. *The History of Rasselas Prince of Abissinia.* 1759. Edited by J. P. Hardy. Oxford: Oxford University Press, 1988.

Jones, Eldred. *Othello's Countrymen.* London: Oxford University Press, 1965.

Jonson, Ben. *The Works.* Edited by William Gifford. London: Edward Moxon, 1853.

Kanitkar, Helen, and Hemant Kanitkar. *Asoka and Indian Culture.* Edited by Malcolm Yapp. San Diego: Greenhaven, 1980.

Karenga, Maulana. *The African-American Holilday of Kwanzaa: A Celebration for Family, Community, and Culture.* Los Angeles: University of Sankore Press, 1988.

Keightley, David W., ed. *The Origins of Chinese Civilization.* Berkeley: University of California Press, 1983.

King, Bruce. *Literatures of the World in English*. London: Routledge & Kegan Paul, 1974.

Knappert, Jan. *A Choice of Flowers*. London: Heinemann, 1972.

Komroff, Manuel, ed. *Contemporaries of Marco Polo*. New York: Dorset, 1989.

Kravath, Fred F. *Christopher Columbus, Cosmographer*. Rancho Cordova, CA: Landmark Enterprises, 1987.

Lahiri, Latika. *Chinese Monks in India*. Delhi: Motilal Banarsidass, 1986.

Langlois, John D. *China Under Mongol Rule*. Princeton: Princeton University Press, 1981.

Lattimore, Owen. *Inner Asian Encounters of China*. Boston: Beacon Press, 1962.

———. *Inner Asian Frontiers of China*. Boston: Beacon Press, 1951.

Lawrence, D. H. *Classic American Literature*. 1923. London: Penguin, 1971.

Legge, James ed. *The Chinese Classics*. 5 vols. Hong Kong: Hong Kong University Press, 1960. These are as follows: *Confucian Analects, Great Learning, Doctrine of the Mean*, vol 1; *The Works of Mencius*, vol 2; *The Shoo King, or the Book of Historical Documents*, vol 3; *The She King, or the Book of Poetry*, vol 4; *The Ch'un Ts'ew, with the Tso Chuen*, vol 5.

———. trans. and ed. *The I Ching*. New York: Dover Publications, 1963.

———. trans. and ed. *The Texts of Taoism: The Tao Te Ching of Lao Tzu*, [and] *The Writings of Chuang Tzu*, 2 vols. New York: Dover Publications, 1962.

Le Maire, Jacob. "The Australian Adventures of Jacob Le Maire." In *The East and West Indian Mirror* translated by J.A.J. de Villiers. London: Hakluyt Society, 1906. Reprint, Nendeln, Lechtenstein: Kraus Reprint, 1967. 165–234.

Léon-Portilla, Miguel. "The Aztec Gods: How Many?" In *Circa 1492*. edited by Jay A. Levinson. Washington: National Gallery of Art; New Haven: Yale University Press, 1991. 507–8.

———. ed. *The Broken Spears: The Aztec Account of the Conquest of Mexico*. Boston: Beacon Press, 1962.

———. ed. *Pre-Columbian Literatures of Mexico*. Norman: University of Oklahoma Press, 1969.

Lerner, Max. *America as a Civilization*. New York: Henry Holt, 1957.

Levinson, Jay A. *Circa 1492*. Washington: National Gallery of Art; New Haven: Yale University Press, 1991.

Levy, Howard S., trans. *Biography of An Lu-shan*. Berkeley: University of California Press, 1960.

Lewis, Bernard. "What Went Wrong? Some Reflections on Arab History." *American Scholar* 62, no. 4 (Autumn 1993).

Lewis, R.W.B. *The American Adam: Innocence, Tragedy, and Tradition in the Nineteenth Century*. Chicago: University of Chicago Press, 1955.

Li Yu-ning, ed. *The First Emperor of China: The Politics of Historiography*. White Plains, NY: International Arts & Sciences Press, 1974.

Li Zhisui. *The Private Life of Chairman Mao*. London: Chatto and Windus, 1994.

Link, Frederick M. *Aphra Behn*. New York: Twayne Publishers, 1968.

Lister, R. P. *The Secret History of Genghis Khan*. London: Peter Davies, 1969.

Little, Kenneth. *Negroes in Britain: A Study of Racial Relations in English Society*. London: Kegan Paul, 1947.

Liu Jung-en, ed. *Six Yüan Plays*. London: Penguin, 1972.

Liyong, Taban lo. "Negroes Are Not Africans." In *The Last Word*. Nairobi: East African Publishing House, 1969.

Loewe, Michael. *Ways to Paradise: The Chinese Quest for Immortality*. London: George Allen & Unwin, 1979.

Long, Edward. *A History of Jamaica*. London: Printed for T. Lowndes, 1774.

The Lotus Sutra. Translated and edited by Burton Watson. New York: Columbia University Press, 1993.

Ma Huan. *Ying-yai Sheng-lan: The Overall Survey of the Ocean's Shores*. 1433. Translated and edited by Feng Ch'eng-Chün. Introduction by J.V.G. Mills. Cambridge: The University Press, Hakluyt Second Series, 1970.

Malo, David. *Hawaiian Antiquities*. Translated by Nathaniel R. Emerson. 1898. Reprint, Honolulu: Bernice P. Bishop Museum, 1951.

Mao Zedong. *Mao Tse-tung on Literature and Art*. Beijing: Foreign Language Press, 1987.

Marcou, Jules."Nouvelles Recherches sur L'Origine du Nom d'Amérique." *Bulletin de la Société de Géographie* (Paris) 9, 7th series (1888), 480–520.

———. "Sur L'Origine du Nom d'Amérique." *Bulletin de la Société de Géographie* (Paris) 9, 6th Series (1875), 587–97.

Marshall, Robert. *Storm from the East*. Berkeley: University of California Press, 1993.

Martyr, Peter. *De Orbe Novo*. Translated by Francis Augustus MacNutt. 2 vols. New York: Burt Franklin, 1912.

Masao, F. T., and H. W. Muturo, "The East African Coast and the Comoro Islands." In *UNESCO General History of Africa*. Berkeley: University of California Press, 1988. vol. 3, 586–615.

Maxwell, William. "Stevenson Revealed." Review of *The Collected Letters of Robert Louis Stevenson*. 8 vols projected. Ed. Bradford A. Booth and Ernest Mehew. New Haven: Yale University Press, 1994–1995 in *The New Yorker*,

LXX (December 26, 1994), 134–41.

Mazrui, Ali. *The Africans*. Boston: Little, Brown, 1986.

McClellan, Robert. *The Heathen Chinee*. Columbus: Ohio State University Press, 1971.

McClintock, Anne M. *Imperial Leather: Race, Gender and Sexuality in the Colonial Context*. New York: Routledge, 1995.

McCrum, Robert, William Cran, and Robert McNeil. *The Story of English*. New York: Penguin, 1993.

McCullough, N. V. *The Negro in English Literature*. Ilfracombe, UK: Stockwell,. 1962.

McGregor, Gaile. *The Noble Savage in the New World Garden: Notes Toward the Syntactics of Place*. Toronto: University of Toronto Press, 1988.

Mead, Margaret. *Coming of Age in Samoa*. New York: William Morrow, 1928.

Melville, Herman. *John Marr and Other Sailors, with Some Sea Pieces*. New York: DeVinne Press, 1888.

———. *Moby-Dick, or, the Whale*. 1851. Reprint, Norwalk, CT: Easton Press, 1977.

———. *Typee*. New York: Dodd, Mead, n.d. [1846?]

Mencius. Translated by D. C.Lau. London: Penguin, 1970.

Menguin, Ernest. "Commentaire du Codex Mexicanus Nos. 23–24 de la Bibliothèque Nationale de Paris."*Journal de la Société des Américanistes*, Nouvelle Série, 41 (1952): 387–499.

Métraux, Alfred. *Easter Island*. New York: Oxford University Press, 1957.

———. *Voodoo in Haiti*. London: André Deutsch, 1959.

Mirsky, Jeanette. "Silent Upon a Peak in Darien—Balboa Discovers the Pacific." In *The Great Explorers*, edited by Helen Wright and Samuel Rapport. New York: Harper & Brothers, 1957. 250–61.

———. *The Westward Crossings*. New York: Alfred A Knopf, 1946.

Mochtar, Lubis. *Indonesia: Island Under the Rainbow*. Singapore: Oxford University Press, 1987.

Montaigne, Michel Eyquem de. *The Essays*. [1580–1595]. Translated and edited by M. A. Screech. London: Allen Lane, Penguin Press, 1987.

Moore, Carlos. *Castro, the Blacks and Africa*. Los Angeles: Center for Afro-American Studies, UCLA, 1988.

Moore, Gerald. *The Chosen Tongue*. London: Longmans, 1969.

Morgan, David. *The Mongols*. Oxford: Blackwell, 1986.

Morison, Samuel Eliot. *The European Discovery of America: The Northern Voyages, A.D.500–1600*. New York: Oxford University Press, 1971.

————. *The European Discovery of America: The Southern Voyages, A.D. 1492–1616.* New York: Oxford University Press, 1974.

————. *Portuguese Voyages to America in the Fifteenth Century.* Cambridge: Harvard University Press, 1940.

Mudrooroo, see Narogin.

Mulvaney, D. J. *The PreHistory of Australia.* New York: Frederick A. Praeger, 1969.

Murphy, Joseph M. *Santería: An African Religion in America.* Boston: Beacon Press, 1988.

————. *Working the Spirit.* Boston: Beacon Press, 1994.

Narasimhaiah, C. D., ed. *Awakened Conscience: Studies in Commonwealth Literature.* Atlantic Highlands, NJ: Humantities Press, 1978.

Narogin, Mudrooroo. *Writing for the Fringe: A Study of Modern Aboriginal Literature.* Melbourne: Hyland House, 1990.

Newton, Arthur Percival, ed. *Travel and Travellers of the Middle Ages.* London: Routledge & Kegan Paul, 1926.

Ngugi wa Thiong'o. *Homecoming.* London: Heinemann, 1972.

Nicol, Davidson."The Meaning of Africa." In *A Book of African Verse,* edited by John Reed and Clive Wake. London: Heinemann, 1964.

Nordhoff, Charles, and James Norman Hall. *The Bounty Trilogy.* Boston: Little, Brown, 1985.

Nuttall, Zelia, ed. *Codex Nuttall.* 1902. Reprint, New York: Dover, 1975.

Obeyesekere, Ganath. *The Apotheosis of Captain Cook: European Mythmaking in the Pacific.* Princeton: Princeton University Press, 1992.

Odoric.*The Voyage and Travayle of Syr John Mandeville Knight with the Journall of Frier Odoricus.* London: J. M. Dent, c.1887.

Oliver, Douglas. "Friendship Pacts in Ancient Tahiti." In *Polynesian Culture History: Essays in Honour of Kenneth P. Emory,* edited by Genevieve A. Highland et al. Honolulu: Bishop Museum Press, 1967, 439–450.

O'Neill, Hugh B. *Companion to Chinese History.* New York: Facts on File Publication, 1987.

Orwell, George. "Marrakesh." In *A Collection of Essays.* New York: Doubleday Anchor, 1954.

O'Sullivan, John L. *United States Magazine and Democratic Review,* July-August, 1845 in Foner and Garaty.

Owen, J. B., ed. *Lyrical Ballads, 1798.* London: Oxford University Press, 1969.

Owomoyela, Oyekan. *A History of Twentieth Century African Literature.* Lincoln: Universiy of Nebraska Press, 1993.

Pan Ku [pinyin, Ban Gu]. *Courtier and Commoner in Ancient China: Sections from the "History of the Former Han."* Translated by Burton Watson. New York: Columbia University Press, 1974.

————. *The History of the Former Han Dynasty.* ed Homer Dubbs. 3 vols. Baltimore: Waverly Press, 1955.

Parekh, Bhikhu. "Incurious Mill." Review of Lynn Zastoupil, *John Stuart Mill and India.* Stanford: Stanford University Press, 1994. In London *Times Literary Supplement,* November 11, 1994 (No 4780), 23.

Peacock, Seth, and Ruth Peacock. *Spirits of the Deep.* Garden City, NY: Anchor Press, Doubleday, 1975.

Pearson, Noel. "A Troubling Inheritance." *Race & Class* 35, no. 4 (April-June, 1994): 1–9.

Pigafetta, Antonio. *Magellan's Voyage.* Translated and edited by R. A. Skelton. 2 vols. New Haven: Yale University Press, 1969.

Pliny. *Natural History.* Edited by H. Rackham et al. 10 vols. Cambridge: Harvard University Press, 1938–1967.

Pollak-Elzt, Angelina. *Black Culture and Society in Venezuela.* Caracas: Lagoven, 1994.

Polo, Marco. *The Description of the World.* Edited by A. C. Moule and Paul Pelliot. 2 vols. London: George Routledge & Sons, 1938.

Popul Vuh. Translated by Dennis Tedlock. New York: Simon & Schuster, 1985.

Prescott, William Hickling. *The Conquest of Mexico.* New York: Henry Holt, 1922.

————. *The Complete and Unexpurgated History of the Conquest of Mexico* [1843, 3 vols.] *and History of the Conquest of Peru* [1847, 2 vols]. Reprinted in 1 vol. London: Random House, n.d.

Press, John, ed. *Commonwealth Literature: Unity and Diversity in a Common Culture.* London: Heienmann, 1965.

Price, A. Grenfell, ed. *The Explorations of Captain James Cook in the Pacific.* New York: Dover, 1971.

Price, Lawrence M. *Inkle and Yarico Album.* Berkeley: University of California Press, 1937.

Price, Richard, and Sidney M. Mintz. *An Anthropological Approach to the Afro-American Past: A Caribbean Perspective.* Philadelphia: ISHU, 1976.

Pulleybank, E. G. *The Background of the Rebellion of An Lu-shan.* London: Oxford University Press, 1955.

Purchas, Samuel. *Hakluytus Posthumus, or Purchas his Pilgrimes, contayning a History of the World in Sea Voyages and Land Travell by Englishmen and Others.* 1625. 20 vols. Reprint, Glasgow: James MacLehose & Sons, 1905.

Quinn, David Beers. *The Roanoke Voyages, 1584–1590.* London: The Hakluyt

Society, 1955.

Quirós, Pedro Fernandez de. *The Voyages: 1539–1606.* 1906. Translated and edited by Clements Markham. Nendeln, Liechtenstein: Kraus Reprint, 1967.

Rabasa, José. "Dialogue as Conquest: Mapping Spaces for Counter Discourse." In *The Nature and Context of Minority Discourse,* edited by Abdul R. JanMohammed and David Lloyd. Oxford: Oxford University Press, 1990. 187–215.

Rachewiltz, I. de. *Papal Envoys to the Great Khans.* London: Faber and Faber, 1971.

Radhakumund, Mookerji. *Asoka.* New Delhi: Motilal Banarsiduss, 1986.

Raleigh, Walter. *The Discoverie of the Large, Rich and Bewtiful Empyre of Guiana.* 1506. Reprint,Amsterdam: Da Capo Press, 1968.

Reed, John, and Clive Wake. *A Book of African Verse.* London: Heinemann, 1964.

Reid, Anthony. "Early Southeast Asian Categorizations of Europeans." In *Implicit Understandings,* edited by Stuart B. Schwartz. New York: Cambridge University Press, 1994, 268–294

Reischauer, Edwin O., ed. *Ennin's Diary.* New York: Ronald Press, 1955.

Remacle, Jeanne."'Le Noir du Blanc': An Exhibition of Clichés and Racial Stereotypes." In *The Courier* 130 (Nov–Dec, 1991), 91–93.

Roberts, J. M. *The Triumph of the West.* London: British Broadcasting Corporation, 1985.

Robertson, George. *The Discovery of Tahiti.* Edited by Hugh Carrington. London: Hakluyt Society, 1948.

Rockhill, W. W. "Notes on the Relations and Trade of China with the Eastern Archipelago and the Coasts of the Indian Ocean During the Fourteenth Century, Ormuz, Coast of Arabia and Africa." Part 1, *T'oung Pao,* 15 (1915), 419–47. Part 2, *T'oung Pao,* 16 (1915), 604–26.

Rogers, Woodes. *A Cruising Voyage Round the World.* 1712. London: Longman, Green & Co., 1928.

Roosevelt, Theodore. *African Game Trails.* New York: Charles Scribner's Sons, 1910.

Ross, James Bruce, and Mary Martin McLaughlin, *The Portable Medieval Reader.* London: Penguin, 1949.

Rouse, Irving. *The Taínos: Rise and Decline of the People Who Greeted Columbus.* New Haven: Yale University Press, 1992.

Rugoff, Milton, ed. *The Travels of Marco Polo.* New York: New American Library, 1961.

Sahagún, Fray Bernardino de. *Florentine Codex, General History of the Things of New Spain.* 12 vols. Edited by Arthur J.O. Anderson and Charles Dibble. Salt Lake City: School of American Research and University of Utah, 1950–1982.

Sahlins, Marshall. *How "Natives" Think About Captain Cook, for Example*. Chicago: University of Chicago Press, 1995.

Said, Edward. *Orientalism*. New York: Vintage, 1979.

Saint-Pierre, Jacques-Henri Bernardin de, *Paul and Virginia*. 1796. Translated by Helen Maria Williams. Oxford: Woodstock Books, 1989.

Sancho, Ignatius. *Letters of the Late Ignatius Sancho*. 1782. Reprint edited by Paul Edwards. London: Dawsons of Pall Mall, 1968.

Sandiford, Keith A. *Measuring the Moment: Strategies of Protest in Eighteenth Century Writing*. Cranbury, NJ: Associated University Presses, 1988.

Schwartz, Stuart B., ed. *Implicit Understandings*. New York: Cambridge University Press, 1994.

Scobie, Edward. *Black Britannia*. Chicago: Johnson Publishing, 1972.

Scott, A. C., ed. *Traditional Chinese Plays*. 3 vols. Madison: University of Wisconsin Press, vol 1 (1964); vol 2 (1969); vol 3 (1973).

Seneca, *Selections*. Edited by Umberto Moricca. Turin, Italy: I. B. Paravia, 1947.

Severin, Tim. *The China Voyage*. Boston: Little, Brown, 1994.

Shirley, Rodney W. *The Mapping of the World*. London: Holland Press Cartographica, 1984.

Shyllon, Folarin. *Black People in Britain*. London: Oxford University Press, 1977.

Siikala, Jukka. *Cultural Conflict in Tropical Polynesia*. Helsinki: Suomalainen Tredeakatemia Academia Scientiarum Fennica [The Finnish Academy of Science and Letters], 1982.

Sima Qian, see Ssu-ma Chien.

Simpson, George Eaton. *Black Religions in the New World*. New York: Columbia University Press, 1978.

Slessarev, Vsevold. *Prester John: The Letter and the Legend*. Minneapolis:University of Minnesota Press, 1959.

Smith, Marian W. "Towards a Classification of Cult Movements." *Man* 59, no. 2 (January 1959): 8–12.

Smitherman, Geneva. *Talkin' and Testifyin': The Language of Black America*. Boston: Houghton Mifflin, 1977.

Snow, Phillip. *Star Raft: China's Encounter with Africa*. Ithaca: Cornell University Press, 1988.

Sollors, Werner, ed. *The Invention of Ethnicity*. New York: Oxford University Press, 1989.

Ssu-ma Chien [pinyin, Sima Qian]. *Records of the Grand Historian of China*. Translated by Burton Watson. 2 vols. New York: Columbia University Press, 1961.

Steele, Richard. *The Englishman,* no. 26, December 3, 1713.

————. *Spectator,* no.11, March 13, 1711.

Stein, Aurel. *Innermost Asia.* 2 vols. Oxford: Oxford University Press, 1928.

————. *Ruins of Desert Cathay.* 2 vols. New York: Benjamin Bloom, 1912.

Stevens, Henry N., and George F. Barwick, eds. *New Light on the Discovery of Australia as Revealed by the Journal of Captain Don Diego de Prado y Tovar.* London: Hakluyt Society, 1930.

Stevenson, Robert Louis. *The Collected Letters of Robert Louis Stevenson.* 8 vols. Edited by Bradford A. Booth and Ernest Mehew. New Haven: Yale University Press, 1994–1995. Vols. 7 and 8 are relevant for the South Seas.

————. *In the South Seas.* New York: Charles Scribner's Sons, 1890.

————. *Island Night's Entertainment.* New York: Charles Scribner's Sons, 1893.

Stoneman, Richard. Trans. *The Great Alexander Romance* London: Penguin, 1991.

Stowe, William W. *Going Abroad: European Travel in Nineteenth Century American Culture.* Princeton: Princeton University Press, 1994.

Stroven, Carl, and A. Grove Day. *The Spell of the Pacific.* New York: Macmillan, 1949.

Suggs, Robert C. *The Island Civilization of Polynesia.* New York: Mentor, 1960.

Suntzu. *The Art of War.* Translated by Samuel B. Griffith. London: Oxford University Press, 1963.

Susuki, D. T. *Manual of Zen Buddhism.* New York: Grove Press, 1960.

Sutra of Hui-neng, see *The Diamond Sutra.*

Sypher, Wylie. *Guinea's Captive Kings.* Chapel Hill: University of North Carolina Press, 1942.

Teng, Ssu-yü. *New Light on the History of the T'ai-p'ing Rebellion.* Cambridge: Harvard University Press, 1950.

Theroux, Paul. *The Happy Isles of Oceania.* New York: G. P. Putnam's Sons, 1992.

————. "Poetry Lesson," *The New Yorker,* LXXI, no 18 (June 26 and July 3, 1995), 153–65.

Thomas, David, and Karin Ronnefeldt, eds. *People of the First Man: Life Among the Plain Indians in Their Final Days of Glory.* New York: E. P. Dutton, 1976.

Thumboo, Edwin, ed. *The Second Tongue.* Singapore: Heinemann Educational Books (Asia), 1976.

Todorov, Tzvetan. *The Conquest of America: The Question of the Other.* New York: Harper & Row, 1984.

Torgovnick, Marianna. *Gone Primitive: Savage Intellects, Modern Lives.* Chicago: University of Chicago Press, 1990.

Townsend, E. R., ed. *President Tubman of Liberia Speaks*. London: Consolidated, 1959.

Toynbee, Paget, ed. *Letters of Horace Walpole*. 16 vols. Oxford: Clarendon Press, 1903–1905.

Tso Chuan. See James Legge, *The Chinese Classics: The Ch'un Ts'ew, with the Tso Chuen*, vol. 5, and Watson, *Tso Chuan*.

Turner, Frederick Jackson. "The Significance of the Frontier in American History." 1893. In *America: One Land One People*, edited by Robert C. Baron. Golden, CO: Fulcrum, 1987. 245–77.

Turner, Lorenzo. *Africanisms in the Gullah Dialect*. Chicago: University of Chicago Press, 1949.

Twain, Mark. *Following the Equator: A Journey Around the World*. 1897. Reprint, New York: Dover, 1989.

———. *More Tramps Abroad*. London: Chatto & Windus, 1898.

———. *The Works of Mark Twain*. 2 vols. as of 1995. Edited by Harriet Elinor Smith and Edgar Marquess Branch. Berkeley: University of California Press, 1994.

Twitchett, Denis, and John K. Fairbank, series eds. *The Cambridge History of China*. 15 vols. projected. Cambridge: Cambridge University Press, from 1979 in progress. Vol. 1 (1986); Vol. 3, Part 1 (1979); Vol. 6 (1994); Vol. 7, Part 1 (1988); Vol. 10 (1978); Vol. 11, Part 2 (1980); Vol. 12, Part 1 (1983); Vol. 13, Part 2 (1986); Vol. 14, Part 1 (1987); Vol. 15, Part 2 (1991).

UNESCO General History of Africa, 8 vols. Berkeley: University of California Press, 1980–1993. Vol. 1, "Methodology and African Prehistory" ed. J. Ki-Zerbo(1980); Vol. 2, "Ancient Civilizations of Africa" ed. G. Mokhtar (1980); Vol. 3, "Africa from the Seventh to the Eleventh Century" ed. M. El Fasi and I. Hrbek (1988); Vol. 4, "Africa from the Twelfth to the Sixteenth Century" ed. D.T. Niane (1984); Vol. 5, "Africa from the Sixteenth to the Eighteenth Century" ed. B.A.Ogot (1992); Vol. 6, "The Nineteenth Century until 1880" ed. J.F.A. Ajayi (1989); Vol. 7, "Africa under Foreign Domination, 1880–1935" ed. A. A. Boahen (1985); Vol. 8, "Africa since 1935" ed. A. A. Mazrui and C. Wondji (1993).

Utley, Robert, ed. *Battlefield and Classroom: Four Decades with the American Indian, the Memoirs of Richard H. Pratt*. New Haven: Yale University Press, 1964.

Validi, Ahmad Zaki. "Muslim Geography." *Islamic Culture*, 8, 1934.

Van Sertima, Ivan, and Runoko Rashdi, eds. *African Presence in Early Asia*. New Brunswick, NJ: Transaction Publishers, 1988.

Van Speilbergen, Joris. "Speilbergen's Journal." In *East and West Indian Mirror*. Edited and translated by J. A. J. de Villiers. London: Hakluyt Society, 1906. 24-163.

Vass, Winifred K. *The Bantu Speaking Heritage of the United States*. Los Angeles: Center for Afro-American Studies, UCLA, 1979.

Vaughan, Richard, ed. *The Illustrated Chronicles of Matthew Paris*. Cambridge, UK: Alan Sutton, 1993.

Voget, Fred W. "Shorter Notes Towards a Classification of Cult Movements: Some Further Contributions II," *Man* 59, no. 26 (February 1959): 26–28.

Voltaire. *Candide*. 1759. New York: Literary Guild, 1929.

Waddell, L. Augustus. *Lhasa and Its Mysteries*. New York: E. P. Dutton, 1905.

Walcott, Derek. "What the Twilight Says: An Overture." In *Dream on Monkey Mountain and Other Plays*. New York: Farrar, Strauss, and Giroux, 1970.

Wadley, Nicholas, ed. *Noa Noa: Gauguin's Tahiti*. Salem, NH: Salem House, 1985.

Waley, Arthur. "The Heavenly Horses of Ferghana: A New View." *History Today* 5, no. 2 (February 1955): 95–103.

———. Introduction to *One Hundred & Seventy Chinese Poems*. London: Constable & Co., 1918.

———. *The Real Tripitaka*. London: George Allen & Unwin, 1952.

———. *Three Ways of Thought in Ancient China*. London: George Allen & Unwin, 1939.

———. *The Way and Its Power: A Study of the Tao Te Ching*. New York: Grove and Weidenfeld, 1958.

Walker, Alice. *Possessing the Secret of Joy*. New York: Harcourt Brace Jovanovich, 1972.

Wallis, Helen, ed. *Carteret's Voyage Round the World, 1766–1769*. 2 vols. Cambridge: Hakluyt Society, 1965.

Watson, Burton, ed. and trans. *Basic Writings of Mo Tzu, Hsün Tzu, and Han Fei Tzu*. New York: Columbia University Press, 1963.

———. ed. and trans. *The Tso Chuan*. New York: Columbia University Press, 1989.

Watters, Thomas, ed. *On Yuan Chwang's Travels in India*. London: Royal Asiatic Society, 1973.

Welty, Paul Thomas. *The Asians: Their Heritage and Their Destiny*. Philadelphia: J.P. Lippincott, 1970.

Whitely, W. H., ed. *A Selection of African Prose*. 2 vols. Oxford: Clarendon Press, 1964.

Willetts, William. *Chinese Art*. 2 vols. Harmondsworth,UK: Penguin, 1958.

Williams, Chancellor. *The Destruction of Black Civilization*. Chicago: Third World Press, 1974.

Wilson, Derek. *The Circumnavigators*. New York: M. Evans, 1989.

Winchester, Simon. "After Dire Straits, An Agonizing Haul across the Pacific," *Smithsonian*, 22, no. 1 (April 1991): 84–93.

Worsley, Peter. *The Three Worlds: Culture and World Development*. Chicago: University of Chicago Press, 1984.

Wright, Helen, and Samuel Rapport, eds. *The Great Explorers*. New York: Harper & Brothers, 1957.

Wu Ch'eng-en. *The Journey to the West*. 4 vols. Translated by Anthony C. Yu. Chicago: University of Chicago Press, 1974–1983.

Yampolsky, Philip B., ed. *Selected Writings of Nichiren*. New York: Columbia University Press, 1990.

Yap, Yong, and Arthur Cotterell. *The Early Civilization of China*. New York: G. P. Putnam's Sons, 1975.

Yawata, I., and Sinoto, Y. H., eds. *Prehistoric Culture in Oceania* [Eleventh Pacific Science Congress]. Honolulu: Bishop Museum Press, 1968.

Zastoupil, Lynn. *John Stuart Mill and India*. Stanford: Stanford University Press, 1994.

Zenkovsky, Serge A., ed. *Medieval Russia's Epics, Chronicles, and Tales*. New York: Penguin, 1963.

Zhao Rugua, see Chau Ju-kua.

Ziff, Larzer. *Literary Democracy: The Declaration of Cultural Independence in America*. New York: Viking, 1981.

INDEX

About the Author

O. R. DATHORNE is Professor of English at the University of Kentucky and founder and director of the Association of Caribbean Studies. A native of Guyana, Dathorne represents a "postcolonialist" viewpoint, marginalized by majority discourse. He has taught at four African universities and five American universities, including Yale. He is a prolific novelist and poet and the author of more than fifteen books, including *The Black Mind* (1974), *Dark Ancestor* (1981), *Dele's Child* (1986), *In Europe's Image* (Bergin & Garvey, 1994), and *Imagining the World* (Bergin & Garvey, 1994).